A Decade of Progress in Primary Prevention

Primary Prevention of Psychopathology
George W. Albee and Justin M. Joffe, *General Editors*

I. *The Issues: An Overview of Primary Prevention, 1977*
George W. Albee and Justin M. Joffe, *Editors*

II. *Environmental Influences and Strategies in Primary Prevention, 1978*
Donald G. Forgays, *Editor*

III. *Social Competence in Children, 1979*
Martha Whalen Kent and Jon E. Rolf, *Editors*

IV. *Competence and Coping during Adulthood, 1980*
Lynne A. Bond and James C. Rosen, *Editors*

V. *Prevention through Political Action and Social Change, 1981*
Justin M. Joffe and George W. Albee, *Editors*

VI. *Facilitating Infant and Early Childhood Development, 1982*
Lynne A. Bond and Justin M. Joffe, *Editors*

VII. *Promoting Sexual Responsibility and Preventing Sexual Problems, 1983*
George Albee, Sol Gordon, and Harold Leitenberg, *Editors*

VIII. *Prevention in Health Psychology, 1985*
James C. Rosen and Laura J. Solomon, *Editors*

IX. *A Decade of Progress in Primary Prevention, 1986*
Marc Kessler and Stephen E. Goldston, *Editors*

A Decade of Progress in Primary Prevention

Marc Kessler and
Stephen E. Goldston, editors

Published for the University of Vermont and the Vermont Conference on the Primary Prevention of Psychopathology by
University Press of New England
Hanover and London, 1986

University Press of New England

Brandeis University

Brown University

Clark University

University of Connecticut

Dartmouth College

University of New Hampshire

University of Rhode Island

Tufts University

University of Vermont

Printed in the United States of America

LIBRARY OF CONGRESS IN PUBLICATION DATA

Vermont Conference on the Primary Prevention of Psychopathology (9th : 1984 : University of Vermont)
A decade of progress in primary prevention.
(Primary prevention of psychopathology ; 9)
Papers presented at the 1984 Vermont Conference on the Primary Prevention of Psychopathology held at the University of Vermont.
Includes bibliographies and indexes.
1. Mental illness—United States—Prevention—Congresses. 2. Mental health—Research—United States—Congresses. 3. Mental health services—United States—Congresses. I. Kessler, Marc. II. Goldston, Stephen E. III. Title. IV. Series: Vermont Conference on the Primary Prevention of Psychopathology. Primary prevention of psychopathology ; v. 9 [DNLM: 1. Mental Disorders—prevention & control—congresses. 2. Primary Prevention—trends—congresses. 3. Psychopathology—trends—congresses. W3 PR945CK v. 9 / WM 31.5 V527 1984d]
RC454.V46 1977 vol. 9 616.89 s [362.2'0973] 86-40114
ISBN 0-87451-377-4
ISBN 0-87451-378-2 (pbk).

Dedication

One of the editors of this volume, Steve Goldston, is one of the heroes of primary prevention. He fought a lonely battle within the federal government to keep prevention visible and viable. He has avidly attended and contributed to all the VCPPPs. He was recently honored by The American Psychological Association with its award for Distinguished Professional Contributions to Public Service—recognition that was long overdue. VCPPP takes pleasure in dedicating this volume to Stephen E. Goldston in recognition of his contributions to the decade of progress that this volume celebrates.

Contents

Preface

In 1974, George Albee met with Jim and Faith Waters of the Waters Foundation to discuss ways in which the foundation could support efforts in mental health. They decided that a series of conferences to bring together researchers and practitioners of primary prevention of psychopathology would have a salubrious effect on the field. Thus was born the Vermont Conference on the Primary Prevention of Psychopathology. Hosted by and held at the University of Vermont, eight conferences over the subsequent ten years were held and the papers from these conferences published for wider distribution. As Emory Cowen notes in his chapter in this volume, these conferences and the published volumes were a major event in the recent history of primary prevention.

The Waters Foundation continued its support until other funding could be found, and in 1983 the National Institute of Mental Health began to provide partial support for the conference. That support has continued uninterrupted.

In planning for the 1984 conference we were aware that a decade would have passed since that meeting between Albee and the Waters, and we felt that sufficient time had passed and sufficient changes had occurred in the field to warrant a review of the progress that had been made. Realizing, too, the gap that still exists between an idealized state and the realities of the current situation, we knew too that there was room to discuss ways to bridge that gap.

The 1984 conference thus offered the opportunity for both a summing up and a look to the future. Bringing together some of the important progenitors of the field, such as Gerald Caplan, whose early work in community psychology was a herald of prevention, and what could be called the second (or perhaps even the third) generation of preventionists, such as Ricardo Muñoz, who was intellectually nurtured by Jim Kelly, one of the participants at the first Conference, we saw this conference as laying the groundwork for filling the gap between the ideal and the actual.

The chapters in this volume were initially presented as papers at the conference. Each is two-headed, looking to the past with an eye on the future or, if you prefer, looking to the future with a clear vision of from where the field has come. The authors both sum up and give direction for the future. In pure and applied research, in programs and politics, progress has been noted, and the prospects for the future are laid out. While it is dangerous to be a prophet we asked the authors to share the risk and prophesize. We believe that you will be intrigued with the results.

Just as the field of primary prevention is dynamic and unpredictable, so too are the chapters in this volume. You will find much that is controversial and unexpected—and enough to digest, if not for the next decade then at least for the next few years, as these authors continue to shape and give direction to the field.

In 1977 Klein and Goldston edited a volume that had an implied interrogative title: *Primary Prevention, An Idea Whose Time Has Come*. During the past decade, at every VCPPP conference, that question has plagued many, if not all, of the participants. This year, too, the phrase recurred and the response was almost unanimously yes ("almost" because, as we said, there is controversy still).

This volume is divided into five parts, but these divisions are artificial. Each author, while maintaining a particular focus, ranges broadly. You will find recurring themes and multiple perspectives on similar problems.

Part I

Cowen reviews the history of primary prevention in exquisite detail. He highlights events that illuminate the progress of the field and the substantive contributions that have been made to it. He delineates two programmatic approaches to prevention: *systems centered* and *person centered*. The first has two foci, one on forestalling the sequalae of stressful life events and the second on developing skills and competencies in unaffected people to strengthen adaptive capacities. System-centered strategies focus on social action and change. Cowen presents a five-step conceptual model for developing and evaluating primary prevention programs.

Part II

As is true for other applied sciences, prevention requires a research base. Because the field is so diverse, a number of lines of research converge on the problems that prevention programs address. The authors of the papers in this part provide information about those lines of research.

McGuffin and Katz review the current findings on psychiatric genetics in general and for schizophrenia, affective disorders, neurotic and personality disorders and alcoholism more particularly. Although, the evidence for a genetic contribution to the etiology of schizophrenia is clear, that for the other disorders is less so. They caution that even for schizophrenia, in which the genetic contribution is significant, environmental factors cannot be neglected. McGuffin and Katz present a discussion of the liability and threshold models of the genetic transmission of disorders and ways of partialling the variance of genetic and environmental contributions. They also discuss the contribution of new and exciting biological technologies to the study of genetics.

Dohrenwend reviews the evidence for the effects of socioenvironmental factors and environmentally induced stress on the development of psychopathology. The relationships of psychopathology to gender, social class, and recent and long-term stress are reviewed. He examines five models of the relationship between life stress and psychopathology in the light of his current research.

Watt reviews the advances in knowledge of risk factors in schizophrenia and other major psychological disorders. Risk factors are associative and not causative variables that point to the causative research needed subsequent to their identification. In his review Watt finds evidence for maturational variables underlying many psychopathologies; that is, in a number of disorders, early and persistent differences exist between those who do and those who do not develop later problems. Watt discusses the methodological problems inherent in risk research and the large payoff anticipated from the multidisciplinary, multiorientations of the Risk Consortium.

Kellam and Werthamer-Larsson present the methodology and findings of child psychiatric developmental epidemiology. Derived from community epidemiology and from a lifespan developmental orientation, child psychiatric developmental epidemiology studies the distribution of cases in populations and the distribution of developmental patterns leading to caseness. It provides a basis for specific preventive interventions. Their review focuses on four domains of antecedents of mental health problems: social field, social adaptation, psychological status and biological status. These domains provide a framework for a review of preventive interventions. Following the review of the literature Kellam and Werthamer-Larsson discuss core methodological issues in preventive research and then describe the work based on their epidemiological model being carried out at their Prevention Research Center.

Osofsky reviews the literature on infant development that relates to the affective and emotional development of the child and to the emotional availability of the mothering person. She presents research that emphasizes the interactive nature of emotional communication between the mother and child and the importance of this interaction for the development of the infant. The importance of continuities and discontinuities for the predictability of later behavior are discussed as are the biobehavioral stage changes that make prediction difficult.

Part III

While research makes the world go round, at some point research leads to practice. It is also true that practice informs research. Reported in this part are results from some of the innovative prevention projects that have been mounted—and ideas for developing more such projects.

While most prevention research focuses on the usual standards of research validation, Swift's work has added the element of constituent validation, i.e., ensuring that the program makes sense to the people who are going to use it and benefit by it, which he has shown is necessary for the activities to continue after the researchers have left. He presents information on how to achieve constituent validation and examples of successful prevention programs that his center has developed.

Caplan's chapter demonstrates that he is not a man who rests on his laurels. After presenting a model for prevention efforts, he elaborates on the model by drawing on his current work with adults and children facing the stress of surgery and/or death. He also discusses the importance of social support systems in increasing the ability of the individual to master stressful situations.

Segal addresses two issues: (1) the factors that develop resiliency and invulnerability to severe stressors; and (2) the problems of communicating findings about these factors to the public. He notes the recent shift of emphasis from a pathology orientation and a search for causes of illness to an interest in the roots of health, relative invulnerability to severe disruptions in life, and those factors that promote competence. He strikes a note of caution about our communication with the public: Too frequently we have been quick to rush to print advice that is soon out of date, and we have neglected the diversity of our audience.

As early as at the time of President Kennedy's Commission on Mental Health, it was recognized that the need for human services far outstrips the professional services available. It took longer to recognize that needs far outstrip what *professional* services can ever provide. The greatest potential resource available, then, is the nonprofessional helpgiving already taking place and the enormous amount that remains untapped. Reissman documents the help that is already available in self-help organizations and discusses why and how they are effective.

Price reviews the history of education for prevention and the lack of its penetration into academic settings. He provides a schema for delineating the skills needed by preventionists, a schema that can direct systematic training activities to replace the haphazard approach that now exists.

Part IV

Any endeavor that depends on governmental support, as programs in mental health do, cannot ignore the realities of the political marketplace. Fortunately for prevention, as you will see in reading the chapters in this section, many of the advocates of prevention are astute politicians. Without their astuteness and hard work, progress would have been a lot slower.

As a politician Albee is in a good position to identify those individuals and ideologies that oppose prevention efforts. His chapter takes the critics to task for ignoring relevant research, supporting the status quo, and supporting outmoded and demonstrably invalid practices.

Tableman reviews the status of prevention programs in state departments of mental health and, based on her experience, provides guidelines for developing programs within the political and administrative framework of state government.

Long reviews the political climate surrounding prevention efforts over the past decade. She astutely delineates the reasons for successes and, more importantly, points to the reasons for failures. She also charts the current situation and emphasizes the need for continuing vigilance (against the forces that Albee discusses) and suggests ways of having an impact on the political process to foster the growth of prevention efforts.

Goldston reviews the history of primary prevention efforts at the federal level, especially those of NIMH. In an earlier presentation at the VCPPP in 1975, Goldston discussed the gaps that existed in primary prevention program efforts. He now brings us up to date on the status of efforts to fill those gaps.

Part V

Muñoz provides an integrative summary of the themes and concepts presented in the preceding chapters. He identifies recurring themes, and points to conceptual and methodological problems in program development and evaluation.

Burlington, Vermont M.K.
March 1986 S.E.G.

PART I

An Overview

Primary Prevention in Mental Health

Ten Years of Retrospect and Ten Years of Prospect

Emory L. Cowen

The goals of this chapter are to provide a global overview of the recent accomplishments in the field and to gaze into the crystal ball regarding its needed future directions. The task is both timely and challenging.

In meandering through some of primary prevention's known pastures and fantasied open ranges, I address the topic both structurally and substantively. I use the term *structural* to describe marker events that seem to bespeak growing interest and progress in the field. One good example is the occurrence of ten Vermont Conferences on the Primary Prevention of Psychopathology during the decade. A second is the Report of the President's Commission on Mental Health (1978), including a subreport by its Prevention Task Panel (1978). A third is the appearance of five separate chapters on community psychology and primary prevention in the *Annual Review of Psychology* (Cowen, 1973; Kessler and Albee, 1975; Kelly, Snowden, and Muñoz, 1977; Bloom, 1980; Iscoe and Harris, 1984).

Beyond those events, municipal, county, and state offices—indeed even academic departments, which rarely change short of nuclear fusion—have all taken visibly greater cognizance of primary prevention. For example, NIMH recently published a directory of State Government Mental Health Prevention Contacts (1983), listing for all 50 states and the territories the name, title, and address of a designated Prevention Administrator. Importantly, NIMH also created an Office of Prevention and launched a network of Preventive Intervention Research Centers (PIRC). Similarly, the American Psychological Association appointed a Task Force on Promotion and Prevention, which is currently surveying innovative prevention program models both to codify existing knowledge and to make recommendations about the field's future development.

Another indicator, the printed literature, has also grown significantly. Representative of this growth is the pioneering series of primary prevention volumes published by the Vermont Conference and at least ten other books devoted primarily or exclusively to that topic (e.g., Aronovitz, 1982; Felner, Jason, Moritsugu, and Farber, 1983; Goldstein, 1982; Joffe, Albee, and Kelly, 1984; Klein and Goldston, 1977; Manson, 1982; Marlowe and Weinberg, 1983, Muñoz and Kelly, 1975; Muñoz, Snowden, and Kelly, 1979; Price, Ketterer, Bader, and Monahan, 1980; Roberts and Peterson, 1984). Of these, two new volumes provide outstanding coverage of the current status of the field-at-large (Felner et al., 1983) and prevention work with children (Roberts and Peterson, 1984). The very appearance of these two substance-filled volumes is one form of testimony to the field's rapid, productive maturation. The title of an earlier volume, *Primary Prevention: An Idea Whose Time Has Come* (Klein and Goldston, 1977), offers a clue about why this development has mushroomed so rapidly.

Similarly, volumes on topical subareas in primary prevention such as social environments, social system intervention, competence training, stressful life events, and social support have surfaced at a geometrically increasing rate, as have individual book chapters on such topics. Even texts in staid fields such as abnormal psychology have extended their boundary limits to include a preventive–community focus.

Several new journals dedicated in whole or part to primary prevention were started this past decade. One, the *Journal of Primary Prevention,* includes a clearinghouse that abstracts 25–30 primary prevention projects each issue. With increasing frequency, journals have published "special numbers" (SNs) on major primary prevention themes, e.g., training (Lorion and Stenmark, 1984), research (Cowen, 1982a), social systems change (Sandler, 1985), helping- and support-systems (Gottlieb, 1982; Lieberman and Glidewell, 1978), work in schools (Shaw and Goodyear, 1984), and empowerment (Rappaport, Swift, and Hess, 1984). And, finally, the field's research growth made possible in 1984 a first step toward "science heaven," i.e., a meta-analysis of 40 primary prevention studies, which yielded encouragingly positive findings (Baker, Swisher, Nadenichek, and Popowicz, 1984). Thus the field's rapid crystallization makes this an entirely natural and appropriate time to assess accomplishments and identify future needs; in fact, several such attempts have recently been made (Jason, Felner, Moritsugu, and Farber, 1983; Newbrough, 1984).

At least on the surface, then, we seem to have completed a decade of quantum leaps in primary prevention's visibility and salience. But there is a rub! Structural evolution is not the same as substantive gain; indeed, even intoxicating signs of the former can be grossly misleading. Let me illustrate by "turning" on several of the above examples:

• A complete roster of state and territory contact persons in prevention is fine, but I would prefer to know what those states are actually *doing* in primary prevention.

• The mere listing of 30 (self-proclaimed) primary prevention abstracts per journal issue is less persuasive than the primary prevention substance of those abstracts (Cowen, 1982b).

• Our enthusiasm about sophisticated meta-analyses, even those that yield flattering findings for primary prevention, must be tempered by recognition of the nature of the studies that feed into them.

• I am skeptical when, after a President's Commission Report (1978) that praises the concept of prevention throughout, an NIH branch proclaims that 65 percent of its activities are prevention. I would prefer to know the ground rules by which those activities were so classified.

I cite these examples to suggest that some of the decade's primary-prevention music has had a high noise-to-signal ratio. But that is not all bad; being able to detect a signal can be a useful precondition for fine tuning receivers and improving signal-to-noise ratios. If we can resist being dazzled by signs of structural evolution, the important questions that still remain are: "How much *real* substantive change has there been?" and "How does that change inform the future?"

One factor that helps explain the discrepancy between primary prevention's structural and substantive evolution this past decade is how the concept is viewed and defined. It is not too much of an exaggeration to say that the single most important de facto reason for classification of something as primary prevention is whether its creator *calls* it that. That, I believe, is how we get 30 primary prevention abstracts per issue in the journal clearinghouse (Cowen, 1982b) and how an agency suddenly discovers that 65 percent of its work is prevention. *Why* that happens is less clear, though I suspect that the reasons range from a genuinely poor understanding of the concept to a wish to be identified with a movement perceived as avant-garde to pragmatic (i.e., money-related) considerations (Cowen, 1977).

Elsewhere (Cowen, 1983), I suggested that four very different concepts (with different goals and operations), i.e., prevention, prevention in mental health, primary prevention, and primary prevention in mental health have been used indiscriminately and interchangeably in practice. Several of those concepts are sufficiently elastic to accommodate most existing mental health practices. When such an elastic concept is used, it inflates primary prevention number counts and yields seductive, but misleading, signs of structural evolution. In the final analysis, the practice is more harmful than helpful because it dilutes the movement's most important potential contribution: highlighting conceptual and operational contrasts with mental health's regnant but insufficient ways. Of the four terms, the one that maximizes such contrast is primary prevention in mental health. Since that is the concept that frames this overview chapter, I need to clarify my meaning.

The ultimate goal of primary prevention in mental health is to develop programs (interventions/actions) to forestall psychological problems and/or to build strengths or competencies that favor psychological wellness. It is an intentional, outreaching approach, targeted to groups of well people (including some at risk) before the fact of maladjustment (Cowen, 1982c). So viewed, its two main strategies are: (1) to reduce sources of stress on, and increase life opportunities for, people, i.e., a *systems-level* strategy; and (2) to develop interventions to enhance people's capacity to adapt effectively and to deal with stressful situations and events, i.e., a *person-centered* strategy (Cowen, 1985).

System-Level Strategies

Empowerment

Intrinsic to system-level approaches are the convictions that profound, widespread social injustices such as racism, sexism, ageism—indeed, most basically, *lack of empowerment*—are root sources of psychological (and other) malaise, and change that fails to address such core problems will at best be socially palliative or, in Watzlawick, Weakland, and Fisch's (1974) idiom, "first-order" change (Rappaport, 1977, 1981). From that view it follows that informed social action, policy change, and reform based on concepts such as justice, empowerment and the provision of life opportunities are the real keys to achieving primary prevention's basic goals (Rappaport, 1981).

Some preliminary support of that view was presented at the end of Kessler and Albee's (1975) *Annual Review* chapter.

> Everywhere we looked, every research study we examined, suggested that major sources of human stress and distress generally involve some form of excessive power. It is enough to suggest the hypothesis that a dramatic reduction and control of power might improve the mental health of people. It is a tempting oversimplification, an hypothesis we will not propose seriously, but recommend for quiet contemplation. We have found it particularly satisfying under relaxed environmental conditions—in a rowboat on a quiet Vermont lake, on a sleepy summer day, just before the fish begin to bite. (1975, p. 578)

Albee (1982) later developed that germinal thesis further and more strongly.

But the Vermont group has hardly been alone in promoting that concept. Rappaport's (1981) brilliant and provocative essay, "In Praise of Paradox," is among the strongest and most challenging formulations of the position. Rappaport's thesis, with deep roots in his 1977 volume, is built around the urgency of constructs such as empowerment, justice, and the provision of life opportunities. Given the nature and extent of existing social problems and what it will take to solve them, Rappaport argues that most of primary prevention's person-centered ways are at best a pimple on the ocean and at worst a "cruel joke." His choice of words reflects the depth of his conviction. At one point he describes primary prevention as "name trading" [i.e., using "in" terms such as "teaching competencies," (p. 12) rather than doing psychotherapy—a new form of paternalism, if you will]. At another, he calls it a "new area of colonization" which "leaves no doubt about who is up and who is down" (p. 12). The argument culminates with the following critique:

> This is what underlies much of prevention: Find so-called high risk people and save them from themselves if they like it or not by giving them, or even better, their children, programs which we develop, package, sell, operate or otherwise control. Teach them how to fit in and be less of a nuisance. Convince them that a change in their test scores is somehow a change in their life. (1981, p. 13)

To sum up, as Rappaport has done elsewhere (1984), empowerment is "hypothesized as the key to a genuine psychology of prevention in human services" (p. 7). That view has important implications for how those involved in primary prevention should think (i.e., the levels-of-analysis issue), the settings in which they should work, their activities in those settings, and associated training needs. Interestingly in that regard, several articles in the recent *American Journal of Community Psychology* Special Issue on training in community psychology (Lorion and Stenmark, 1984) deal primarily with training in social policy formulation and/or social action (Glidewell, 1984; Iscoe, 1984; Murrell, 1984; Sarason, 1984).

Several exploratory projects clustering around the empowerment theme of enhancing the likelihood of people controlling their own lives have been reported. Rappaport, Davidson, Wilson, and Mitchell (1975), for example, developed an inner-city action center, modeling that approach on a small scale. They first identified and then built upon existing competencies in the community (e.g., through the establishment of productive business enterprises based on identified skills) as a viable alternative both to blaming the victim (Ryan, 1971) and to dealing reactively with people's so-called psychological problems.

Hodgson's (1979) program mirrors a similar concept. That program, set in a noncohesive, urban subcommunity characterized by isolation and anomie, promoted involvement by neighborhood mothers in a day-care setting and engineered mechanisms to facilitate mutual support and interactions with peers living under similar circumstances. We note, in that context, that support has been seen by some (Gottlieb, 1981, 1983; Rappaport, Seidman, Toro, McFadden, Reischl, Roberts, Salem, Stein, and Zimmerman, 1985; Riessman, 1985) as one key access route to empowerment. Dinges's (1982) program, in an American Indian community, sought to enhance competence through the use of family-based developmental tasks to train parents in intervention skills with their young children. The program strengthened both family cohesiveness and the personal adjustment of participants.

Most recently, Rappaport et al. (1984) edited a special journal issue describing nine very diverse empowerment related projects—diverse in the disciplines represented, issues addressed, methodologies used, and, critically, in the underlying concepts of empowerment reflected. The articles included a sophisticated statistical analysis of predictor variables of empowerment, based on a 2-year longitudinal, observational study of a religious group (Maton and Rappaport, 1984); an anthropologist's analysis of the empowering quality of synergistic healing systems in several primitive societies (Katz, 1984); a series of case studies of disenfranchised people who gained power through participation in social action processes, illuminating the developmental progression from a sense of helplessness to one of empowerment (Kieffer, 1984); a clinical report of the empowering process in an American Indian community, which coalesced in a struggle to prevent construction of a dam that would have overrun its homeland (O'Sullivan, Waugh, and Espeland, 1984); and a project designed to catalyze empowerment in a poor Puerto Rican community (Serrano-Garcia, 1984). The Special Issue is a true pot-pourri in and around the guiding notion of empowerment.

Thus the system-level notion of empowerment, including the concept of the competent community (Iscoe, 1974; Rhoads and Raymond, 1981), is far more salient in 1984 than it was in 1974. Although it is a sensible, attractive and energizing concept, some of its important byways remain fuzzy and unanchored. That fuzziness begets questions. Swift (1984) asked one such question: Is empowerment "an extension and refinement of prevention theory, or an alternative"? (p. xi). Another deceptively simple one, i.e., "What exactly do we *mean* by empowerment?" suggests that the concept means different things when defined as equal access to resources and opportunities in contrast to a phenomenological sense of empowerment. Still others are: What actions/operations are necessary conditions for defining these two empowering processes? Are they the same? To what extent do mental health people or social scientists more generally have (or can develop) the knowledge, skills, resources, and, indeed, the needed power, to bring about empowerment? Within what time frame do we envision those things happening? Can fully empowered people nevertheless develop psychological problems? What are the limits of applicability of the concept (e.g., developmentally)? However we define empowerment, what measurable or observable objectives can we accept as demonstrating its efficacy in fostering psychological wellness? And, importantly, what evidence is there that those goals have been or can be achieved?

I raise these questions to stimulate and to caution, not to detract from what I consider to be an exciting and promising development. And I see these conceptual, logistic, temporal, and empirical issues as an agenda for the upcoming decade.

Person-Centered Strategies

To lay my values on the table, I believe that *both* system-level and person-centered approaches to primary prevention are needed and are important strategies—and that they are complementary (though calibrated to different operations and time frames), not antagonistic (Cowen, 1985). With that value judgment as prologue let us next consider accomplishments and prospects for the two main families of person-centered strategies. The first, based on linkages shown between certain life situations and/or stressful events and psychological problems, is to develop interventions for well people who have experienced such situations and/or events to forestall predictably negative psychological sequelae; these are *event-* or *situation-*focused approaches. The second is to develop programs that provide relevant skills, competencies, and experiences to as yet unaffected people to strengthen their adaptive capacities; these are *competence-enhancement* approaches. One type of approach is reactive, the other proactive (Cowen, 1985).

Situation-Focused Approaches

Rutter's (1983) review concludes that the role of stressful events in adult disorders is now well-documented. Kornberg and Caplan's (1980) exhaustive review and Garmezy and Rutter's (1983) volume present strong evidence for extending that conclusion to children. Since Holmes and Rahe's (1967) pioneering study that charted the stressfulness of life events, this line of inquiry seems to have advanced exponentially. We have moved well beyond the simple unidimensional conclusion that stressful events predispose negative psychological outcomes. We now better understand that the effects of stress differ for different situations and events and that they are tempered by such factors as the person's age, sex, cognitive appraisal systems, sense of control or sense of powerlessness, coping styles and prior mastery experiences, problem-solving skills, and available sources of psychological support (Felner, Farber, and Primavera, 1983; Kobasa, 1979; Kobasa, Maddi, and Kahn, 1982; Lazarus, 1981; Monroe, 1982).

We have also learned much about the specific problems that stressful situations and events predispose in particular groups. That point can be illuminated by several examples from the divorce literature: Bloom, Asher, and White's (1978) extensive review showed that divorce had systematic negative physical and psychological consequences for adults and also identified specific problems that marital dissolution poses, e.g., loss of significant support, feelings of isolation and loneliness, and having new financial, legal, home-management and child-care problems. Similarly, Wallerstein and Kelly's longitudinal clinical study of children of divorce (Kelly and Wallerstein, 1976; Wallerstein, 1983; Wallerstein and Kelly, 1974, 1975, 1976, 1979, 1980) identified the differential concerns, problems, and mastery challenges facing children at different age levels—vital raw material for programs that are designed to forestall predictable psychological problems.

That raw material, however, has not yet been fully utilized to form sound preventive interventions. The stumbling blocks are more conceptual and logistic than empirical. In the past, victims of stressful circumstances entered the formal mental health system only when their problems reached serious proportions *and* if they had access to the system's resources. Such timing and circumstances limit constructive change. The attractive, evolving alternative is to take the very occurrence of events as a warning sign and to develop before-the-fact interventions to short-circuit otherwise predictable psychological problems and to bolster wellness (Cowen, 1985)—a sensible approach that remains largely untried. Thus, although the Bloom et al. (1978) review clearly documented the devastating effects of marital disruption on adults, it noted ironically at the end that, to that point, there had not been a single controlled study of an effective preventive intervention for divorcing adults.

Halting steps in that direction have since been reported. Illustratively, shaped by the earlier review, Bloom, Hodges, and Caldwell (1982) conducted a successful 6-month preventive intervention for 100 newly divorcing adults. The program's two key components were (1) provision of support both from peers and paraprofessional help agents; and (2) training specific, situationally relevant problem-solving skills. Participants exceeded controls in overall adjustment and had lower anxiety and neuraesthenia scores on a symptom checklist. Program gains were either maintained or were stronger at the 30- and 48-month follow-up points (Bloom, Hodges, Kern, and McFaddin, 1985). The program, in other words, met the primary prevention goal of reducing psychological problems known on base-rate to follow marital dissolution.

Similar studies and reviews (Emery, 1982; Felner, Farber, and Primavera, 1980; Guidubaldi, Cleminshaw, Perry, and Mcloughlin, 1983; Hetherington, 1979; Hetherington, Cox, and Cox, 1978; Kalter, 1977; Kurdek, 1981; Wallerstein and Kelly, 1979) with similar conclusions have stimulated the recent development of several effective preventive interventions for children of divorce (Stolberg and Garrison, 1985; Pedro-Carroll and Cowen, 1985). In brief, those programs provide experiences and skills known on generative grounds to be important to the psychological well-being of such youngsters: learning to better identify, express, and deal with feelings of fear, guilt, anger, and being different; support from understanding, credible peers who have had the same experiences; and acquiring the communication, anger-control, and problem-solving skills needed to cope with the new realities.

Although divorce is certainly one good example of a stressful event that predisposes systematic, negative psychological sequelae, it is far from the only one. A recent volume (Osterweis, Solomon, and Green, 1984) presents detailed evidence documenting the adverse consequences of bereavement on people's physical and psychological well-being and factors known to maximize or minimize such consequences. It also reviews a number of preventive interventions for bereaved people. One such project (Vachon, Lyall, Rogers, Freedman-Letofsky, and Freeman, 1980) evaluated the effectiveness of Silverman's (1969, 1976, 1981) widely cited widow-to-widow program, which typically includes (a) pairing recently bereaved widows with trained, longer standing widow-helpers, both for support and practical assistance with financial, legal, insurance, housing, and social service matters; and (b) mutual support group meetings. The research was based on 162 recently bereaved women who participated in widow-to-widow programs conducted by seven hospitals in Toronto. Half the sample, randomly assigned, participated in the program, and half served as nonprogram controls. Interviews conducted 1, 6, 12 and 24 months after the bereavement, as well as periodic health questionnaire data, were used to evaluate the program's efficacy. Participants significantly exceeded controls on all adjustment measures at the two-year follow-up point. Among women judged to be at high risk when the study started, significantly more *E*s than *C*s had shifted to the low-risk group, after two years.

Similar research (Lieberman and Borman, 1981) evaluated outcomes for more than 500 participants in 71 THEOS (i.e., post-bereavement mutual support) groups around the country. Those people were surveyed at several different times to evaluate their status on such variables as self-esteem, anxiety, somatic symptoms, and depression. People who had experienced the most enduring, intense THEOS involvements had the best adjustive outcomes. A similar finding was reported by Videka-Sherman (1982) based on a study of people who participated in the Compassionate Friends program (i.e., a program for parents who had lost a child in the past 18 months).

Beyond death and divorce, many other life events and situations, identified through their own generative bases, increase people's susceptibility to psychological difficulties, e.g., chronic situations involving growing up in poverty or being the offspring of psychologically disturbed parents (Goodman, 1984a) and specific events involving a major life transition (Bronfenbrenner, 1979; Felner, 1974; Felner et al., 1983; Felner, Ginter, and Primavera, 1982; Felner, Primavera, and Cauce, 1981); economic disaster and/or job loss (Buss and Redburn, 1983; Dooley and Catalano, 1979, 1980; Monahan and Vaux, 1980; Seidman and Rapkin, 1983); illness and hospitalization (Kornberg and Caplan, 1980; Roberts, Elkins, and Royal, 1984); natural disaster (Baisden and Quarantelli, 1981; Hartsough and Savitsky, 1984; Levine, 1982; Lindemann, 1944; Tierney and Baisden, 1979); and captivity (Segal, 1983, 1985).

Let us look at a concrete example of the application of research findings to primary prevention actions. A large amount of evidence had been amassed showing that hospitalization and surgery increase children's risk for short- and long-term negative psychological consequences (Kornberg and Caplan, 1980; Peterson and Brownlee-Duffeck, 1984; Shore, 1965). That body of data, combined with laboratory findings on the cognitive appraisal of stress (Lazarus, 1981) and the efficacy of various coping strategies in dealing with it (Graziano, DeGiovanni, and Garcia, 1979; Thelen, Fry, Fehrenbach, and Frautschi, 1979), fueled the development of effective preventive interventions (Melamed and Siegel, 1975; Drotar, Crawford, and Ganofsky, 1984), based on expressive and modeling procedures, to short-circuit such negative effects. The primary prevention import of that work has been noted (Graziano et al., 1979). One practical outcome is that many hospitals around the country now routinely incorporate preventive measures for hospitalized and presurgical children.

Stressful events sometimes come in bunches. When they do, their negative effects seem to cumulate like lead poisoning (Felner, 1984; Felner et al., 1983; Monroe, 1982; Vaux and Ruggiero, 1983). Rutter's (1983) suggestion that the cumulation is more nearly multiplicative than additive has already found empirical support (Lotyczewski, Cowen, and Weissberg, 1984; Sterling, Cowen, Weissberg, Lotyczewski, and Boike, 1985). Such generative data have also been used to frame primary preventive interventions. Roskin's (1982) program for adults who had recently experienced multiple stressful events, emphasized mutual aid and support and provided problem-solving skills needed to surmount current difficulties. Program evaluation, based on a within subject design, demonstrated significant reductions in participants' somatic complaints, depression, and anxiety.

Conceptually related approaches have also evolved for chronically stressful life circumstances. Tableman, Marciniak, Johnson, and Rodgers (1982) for example, developed a 10-week preventive intervention for low-income, single mothers on public assistance, who faced the combined stressors of meager finances, heavy responsibilities for young children, and the seeming absence of viable alternatives. The intervention sought to teach concrete life-coping and stress-management skills, provide genuine psychological support and strengthen self-concept. Program participants gained more than those in the control group in overall adjustment and on specific measures of depression, anxiety, feelings of inadequacy, ego strength, and self-confidence. Although the intervention was effective, some would argue that a system-level empowerment approach might be even more useful over a long period of time.

The decade 1974–1984 was an important period for accreting knowledge and building blocks for event- or situation-focused, person-centered preventive approaches. The next decade must extend that accretion process and convert such knowledge into effective applications of primary prevention programs. Among the areas in which existing knowledge must be augmented, one instrumental need is to refine measures of life stressors and their effects (Sandler and Guenther, 1985). Another is to chart more fully the *specific* adverse outcomes associated with diverse life situations and stressful events (Rutter, 1983). There is already the strong suggestion that such effects do, indeed, differ across events and circumstances (Rutter, 1983; Felner, Ginter, Boike, and Cowen, 1981; Felner, Stolberg, and Cowen, 1975). We also need to know more about parametric variables (e.g., age, sociodemographic variables) that shape people's reactions to stressful events and factors, e.g., social support and problem-solving skills (Cowen, 1982d; Gottlieb, 1984, 1985;

Heller and Swindle, 1983; Pedro-Carroll and Cowen, 1985; Sandler, Wolchik, and Braver, 1985) that moderate the deleterious effects of such events.

The preceding are building blocks that can be used to shape more meaningful and developmentally appropriate primary prevention interventions. In this area, however, our most urgent need, by far, is to develop, conduct, and document the efficacy of primary preventive interventions for the many in society whose risk status has been exacerbated by circumstances known on base-rate to predispose to maladjustment (Cowen, 1982c); in other words, program models that hold promise for preventing problems and promoting wellness, as an alternative to past frustrating efforts to contain already rooted misery and ineffectuality.

Competence-Enhancement Approaches

Analysis and Change of Social Environments

Earlier, I pictured major social change and empowerment in pursuit of a just environment as an important but complex challenge. On the other hand, engineering physical environments (Wandersman, Andrews, Riddle, and Fawcett, 1983) and/or specific microenvironments (Vincent and Trickett, 1983) with significant shaping impact, may offer more realistic, accessible, and better controlled targets for such intervention. Work toward the latter goal rests on two key preparatory steps: (1) developing methodologies that accurately assess high-impact dimensions of social environments and sensitively reflect individual differences among them; and (2) demonstrating systematic relationships between properties of social environments and inhabitants' behavior, performance, and adjustment. The approach assumes that the effects of the social environment are *not* neutral; they either facilitate or hinder people's adaptation. If so, the choice is to accept such effects as they fall randomly or to engineer microenvironments designed to enhance competence and facilitate adjustment.

The past decade has witnessed major progress with respect to those two preparatory steps. Moos and colleagues (Insel and Moos, 1974; Moos, 1973, 1974, 1976, 1979a, 1979b, 1984) have: (1) pioneered the development of measures of the properties of diverse microenvironments, ranging from hospital wards to therapy groups to military, work, and family units to high school and junior high school classes; and (2) pinpointed adaptive behavioral correlates of environmental variation. Others have extended that work to develop comprehensive assessment frameworks for specific environments, such as that of the primary grade classroom (Stallings, 1975).

That growing body of generative research has catalyzed exploration of environment-change interventions designed to foster competence and adaptation. Moos (1979a), for example, sought to modify environments based on direct consensual feedback from inhabitants. Diverse environment-change strategies designed to enhance learning and adaptation have been explored in school settings. They include: (1) the use of open-space structures (Reiss and Dyhdalo, 1975; Reiss and Martell, 1974); (2) changing specific classroom practices, e.g., teaching methods that encourage curiosity behavior in pupils (Susskind, 1979); and (3) nontraditional educational formats including cooperative learning or peer teaching approaches, peer counseling and role taking, cross-age tutoring (Aronson, Blaney, Stephan, Sikes, and Snapp, 1978; Gump, 1980; Slavin, 1977; Wright and Cowen, 1985), and active involvements in live community helping programs (Sarason, 1983). Sprinthall (1984) clusters the latter approaches under the term *deliberate psychological education* (DPE), i.e., learning by doing, "particularly . . . helping others through active participation" (p. 494). Sprinthall views DPE as a form of redistribution of power, which breaks down the stereotypes of teacher as authority and pupil as the passive recipient of formal knowledge. His reviews of DPE outcome studies (Sprinthall, 1981, 1984) provide evidence of important gains on measures of ego development, self-reliance, internality, empathy, moral judgment, and decreased egocentricity. He concludes: "This is the whole point of primary prevention, namely to create . . . educative experiences that affect students' intellectual and personal development simultaneously" (1984, p. 494). Sarason's (1983) intriguing volume richly develops that view.

Although the microsystem approaches considered are hardly societal in scope, they are significant in their own right and illustrate an important grey zone between pure system- and person-oriented approaches to primary prevention in mental health. More explicitly, person-centered approaches include direct training in age- and situationally appropriate skills and engineering experiences that enhance competence. Relevant skills or experiences are identified through generative knowledge bases linking their presence to good adjustment or their absence to maladjustment (Cowen, 1985). The interventions are simply to provide those skills or experience.

Early Child Stimulation and Enrichment

One cluster of such approaches, i.e., those designed to enhance the early psychological development of infants and very young children, immediately met expectations. Klaus and Kennell (1976), based on Bowlby's (1969) earlier work in attachment theory, argued the importance of the mother–child bonding process to the child's early development. Within that framework, Broussard (1976, 1977, 1979) developed a longitudinal preventive intervention for high-risk families with newborn infants. The program, which ran from the time the infants were 2–3 months old until they were age 3½, featured regular 1½-hour biweekly meetings with mothers and infants, as well as home visits by child-development specialists. The latter included observation of parent-child interactions and intervention around perceived developmental needs. Comprehensive program evaluation, including observation of free play and mother–child separation and reunion episodes, showed striking differences and favored the intervention sample on such adjustive variables as confidence, balance of affect, coping and communication skills, and less aggression.

Work by Greenspan (1981, 1982) with infants from multirisk families is based on the assumption that intensive longitudinal intervention in the earliest years can prevent the occurrence of otherwise predictable maladaption (i.e., morbidity). His comprehensive intervention was designed to meet families' survival needs, provide support and a trusting relationship, and offer family training and specific, individualized clinical services to help children master relevant cognitive, social, and sensorimotor tasks. Although this study is still in progress, findings to date regarding children's development up to age six suggest that the program succeeded in reversing the base-rate maladaptive trends ordinarily found in infants from multirisk families (Greenspan, 1982). Osofsky (1986) reviews other proactive, preventive interventions with infants from high-risk families that are designed to inculcate needed adaptive skills and competencies.

The decade also witnessed parallel strides in the development of promising prevention programs for preschool and grade-school children. Head Start is perhaps the oldest and best known such example. Although Head Start's unfolding period witnessed major controversies based on early evaluations challenging its efficacy (e.g., Westinghouse Report, 1969), more recent evaluations have produced impressive evidence of significant, enduring gains on key dimensions of later academic performance and adjustment (Darlington, Royce, Snipper, Murray, and Lazar, 1980; Lazar and Darlington, 1982; Lazar, Hubbell, Murray, Rosche, and Royce, 1977; Muenchow and Shays, 1980; Rickel, Dyhdalo, and Smith, 1984; Seitz, Apfel, and Efron, 1979).

One such program, tracked comprehensively for 22 years, is the Perry preschool intervention for disadvantaged children (Berrueta-Clement, Schweinhart, Barnett, Epstein, and Weikart, 1984; Schweinhart and Weikart, 1980; Weikart, Bond, and McNeil, 1978). The highly disadvantaged, relatively low IQ (i.e., 70–85) children in this project, all black, came from a slum area. They were children "who entered life with all the odds against their success" (Schweinhart and Weikart, 1980, p. 17). Each year, for five years, matched subgroups were randomly assigned to the experimental (program) and control (nonprogram) conditions. Children stayed in the program for two years. The program included: (1) a preschool experience, with highly favorable (1:5) teacher/pupil ratios, that emphasized active learning, problem-solving and skill acquisition, and close interpersonal interactions, and was designed to provide children with tools needed to cope in school; and (2) weekly 1½-hour home visits to stimulate parents' awareness and interest in children's curiosity to learn, as well as to provide specific teaching skills. The study's complex design involved repeated assessments of participants (parents and children) over a 15-year period, based on measurement of 48 criteria, including interview, cognitive–intellectual, adjustment–behavioral, and attitude measures. The following were among the study's important findings: (1) participants exceeded controls in school attitudes and achievement through 8th grade; (2) they were rated more positively in social development, required significantly fewer special education services, and their parents were more satisfied with their education; and (3) throughout, *E* children received more favorable conduct and behavior ratings and were superior on such behavioral indicants as being kept after school less often, exhibiting fewer delinquencies or serious delinquencies, and having higher rates of after-school jobs. The most recent program evaluation (Berrueta-Clement et al., 1984) confirmed the across-the-board superiority of *E*s on such bellweather criteria as better academic performance, lower crime and delinquency rates, and superior earning records and prospects. The uniqueness of this program lies both in the comprehensiveness of its evaluation and its demonstration of enduring preventive outcomes for youngsters who, initially, were unquestionably at high risk.

The Houston Parent Child Development Project (Johnson, 1975; Johnson and Breckenridge, 1982; Johnson, Kahn, and Leler, 1976; Johnson and Walker, 1984), a family-oriented program designed to prepare economically disadvantaged Hispanic children for school entry, used a similar longitudinal approach. The program featured three components: (1) training children for two years (aged 1–3) in requisite social, cognitive, and language skills; (2) yoking parents to train mothers as effective teachers of their children; and (3) providing comprehensive services to address the pervasive problems of parenting for this group. Program children and matched nonprogram controls have been evaluated on intellective and behavior measures at several follow-up points through age eight. Early outcome studies (Johnson et al., 1976) showed that *E*s made important cognitive gains and, based on videotapes of actual parent–

child interactions, that their mothers were more affectionate, encouraged more child verbalization, and used more praise. They also provided more appropriate play materials and had fewer restrictive or punitive responses. The 1–4-year follow-up (Johnson and Breckenridge, 1982) offered further evidence that program families had provided more positive, facilitating home environments and that program children (especially boys) were less destructive, overactive, or attention-seeking than controls. The most recent follow-up (5½–8 years later) was based on 2nd–5th-grade teachers' judgments of children's classroom behavior. At that time, program children were doing significantly better than controls; they were less impulsive, obstinate, moody, restless, and disruptive and getting into fewer fights with peers (Johnson and Walker, 1984).

The Brookline Early Education Program—BEEP (Pierson, Bronson, Dromey, Swartz, Tivnan, and Walker, 1983; Pierson, Klein-Walker, and Tivnan, 1984) is a preschool preventive program with three main components: (1) parent education and support; (2) diagnostic monitoring and feedback; and (3) a graded sequence of direct early childhood education experiences. Half the study's 285 families had access to one or more program components; some to all three. There was also a nonprogram comparison group. The interventions took place from birth through entry into kindergarten. Formal program evaluation at the end of 2nd grade highlighted two conclusions: (1) program children were doing much better than controls; and (2) the more saturated the program experience, the greater the benefit to children. Gains were evident on standard academic criteria such as reading performance; on such measures program children had approximately 15–40 percent of the number of problems shown by controls. They were also superior in working independently, following directions, getting along with peers, and participating in classroom activities (Pierson et al., 1984).

The preceding early intervention programs were for disadvantaged children. A related program, Project PACT (Goodman, 1984b; Goodman and Isaacs, 1985) sharing the same general focus, is targeted more specifically to the offspring of severely disturbed, inner-city mothers. The program includes: (1) regular home visits by family workers to provide support and help with concrete family needs (e.g., health, income, and housing; (2) parent education to augment parenting skills and clarify roles and expectations; and (3) child interventions, including a stimulating day-care program for children over 2½ years of age; and (4) for younger children, mother–infant groups oriented to experiential learning. Subjects in the current PACT program include 82 poverty-level families with "disturbed" (56 schizophrenic, 26 depressed) mothers. Comprehensive program evaluation, including 29 demographically comparable well mothers, is now in process.

At yet another level, Olweus (1978) documented the frequency and negative consequences of so-called bullying behavior in Scandinavian school children and marshalled evidence of the stability of such behavior over time (Olweus, 1979). The combination of those findings paved the way for a large-scale (3000 children), school-based preventive intervention in Norway based on a comprehensive program package for teachers, administrators, parents, and children (Olweus, 1984).

One hallmark of primary prevention programs is their focus on well people. As suggested elsewhere (Cowen, 1985), however, the dividing line between primary and certain types of ontogenetically early secondary prevention programs is sometimes thin. Accordingly, we also note the development during the decade of a number of broadly targeted school-based programs in early detection and prevention (e.g., Glidewell, Gildea, and Kaufman, 1973; Kellam, Branch, Agrawal, and Ensminger, 1975; Kirschenbaum, DeVoge, Marsh, and Steffen, 1980; Kirschenbaum, 1979; Kirschenbaum, Pedro-Carroll, and DeVoge, 1983; Lorion, Work, and Hightower, 1984; Rickel et al., 1984; Rickel and Lampi, 1981; Rickel and Smith, 1979). One long-standing example of such work is the Primary Mental Health Project (PMHP), a program for systematic early detection and prevention of young children's school adjustment problems (Cowen, 1980; Cowen, Gesten, and Weissberg, 1980; Cowen, Trost, Lorion, Dorr, Izzo, and Isaacson, 1975). The project's four main features are its: (1) focus on very young (primary-grade children; (2) use of systematic screening and early identification techniques to identify youngsters at risk; (3) use of carefully selected, trained nonprofessionals as help agents; and (4) recasting of professional roles to nourish an effective, geometrically expanded service-delivery system. One of PMHP's distinguishing qualities is its emphasis on program dissemination (Cowen, Davidson, and Gesten, 1980; Cowen, Spinell, Wright, and Weissberg, 1983). Currently some 500 schools in 200 school districts around the world are implementing the approach. Program expansion was facilitated by some 20 separate PMHP-conducted evaluation studies, the most recent of which (Weissberg, Cowen, Lotyczewski, and Gesten, 1983) was based on seven independent annual child cohorts. A number of independent evaluations also testifying to PMHP's efficacy have been conducted by other implementing groups (e.g., Cowen, Weissberg, and Lotyczewski, 1983). Data from follow-up studies (e.g., Cowen, Dorr, Trost, and Izzo, 1972; Chandler, Weissberg, Cowen, and Guare, 1984) indicate that early gains in adjustment endure over time.

The preceding examples suggest that the development of prevention programs for young children, particularly those at risk, yielded important dividends this past decade. The present need is to expand and accelerate such programs and to make their benefits available to many more children. The approach offers a bona fide and refreshing contrast to mental health's past, predominantly restorative ways.

Skill Training for Well Groups

A related thrust of major proportions during the decade was the development, application, and evaluation of mass, curriculum-based programs to teach well children specific skills that are believed, on generative grounds, to enhance competence in ways that radiate positively to adjustment. Social or interpersonal cognitive problem solving (ICPS) is perhaps the best known example of this approach. A series of generative studies by workers at the Hahnemann Medical Center documented consistent linkages between deficiencies in a family of ICPS skills (such as the abilities to generate alternative solutions to interpersonal problems, evaluate the consequences of such solutions, take the role of the other, and do step-by-step, means–end planning) and maladjustment. (Shure, 1979; Spivack, Platt, and Shure, 1976). The preventive leap was taken by developing training programs to teach age-appropriate ICPS skills to children. Inner-city Head Start children were the first targets. In separate projects, college students (Shure, Spivack, and Gordon, 1972), teachers (Spivack and Shure, 1974), and parents (Shure and Spivack, 1978) were used to train such youngsters.

Several important and challenging findings emerged from that work. First, trained children exceeded controls in acquiring the component skills. They also improved more in behavioral adjustment. There were significant linkages between the two sets of gains, and both generalized to new classrooms and teachers one year later (Shure and Spivack, 1982; Spivack and Shure, 1974). The primary prevention import of that work resides in the fact that young children's behavior problems were reduced and their adjustment enhanced by a preventive, primarily cognitive, training program—a clear alternative to dealing reactively, as we have in the past, with out-of-hand conflagration. A similar strategy is reflected in Ojemann and others' (Bruce, 1958; Griggs and Bonney, 1970; Muuss, 1960; Ojemann, 1961, 1969) earlier demonstrations that a predominantly cognitive program to teach young children *causal* (analytic) thinking skills also yielded significant adjustive gain.

In terms of heuristic value, the Hahnemann program has been an unqualified success. Later replications have largely confirmed its skill acquisition findings (e.g., Elardo and Caldwell, 1979; Weissberg, Gesten, Carnrike, Toro, Rapkin, Davidson, and Cowen, 1981; Weissberg, Gesten, Rapkin, Cowen, Davidson, Flores de Apodaca, and McKim, 1981) and have shown that those skills generalize to new situations, separated in person, place, and time from the initial training (Allen, Chinsky, Larcen, Lochman, and Selinger, 1976; Gesten, Rains, Rapkin, Weissberg, Flores de Apodaca, Cowen, and Bowen, 1982). They have *not,* however, consistently confirmed either adjustive increments or linkages between cognitive and adjustive gain. Those failures may in part reflect changes in program content, teaching formats, and evaluation frameworks, not to mention age and sociodemographic differences among target populations (Durlak, 1983; Urbain and Kendall, 1980; Weissberg and Gesten, 1982).

Although the decade's ICPS development pioneered a sorely needed conceptual alternative, the approach's early successes may have had an (unintended) imprisoning effect, i.e., too strong an emphasis on ICPS, relative to many other potential adjustment mediating skills relevant to different groups at different points in the life-span. Even so, several budding examples of preventive interventions from the same (competence enhancement) conceptual womb can be cited, if only as potential harbingers of things to come.

Based on studies showing linkages between self-awareness, assertiveness and social contact skills on the one side, and adjustment on the other, Rotheram and her associates (Rotheram, 1980, 1982; Rotheram, Armstrong, and Booraem, 1982) developed a 12-week program to teach fourth and fifth graders a family of skills, including the use of eye contact; postural, gestural, and touch cues; giving and receiving compliments; recognizing feelings; and engaging people and making friends. Collectively, those skills were intended to facilitate socially effective thinking, feeling, and behavior. In an overall sample of 343 *S*s, program children improved significantly more than controls in student-initiated contacts, teacher behavior ratings, peer popularity, and academic performance. Those gains were maintained a year later. Based on different generative knowledge bases, Stamps (1975) taught young, inner-city children to set realistic goals; Susskind (1979) did a program to enhance children's curiosity skills; Vogelsong, Most, and Yanchko (1979) taught children relationship-forming skills; Stone, Hinds, and Schmidt (1975) taught children to deal independently with critical problems of living; and Jason, Robson, and Lipshutz (1980) taught sharing behaviors. Although all these programs are embryonic, each offers preliminary evidence that the targeted skills were acquired and adjustive gain ensued.

Other preventively intended skill enhancement programs were targeted to specific outcomes. Thus Englander-Golden and associates (Englander-Golden, Elconin, and Miller, 1985; Englander-Golden, Elconin, and Satir, 1986) developed and evaluated a large-scale preventive intervention to teach young adolescents appropriate communication and assertiveness skills for refusing offers of alcohol or drugs. The program improved assertive skills and led to significant reductions in alcohol- and/or drug-related referrals or suspensions. Schinke and associates (Schinke, Blythe, and Gilchrist, 1981; Schinke, Blythe, Gilchrist, and Burt, 1981; Schinke, Gilchrist, and Small, 1979) developed a multiphased program to prevent unwanted teenage pregnancy. Role playing and discussion were used to provide accurate sex information and help students to integrate such information into their value systems; participants were then trained in communication, problem-solving, and assertiveness skills. Program youth acquired relevant program information, improved both in problem-solving skills and behaviors, felt more confident, and used more effective methods of contraception (Gilchrist and Schinke, 1983; Schinke et al., 1981). Bry and associates (Bry, 1982; Bry and George, 1980) reported behavioral effectiveness data following a preventive intervention for youth at risk of delinquency.

An ongoing, downward age extension of the competence-enhancement approach is reflected in Strayhorn's (1983) program that was designed to train inner-city preschool children in three families of competencies incompatible with the development of disabling childhood acting-out and withdrawal problems and academic failure: (1) cooperative–kind behaviors; (2) social interaction skills; and (3) language proficiencies. The third cluster is of special interest in light of data from the earlier cited meta-analysis of school-based preventive interventions (Baker et al., 1984) that the single largest primary prevention effect size, based on 13 different competence domains, was for communication skills. In Strayhorn's highly structured approach, lay preceptors meet individually with target children four to five times a week for a year.

The decade's strong competence-enhancement thrust implicates a three-step paradigm shift from mental health's classic restorative model:

1. Identify competencies with generative bases linking their presence to adjustment or their underdevelopment to maladjustment.

2. Develop age- and situationally appropriate programs to impart those skills to well people.

3. Demonstrate that the targeted skills are acquired, adjustment enhanced, and that the two sets of gains are linked (Cowen, 1977).

Experiential Approaches to Competence Enhancement

Earlier, I suggested that competence can be enhanced by engineering facilitative experiences as well as by training specific skills. That point is illustrated by Riessman's (1965) helper-therapy principle (i.e., that people help themselves through the process of being genuinely helpful to others), as well as by the burgeoning mutual-help movement (Riessman, 1985). Riessman's principle has special relevance for society's many alienated, low-status, disenfranchised groups, e.g., inner-city residents, retired people, and disinvolved high school students, who (as chronic "have nots") are susceptible to the psychological problems that stem from diminished stake and empowerment.

One of its early applications involved the use of indigenous, inner-city residents as help agents with community peers in a neighborhood storefront setting (Reiff and Riessman, 1965; Riessman, 1967). Since then, the concept has been harnessed intentionally in diverse contexts as a person-centered primary prevention strategy. Simultaneous benefits to helpers and those helped have, for example, been reported in programs using retirees (Cowen, Leibowitz, and Leibowitz, 1968; Matefy, 1978) and tuned out high school students (Tefft and Kloba, 1981) as help agents with maladapting primary-grade children, and retirees as facilitators for community peers (Crowe and Middleman, 1982; Gatz, Barbarin, Tyler, Mitchell, Moran, Wirzbicki, Crawford, and Engelman, 1982). Yoking a person-centered primary prevention strategy for helpers with a secondary prevention approach for those helped can advance mutually supportive solutions to pressing social problems. The sense of worth (or, perhaps, empowerment) that derives from giving such help may well be the motor force in the ensuing adjustive gain. Being genuinely helpful to others in real need may have the same adjustively liberating potential for adults as certain types of "do it" (DPE) programs seem to have for children (Sprinthall, 1984). That possibility recalls Staub's (1979) conclusion, based on his two-volume literature review, that significant experience in the interpersonal helping role is a key shaping factor in the development of positive social behavior in children.

Invulnerability

So far, I have identified several promising directions for primary prevention for the coming decade; empowerment, justice, stress inoculation, and competence enhancement. Another that bears mention is Garmezy's concept of invulnerability (Garmezy, 1975, 1976, 1981, 1983; Garmezy, Masten, Nordstrom, and Ferrarese, 1979), or resilience, as some (Werner and Smith, 1982) call it.

The crux of the invulnerability concept is this: Given the most profound adversities that we can imagine—the ravages of war or concentration camps, death of a loved one, separation, victimization by chronic brutality, or combinations of such experiences, described by Garmezy (1983) as "stressors of *marked* gravity"—some few people not only surmount the adversity but show excellent "behavioral adaptation and manifest competence" in spite of it. How does that happen? What factors enable them to overcome the adversity? Garmezy (1982) cites the rich dividends that can accrue from answers to those questions:

> Were we to study the forces that move such children to survival and adaptation, the long range benefits to our society might be far more significant than are the many efforts to construct models of primary prevention to curtail the incidence of vulnerability. (p. xix)

Garmezy thus suggests that knowledge about the determinants of invulnerability has broad implications for engineering health in people in general.

Most of what we now know about invulnerability comes from scattered clinical observations, although several germinal research answers are forming. The appearance of Werner and Smith's (1982) fascinating book *Vulnerable But Invincible: A Study of Resilient Children,* the third volume in their 20-year longitudinal study of 700 children of Kauai (Werner, Bierman, and French, 1971; Werner and Smith, 1977, 1982), is a monumental stride in that direction. About 200 of those 700 youngsters—exposed to profound insults of biology, poverty, squalor, and familial disorganization—developed a serious learning and/or behavior problem at some time during their first 20 years. But some 70 others, exposed to the same profound stressors, "remained invincible and developed into competent autonomous young adults" (1982, p. 3). The book describes an empirical treasure hunt for the ingredients of invincibility. The study's findings were complex in that the balance of crucial determinants differed as a function of age, sex, and the cultural context in which the children were reared. Even so, three influential clusters favored invincibility: (1) predisposing factors, such as activity, social responsivity, and autonomy in infancy and early childhood; (2) familial closeness and supportiveness; and (3) the presence of external support from peers and nonfamily identification models, e.g., teachers, neighbors, and ministers. Those empirical findings agree well with the cluster of invulnerability factors identified in Garmezy's (1981) review of the literature. The strong positioning of psychological support in that preliminary ingredient list should be noted by those with interest in the development of primary prevention interventions (Gottlieb, 1984).

The concept of invulnerability should not be viewed in splendid isolation; rather, it illustrates well a broader alteration in mental health's course away from its past, or from a predominant emphasis on illness toward a focus on health (Kelly, 1974). Although that development has visible antecedents (e.g., Anderson and Messick, 1974; Finkel, 1974, 1975; Gesten, 1976; Harter, 1974, 1979, 1981; Hollister, 1965, 1967; White, 1959, 1979) and, indeed, is reflected in currently active, related research areas such as hardiness (Kobasa, 1979; Kobasa, Maddi, and Kahn, 1979) and quality of life (Barker and Schoggen, 1973; Reich and Zautra, 1983; Rhoads and Raymond, 1981; Zautra, 1983a, 1983b; Zautra and Goodbart, 1979; Zautra and Reich, 1980, 1983; Zautra and Simons, 1979), knowledge of the determinants of psychological well-being is a critical aspect of primary prevention's infrastructure, and gaining more should be an important activity for the coming decade.

In sum, findings of the past decade based on programs to engineer facilitative experiences and environments and to train well people in specific skills and competencies reflect a conceptually appealing development that captures primary prevention's educational, health-building thrust. The approach is potentially targetable to the many and is, indeed, adaptable to mass media interventions such as those used in the Stanford Heart Disease Prevention Project (Maccoby and Alexander, 1979; Maccoby and Farquhar, 1975, 1976), a depression prevention project (Muñoz, Glish, Soo-Hoo, and Robertson, 1982), and a preventive program in mental health and mental retardation (Schanie and Sundel, 1978). It offers flexible options both in the developmental (life span) sense and in terms of selecting a program's target group, setting, optimal time, and methodology (Cowen, 1980). It is well-suited to educational settings, and it is easy to imagine a scenario in which diverse adjustment-linked competences are built into integrated, sequential educational curricula, much as is now done with the 3 Rs.

An important competence beachhead has been established, but vital questions remain: How central and important are the adjustive gains produced by such programs? To what extent do they generalize to new adjustment domains? How well do they endure the harsh test of time?

Normal development affords diverse competence challenges. Certainly competence for a toddler is not the same as competence for a kindergartner or competence for an adolescent. We have scarcely begun to glimpse and probe a few such options from a potentially vast universe of alternatives (Sarason, 1971). Such work should be expanded in a life-span framework to reflect many instrumental competencies, groups, and settings to provide a more comprehensive psychology of health promotion.

A Structural Model for Primary Prevention in Mental Health

Primary prevention in mental health has, in my view, been more mysterious than it need be (Cowen, 1977, 1980, 1983, 1985). I used to think (Cowen, 1977) that primary prevention's worst enemy was lack of clarity about its precise definition and boundary limits, and I still worry about that. But I came to see that the absence of a clearly articulated step-by-step sequence for achieving primary prevention's cherished goals is a major deterrent to progress in this field. With that concern in mind, I recently proposed (Cowen, 1984) a sequential five-step model for developing and documenting primary prevention programs. (See Figure 1.) Although it is somewhat easier to introduce the model in the context of person-centered approaches, it is, I believe, sufficiently flexible to accomodate the operations of most system-level approaches.

Key Steps

The key steps (along the middle axis) are numbered 1–5, respectively. For me, all primary prevention programming starts with a generative knowledge base, showing for competence-enhancement programs (labeled Type 1) that the presence/absence of certain competencies relates to adjustment/maladjustment or, for situation-focused interventions (labeled Type 2), that certain life situations or events are characteristically

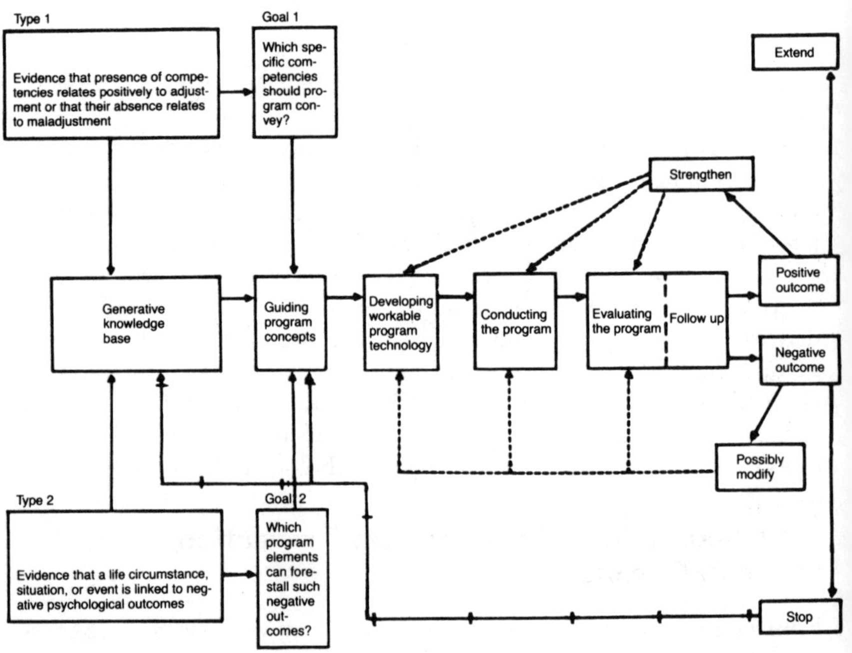

Figure 1. General structural model for primary prevention program development in mental health

followed by negative psychological outcomes. Some of those knowledge bases already exist; others remain to be carved out or filled in. Not all will be found in pigeon holes that mental health professionals best know or typically seek out; rather, they tap domains as diverse as education, sociology, social ecology, family relations, epidemiology, urban planning, political science and social policy formulation, public health, architecture, environmental engineering, and sundry other exotic areas, some noted facetiously in Kessler and Albee's (1975) review.

From those same knowledge bases, we may also learn which specific competencies mediate adjustment for particular target groups or which types of program elements (e.g., support and training situationally relevant skills) may forestall probable negative outcomes. Such knowledge (at least at the conceptual level) establishes in step two what, in general terms, a program should include and convey.

The third step (developing workable program technology) involves translating broad, guiding program concepts into specific curricula and program methodologies. This step requires detailed knowledge of the characteristics, abilities, and motivational levels of specific target groups. Thus preventive programs for 6–8- and 10–12-year-old children of divorce may have very similar objectives, but require very different technologies. System-level approaches are likely to differ most from person-centered approaches in terms of those technological differences.

The fourth step (conducting the program) is more complex than it sounds. People who conduct a program must know the program's components well and provide conditions (e.g., group processes) that allow those components to take hold. Program components must be closely monitored to ensure that sound guesses about optimal methodology have, in fact, been made. Deft program adaptations, in course, may be needed if wrong guesses, weak operational efforts, or poor sequencing of program concepts are identified. These are quality control requirements, which, again, may differ for system-level approaches.

Finally, in step five, program outcomes must be assessed to establish whether intended adjustive outcomes (be they proactive or preventive) have in fact occurred (Lorion, 1983; Lorion and Lounsbury, 1982). Follow-up is included as an integral part of this step, on the assumption that stable, meaningful, and adjustive gain (Cowen, 1978, 1982c), is a key criterion for judging the efficacy of primary prevention programs.

Program and Conceptual Modifications

With positive outcomes, decisions can be made to extend or strengthen the programs. Even effective programs can be improved through modifications that correct perceived weaknesses at steps 3, 4, and 5. With negative outcomes, however, the *source* of error has to be determined and should, in large measure, influence decisions about trying again. If false turns occurred at step 2, modification may be extremely difficult, requiring perhaps literally a return to "Square 1."

Limitations

The approach suggested in this general structural model may have broad applicability to many different primary prevention approaches and methodologies and to diverse age and sociodemographic target groups. However, there is nothing special about the model; others (e.g., Price, 1983) have developed similar representations. I offer this one because it happens to be the one I know best. Moreover, a model per se cannot generate substantive primary prevention concepts or programs; it can simply offer an orderly, systematic framework for developing and pursuing them.

Summary

In the past decade an appealing notion, *primary prevention in mental health,* has taken form and run its early unbridled course. Assessing that course realistically can help us to make the next one a more disciplined, more productive decade of accomplishment.

The decade 1974–84 was a period of gathering and codifying germinal ideas which, in my view, hold the seeds of a fourth mental health revolution. Importantly, a small number of primary prevention interventions, some quite innovative, have been developed and implemented and shown to have at least short-term effectiveness. Those are not insignificant accomplishments for so short a time period. But "baby-step" gains (Cowen, 1977) and fantasy systems should not be confused with enduring, significant accomplishment worthy of the appelative *revolution.*

And so, primary prevention's system and person-centered components face difficult tasks in the decade to come. Although I am warmly disposed to the notions of diversity and pluralism in what we choose to pursue, the methodologies we use, and the people (by discipline or subdiscipline) who engineer and perpetrate pursuit, I am skeptical that there can be real gain unless we insist on a clear, discriminating definition of the concept. Maximizing contrast among options is necessary both for sane planning and for distinguishing between true and pseudo revolutions. Although it is really quite easy to indulge the pleasure principle by cutting definitional corners, such legerdemain will not effectively serve the long-term reality principle of a better psychological world for the many. Primary prevention interventions are for well people: They are intentional (i.e., knowledge-grounded), before-the-fact steps that seek to enhance psychological wellness and/or to forestall predictable dysfunction (Cowen, 1980, 1985). The so-called general structural model that I and others have proposed is less important; it is simply a potentially useful tool, not an imperative.

Our immediate and strongest need is to extend the limited number of documented effective system- or person-centered primary prevention demonstration models. In such work to date, sufficient hard-nosed evaluation has been lacking and has been virtually nonexistent for long-term outcomes. The movement's future credibility depends both on the solidification of its empirical ground (Cowen, 1982c) and an appropriate emphasis on the dissemination of documented models in usable forms and suited to widespread implementation (Masterpasqua and Swift, 1984; Stolz, 1984).

We would be well advised to insist on quality, not quantity, during the next decade. When I use the word *quality,* I mean to imply several things beyond sound research. First, primary prevention's chosen battlefields must be demonstrably important to the domain of psychological well-being. Second, changes that such programs bring about must be real and robust (in the human, rather than just the DSM-III sense); they must be enduring rather than ephemeral, and they must radiate to new adaptive domains. Demonstrating those very qualities is per se a complex, labor intensive challenge for the future. Solid, well documented, quality primary prevention models will produce their own major ripple effects and generalize to other age and sociodemographic groups, and conceptual generalization to productive variants on established themes.

We pay respect to a good, productive, ground-breaking decade. The challenges of the next decade are at once exciting and scary. Well pursued, they should leave us better positioned a decade hence to know whether the now unfolding primary prevention movement will indeed be a fourth mental health revolution with true and distinctive essences.

References

Albee, G. W. (1982). Preventing psychopathology and promoting human potential. *American Psychologist, 37,* 1043–1050.

Allen, G. J., Chinsky, J. M., Larcen, S. W., Lochman, J. E., and Selinger, H. V. (1976). *Community psychology and the schools: A behaviorally oriented multi-level preventive approach.* Hillsdale, N.J.: Lawrence Erlbaum Associates.

Anderson, S., and Messick, S. (1974). Social competence in young children. *Developmental Psychology, 10,* 282–293.

Aronson, E., Blaney, N., Stephan, C., Sikes, J., and Snapp, M. (1978). *The jigsaw classroom.* Beverly Hills, Calif.: Sage.

Aronovitz, E. (1982). *Prevention strategies for mental health*. New York: Westchester County Department of Community Mental Health.

Baisden, B., and Quarantelli, E. L. (1981). The delivery of mental health services in community disasters: An outline of research findings. *Journal of Community Psychology, 9,* 195–203.

Baker, S. B., Swisher, J. D., Nadenichek, P. E., and Popowicz, C. L. (1984). Measured effects of primary prevention strategies. *Personnel and Guidance Journal, 62* 459–464.

Barker, R. G., and Schoggen, P. (1973). *Qualities of community life*. San Francisco: Jossey-Bass.

Berrueta-Clement, J. R., Schweinhart, L. J., Barnett, M. W., Epstein, A. S., and Weikart, D. P. (1984). *Changed lives: The effects of the Perry Preschool Program on youths through age 19*. Ypsilanti, Mich.: High/Scope Educational Research Foundation.

Bloom, B. L. (1980). Social and community interventions. In M. Rosenzweig and L. W. Porter (Eds.), *Annual Review of Psychology, 31,* 111–142.

Bloom, B. L., Asher, S. J., and White, S. W. (1978). Marital disruption as a stressor: A review and analysis. *Psychological Bulletin, 85,* 867–894.

Bloom, B. L., Hodges, W. F., and Caldwell, R. A. (1982). A preventive program for the newly separated. *American Journal of Community Psychology, 10,* 251–264.

Bloom, B. L., Hodges, W. F., Kern, M. B., and McFaddin, S. C. (1985). A preventive intervention program for the newly separated: Final report. *American Journal of Orthopsychiatry, 55.*

Bowlby, J. (1969). *Attachment and loss: I. Attachment*. London: Hogarth Press.

Bronfenbrenner, U. (1979). *The ecology of human development. Experiments by nature and design*. Cambridge, Mass.: Harvard University Press.

Broussard, E. R. (1976). Neonatal predictions and outcome at 10/11 years. *Child Psychiatry and Human Development, 7,* 85–93.

Broussard, E. R. (1977). Primary prevention program for newborn infants at high risk for emotional disorder. In D. C. Klein and S. E. Goldston (Eds.), *Primary prevention: An idea whose time has come.* (pp. 63–68). Rockville, Md.: U. S. Department of Health, Education and Welfare.

Broussard, E. R. (1979). Assessment of the adaptive potential of the mother-infant system: The Neonatal Perception Inventories. In *Seminar in Perinatology: Vol. 3* (pp. 91–100). New York: Grune and Stratton.

Bruce, P. (1958). Relationship of self-acceptance to other variables with sixth-grade children oriented in self-understanding. *Journal of Educational Psychology, 49,* 229–238.

Bry, B. H. (1982). Reducing the incidence of adolescent problems through preventive intervention: One and five year follow-up. *American Journal of Community Psychology, 10,* 265–276.

Bry, B. H., and George, F. E. (1980). The preventive effects of early intervention on the attendance and grades of urban adolescents. *Professional Psychology, 11,* 252–260.

Buss, T., and Redburn, F. S. (1983). *Mass employment: Plant closings and community mental health*. Beverly Hills, Calif.: Sage.

Chandler, C., Weissberg, R. P., Cowen, E. L., and Guare, J. (1984). The long-term effects of a school-based secondary prevention program for young maladapting children. *Journal of Consulting and Clinical Psychology, 52,* 165–170.

Cowen, E. L. (1973). Social and community interventions. In P. Mussen and M. Rosenzweig (Eds.), *Annual Review of Psychology, 24,* 423–472.
Cowen, E. L. (1977). Baby-steps toward primary prevention. *American Journal of Community Psychology, 5,* 1–22.
Cowen, E. L. (1978). Some problems in community program evaluation research. *Journal of Consulting and Clinical Psychology, 46,* 792–805.
Cowen, E. L. (1980). The wooing of primary prevention. *American Journal of Community Psychology, 8,* 258–284.
Cowen, E. L. (Ed.). (1982a). *Research in primary prevention in mental health. American Journal of Community Psychology, 10,* 239–367.
Cowen, E. L. (1982b). Primary prevention research: Barriers, needs and opportunities. *Journal of Primary Prevention, 2,* 131–137.
Cowen, E. L. (1982c). The special number: A compleat roadmap. In E. L. Cowen (Ed.), *Research in primary prevention in mental health. American Journal of Community Psychology, 10,* 239–250.
Cowen, E. L. (1982d). Help is where you find it: Four informal helpgiving groups. *American Psychologist, 37,* 385–395.
Cowen, E. L. (1983). Primary prevention in mental health: Past, present and future. In R. D. Felner, L. Jason, J. Moritsugu, and S. S. Farber (Eds.), *Preventive psychology: Theory, research and practice in community interventions.* New York: Pergamon.
Cowen, E. L. (1984). A general structural model for primary prevention program development in mental health. *Personnel and Guidance Journal, 62,* 485–490.
Cowen, E. L. (1985). Person centered approaches to primary prevention in mental health: Situation focused and competence enhancement. *American Journal of Community Psychology, 13,* 87–98.
Cowen, E. L., Davidson, E. R., and Gesten, E. L. (1980). Program dissemination and the modification of delivery practices in school mental health. *Professional Psychology, 11,* 36–47.
Cowen, E. L., Dorr, D. A., Trost, M. A., and Izzo, L. D. (1972). A follow-up study of maladapting school children seen by nonprofessionals. *Journal of Consulting and Clinical Psychology, 39,* 235–238.
Cowen, E. L., Gesten, E. L., and Weissberg, R. P. (1980). An integrated network of preventively oriented school-based mental health approaches. In R. H. Price and P. Politzer (Eds.), *Evaluation and action in the social environment* (pp. 173–210). New York: Academic Press.
Cowen, E. L., Leibowitz, E., and Leibowitz, G. (1968). Utilization of retired people as mental health aides with children. *American Journal of Orthopsychiatry, 39,* 900–909.
Cowen, E. L., Spinell, A., Wright, S., and Weissberg, R. P. (1983). Continuing dissemination of a school-based early detection and prevention model. *Professional Psychology, 14,* 118–127.
Cowen, E. L., Trost, M. A., Lorion, R. P., Dorr, D., Izzo, L. D., and Isaacson, R. V. (1975). *New ways in school mental health: Early detection and prevention of school maladaptation.* New York: Human Sciences Press, Inc.
Cowen, E. L., Weissberg, R. P., Lotyczewski, B. S., Bromley, M. L., Gilliand-Mallo, G., De Meis, J. L., Farago, J. P., Grassi, R. J., Haffey, W. G., Weiner, M. J. and Woods, A. (1983). Validity generalization of school-based preventive mental health program. *Professional Psychology, 14,* 613–623.

Crowe, A. H., and Middleman, R. R. (1982). The elder program: A strategy for prevention. *Journal of Primary Prevention, 3,* 133–138.

Darlington, R. B., Royce, J. M., Snipper, A. S., Murray, H. W., and Lazar, I. (1980). Preschool programs and later school competence of children from low-income families. *Science, 208,* 202–204.

Dinges, N. G. (1982). Mental health promotion with Navajo families. In S. M. Manson (Ed.), *New directions in prevention among native American and Alaska native communities* (pp. 119–141). Portland, Ore.: Health Sciences University.

Dooley, D., and Catalano, R. (1979). Economic, life, and disorder changes: Time-series analyses. *American Journal of Community Psychology, 7,* 381–396.

Dooley, D., and Catalano, R. (1980). Economic change as a cause of behavior disorder. *Psychological Bulletin, 87,* 450–468.

Drotar, D., Crawford, P., and Ganofsky, M. A. (1984). Prevention with chronically ill children. In M. C. Roberts and L. Peterson (Eds.), *Prevention of problems in childhood: Psychological research and applications* (pp. 232–265). New York: Wiley.

Durlak, J. A. (1983). Social problem-solving as a primary prevention strategy. In R. D. Felner, L. A. Jason, J. N. Moritsugu, and S. S. Farber (Eds.), *Preventive psychology: Theory, research and practice* (pp. 31–48). New York: Pergamon.

Elardo, P. T., and Caldwell, B. M. (1979). The effects of an experimental social development program on children in the middle childhood period. *Psychology in the Schools, 16,* 93–100.

Emery, R. E. (1982). Interpersonal conflict and the children of discord and divorce. *Psychological Bulletin, 92,* 310–330.

Englander-Golden, P., Elconin, J., and Miller, K. J. (1985). Say it straight: Adolescent substance abuse prevention training. *Academic Psychological Bulletin, 7.*

Englander-Golden, P., Elconin, J., and Satir, V. (1986). Assertive/leveling communication and empathy in adolescent drug abuse prevention. *Journal of Primary Prevention, 6* (4) (in press).

Felner, R. D. (1984). Vulnerability in childhood: A preventive framework for understanding children's efforts to cope with life stresses and transitions. In M. C. Roberts and L. Peterson (Eds.), *Prevention of problems in childhood: Psychological research and applications* (pp. 232–265). New York: Wiley.

Felner, R. D., Farber, S. S., and Primavera, J. (1980). Children of divorce, stressful life events, and transitions: A framework for preventive efforts. In R. H. Price, R. F. Ketterer, B. C. Bader, and J. Monahan (Eds.), *Prevention in mental health: Research, policy and practice* (pp. 81–108). Beverly Hills, Calif.: Sage.

Felner, R. D., Farber, S. S., and Primavera, J. (1983). Transition and stressful events: A model for primary prevention. In R. D. Felner, L. A. Jason, J. N. Moritsugu, and S. S. Farber (Eds.), *Preventive psychology: Theory, research and practice* (pp. 199–215). New York: Pergamon.

Felner, R. D., Ginter, M. A., Boike, M. F., and Cowen, E. L. (1981). Parental death or divorce and the school adjustment of young children. *American Journal of Community Psychology, 9,* 181–191.

Felner, R. D., Ginter, M., and Primavera, J. (1982). Primary prevention and school transitions: Social support and environmental structure. *American Journal of Community Psychology, 10,* 277–290.

Felner, R. D., Jason, L. A., Moritsugu, J. N., and Farber, S. S. (1983). *Preventive psychology: Theory, research and practice.* New York: Pergamon.
Felner, R. D., Primavera, J., and Cauce, A. M. (1981). The impact of social transitions: A focus for preventive efforts. *American Journal of Community Psychology, 9,* 449–459.
Felner, R. D., Stolberg, A. L., and Cowen, E. L. (1975). Crisis events and school mental health referral patterns of young children. *Journal of Consulting and Clinical Psychology, 43,* 305–310.
Finkel, N. J. (1974). Strens and traumas: An attempt at categorization. *American Journal of Community Psychology, 2,* 265–275.
Finkel, N. J. (1975). Strens, traumas, and trauma resolution. *American Journal of Community Psychology, 3,* 173–178.
Garmezy, N. (1975). The experimental study of children vulnerable to psychopathology. In A. Davis (Ed.), *Child personality and psychopathology: Current topics,* Vol. 2 (pp. 171–217). New York: Wiley-Interscience.
Garmezy, N. (1976). *Vulnerable and invulnerable children: Theory, research and intervention.* Washington, D. C.: American Psychological Association.
Garmezy, N. (1981). Children under stress: Perspectives on antecedents and correlates of vulnerability and resistance of psychopathology. In A. I. Robin, J. Aronoff, A. M. Barclay, and R. A. Zucker (Eds.), *Further explorations in personality.* New York: Wiley.
Garmezy, N. (1982). Foreword. In E. Werner and R. S. Smith, *Vulnerable but invincible: A study of resilient children* (xiii–xix). New York: McGraw-Hill.
Garmezy, N. (1983). Stressors of childhood. In N. Garmezy and M. Rutter (Eds.), *Stress, coping, and development in children* (pp. 73–84). New York: McGraw-Hill.
Garmezy, N., Masten, A., Nordstrom, L., and Ferrarese, M. (1979). The nature of competence in normal and deviant children. In M. W. Kent and J. E. Rolf (Eds.), *The primary prevention of psychopathology: Vol. 3. Social competence in children* (pp. 23–43). Hanover, N.H.: University Press of New England.
Garmezy, N., and Rutter, M. (1983). *Stress, coping, and development in children.* New York: McGraw-Hill.
Gatz, M., Barbarin, O. A., Tyler, F. B., Mitchell, R. B., Moran, J. A., Wirzbicki, P. J., Crawford, J., and Engelman, A. (1982). Enhancement of individual and community competence: The older adult as community worker. *American Journal of Community Psychology, 10,* 291–303.
Gesten, E. L. (1976). A health resources inventory: The development of a measure of the personal and social competence of primary grade children. *Journal of Consulting and Clinical Psychology, 44,* 775–786.
Gesten, E. L., Rains, M. H. Rapkin, B. D., Weissberg, R. P., Flores de Apodaca, R., Cowen, E. L., and Bowen, R. (1982). Training children in social problem-solving competencies: A first and second look. *American Journal of Community Psychology, 10,* 95–115.
Gilchrist, L. D. and Schinke, S. P. (1983). Coping with contraception: Cognitive and behavioral methods with adolescents. *Cognitive Therapy and Research, 7,* 379–388.
Glidewell, J. C. (1984). Training for the role of advocate. *American Journal of Community Psychology, 12,* 193–198.
Glidewell, J. C., Gildea, M. C.-L., and Kaufman, M. K. (1973). The preventive

and therapeutic effects of two school mental health programs. *American Journal of Community Psychology, 1,* 295–329.

Goldstein, M. J. (1982). *Preventive intervention in schizophrenia: Are we ready?* Washington, D.C.: U.S. Department of Health and Human Services, National Institute of Mental Health.

Goodman, S. H. (1984a). Children of disturbed parents: The interface between research and intervention. *American Journal of Community Psychology, 12,* 663–687.

Goodman, S. H. (1984b). Children of disturbed parents: A research based model for intervention. In B. Cohler and J. Musick (Eds.), *Intervention with psychiatrically disabled parents and their young children* (pp. 33–51). San Francisco, Calif.: Jossey-Bass.

Goodman, S. H., and Isaacs, L. D. (1985). Primary prevention with children of severely disturbed mothers. *Journal of Preventive Psychiatry, 3.*

Gottlieb, B. H. (Ed.). (1981). *Social networks and social support.* Beverly Hills, Calif.: Sage.

Gottlieb, B. H. (Ed.). 1982. Social support and risk reduction. *Journal of Primary Prevention, 3,* 71–132.

Gottlieb, B. H. (1983). Social support as a focus for integrative research in psychology. *American Psychologist, 38,* 278–287.

Gottlieb, B. H. (1984). *Social support strategies: Guidelines for mental health practice.* Beverly Hills, Calif.: Sage.

Gottlieb, B. H. (1985). Social support and community mental health. In S. Cohen and L. Syme (Eds.), *Social support and health* (pp. 303–326). New York: Academic Press.

Graziano, A. M., DeGiovanni, I. S., and Garcia, K. A. (1979). Behavioral treatment of children's fears: A review. *Psychological Bulletin, 86,* 804–830.

Greenspan, S. I. (1981). *Psychopathology and adaptation in infancy and early childhood: Principles of clinical diagnosis and preventive intervention.* Clinical Infant Report No. 1. New York: International Universities Press.

Greenspan, S. I. (1982). Developmental morbidity in infants in multi-risk-factor families. *Public Health Reports, 97,* 16–23.

Griggs, J. W., and Bonney, M. E. (1970). Relationship between "causal" orientation and acceptance of others, "self-ideal self" congruence, and mental health changes for fourth- and fifth-grade children. *Journal of Educational Research, 63,* 471–477.

Guidubaldi, J., Cleminshaw, A. K., Perry, J. D., and Mcloughlin, C. S. (1983). The impact of parental divorce on children: Report of the nationwide NASP study. *School Psychology Review, 12,* 300–323.

Gump, P. V. (1980). The school as a social situation. In M. R. Rosenweig and L. W. Porter (Eds.), *Annual Review of Psychology, 31,* 553–582.

Harter, S. (1974). Pleasure derived by children from cognitive challenge and mastery. *Child Development, 45,* 661–669.

Harter, S. (1979). The effects of social support: Prevention and treatment implications. In A. P. Goldstein and F. H. Kanfer (Eds.), *Maximizing treatment gains: Transfer enhancement in psychotherapy* (pp. 353–375). New York: Academic Press.

Harter, S. (1981). A model of mastery motivation in children: Individual differences and developmental changes. In W. A. Collins (Ed.), *Aspects of the development of competence* (pp. 215–255). Hillsdale, N.J.: L. E. Erlbaum Associates.

Hartsough, D. M., and Savitsky, J. C. (1984). Three Mile Island: Psychology and environmental policy at the crossroads. *American Psychologist, 39,* 1113–1122.

Heller, K., and Swindle, R. W. (1984). Social networks, perceived social support, and coping with stress. In R. D. Felner, L. A. Jason, J. N Moritsugu, and S. S. Farber (Eds.), *Preventive psychology: Theory, research and practice* (pp. 31–48). New York: Pergamon.

Hetherington, E. M. (1979). Divorce: A child's perspective. *American Psychologist, 34,* 851–858.

Hetherington, E. M., Cox, M., and Cox, R. (1978). The aftermath of divorce. In J. H. Stevens and M. Mathews (Eds.), *Mother–child, father–child relationships* (pp. 149–176). Washington, D.C.: National Association for the Education of Young Children.

Hodgson, S. (1979). *Intervening to support parents in high-risk populations.* Toronto, Canada: University of Toronto Press.

Hollister, W. G. (1965). The concept of "strens" in preventive interventions and ego-strength building in the schools. In N. M. Lambert (Ed.), *The protection and promotion of mental health in schools* (pp. 30–35). Washington, D.C.: U.S. Department of Health, Education, and Welfare.

Hollister, W. G. (1967). Concept of strens in education: A challenge to curriculum development. In E. M. Bower and W. G. Hollister (Eds.), *Behavioral science frontiers in education* (pp. 193–206). New York: Wiley.

Holmes, T. H., and Rahe, R. H. (1967). The social readjustment rating scale. *Journal of Psychosomatic Research, 11,* 213–218.

Insel, P. M., and Moos, R. H. (1974). Psychosocial environments: Expanding the scope of human ecology. *American Psychologist, 29,* 179–188.

Iscoe, I. (1974). Community psychology and the competent community. *American Psychologist, 29,* 607–613.

Iscoe, I. (1984). Austin—A decade later: Preparing community psychology students for work in social policy areas. *American Journal of Community Psychology, 12,* 175–184.

Iscoe, I., and Harris, L. C. (1984). Social and community interventions. In M. R. Rosenzweig and L. W. Porter (Eds.), *Annual Review of Psychology, 35,* 333–360.

Jason, L. A., Felner, R. D., Moritsugu, J. N., and Farber, S. S. (1983). Future directions for preventive psychology. In R. D. Felner, L. A. Jason, J. N. Moritsugu, and S. S. Farber (Eds.), *Preventive psychology: Theory, research and practice* (pp. 31–48). New York: Pergamon.

Jason, L. A., Robson, S. D., and Lipshutz, S. A. (1980). Enhancing sharing behaviors through the use of naturalistic contingencies. *Journal of Community Psychology, 8,* 237–244.

Joffe, J. M., Albee, G. N., and Kelly, L. D. (Eds.). (1984). *Readings in primary prevention of psychopathology.* Hanover, N.H.: University Press of New England.

Johnson, D. L. (1975). The development of a program for parent–child education among Mexican-Americans in Texas. In B. Z. Friedlander, G. M. Sterritt, and G. E. Kirk (Eds.), *Exceptional Infant,* Vol. 3 (pp. 374–398). New York: Brunner-Mazel.

Johnson, D. L., and Breckenridge, J. N. (1982). The Houston Parent–Child Development Center and the primary prevention of behavior problems in young children. *American Journal of Community Psychology, 10,* 305–316.

Johnson, D. L., Kahn, A. J., and Leler, H. (1976). *Parent–Child Development Center Program.* Houston: Houston Parent Child Development Center. (ERIC Document Reproduction Service No. ED 135-459)

Johnson, D. L., and Walker, T. (1984). *The primary prevention of behavior problems in Mexican-American children.* Paper presented at American Psychological Association Meeting, Toronto, Canada.

Kalter, N. (1977). Children of divorce in an outpatient psychiatric population. *American Journal of Orthopsychiatry, 47,* 40–51.

Katz, R. (1984). Empowerment and synergy: Expanding the community's healing resources. *Prevention in Human Services, 3,* 201–226.

Kellam, S. G., Branch, J. D., Agrawal, K. C., and Ensminger, M. E. (1975). *Mental Health and going to school: The Woodlawn program of assessment, early intervention, and evaluation.* Chicago: University of Chicago Press.

Kelly, J. B., and Wallerstein, J. S. (1976). The effects of parental divorce: Experiences of the child in early latency. *American Journal of Orthopsychiatry, 46,* 20–32.

Kelly, J. G. (1974). *Toward a psychology of healthiness.* Address presented at the meeting of Western Psychological Association.

Kelly, J. G., Snowden, L. E. and Muñoz, R. F. (1977). Social and community interventions. In M. R. Rosenzweig and L. W. Porter (Eds.), *Annual Review of Psychology, 28,* 323–361.

Kessler, M., and Albee, G. W. (1975). Primary prevention. In M. R. Rosenzweig and L. W. Porter (Eds.), *Annual Review of Psychology, 26,* 557–591.

Kieffer, C. H. (1984). Citizen empowerment: A developmental perspective. *Prevention in Human Services, 3,* 9–36.

Kirschenbaum, D. (1979). Social competence intervention and evaluation in the inner city: Cincinnati's Social Skills Development Program. *Journal of Consulting and Clinical Psychology, 47,* 778–780.

Kirschenbaum, D., DeVoge, J. B., Marsh, M. E., and Steffen, J. J. (1980). Multimodal evaluation of therapy vs. consultation components in a large inner-city early intervention program. *American Journal of Community Psychology 8,* 587–601.

Kirschenbaum, D., Pedro, J., and DeVoge, J. B. (1983). A social competency model meets an early intervention program: Description and evaluation of Cincinnati's Social skills Development Program. In D. F. Ricks, and B. S. Dohrenwend (Eds.), *Prevention of mental illness: Research frontiers* (pp. 215–250). New York: Pergamon.

Klaus, M. H., and Kennell, J. H. (1976). *Maternal–infant bonding.* St. Louis: C. V. Mosby.

Klein, D. C., and Goldston, S. E. (Eds.). (1977). *Primary prevention: An idea whose time has come.* Washington, D.C.: U.S. Government Printing Office. Department of Health, Education, and Welfare Publication No. (ADM) 77-447.

Kobasa, S. C. (1979). Personality and resistance to illness. *American Journal of community Psychology, 7,* 413–424.

Kobasa, S. C., Maddi, S. R., and Kahn, S. (1982). Hardiness and health: A prospective study. *Journal of Personality and Social Psychology, 42,* 168–177.

Kornberg, M. S., and Caplan, G. (1980). Risk factors and preventive intervention in child therapy: A review. *Journal of Prevention, 1,* 71–133.

Kurdek, L. A. (1981). An integrative perspective on children's divorce adjustment. *American Psychologist, 36,* 856–866.

Lazar, I., and Darlington, R. (1982). Lasting effects of early education: A report from the Consortium for Longitudinal Studies. *Monographs of the Society for Research in Child Development, 47,* Serial No. 195, Nos. 2–3.

Lazar, I., Hubbell, V., Murray, H. W., Rosche, M., and Royce, J. (1977). *The persistence of preschool effects: A long-term follow-up of fourteen infant and preschool experiments.* Washington, D.C.: U.S. Department of Health, Education, and Welfare.

Lazarus, R. S. (1981). The stress and coping paradigm. In C. Eisdorfer, D. Cohen, A. Kleinman, and P. Maxim (Eds.), *Models for clinical psychological pathology* (pp. 177–214). New York: Spectrum.

Levine, A. (1982). *The Love Canal: Science, politics and people.* New York: Lexington Books.

Lieberman, M. A., and Borman, L. D. (1981). Researchers study THEOS: Report group's effect big help to members. *THEOS, 20,* 3–6.

Lieberman, M. A., and Glidewell, J. C. (Eds.). (1978). The helping process. *American Journal of Community Psychology, 6,* 405–507.

Lindemann, E. (1944). Symptomatology and management of acute grief. *American Journal of Psychiatry, 101,* 141–148.

Lorion, R. P. (1983). Evaluating preventive interventions: Guidelines for the serious social change-agent. In R. D. Felner, L. A. Jason, J. N. Moritsugu, and S. S. Farber (Eds.), *Preventive psychology: Theory, research and practice* (pp. 251–268). New York: Pergamon.

Lorion, R. P., and Lounsbury, J. (1982). Conceptual and methodological considerations in evaluating preventive interventions. In W. R. Task and G. Stahler (Eds.), *Innovative approaches to mental health evaluation* (pp. 24–57). New York: Academic Press.

Lorion, R. P., and Stenmark, D. E. (Eds.). (1984). Training in community psychology. *American Journal of Community Psychology, 12,* 133–259.

Lorion, R. P., Work, W. C., and Hightower, A. D. (1984). A school-based multilevel preventive intervention: Issues in program development and evaluation. *Personnel and Guidance Journal, 62,* 479–484.

Lotyczewski, B. S., Cowen, E. L., and Weissberg, R. P. (1984). Adjustment correlates of physical and health problems in young children. *Journal of Special Education, 18.*

Maccoby, N., and Alexander, J. (1979). Reducing heart disease risk using the mass media: Comparing the effects on three communities. In R. F. Muñoz, L. R. Snowden, and J. G. Kelly (Eds.), *Social and psychological research in community settings* (pp. 69–100). San Francisco: Jossey-Bass.

Maccoby, N., and Farquhar, J. W. (1975). Communication for health: Unselling heart disease. *Journal of Communication, 25,* 114–126.

Maccoby, N., and Farquhar, J. W. (1976). Bringing California's health report up to date. *Journal of Communication, 26,* 56–57.

Manson, S. M. (Ed.). (1982). *New directions in prevention among native American and Alaska native communities.* Portland, Ore. Oregon Health Sciences University.

Marlowe, H. A., and Weinberg, R. B. (1983). *Primary prevention: Fact or fallacy?* Tampa: University of South Florida.

Masterpasqua, F., and Swift, M. (1984). Prevention of problems in childhood on a community wide basis. In M. C. Roberts and L. Peterson (Eds.), *Prevention of problems in childhood: Psychological research and applications* (pp. 369–388). New York: Wiley.

Matefy, R. E. (1978). Evaluation of a remediation program using senior citizens as psychoeducational agents. *Community Mental Health Journal, 14,* 327–336.

Maton, K. I., and Rappaport, J. (1984). Empowerment in a religious setting. *Prevention in Human Services, 3,* 38–72.

Melamed, B. G., and Siegel, L. J. (1975). Reduction of anxiety on children facing hospitalization and surgery, by use of filmed modeling. *Journal of Consulting and Clinical Psychology, 43,* 511–521.

Monahan, J., and Vaux, A. (1980). Task force report: The macroenvironment and community mental health. *Community Mental Health Journal, 16,* 14–26.

Monroe, S. M. (1982). Life events assessment: Current practices, emerging trends. *Clinical Psychology Review, 2,* 435–454.

Moos, R. H. (1973). Conceptualizations of human environments. *American Psychologist, 28,* 652–665.

Moos, R. H. (1974). *Evaluating treatment environments: A social ecological approach.* New York: Wiley.

Moos, R. H. (1976). Evaluating and changing community settings. *American Journal of Community Psychology, 4,* 313–326.

Moos, R. H. (1979a). *Evaluating educational environments.* San Francisco: Jossey-Bass.

Moos, R. H. (1979b). Improving social settings by social climate measurement and feedback. In R. F. Muñoz, L. R. Snowden, and J. G. Kelly (Eds.), *Social and psychological research in community settings* (pp. 145–182). San Francisco: Jossey-Bass.

Moos, R. H. (1984). Context and coping: Toward a unifying conceptual framework. *American Journal of Community Psychology, 12,* 5–23.

Muenchow, S., and Shays, S. (1980). *Head Start in the 1980's: Review and recommendations.* St. Paul, Minn.: Bush Foundation.

Muñoz, R. F., Glish, M., Soo-Hoo, T., and Robertson, J. (1982). The San Francisco Mood Survey Project: Preliminary work toward the prevention of depression. *American Journal of Community Psychology, 10,* 317–329.

Muñoz, R. F., and Kelly, J. G. (1975). *The prevention of mental disorders.* Homewood, Ill.: Learning Systems, Inc.

Muñoz, R. F., Snowden, L. F., and Kelly, J. G. (Eds.). (1979). *Social and psychological research in community settings.* San Francisco: Jossey-Bass.

Murrell, S. A. (1984). The social policy process and community psychology training. *American Journal of Community Psychology, 12,* 209–216.

Muuss, R. E. (1960). The effects of a one and two year causal learning program. *Journal of Personality, 28,* 479–491.

Newbrough, J. R. (1984). Editorial: 1984—Prospects for the field of community psychology. *Journal of Community Psychology, 12,* 91–98.

Ojemann, R. H. (1961). Investigations on the effects of teacher understanding and appreciation of behavior dynamics. In G. Caplan (Ed.), *Prevention of mental disorders in children* (pp. 378–397). New York: Basic Books.

Ojemann, R. H. (1969). Incorporating psychological concepts in the school curriculum. In H. P. Clarizio (Ed.), *Mental health and the educative process* (pp. 360–368). Chicago: Rand McNally.

Olweus, D. (1978). *Aggression in the schools.* Washington, D.C.: Hemisphere.

Olweus, D. (1979). Stability of aggressive reaction patterns in males: A review. *Psychological Bulletin, 86,* 852–875.

Olweus, D. (1984). *Bullying and harassment among school children in Scandinavia: Research and a nationwide campaign in Norway.* Unpublished manuscript, May, 1984.

Osofsky, J. (1986). Perspectives on infant mental health. In M. Kessler and S. E. Goldston (Eds.), *A decade of progress in primary prevention.* Hanover, N.H.: University Press of New England.

Osterweis, M., Solomon, F., and Green, M. (Eds.). (1984). *Bereavement: Reactions, consequences and care.* Washington, D.C.: National Academy Press.

O'Sullivan, M. J., Waugh, N., and Espeland, W. (1984). The Fort McDowell Yavapai: From pawns to powerbrokers. *Prevention in Human Services, 3,* 73–97.

Pedro-Carroll, J. L., and Cowen, E. L. (1985). The Children of Divorce Intervention Project: An investigation of the efficacy of a school based prevention project. *Journal of Consulting and Clinical Psychology, 54.*

Peterson, L. C., and Brownlee-Duffeck, M. (1984). Prevention of anxiety and pain due to medical and dental procedures. In M. C. Roberts and L. Peterson (Eds.), *Prevention of problems in childhood: Psychological research and applications* (pp. 263–308). New York: Wiley.

Pierson, D. E., Bronson, M. B. Dromey, E., Swartz, J. P. Tivnan, T., and Walker, D. K. (1983). The impact of early education measured by classroom observations and teacher ratings of children in kindergarten. *Evaluation Review, 7,* 191–216.

Pierson, D. E., Klein-Walker, D., and Tivnan, T. (1984). A school-based program from infancy to kindergarten for parents and their children. *Personnel and Guidance Journal, 62,* 448–455.

President's Commission on Mental Health (1978). *Report to the President,* Vol. 1. Washington, D.C.: U.S. Government Printing Office, Stock No. 040-000-00390-8.

Prevention Task Panel Report. (1978). *Task Panel reports submitted to the President's Commission on Mental Health,* Vol. 4. (pp. 1822–1863). Washington, D.C.: U.S. Government Printing Office, Stock No. 040-000-00393-2.

Price, R. H. (1983). The education of a prevention psychologist. In R. D. Felner, L. A. Jason, J. N. Moritsugu, and S. S. Farber (Eds.), *Preventive psychology: Theory, research and practice)* (pp. 290–296). New York: Pergamon.

Price, R. H., Ketterer, R. F., Bader, B. C., and Monahan, J. (Eds.). (1980). *Prevention in mental health: Research, policy and practice.* Beverly Hills, Calif.: Sage.

Rappaport, J. (1977). *Community psychology: Values, research, and action.* New York: Holt, Rinehart and Winston.

Rappaport, J. (1981). In praise of paradox: A social policy of empowerment over prevention. *American Journal of Community Psychology, 9,* 1–25.

Rappaport, J. (1984). Studies in empowerment: Introduction to the issue. *Prevention in Human Services, 3,* 1–7.

Rappaport, J., Davidson, W. S., Wilson, M. N., and Mitchell, A. (1975). Alternatives to blaming the victim or the environment: Our places to stand have not moved the earth. *American Psychologist, 30,* 525–528.

Rappaport, J., Seidman, E., Toro, P. A., McFadden, L. S., Reischl, T. M., Roberts, L. J., Salem, D. A., Stein, C. H., and Zimmerman, M. A. (1985). Collaborative research with a mutual help organization. *Social Policy, 15,* 12–24.

Rappaport, J., Swift, C., and Hess, R. D. (Eds.). (1984). *Studies in empowerment: Steps toward understanding and action. Prevention in Human Services, 3,* 1–230.

Reich, J. W., and Zautra, A. J. (1983). Demands and desires in daily life: Some influences on well-being. *American Journal of Community Psychology, 11,* 41–58.

Reiff, R., and Riessman, F. (1965). The indigenous nonprofessional: A strategy of change in community action and community mental health programs. *Community Mental Health Journal,* Monograph No. 1.

Reiss, S., and Dyhdalo, N. (1975). Persistence, achievement and open-space environments. *Journal of Educational Psychology, 67,* 506–513.

Reiss, S., and Martell, R. (1974), *Educational and psychological effects of open space education in Oak Park, Illinois.* Final Report to Board of Education, District 97, Oak Park, Illinois.

Rhoads, D. L., and Raymond, J. S. (1981). Quality of life and the competent community. *American Journal of Community Psychology, 9,* 293–301.

Rickel, A. U., Dyhdalo, L. L., and Smith, R. L. (1984). Prevention with preschoolers. In M. C. Roberts and L. Peterson (Eds.), *Prevention of problems in childhood: Psychological research and applications* (pp. 74–102). New York: Wiley.

Rickel, A. U., and Lampi, L. A. (1981). A two-year follow-up study of a preventive mental health program for preschoolers. *Journal of Abnormal Child Psychology, 9,* 455–464.

Rickel, A. U., and Smith, R. L. (1979). Maladapting preschool children: Identification, diagnosis and remediation. *American Journal of Community Psychology, 7,* 197–208.

Riessman, F. (1965). The "helper therapy" principle. *Social Work, 10,* 27–32.

Riessman, F. (1967). A neighborhood-based mental health approach. In E. L. Cowen, E. A. Gardner, and M. Zax (Eds.), *Emergent approaches to mental health problems* (pp. 162–184). New York: Appleton-Century-Crofts.

Riessman, F. (1986). Support groups as preventive intervention. In M. Kessler and S. E. Goldston (Eds.), *A decade of progress in primary prevention.* Hanover, N.H.: University Press of New England.

Roberts, M. C., Elkins, P. D., and Royal, G. P. (1984). Psychological applications to the prevention of accidents and illness. In M. C. Roberts and L. Peterson (Eds.), *Prevention of problems in childhood: Psychological research and applications.* (pp. 173–199). New York: Wiley.

Roberts, M. C., and Peterson, L. (Eds.) (1984). *Prevention of problems in childhood: Psychological research and applications.* New York: Wiley.

Roskin, M. (1982). Coping with life changes: A preventive social work approach. *American Journal of Community Psychology, 10,* 331–340.

Rotheram, M. J. (1980). Social skills training programs in elementary and high school classrooms. In D. Rathgen and J. Foreyt (Eds.), *Social competence throughout the life span* (pp. 69–112). New York: Pergamon.

Rotheram, M. J. (1982). Social skills training with underachieving, disruptive and exceptional children. *Psychology in the Schools, 19,* 532–539.

Rotheram, M. J., Armstrong, M., and Booraem, C. (1982). Assertiveness training in fourth- and fifth-grade children. *American Journal of Community Psychology, 10,* 567–582.

Rutter, M. (1983). Stress, coping and development: Some issues and some questions. In N. Garmezy and M. Rutter (Eds.), *Stress, coping and development in children* (pp. 1–41). New York: McGraw-Hill.

Ryan, W. (1971). *Blaming the victim*. New York: Random House.

Sandler, I. N. (Ed.). (1985). Children's environments: Maximizing the mental health of children. *American Journal of Community Psychology, 13,* 335–337.

Sandler, I. N., and Guenther, R. (1985). Assessment of life stress events. In P. Karoly (Ed.), *Measurement strategies in health psychology* (pp. 555–600). New York: Wiley.

Sandler, I. N., Wolchik, S., and Braver, S. (1985). Social support and children of divorce. In I. G. Sarason and B. R. Sarason (Eds.), *Social support: Theory, research and application* (pp. 371–389). The Hague, Netherlands: Martinus Nijhoff.

Sarason, S. B. (1971). *The culture of the school and the problem of change*. Boston: Allyn-Bacon.

Sarason, S. B. (1983). *Schooling in America: Scapegoat and salvation*. New York: The Free Press.

Sarason, S. B. (1984). Community psychology and public policy: Missed opportunity. *American Journal of Community Psychology, 12,* 199–208.

Schanie, C. F., and Sundel, M. (1978). A community mental health innovation in mass media prevention evaluation: The Alternatives Project. *American Journal of Community Psychology, 6,* 573–581.

Schinke, S. P., Blythe, B. J., and Gilchrist, L. D. (1981). Cognitive and behavioral prevention of adolescent pregnancy. *Journal of Counseling Psychology, 28,* 451–454.

Schinke, S. P., Gilchrist, L. D., and Small, R. W. (1979). Preventing unwanted adolescent pregnancy: A cognitive behavioral approach. *American Journal of Orthopsychiatry, 49,* 81–88.

Schweinhart, L. J., and Weikart, D. P. (1980). *Young children grown up: The effects of the Perry Preschool Program on youths through age 15*. Ypsilanti, Mich.: High-Scope Educational Research Foundation.

Segal, J. (1983). Utilization of stress and coping research: Issues of public education and public policy. In N. Garmezy & M. Rutter, *Stress, coping and development in children* (pp. 303–334). New York: McGraw-Hill.

Segal, J. (1986). Stress and resiliency: A developmental perspective. In M. Kessler and S. E. Goldston (Eds.), *A decade of progress in primary prevention*. Hanover, N.H.: University Press of New England.

Seidman, E., and Rapkin, B. (1983). Economics and psychosocial dysfunction: Toward a conceptual framework and prevention strategies. In R. D. Felner, L. A. Jason, J. N. Moritsugu, and S. S. Farber (Eds.), *Preventive psychology: Theory, research & practice* (pp. 175–198). New York: Pergamon.

Seitz, V., Apfel, N. H., and Efron, C. (1979). Long-term effects of early intervention: The New Haven Project. In B. Brown (Ed.), *Found: Long-term gains from early intervention*. Boulder, Colo.: Westview.

Serrano-Garcia, I. (1984). The illusion of empowerment: Community development within a colonial context. *Prevention in Human Services, 3,* 173–200.

Shaw, M. C., and Goodyear, R. K. (Eds.). (1984). Primary prevention in the schools. *Personnel and Guidance Journal, 62,* 443–495.

Shore, M. F. (Ed.). (1965). *Red is the color of hurting*. Rockville, Md.: National Institute of Mental Health.

Shure, M. B. (1979). Training children to solve interpersonal problems: A preventive approach. In R. F. Muñoz, L. F. Snowden, and J. G. Kelly (Eds.), *Social and psychological research in community settings* (pp. 50–68). San Francisco: Jossey-Bass.

Shure, M. B., and Spivack, G. (1978). *Problem-solving techniques in childrearing.* San Francisco: Jossey-Bass.

Shure, M. B., and Spivack, G. (1982). Interpersonal problem-solving in young children: A cognitive approach to prevention. *American Journal of Community Psychology, 10,* 341–356.

Shure, M. B., Spivack, G., and Gordon, R. (1972). Problem-solving thinking: A preventive mental health program for preschool children. *Reading World, 11,* 259–274.

Silverman, P. R. (1969). The widow–widow program: An experiment in preventive intervention. *Mental Hygiene, 53,* 333–337.

Silverman, P. R. (1976). The widow as a caregiver in a program of preventive intervention with other widows. In G. Caplan and M. Killilea (Eds.), *Support systems and mutual help: Multidisciplinary explorations* (pp. 233–243). New York: Grune and Stratton.

Silverman, P. R. (1981). *Helping women cope with grief.* Beverly Hills, Calif.: Sage.

Slavin, R. (1977). Classroom reward structure: An analytical and practical review. *Review of Educational Research, 44,* 633–650.

Spivack, G., Platt, J. J., and Shure, M. B. (1976). *The problem-solving approach to adjustment.* San Francisco: Jossey-Bass.

Spivack, G., and Shure, M. B. (1974). *Social adjustment of young children: A cognitive approach to solving real-life problems.* San Francisco: Jossey-Bass.

Sprinthall, N. A. (1981). A new model for research in the service of guidance and counseling. *Personnel and Guidance Journal, 58,* 487–494.

Sprinthall, N. A. (1984). Primary prevention: A road paved with a plethora of promises and procrastinations. *Personnel and Guidance Journal, 62,* 491–495.

Stallings, J. (1975). Implementation and child effects of teaching practices in follow-through classrooms. *Monographs of the Society for Research on Child Development, 40,* Serial No. 163.

Stamps, L. W. (1975). *Enhancing success in school for deprived children by teaching realistic goal setting.* Paper presented at Society for Research in Child Development, Denver.

State Government Mental Health Prevention Contacts (1983). *Directory.* Rockville, Md.: Office of Prevention, National Institute of Mental Health.

Staub, E. (1979). *Positive social behavior and morality: Socialization and development,* Vol. 2. New York: Academic Press.

Sterling, S., Cowen, E. L., Weissberg, R. P., Lotyczewski, B. S., and Boike, M. (1985). Recent stressful life events and young children's school adjustment. *American Journal of Community Psychology, 13,* 31–48.

Stolberg, A. L., and Garrison, K. M. (1985). Evaluating a primary prevention program for children of divorce: The Divorce Adjustment Project. *American Journal of Community Psychology, 13,* 111–124.

Stolz, S. B. (1984). Preventive models: Implications for a technology of practice. In M. C. Roberts and L. Peterson (Eds.), *Prevention of problems in childhood: Psychological research and applications* (pp. 391–413). New York: Wiley.

Stone, G., Hinds, W. C., and Schmidt, G. W. (1975). Teaching mental health behaviors to elementary school children. *Professional Psychology, 6*, 34–40.

Strayhorn, J. M. (1983). *Preventive mental health intervention for preschoolers.* Unpublished manuscript.

Susskind, E. (1979). Encouraging teachers to encourage children's curiosity: A pivotal competence. *Journal of Clinical Child Psychology, 8*, 101–106.

Swift, C. (1984). Empowerment: An antidote for folly. *Prevention in Human Services, 3*, ix–xv.

Tableman, B., Marciniak, D., Johnson, D., and Rodgers, R. Stress management training for women on public assistance. *American Journal of Community Psychology, 10*, 359–367.

Tefft, B. M., and Kloba, J. A. (1981). Underachieving high-school students as mental health aides with maladapting primary grade children. *American Journal of Community Psychology, 9*, 303–319.

Thelen, M. H., Fry, R. A., Fehrenback, P. A., and Frautschi, N. M. (1979). Therapeutic videotape modeling: A review. *Psychological Bulletin, 86*, 701–720.

Tierney, K. H., and Baisden, B. (1979). *Crisis intervention for disaster victims: A sourcebook and manual for smaller communities.* Washington, D.C.: U.S. Government Printing Office.

Urbain, E. S., and Kendall, P. C. (1980). Review of social-cognitive-problem-solving interventions with children. *Psychological Bulletin, 88*, 109–143.

Vachon, M., Lyall, W. A., Rogers, J., Freedman-Letofsky, K., and Freeman, S. (1980). A controlled study of a self-help intervention for widows. *American Journal of Psychiatry, 137*, 1380–1384.

Vaux, A., and Ruggiero, M. (1983). Stressful life change and delinquent behavior. *American Journal of Community Psychology, 11*, 169–183.

Videka-Sherman, L. (1982). Effects of participation in self-help groups for bereaved parents: Compassionate Friends. *Prevention in Human Services, 1*, 69–77.

Vincent, T. A., and Trickett, E. J. (1983). Preventive intervention and the human context: Ecological approaches to environmental assessment and change. In R. D. Felner, L. A. Jason, J. N. Moritsugu, and S. S. Farber (Eds.), *Preventive psychology: Theory, research and practice* (pp. 67–86). New York: Pergamon.

Vogelsong, E. L., Most, R. K., and Yanchko, A. (1979). Relationship enhancement training for preadolescents in public schools. *Journal of Clinical Child Psychology, 8*, 97–100.

Wallerstein, J. S. (1983). Children of divorce: Stress and developmental tasks. In N. Garmezy and M. Rutter (Eds.), *Stress, coping and development in children* (pp. 265–302). New York: McGraw-Hill.

Wallerstein J. S, and Kelly, J. B. (1974). The effects of parental divorce: The adolescent experience. In E. Anthony and C. Koupernik (Eds.), *The child and his family,* Vol. 3 (pp. 479–505). New York: Wiley.

Wallerstein, J. S., and Kelly, J. B. (1975). The effects of parental divorce: Experiences of the preschool child. *Journal of the American Academy of Child Psychiatry, 14*, 600–616.

Wallerstein, J. S., and Kelly, J. B. (1976). The effects of parental divorce: Experiences of the child in later latency. *American Journal of Orthopsychiatry, 46*, 256–269.

Wallerstein, J. S., and Kelly, J. B. (1976). Children and divorce: A review. *Social Work, 24,* 468–475.

Wallerstein, J. S., and Kelly, J. B. (1980). *Surviving the breakup: How children and parents cope with divorce.* New York: Basic Books.

Wandersman, A., Andrews, A., Riddle, D., and Fawcett, C. (1983). Environmental psychology and prevention. In R. D. Felner, L. A. Jason, J. N. Moritsugu, and S. S. Farber (Eds.), *Preventive psychology: Theory, research and practice* (pp. 104–127). New York: Pergamon.

Watzlawick, P., Weakland, J., and Fisch, R. (1974). *Change: Principles of problem formation and problem resolution.* New York: W. W. Norton.

Weikart, D. P., Bond, J. T., and McNeil, J. T. (1978). *The Ypsilanti Perry Preschool Project: Preschool years and longitudinal results through 4th grade.* Ypsilanti, Mich.: High/Scope Educational Research Foundation.

Weissberg, R. P., Cowen, E. L., Lotyczewski, B. S., and Gesten, E. L. (1983). The Primary Mental Health Project: Seven consecutive years of program outcome research. *Journal of Consulting and Clinical Psychology, 51,* 100–107.

Weissberg, R. P., and Gesten, E. L. (1982). Considerations for developing effective school-based social problem-solving programs. *Schools Psychology Review, 11,* 56–63.

Weissberg, R. P., Gesten, E. L., Carnrike, C. L., Toro, P. A., Rapkin, B. D., Davidson, E., and Cowen, E. L. (1981). Social problem-solving skills training: A competence building intervention with 2nd–4th grade children. *American Journal of Community Psychology, 9,* 411–424.

Weissberg, R. P., Gesten, E. L., Rapkin, B. D., Cowen, E. L., Davidson, E., Flores de Apodaca, R., and McKim, B. J. (1981). Evaluation of a social problem-solving training program for suburban and inner-city third-grade children. *Journal of Consulting and Clinical Psychology, 49,* 251–261.

Werner, E. E., Bierman, J. M., and French, F. E. (1971). *The children of Kauai: A longitudinal study from the prenatal period to age ten.* Honolulu: University of Hawaii Press.

Werner, E. E., and Smith, R. S. (1977). *Kauai's children come of age.* Honolulu: University of Hawaii Press.

Werner, E. E., and Smith, R. S. (1982). *Vulnerable but invincible: A study of resilient children.* New York: McGraw-Hill.

Westinghouse Learning Corporation. (1969). *The impact of Head Start: An evaluation of the effects of Head Start on children's cognitive and affective development.* Washington, D.C.: U.S. Office of Economic Opportunity.

White, R. W. (1959). Motivation reconsidered: The concept of competence. *Psychological Review, 66,* 297–333.

White, R. W. (1979). Competence as an aspect of personal growth. In M. W. Kent and J. E. Rolf (Eds.), *Primary prevention of psychopathology,* Vol. 3. *Social competence in children.* Hanover, N.H.: University Press of New England.

Wright, S., and Cowen, E. L. (1985). The effects of peer teaching on student perceptions of class environment, adjustment and academic performance. *American Journal of Community Psychology, 13,* 417–431.

Zautra, A. J. (1983a). Social support and the quality of life. *American Journal of Community Psychology, 11,* 275–290.

Zautra, A. J. (Ed.). (1983b). The measurement of quality in community life. *American Journal of Community Psychology, 11,* 83–181.

Zautra, A. J., and Goodbart, D. (1979). Quality of life indicators: A review of the literature. *Community Mental Health Review, 4,* 1–10.
Zautra, A. J., and Reich, J. W. (1980). Positive life events and reports of well-being: Some useful distinctions. *American Journal of Community Psychology, 8,* 657–670.
Zautra, A. J., and Reich, J. W. (1983). Life events and perceptions of life quality: Developments in a two factor approach. *Journal of Community Psychology, 11,* 121–132.
Zautra, A. J., and Simons, L. S. (1979). Some effects of positive life events on community mental health. *American Journal of Community Psychology, 7,* 441–451.

PART II

Research Bases for Prevention

Genetics and Psychopathology

Prospects for Prevention

Peter McGuffin and Randy Katz

Psychiatric Genetics and Primary Prevention

Despite the recent resurgence of interest in biological psychiatry, it remains somewhat unfashionable to discuss the possible implications of genetic findings for prevention of psychopathology. Individually, the terms *psychiatric genetics* and *primary prevention* sound innocuous. Combine and juxtapose the two, however, and we create a perceived challenge to liberalism, freedom of choice, and all the things that we in the helping professions hold dear. Perhaps the time has come to try to remove unfavorable preconceptions—to try to carry out some cognitive therapy so that the actual circumstances are perceived in a more optimistic and unthreatening light. The historical context of this misperception is well known. The enthusiasms of the eugenics movement in the early part of this century had unhappy outcomes on both sides of the Atlantic. A misguided determinism based on faith in the power of genes was allegedly responsible for antiliberal federal policies in the United States, relating, for example to immigration (Kamin, 1974). Far worse still, a tragic travesty of eugenic principles was used to justify some of the unspeakable excesses of the German Third Reich (Slater, 1936). It is hardly surprising that, in the aftermath, *eugenics* became a term to be avoided. And in some circles behavior genetics or psychiatric genetics were seen as guilty by association.

In the post–World War II years the powerful influence in the United States of post-Freudian psychodynamic psychiatry with its environmental emphasis and the rise of social psychiatry in Europe conspired to keep psychiatric genetics in the background. This was a somewhat unusual period in the history of modern psychiatry. The founding fathers of the

This work was supported by an MRC (UK) Senior Clinical Fellowship (Dr. McGuffin) and an MRC Project Grant. We are grateful to our colleagues in the MRC Social Psychiatry Unit and in the Genetics Section, Institute of Psychiatry (Drs. P. Bebbington, T. Brugha, E. Sturt, Ms. J. Aldrich, and B. McCarthy) for allowing us to quote preliminary results from our joint project on social and genetic factors in depression.

specialty—whether, like Freud, they were primarily concerned with intrapsychic dynamic processes or whether, like Kraepelin, they were interested in description and classification—were in agreement that constitutional and hereditary factors play an important role in the etiology of psychiatric disorders. Over the past two decades there has been a return to this position based on the findings of well-conducted and systematic family, twin, and adoption studies. This renewed interest has also been encouraged by the proven efficacy of physical methods of treatment in psychiatry, strengthening the proposition that there are biological influences at work in the pathogenesis of mental disorder.

How great, then, are the implications of psychiatric genetic research findings for prevention of mental disorder? At the moment we would suggest that they are fairly modest but have the potential of becoming great in the not too distant future. This optimism is based on the belief that a thoroughgoing knowledge of causes inevitably enhances the prevention strategies. (We should mention, though, that hunch and chance have sometimes resulted in the more effective interventions. Thus Snow was able to prevent cholera and Captain Cook and his limey crew successfully avoided scurvy with a far from complete knowledge of etiology.)

We will begin by discussing the territory that psychiatric genetics has covered and the position at which it has currently arrived. We will then try to predict future destinations and will discuss what the discipline has to offer for primary prevention.

Goals and Methods in Psychiatric Genetics

The task of psychiatric genetics is twofold. For any given abnormal behavioral trait we must answer the questions: (1) Are genes involved? and (2) If so, how? The starting point for deciding whether a psychiatric disorder is genetic is to determine whether it is *familial*. That is, we wish to know whether the disorder is more common in the relatives of an index case, or proband, who has the condition than it is in the population at large. This sounds like a straightforward task, but there are some pitfalls for the unwary. The crudest approach (but one that is nevertheless sometimes useful) is to find out how many index cases also have a relative affected by the disorder (family history positive) and how many do not (family history negative). A crucial piece of information required for interpretation of this type of data is the frequency of the trait in the general population. To illustrate the point we list three disorders in Table 1. Childhood autism is an uncommon disorder where there is a family history of brothers or sisters affected in only about 2 percent of cases (Hanson and Gottesman, 1976).

TABLE I
Frequency of Selected Disorders

Disorder	Population frequency (%)	Positive Family History (%)	
		Observed	Expected*
Childhood autism	0.02	2	0.8
Tics/Tourette's	10.0	>30	34.4
Schizophrenia	0.86	37	3.4

*Calculated as $1 - (1 - p)^n \times 100$, where p is the proportion of the general population affected and n is the number of relatives on whom information is available (in this example, $n = 4$).

On these grounds some authors have regarded it as nonfamilial (August et al., 1981). Gilles de la Tourette's Syndrome is also rare, but it has been suggested that the more common trait of motor tics in childhood is genetically related. More than 30 percent of the cases of Tourette's Syndrome are said to have a family history of tics, and hence it has been suggested that tics/Tourette's is a familial syndrome manifesting in either a mild or severe form. However, up to 10 percent of the general population give a positive history of tics (Wilson, Garron, and Klawans, 1978), whereas childhood autism may be diagnosed in only 2 per 10,000 children (Lotter, 1966). Thus if we had reliable information on, say, four first-degree relatives—and assuming that there is *no* familial aggregation—we would by chance alone score a "hit" for a family history in 34 percent of cases of tics/Tourette's but in under 0.1 percent of cases of childhood autism. Viewed in this way, childhood autism would appear to be familial while the tic/Tourette Syndrome would not. About 37 percent of schizophrenics have a family history of the disorder (Bleuler, 1978), whereas the lifetime risk in the population is only 0.86 percent, so that the "hit" rate for positive family history is well above expectation. A more time-consuming but more satisfactory approach is to study the various classes of relatives of a proband and estimate their *morbid risk* of being affected, i.e., the chance that they would develop the disorder, having lived through the period of risk. This is the approach that we will generally follow in this chapter.

Having discovered that a condition is familial, we still ought not assume that it is therefore *genetic*. For example pulmonary tuberculosis and the trait "going to medical school" both show familial aggregation. In both cases we can propose mechanisms that have nothing to do with genes (although even here it is possible that genetic influences play a small and indirect part in "susceptibility"). The classic ways of effecting a separation of genetic and environmental influences are, of course, twin studies and adoption studies. For practical purposes there are two types of twins: (1) identical or monozygotic (MZ), who have all their genes in common; and fraternal or dizygotic (DZ), who (like full siblings) on average share 50 percent of their genes. In both types of twins the other main source of similarity is their shared environment. In genetic studies the assumption is that the effect of shared environment is equally important in both types of twins. This is often criticized on the grounds that identical twins inevitably live within a common microenvironment that is more powerfully embracing than that of nonidentical pairs. However, several pieces of evidence suggest that the assumption is not a bad one. Loehlin and Nichols (1976) attempted to study the degree of environmental similarity in MZ twins but found that it had no influence on the degree to which MZ twins were similar with respect to IQ scores or personality traits. Elsewhere, Scarr and Carter-Saltzman (1979) studied IQ in a large sample consisting of 400 adolescent twin pairs. A surprisingly high proportion, 40 percent, were mistaken about their true zygosity. Nonidentical (DZ) twins who thought they were identical were no more alike on the cognitive tests than DZ pairs who were correct about their zygosity. Similarly identical (MZ) pairs who incorrectly believed themselves to be nonidentical showed only slightly greater differences than MZ pairs who correctly judged themselves to be identical. The effects of shared upbringing on MZ twins have also been assessed by comparing twins reared together with those reared apart. Striking similarities observed in twins reared apart are, at the anecdotal level, sometimes quite uncanny and periodically have caught the imagination of the popular press. Attempts to study twins reared apart in a systematic way are almost inevitably based on small numbers and a somewhat haphazard method of sampling. Nevertheless, interpreted cautiously against a background of data from other sources, the results are of considerable use and have largely been consistent with the inferences drawn from conventional findings for twins reared together.

Some would argue that adoption studies are able to effect a cleaner separation of genetic and environmental factors. There are, however, some methodological difficulties relating to the fact that this "natural experiment" is in itself an abnormal event. For example, adoption studies tend to find higher rates of psychopathology in adoptees, including control adoptees, than in the population at large. The main types of adoption-study strategy are summarized in a simplified form in Table 2. In discussing the ways in which these methods have been applied to psychopathological traits, we will commence at the "hard" end of the psychiatric spectrum with the so-called functional psychoses before going on to the more difficult to define "soft" areas, which include the neuroses, alcoholism, and socially deviant behavior.

TABLE 2
Adoption study designs

Type of study	Who is studied	Comparisons made
Adoptee	Adopted away offspring of patients	Rate of illness versus rate in control adoptees
Adoptee's family	Biological and adoptive relatives of patients who were adopted in early life	Rate of illness in biological versus adoption relatives
Cross-fostering	Individuals with ill biological parents but raised by healthy adopting parents; individuals with healthy biological parents but raised by ill adopting parent	Rate of illness in two types of adoptees

Modified from Murray and McGuffin, 1983.

Genes and Abnormal Behavior: The Basic Evidence

Schizophrenia

Schizophrenia ranks second only to IQ as a topic for nature–nurture controversy. However, as in the IQ debate, a fiercely partisan hereditarian or environmentalist stance is pointless and unproductive. In our opinion a contribution of genes to the etiology of schizophrenia has been proved beyond doubt. However, it is equally clear that schizophrenia is a complex trait with a non-Mendelian pattern of inheritance and that environmental influences are undoubtedly present.

Despite this debate, there has been general agreement among clinicians of whatever theoretical persuasion that schizophrenia has a strong tendency to run in families. The only source of disagreement has been how to interpret the finding. Now, somewhat surprisingly, the latest attack on the genetics of schizophrenia has come from psychiatrists interested in the nosology of psychotic conditions. One of the major changes in psychiatric research since the early 1970s has been that explicit operational definitions of disorder have become virtually mandatory. The great bulk of studies of the relatives of schizophrenics was carried out before this era, and the results are summarized in Table 3. Recently, two groups of workers have questioned the validity of these clinical diagnoses. Pope et al. (1983) applied the DSM-III criteria (American Psychiatric Association, 1980), to family history data in the case records of schizophrenic patients. They claimed to find no cases of DSM-III schizophrenia in 199 first-degree relatives. Using their own rather restrictive criteria, Abrams and Taylor (1983) found a morbid risk of schizophrenia of only 1.61 percent in 128 first-degree relatives of a series of consecutively admitted schizophrenics. These authors asserted that "modern criteria" has clearly demonstrated that schizophrenia is not familial. In our

TABLE 3
Schizophrenia in the relatives of schizophrenics

	Number of relatives at risk (BZ)	Morbid risk (%)
Parents	8020	5.6
Siblings	9920.7	10.1
Siblings, one parent affected	623.5	16.7
Offspring	1577.3	12.8
Offspring, both parents affected	134	46.3
Half-sibling	499.5	4.2
Uncles/aunts/nephews/nieces	6386.5	2.8
Grandchildren	739.5	3.7
Cousins	1600.5	2.4
Spouses	399	2.3

Pooled data from various studies; modified from Gottesman and Shields, 1982.

own view, this is a misguided attempt to encourage the tail to wag the dog. The alternative and more likely conclusion is that Abrams and Taylor's criteria are unsatisfactory. Similarly we would argue that the family-history method of Pope et al. (1983) is likely to have been insensitive and lacking in power. Justification for this view has come from two larger, careful studies based on personal interviews, employing blind diagnoses and using explicit criteria. Both the studies of Tsuang, Winokur, and Crowe (1980) and of Guze and colleagues (1984) found a significant excess of schizophrenics among the first-degree relatives of index cases compared with the relatives of controls.

Returning to Table 3, we note that there is an obvious and direct relationship between the degree of genetic closeness to a schizophrenic proband and an individual's morbid risk of being affected by the disorder. It is also important to note that there is a direct relationship between the individual's risk of schizophrenia and the number of close relatives affected. This favors a multifactorial liability/threshold model of transmission, which is discussed later in this chapter.

The more recent twin studies summarized in Table 4 have all depended on systematic ascertainment through twin registers. This overcomes sources of bias found in earlier studies. Haphazard methods of assembling a twin sample usually result in an excess of the more "interesting" or conspicuous types of twins. There may therefore be an artifactual preponderance of twins who are both monozygotic and concordant. Some older studies sought to overcome this by surveying hospital-based populations and selecting inpatients who were twins, resulting in a bias toward the more severe or chronically institutionalized cases. National registers such as those found in some Scandinavian countries or hospital

TABLE 4
Proband concordance in studies of schizophrenia in twins

Investigator	MZ pairs		DZ pairs	
	N	Concordance (%)	*N*	Concordance (%)
Kringlen (1967)	55	45	90	15
Pollin et al. (1969)	95	43	125	9
Tienari (1971)	16	35	21	13
Fischer (1973)	21	56	41	26
Gottesman and Shields (1982)	22	58	33	12

After Gottesman and Shields, 1982.

registers such as that of the Maudsley Hospital in London, where all inpatients and outpatients who were born one of a pair of twins are included, overcome this problem. As we can see from Table 4, there is a reasonable consistency across studies giving a weighted-average concordance of 46 percent for MZ and 14 percent for DZ twins. The Finnish study of Tienari (1968) originally appeared to be the exception. No concordant MZ pairs were found, suggesting no genetic effect. The results were immediately hailed as a breakthrough by fervent environmentalists. Eliot Slater, the doyen of British psychiatric geneticists of the time, related how a social psychiatrist colleague "whooped for joy" after reading Tienari's paper. Subsequently (Tienari, 1971), however, MZ probands who in fact had organic psychoses were excluded, and cotwins who developed psychotic symptoms were included so that, as we see from Table 4, the findings were not greatly different from those of other studies.

One frequently aired objection to the results for twins concerns the appropriateness of the twin method for studying a disorder because the very fact of being born one of an MZ pair may increase susceptibility to the condition. Jackson (1960) has proposed that MZ twins should have a particularly high risk of developing schizophrenia on psychodynamic theoretical grounds. A less fanciful argument is that MZ twins experience more hazardous birth than singletons, and there is some evidence associating perinatal trauma with the subsequent development of schizophrenia (McNeill and Kaij, 1978). However, the evidence is consistently against there being an increased risk of schizophrenia in individuals born one of a pair of twins.

Once again, the twin studies were carried out before the era of operational diagnostic criteria. Even though one of the studies employed blind ratings from six different clinicians in a careful attempt to ensure diagnostic accuracy, the hard-line advocates of operational criteria might still be skeptical of the results. Aiming to remedy the situation, McGuffin and colleagues (1984) reassessed the Gottesman and Shields twins by examining detailed case abstracts. The raters were blind to zygosity and to the identity or diagnosis in the cotwin, and a variety of operational criteria were used. A summary of some of the results are given in Table 5, illustrating that the Research Diagnostic Criteria of Spitzer, Endicott, and Robins (1975) and the criteria of Feighner et al. (1972) define syndromes that are substantially genetic.

Twins reared apart, where at least one of the pair has developed schizophrenia, are rare. Nevertheless Gottesman and Shields (1982) have culled 12 such pairs from the literature in which the diagnosis was well established and where the twins reared apart formed part of a larger, systematically ascertained twin series. Seven of the 12 pairs (58%) were concordant, a rate which closely approximates that for MZ twins reared together and which suggests that shared environment is unlikely to be a source of overinflated MZ concordance in pairs reared together.

Results of adoption studies have consistently pointed in the same direction as the findings for twins. The first study of note was carried out in Oregon by Heston (1966). He found that 5 of a total of 47 offspring of schizophrenic mothers, removed from their parents in the first 72 hours of life, later became schizophrenic. This contrasted with no schizophrenics among a group of 50 control adoptees who were age and sex matched and whose mothers were free of psychiatric illness.

A series of studies has been carried out by a group of American and Danish researchers based on the Danish Adoption and Psychiatric Registers. In the first of these, using a design similar to Hestons, Rosenthal, and colleagues's (1968) and Wender et al. (1973) found a higher risk of schizophrenia and schizophrenia-like traits, the so-called schizophrenia spectrum disorder, in adoptees who had schizophrenic biological parents, compared with a group of control adoptees. Similarly, Kety et al. (1976), starting with a sample of 63 adoptees who had become schizo-

TABLE 5

Proband concordance for operationally defined schizophrenia

	MZ Twins		DZ Twins	
Criteria	Probands (*N*)	Concordance (%)	Probands (*N*)	Concordance (%)
St. Louis (44)				
Definite	19	47.4	18	9.1
Probable	21	47.6	22	11.1
RDC (45)				
Narrow	19	52.6	21	9.5
Broad	22	45.5	23	8.7

Data from McGuffin et al., 1984.

phrenic, found schizophrenia spectrum disorder in 34 (13.9%) of 173 biological relatives compared with only 2 (2.7%) of 74 adopted relatives. Intrauterine or early maternal influences as a source of transmission of schizophrenia were effectively ruled out by a study of half-siblings for whom the common parent was the father. Thirteen percent of paternal half-siblings of schizophrenic index cases were diagnosed schizophrenic compared with only 1.6 percent of control half-siblings. It is difficult to ascribe such similarities to other than genetic factors.

Once again, however, the adoption studies can be criticized for lack of explicit diagnostic criteria and for use of the rather broad and poorly defined category of schizophrenic spectrum disorder. The material collected by Kety and colleagues has been blindly reassessed by Kendler, Gruenberg, and Strauss (1981), using DSM-III criteria. Of 105 biological relatives of schizophrenics who had been adopted away, 13.3 percent were diagnosed as having schizophrenia or schizotypal personality disorder compared with 1.3 percent of 224 individuals not related to the index cases and comprising their adoptive relatives plus the relatives of control adoptees. Thus the earlier findings were amply confirmed.

Affective Disorders

One of the problems of performing a genetic study on *affective disorders* is that the term is used by various authors to subsume a wide range of differing syndromes. At one end of the spectrum, the term *depression* may signify temporary distress, perhaps related to adverse life circumstances, while at the other it is used to denote a fully blown affective psychosis. This creates two problems. First, there is the difficulty of estimating the appropriate rate of illness in the population at large to be compared with the rate in relatives of probands. Second, there is the difficult practical problem in a family study of deciding who should or should not be classified as ill.

The question of whether so-called endogenous and reactive depressions are truly different entities or whether they merely represent different ends of the same continuum has been hotly debated in the recent past (Kendell, 1975) and remains unresolved. There is, however, general agreement that a typical or endogenous pattern of illness tends to be associated with familial aggregation. It has also now become widely accepted that affective disorder presenting purely with depression (unipolar, or UP, illness) differs from disorder presenting with episodes of both mania and depression or, less commonly, mania alone (bipolar, or BP, illness). The main differences between the two are summarized in Table 6. Table 7 lists the results of recent family studies in which the samples were ascertained via UP or BP probands. Although there is a consider-

TABLE 6

A comparison of unipolar (UP) and bipolar (BP) affective illness

Type of illness	Clinical features	Lifetime expectancy	Sex ratio	Morbidity in first-degree relatives	Type of illness in relatives
UP	Episodes of depression	Common 1–3%	Female to male = 2:1	High 6–12%	UP
BP	Episode of depression and episodes of mania, or (rarely) episodes of mania alone	Less common 0.25–1%	Slight female excess	Very high 15–30%	UP or BP

TABLE 7

Affective illness in first-degree relatives of unipolar (UP) and bipolar (BP) probands

Study	Proband Type	Relatives		
			Morbid Risk(%)	
		N at risk (B2)	BP	UP
Perris (1966)	BP	627	10.2	0.5
Winokur and Clayton (1967)	BP	167	10.2	20.4
Goetzl et al. (1974)	BP	212	2.8	13.7
Helzer and Winokur (1974)	BP	151	4.6	10.6
Mendelwicz et al. (1974)	BP	544		22.4
James and Chapman (1975)	BP	265	6.4	13.2
Gershon et al. (1976)	BP	341	3.8	6.8
Smeraldi et al. (1977)	BP	173	5.7	9.8
Angst et al. (1980)	BP	400.5	2.5	7.0
Winokur et al. (1982)	BP	196	1.5	12.4
Gershon et al. (1982)	BP	572.3	6.4	14.9
Perris (1966)	UP	684	0.3	6.4
Gershon et al. (1975)	UP	96	2.1	11.3
Smeraldi et al. (1977)	UP	185	1.1	11.4
Angst et al. (1980)	UP	766.3	0.1	5.9
Winokur et al. (1982)	UP	305	0.9	11.2
Gershon et al. (1982)	UP	132.9	1.5	16.6
Weissman et al. (1984)	UP	287	1.2	18.4
Pooled results	BP	3710.3	7.8	
		3648.3		11.4
	UP	2319	0.6	9.1

able range in the rates of affective illness in relatives, the direction of the findings is quite similar in that the relatives of BP probands show an excess of both UP and BP disorder, whereas the relatives of the UP probands show an excess of UP disorder only.

It is clear then that major affective disorders, especially those which Kraepelin would have called manic depressive insanity, are highly familial. Interestingly, a genetic interpretation of this finding has never provoked quite the same degree of controversy as it has in the case of schizophrenia. Purely on scientific methodological grounds, this is somewhat surprising since twin and adoption studies have generally been less rigorous and based on smaller numbers than those for schizophrenia. Nevertheless the available evidence does support the genetic position, and Table 8 summarizes six studies selected by Gershon et al. (1976) as having satisfactory methodology. Their findings are strongly supported by a more recent and painstaking piece of work, which has yielded a relatively large sample and clear-cut results (Bertelsen, Harvald, and Hauge, 1977). These findings are summarized in Table 9. This study, based on the Danish National Twin Register, not only shows an important genetic contribution to affective disorder but also illustrates that even in genetically identical individuals it is possible for one to have UP disorder while the other has BP disorder. Even allowing for misclassifications in a proportion of cases where a proband with apparent UP disorder may later "switch" and develop BP disorder, it is unlikely that the two types of affective illness are qualitatively quite distinct at a genetic level.

Adoption studies have been less extensively used in affective illness than in schizophrenia. But again, the available results are consistent with a genetic interpretation. A study of adoptees' families, which took as its

TABLE 8

Pair concordance in studies of affective illness in twins

Investigator	MZ Pairs		DZ Pairs	
	N	Concordance (%)	*N*	Concordance (%)
Luxenburger (1930)	4	75	13	0
Rosanoff et al. (1935)	23	70	67	16
Slater (1953)	7	57	17	24
Kallman (1954)	27	93	55	24
Harvald and Hauge (1965)	15	67	40	5
Allen et al. (1974)	15	33	34	0
Pooled Results	91	69	226	13

Modified after Gershon et al., 1976.

TABLE 9

Proband concordance for unipolar (UP) and bipolar (BP) affective illness in twins

	Proband	Cotwin *N*	UP	BP	Affective illness (%)
MZ	UP	35	15	4	64
	BP	34	6	21	79
DZ	UP	17	3	1	24
	BP	37	4	3	19

Bertelsen et al., 1977.

starting point BP probands, found an excess of affective illness in biological parents (16 of 57) compared with the adopting parents (4 of 57) (Mendelwicz and Rainer, 1977). Twelve of the affectively ill biological parents turned out to have UP disorder, once again suggesting that the same genotype may manifest either as a BP or UP phenotype. A smaller study (Cadoret, 1978), dealing mainly with UP illness in the adopted away offspring of parents with affective disorder, found higher rates of affective illness than in adoptees whose biological parents had other psychiatric conditions or who were psychiatrically well.

Rather more difficult to interpret are findings that have come from von Knorring and colleagues (1983) who studied the families of a mixed group of 115 adoptees with affective disorders or substance abuse. Only five of the index adoptees had BP disorder and these cases were not personally interviewed. There was a marked excess of psychiatric illness among the biological mothers of the index adoptees but no apparent concordance between specific diagnoses in the biological parents and their adopted children. However, there was also an excess of psychiatric illness in the *adoptive* fathers of the psychiatrically ill adoptees compared with the fathers of controls. There would thus appear to be both genetic and cultural transmission in this sample, which comprised a variety of disorders. The results reflect a general trend: Once we leave the area of fairly well circumscribed manic depressive illness, the genetic findings become more blurred and less consistent.

Family studies dealing specifically with neurotic depression are few but nevertheless tend to support familial aggregation (Stenstedt, 1966; Perris et al. 1983). However, as we see in Table 10, twin studies of neurotic or nonpsychotic depression yield inconsistent results. Slater and Shields (1969) found no concordance for hospital diagnosis of neurotic depression in either MZ or DZ pairs but found a slightly higher concordance for "any psychiatric diagnosis" in the MZ group (34%) than in the

TABLE 10
Neurotic/nonpsychotic depression: concordance in twins

	MZ (%)	DZ (%)
Slater and Shields (1969)	0–34	0–25
Shapiro (1970)	60	11
Torgersen (1981)	21	27

DZ group (25%). The two studies carried out in Scandinavia (Shapiro, 1970; Torgersen, 1981) produced markedly different findings, which may reflect differing severities in probands. In the "more genetic" study all of the probands were hospitalized for their illness (Shapiro, 1970).

In summary the genetic evidence at the severe, typical or psychotic, end of the affective disorder spectrum is consistent and compelling. The nearer we move toward the neurotic, or reactive, end the more untidy and troublesome the data become.

Neurotic Disorders

As we have already suggested, one of the major problems about performing a genetic study of neuroses is that of definition. Neurotic symptoms are widespread, affecting as much as 80 percent of the population (Srole et al., 1962; Leighton, 1959). Even when attempts are made to restrict the definition to recognizable syndromes, studies at different places and at different times provide wide variations in the prevalence rates (Carey and Gottesman, 1981). One solution is to restrict consideration to the most clear-cut or severe cases, such as those admitted to a hospital. This, however, has the disadvantage of reducing the number of subjects available for study, so that it might be difficult to collect an acceptably large sample of a less-common disorder, such as obsessive compulsive neurosis. An alternative is a take a wider perspective, including consideration of "normal" neurotic symptoms and related personality traits and to investigate in nonpatient samples, such as volunteer twins. In practice both approaches are utilized.

The study of personality is fraught with difficulties, and the definition of personality types, or traits, is currently beset by controversy (Powell, 1984). Nevertheless, there are three lines of evidence that the relatively stable aspects of a person's behavioral repertoire are likely to be influenced by genes. First, animal studies have now confirmed what animal breeders have known for centuries: Temperament in animals is, to some extent, hereditary and desirable attributes can be selected for by the breeder (Fuller and Thompson, 1978). Second, in human beings, certain psychophysiological characteristics would appear to be genetically influenced, as evidenced by twin studies and may reflect the neural substrate for personality. Third, pencil and paper tests of personality show higher MZ than DZ twin correlations for a wide variety of traits (Loehlin and Nichols, 1976).

Lumping all neurotic and personality disorders together (Table 11) Slater and Shields (1969) found a 47 percent concordance for MZ twins but only a 24 percent concordance for DZ pairs. However, when the sample was split, the genetic effect was apparent only for *anxiety states* and the broad group of personality disorders. A genetic contribution to anxiety states was further supported by a more recent twin study that utilized the Norwegian National Register (Torgersen, 1978) and in which the concordance rate was 30 percent in MZ pairs compared with 9 percent in DZ pairs. There is also good agreement across all studies of anxiety neurosis in families that the condition is familial (Brown, 1942; Cohen et al., 1951; Noyes et al., 1978; Cloninger, Bohman, and Sigvardsson, 1981), with rates in first-degree relatives of 8–15 percent compared with 0–5 percent in controls. So-called *panic disorder,* which may represent a more severe form of anxiety neurosis, was found to be even more highly familial in a recent study (Crowe et al., 1981), occurring in 41 percent of first-degree relatives of index cases.

Phobic disorders also appear to be familial. Two family-history studies found a rate of 12 percent in first-degree relatives of probands compared with 4 percent in the relatives of controls (Solyom et al., 1974; Buglass et al., 1977). A twin study carried out at the Maudsley Hospital in London was based on a small sample, but concordance for phobic symptoms in 7 of 8 MZ pairs, compared with 5 of 13 DZ pairs, suggested a genetic effect. Two other twin studies overcame the problem of small samples by studying "normal" fears in volunteer twins. Both found evidence of a genetic contribution with higher MZ than DZ correlations (Torgersen, 1979; Rose et al., 1981).

TABLE 11
Neurosis in twins

Diagnosis in Probands	Number of Pairs		Cotwins Concordant (%)	
	MZ	DZ	MZ	DZ
Any neurosis or personality disorder	62	84	47	24
Personality disorder	33	35	33	6
Anxiety states	17	28	41	4
Other neurosis	12	21	0	0

Modified after Slater and Shields, 1969.

Obsessional neurosis seems to be more closely associated with preexistent personality traits than with other neurotic disorders (Slater, 1943); clinically, it is often difficult to separate obsessional state from trait. All studies are in agreement that the rate of disorder is higher in first-degree relatives of index patients, but the rates vary widely from 5 percent (Carey, 1978) to 37 percent (Lewis, 1935); this undoubtedly reflects differing diagnostic practice. The disorder is uncommon, so the existence of some concordant MZ pairs is of interest (McGuffin and Mawson, 1980). However, there has only been one small systematic study, again using the Maudsley Hospital Twin Register from London. Five of 15 MZ pairs were concordant for symptoms requiring treatment compared with only one of 15 DZ pairs (Carey and Gottesman, 1981). Once again the strategy of assessing "normal" obsessional traits in twins has proved useful. Murray and colleagues (1981) found a heritability (i.e., a genetic contribution to the variance) of 0.44 for obsessional traits and 0.47 for obsessional symptoms. High obsessional symptom scores tended to be associated with high "neuroticism" or *N*-scores on Eysenck's Personality Questionnaire. The authors therefore speculated that genetic factors contribute to obsessional neurosis via a direct influence on obsessional personality traits and a more general influence on general neurotic tendency. Interestingly, a recent small series on obsessive neurosis following head injury (McKeon, McGuffin, and Robinson, 1984) revives the idea of an organic contribution to the disorder. The series included a pair of identical twins, who were discordant for obsessive compulsive neurosis, in which the affected twin developed his disorder following a serious head injury.

Hysteria is a term that is used in a wide variety of ways and presents particular problems for nosologists. Twin studies suggest that hysteria as a personality trait (Gottesman, 1963) or defined by the presence of classical conversion symptoms (Slater, 1961) has no genetic basis. However, Briquet's Syndrome (or what in England is sometimes called "St. Louis hysteria") does appear to be familial and is associated with a history of asocial behavior in the male relatives of patients affected by the disorder, who are themselves predominantly female (Cloninger, Reich, and Guze, 1975).

Psychopathy is also, as Sir Aubrey Lewis (1974) put it, "a most elusive category." In Europe the term has been applied to a wide variety of personality disorders (Schneider, 1950), whereas English-speaking clinicians tend to restrict the term to antisocial personalities. The possible influences of the genes on antisocial or criminal behavior has again been the subject of some controversy. Early twin studies that purported to show a genetic effect can be criticized on the grounds that ascertainment of the twins was not systematic and will therefore, as we suggested earlier, tend to result in an excess of MZ and concordant pairs. However, as we see from Table 12, MZ concordance across all studies of adult criminality has been higher than DZ concordance. The pattern is consistent and includes comparatively large Scandinavian studies (Christiansen, 1974), for which there is systematic sampling utilizing a twin register. Lest it be thought that twin studies inevitably show higher MZ than DZ rates of concordance for psychopathological traits, Table 12 also summarizes the studies on juvenile delinquency, which show no such pattern.

The results of adoption studies support the view that genetic factors contribute to antisocial personality. Crowe (1974) studied the adopted away offspring of imprisoned women. Six of 46 such offspring, as adults, developed antisocial personality compared with none of a group of control adoptees. At about the same time, a study of male adoptees, using

TABLE 12

Pair concordance rates for twins for juvenile delinquency and crime

Investigator	MZ Twins		DZ Same-Sex Twins	
	Pairs (*N*)	Concordant (%)	Pairs (*N*)	Concordant (%)
Juvenile Delinquency				
Rosanoff et al. (1941) male	29	100	17	71
Rosanoff et al. (1941) female	12	92	9	100
Kranz[b] (1937) combined	16	69	22	59
Hayashi[a] (1967) male	15	80	4	75
Sugamata (cited in Hayashi) male	6	83	—	—
Shields (1977) male	5	80	9	78
Weighted average concordance		87		72
Adult Criminality				
Lange (1931)	13	77	17	12
Rosanoff et al. (1941) male	38	76	23	22
Rosanoff et al. (1941) female	7	86	4	25
Stumpfl (1936) male	15	60	17	41
Kranz (1936) male[c]	31	65	43	54
Yoshimasu (1961) male	28	61	18	11
Dalgaard and Kringlen (1976) male[d]	31	26	54	15
Christiansen (1974) male[e]	73	34	146	18
Christiansen (1974) female[e]	15	20	28	7
Weighted average concordance		51		22

[a]Includes 1 new MZ pair concordant at follow-up (personal communication, 1980) and excludes 1 discordant pair of opposite-sex DZ.

[b]DZ pairs include 14 opposite-sex pairs.

[c]2 DZ probands are female.

[d]For probands 41% and 26%, respectively. Data here for "strict" concept of crime and do not include crimes relating to motor vehicle laws and treason during World War II.

[e]Partial data, preliminary update of Cloninger et al., 1978; for male probands, 51% and 30%, female 33% and 13%.

From McGuffin and Gottesman, 1984.

the Danish register (Hutchings and Mednick, 1975), found a similar effect. The most recent publication of this group (Mednick, Gabrielli, and Hutchings, 1984) shows that where neither biological nor adoptive parents had criminal convictions, 13.5 percent of male adoptees had been convicted. The rate was scarcely higher at 14.7 percent where only the adoptive parents had been convicted. However, where the adoptive parents were free of convictions but one of the biological parents had been convicted, 20 percent of the sons had a criminal record. Those unfortunate male adoptees where both adopting and biological parents were criminal, had a rate of conviction of 24.5 percent. The findings thus suggest a genetic effect plus some nongenetic family environmental effect. Genetic effects appeared to be more closely associated with recidivism than one-time crimes and more strongly associated with property than violent crime. This agrees with the results of Swedish and American workers, using the Swedish Adoption Register (Bohman et al., 1982; Cloninger et al., 1982). The sample here was large and allowed an analysis that took into account the effects of heterogeneity. It was suggested that petty criminality not associated with alcohol abuse and involving mainly nonviolent property offenses showed a genetic effect. The data on men (Cloninger et al., 1982) showed that a low social status alone was not sufficient to lead to criminality but that low status did increase the risk in combination with specific types of genetic diathesis. The authors warn against sweeping conclusions in interpreting these studies. Scandinavian countries, because of their excellent twin and adoption registers, provide a favorite base for genetic studies of criminality. However, these small Northern European nations are socially fairly homogenous and economically prosperous. Extrapolating the results to other larger and more heterogeneous countries such as the United States may be misleading. Also the definition of crime is imposed by society and therefore different from country to country and changes from time to time within a country. Nevertheless it does seem probable that genes, though not conferring the certainty of criminal behavior, can bestow a liability to nonviolent crime.

Alcoholism

There can be little doubt that alcoholism, currently one of our most widespread health hazards, tends to run in families. But it is easy to postulate environmental reasons for this. Indeed, in society as a whole, powerful environmental arguments can be put forward to explain the prevalence of drinking behavior. For example, national rates of alcoholism are closely related to the national consumption of liquor, and the availability of alcohol plays its part in the differing rates of alcoholism in different trades and professions. However, biological factors can also be implicated. Genetic factors appear to play a part in determining alcohol preference in rodents. And in human beings the way in which alcohol is metabolized is influenced by genes. Twin studies of alcoholism in humans have produced conflicting results. Kaij (1960) found a 71 percent concordance for physical addiction to alcohol in 14 MZ pairs compared with a 32 percent concordance in 31 DZ pairs. Preliminary results from a Maudsley Hospital study (Gurling, Clifford, and Murray, 1981) found a pair concordance for alcohol-dependence syndrome that differed little between MZ (21%) and DZ (25%) twins. As with other nonpsychotic conditions, some greater leverage may be applied to the problem by studying the behavior of normal twins. Thus Partanen, Bruun, and Markanen (1966) found that the frequency of drinking and the quantity consumed per session was more similar in MZ than DZ twins. At Maudsley, Clifford et al. (1981) found a heritability of 0.54 for weekly total alcohol consumption in normal male twins and found evidence of a substantial genetic contribution to the same measure in female twins.

Adoption studies have generally been in closer agreement. Although the earliest of these (Roe, 1944) found no evidence of a genetic effect in adoptees separated from biological parents who had been "heavy drinkers," a study by Goodwin and colleagues (1973) using the Danish Adoption Register showed high rates of alcoholism in the adopted away sons of alcoholics. This was actually slightly higher at 25 percent in those adoptees raised by nonalcoholic adoptive parents than in those raised by alcoholic adopting parents, where the rate was 17 percent. Subsequent adoption studies in the United States (Cadoret and Gath, 1978) and Sweden (Cloninger et al., 1981) concur in finding alcoholism to be more common in adoptees where there is a history of either heavy drinking or alcoholism in biological relatives than in those adoptees without such a family history. In general, the adoption studies have found reasonably consistent evidence of a genetic contribution to the disorder in men. In women, however, the situation is less clear-cut. For example Goodwin and colleagues (1973) found that both the adopted away daughters of alcoholics and control adoptees had a higher prevalence of alcoholism than that among normal Danish women.

Current Themes in Psychiatric Genetic Research

The evidence that we have just discussed implicates the action of genes in a wide range of psychopathology. However, looked at in this straightforward way, the classic family, twin, and adoption study designs tell us that a genetic effect is present but tell us little about the likely modes of inheritance, interactions with the environment, or the mechanisms of gene expression. With rare exceptions, such as Huntington's Chorea, familial disorders of interest to the psychiatrist or clinical psychologist show a perplexing and non-Mendelian pattern of segregation within families. In all cases the concordance in identical twins is less than 100 percent, and thus (providing that the twins have lived through the period of risk) environmental influences must certainly be necessary.

The most plausible and heuristically useful class of models to explain the transmission of psychiatric disorders are *liability threshold models* (Falconer, 1965; Reich, James, and Morris, 1972). Here it is assumed that liability to develop a particular disorder is contributed to by the predominantly additive effects of genes at more than one locus, plus multiple environmental effects. Hence, within the population at large, liability has a continuous distribution that will tend to have a normal (i.e., bell-shaped or Gaussian) form. Only those individuals whose liability is beyond a certain threshold will manifest the illness. This model is illustrated in Figure 1. The mean liability among the relatives of affected individuals is higher than that in the population at large; hence the proportion of relatives whose liability exceeds the threshold (and who are therefore affected) is greater than that in the general population. Single major-locus models in which a major gene is the sole cause of resem-

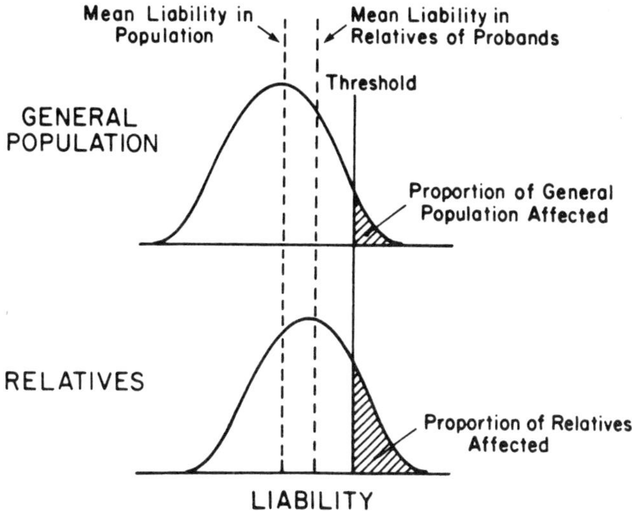

Figure 1. The polygenic-multifactorial/threshold model. Liability is contributed by polygenes plus environment acting in a predominantly additive fashion. Only those individuals beyond the threshold (shaded area) are affected.

blance between pairs of relatives are less satisfactory and have been effectively refuted for schizophrenia (O'Rourke et al., 1982) and for manic depressive illness (Bucher et al., 1981). However, it is still quite possible that genes of major effect operate in these conditions against a background of polygenic or multifactorial influences of the type that we have just described (O'Rourke, McGuffin, and Reich, 1983; Carter and Chung, 1981; Morton, 1982). Mixed models of this type constitute another class of liability threshold models, which, for the purposes of our discussion here, can be treated in the same way as the pure polygenic-multifactorial threshold models.

Genes and the Environment

Because both genes and environment appear to play a part in abnormal behavioral traits, a fundamental question we might ask is: How much does each contribute? One way of conceptualizing the contributors to an observable trait or *phenotype* is in terms of the path diagram given in Figure 2. The phenotype of individual P_1 is the sum of his genetic endowment, or genotype (G), half of which is received from each parent, plus the effects of that part of the environment (CE) that he shares in common with his sibling P_2, plus those environmental effects that are special to him alone and not shared by other members of his family (SE_1). The value of the expected correlation between P_1 and any of his relatives can be worked out as the sum of the permissible connecting paths between them (Li, 1974). If P_1 and P_2 are dizygotic twins, we obtain from Figure 2 the intuitively obvious result that the source of resemblence (r) between DZ twins is that they share half of their genes plus the common environment. Put algebraically, we have the correlation

$$r_{DZ} = \tfrac{1}{2}h^2 + c^2.$$

Similarly, the correlation for MZ twins who share 100 percent of their genes is

$$r_{MZ} = h^2 + c^2.$$

From these equations it is easy to obtain

$$h^2 = 2(r_{MZ} - r_{DZ}),$$

where the commodity h^2 is the heritability, i.e., the proportion of the total phenotypic variance contributed by genes. Rearranging we obtain

$$c^2 = 2r_{DZ} - r_{MZ},$$

where c^2 is the proportion of the variance contributed by the common family environment. For traits measured on continuous scales, such as personality or IQ, correlations between twins or other pairs of relatives

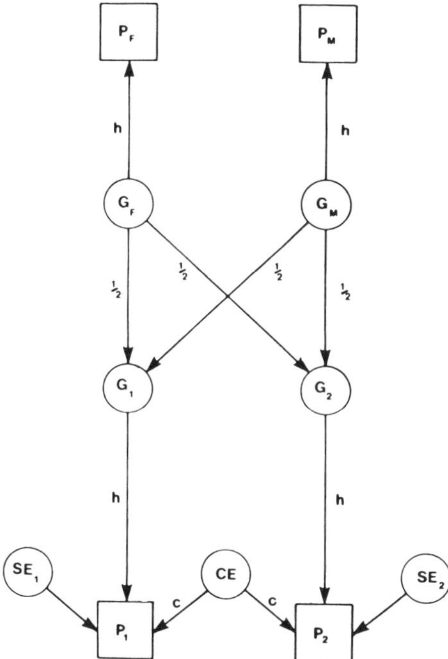

Figure 2. Path diagram illustrating a simple multifactorial model. The observable variables (boxes) are the phenotypes of father and mother (P_F, P_M) and those of the offspring (P_1, P_2, . . ., P_i). The underlying (latent) variables (circles) are the genotype (G), specific environment, with appropriate subscripts (SE) and common environment (CE). The path coefficients are denoted by the lower-case letters h and c or in the case of G(parent) − G(offspring), ½.

can conveniently be expressed as the intraclass correlation coefficient. For present/absent traits such as a psychiatric diagnosis, we can apply a threshold model and—provided that we know the frequency of the disorder in the general population and have an estimate of the proportion of relatives of index cases who are affected—we can calculate the *correlation in liability* (Falconer, 1965; Reich et al., 1972). Taking MZ and DZ twin correlations from a variety of sources, we have used the preceding formulas to partition the variance for various behavioral phenotypes (Table 13). Interestingly, Eysenck's personality factor *E* is the only trait for which the common environmental contribution is effectively zero. This might seem a surprising finding, especially to readers having a psychodynamic orientation, but it is one that is quite consistent across behavioral genetic studies of personality measures. It is supported by studies of twins reared apart, who are actually more alike with regard to person-

TABLE 13
Partitioning the variance for behavioral traits

		Proportion of Variance Contributed (%)		
Scale	Trait	Genes (h^2)	Common Environment (c^2)	Special Environment (s^2)
Continuous	IQ[1]	52	34	14
	Personality[2] (*E*)	66	0	34
Threshold	Schizophrenia[3]	66	19	15
	Affective[4] illness	74	18	8

[1, 2] Based on MZ- and DZ-twin correlations from Bouchard and McGue (1981) and Eaves and Young (1981), respectively.

[3, 4] Based on data from Gottesman and Shields (1982) and Bertelsen et al. (1977), respectively, and correlations in liability calculated by the method of Reich et al. (1972)

ality measures than twins reared together. The only personality trait for which there is some evidence of a family environmental effect is conservatism (Henderson, 1982).

Partitioning the phenotypic variance in this way should be seen only as a starting point. Calculation of heritability is in itself an empty exercise if it does not lead to a more specific consideration of the ways in which genes and environment coact and interact to produce the phenotype in question. (Moreover, it is sometimes forgotten that heritability is simply a proportion of the variance accounted for by genes in a particular population and cannot be extrapolated easily to other, dissimilar populations).

Discordant monozygotic twins provide a potentially important method of identifying specific environmental factors. Since the cotwin provides a genetically identical control, environmental insults that have affected only the proband may be identified as etiologically important. The only circumstances in which this would not apply would be if discordant MZ twins were discordant only because the proband had developed a sporadic or nongenetic form of the disorder. For example, it is still frequently suggested that this is a common cause of discordance for schizophrenia. However, the available evidence argues against this proposition. Thus discordant MZ pairs have a history of schizophrenia among their other relatives as often as do concordant pairs (Kringlen, 1968). Furthermore, the frequency of schizophrenia does not differ significantly between the children of schizophrenic probands and those of their unaffected MZ cotwins (Fischer, 1971).

We have already mentioned that there is some evidence of a relationship between a difficult birth and the risk of developing schizophrenia (McNeil and Kaij, 1978). In the U.S. veterans twin study, the birth histories of discordant pairs revealed that the affected MZ twin more often had low birth weight, birth complications, and a more passive premorbid personality than the unaffected cotwin (Pollin and Stabenau, 1968). Unfortunately, this interesting finding has not been replicated by other investigators of twins (Gottesman and Shields, 1982). More recent investigations have explored a related theme. At Maudsley, Reveley, Reveley, and Murray (1984) have investigated twins discordant for schizophrenia, using a computerized tomographic (CT) brain scanner. They found that the affected twins had cerebral ventricles that were significantly dilated compared with their unaffected cotwins. Cerebral ventricular dilatation has previously been reported in about a third of chronic schizophrenics (Lancet, 1982). The Maudsley findings strongly suggest that this abnormality is not genetic and that it is either a result of the illness or that it reflects some premorbid insult that was of etiological importance. Reveley et al. (1984) favor the latter interpretation and suggest that this may most commonly consist of birth complications.

With some forms of affective disorder, the potential environmental contributors are more intuitively obvious. Connections between stress, adversity, and depression are readily understandable. Recent research has confirmed the relationship between life stresses and depression, and it is discussed in greater detail by Dohrenwend in this volume. Unfortunately there has been little attempt to study both familial predisposition and relevant life events at the same time. We have recently been carrying out a family study which aims to do just that. The approach was attractive to us for two reasons: (1) it offered a means of unraveling the complex relationships between family loading and life happenings; and (2) it offers some leverage upon the difficult problems of classification in depression and the related puzzles of the differing contributions of constitutional factors at the reactive versus the endogenous end of the spectrum. At least one previous study has taken a similar approach but, surprisingly, has received little attention. Pollitt (1972) found a morbid risk of depression that was particularly high at about 21 percent when precipitating factors for the proband's illness were absent or doubtful. The rate in relatives fell to 6–12 percent when the proband's illness was "justifiable" in the sense that it followed severe physical stress, infection or psychological trauma.

In Table 14 we present preliminary results from our own study. Here we have divided the probands into those who have or have not had life events in the three-month period prior to the onset of their depression. Life events were assessed by a semistructured interview and rated according to the methods of Brown and Harris (1978). Thus those in the life-event–positive group have experienced happenings that carry a severe or

TABLE 14

Frequency of hospital-treated depression in the relatives of depressed probands—I

Proband Type	First-Degree Relatives				
	N	BZ	Affected (%)	Morbid Risk (%)	*r**
Life events	80	50	13.8	22.0	.281 ± .134
No life events	176	112	17.0	26.8	.378 ± .082

*Correlation in liability, assuming a population morbid risk of 11%.

TABLE 15

Frequency of hospital-treated depression in the relatives of depressed probands—II

Proband Type	First-Degree Relatives				
	N	Affected (%)	BZ	Morbid Risk (%)	*r**
Adversity	150	16	95.5	25.1	.345 ± .092
No adversity	106	16	66.5	25.6	.355 ± .109

*Correlation in liability, assuming a population morbid risk of 11%.

moderate degree of threat (judged within the context of their life circumstances) and were considered independent of the subjects' mood state. As we see, there was a modest and nonsignificant trend in the expected direction. That is, probands without a stress-related onset of illness show slightly more family loading than those probands whose illness was more explicable in terms of life events.

As shown in Table 15, the effect disappears completely when we take any form of adversity into account. Here those in the adversity group have experienced threatening life events and/or chronic difficulties (stresses that persist for four weeks or more). There appears to be no difference between them and those in the no-adversity group with respect to family loading. However, when we break down the data on the adversity group (Table 16), the highest rate of illness emerges in the relatives of probands with chronic difficulties (whether with or without life events), the next highest rate in the relatives of no-adversity probands, and the lowest rate in the relatives of the probands whose illness followed threatening life events.

Our impression from studying chronic difficulties is that they tend to impinge on the entire family, whereas life events have their greatest impact on particular individuals. Thus it is tempting to speculate that the life-event–positive but chronic-difficulty–negative probands have a type of illness where sporadic happenings (SE in Figure 2) have been of particular importance and therefore have fewer relatives affected than do the

TABLE 16

Frequency of depression in the relatives of depressed probands—III

Proband Type		First-Degree Relatives		
Life Events	Chronic Difficulties	*N*	Affected (%)	Unaffected (%)
Yes	No	55	10.9	89.1
No	Yes	70	18.6	81.4
Yes	Yes	25	20.0	80.0
No	No	106	16.0	84.0

no-adversity probands where genetic factors (G in Figure 2) have a greater influence. However, the highest rate of illness is in the relatives of the probands with chronic difficulties, for whom common environmental adversity (CE) and genetic influences (G) combine (and perhaps interact) to produce familial aggregation of depression.

We should emphasize that the data are preliminary and that none of the differences between rates of illness in the groups of relatives attain conventional significance levels. Nevertheless, we find these early results intriguing and present them here as a first step in our necessary attempts to effect a rapprochement between genetic and social research in psychopathology.

Biological Approaches

So far, almost all of our discussion has concerned syndromes defined by clinical signs and symptoms or traits measured by psychological rating. One of the problems of behavioral genetics is that we must rely heavily on these "exophenotypes," which are somewhat difficult to manage in a genetic analysis. The fact that we are able to demonstrate genetic effects on psychiatric disorder allows us to conclude that there are connecting pathways between abnormal genes and abnormal behavior. Currently these pathways remain obscure, but the search for biological markers aims to establish signposts on these routes. There is little doubt that an ability to move one step nearer to the primary gene products, to discover "endophenotypes" would enhance our abilities to dissect out the genetics of psychiatric disorders more effectively.

We are currently at a stage when biological findings in psychiatric disorders are beginning to emerge in a consistent and reliable way. We have already mentioned CT-scan identified abnormalities in schizophrenia. Two other findings have created great interest over the past decade: (1) that of lowered platelet monoamine oxidase in schizophrenia (Wyatt, Potkin, and Murphy, 1979) and other psychiatric disorders; and (2) that of abnormal dexamethasone suppression found in about 50 percent of endogenous depressives (Carroll, 1982). The difficulties of placing a genetic interpretation on these and allied findings have recently been commented on by McGuffin (1984). Unfortunately, we do not yet have for any psychiatric disorder a biological marker that has all the desirable properties of an endophenotype. Rieder and Gershon (1978) suggested that:

1. A useful biological marker should be associated with an increased risk of psychiatric illness (but the character need not always be more common among a group of patients with a particular syndrome, since there may be biological heterogeneity).

2. The character should be heritable and not therefore a secondary effect of the illness or of treatment for it.

3. The character should be a *trait marker* rather than a *state-dependent* marker, which is no longer observable after recovery from the illness. Platelet MAO fulfills this criteria whereas the dexamethazone suppression test does not).

Some of the problems of stability of findings and the potentially obfuscating effects of medication when studying patients in vivo can be overcome by recent techniques which allow in vitro study of cultured material. An interesting finding of this type was provided by Wright et al. (1984), who were able to show a decrease in betoadrenoreceptors on lymphoblastoid cells in the ill members of families affected by manic depressive psychosis but not among healthy relatives. The abnormalities were detected in cultured cells, which had been serially passaged over many generations so that the defect could be presumed to be genetically coded. Abnormalities in catecholamines have, of course, long been implicated in affective disorder, and it is interesting to speculate whether such receptor abnormalities might also be found in the central nervous system.

Genetic Markers

An area of phenomenal growth in basic human genetics over the past decade and a half has involved the study of genetic markers and the mapping of the human genome, i.e., the 22 pairs of so-called autosomes and a pair of sex chromosomes, which together make up the normal individual's full compliment of 46 chromosomes (McKusick and Ruddle, 1977; McKusick, 1983). Genetic markers are characters that have simple Mendelian modes of inheritance, exist in two or more common forms, which can be reliably detected, and have been mapped or potentially can be mapped to a specific chromosomal location. At present, 317 genes have been assigned to human chromosomes (American Journal of Human Genetics, 1983), but there are perhaps 100,000 genes in the entire genome. The importance of these developments from the point of view of common diseases is that genes of major effect may be identified.

The most straightforward investigation is the *association* study in which the frequency of a particular marker in a patient group is compared with that in healthy controls. Many diseases have now been shown to be associated with the HLA system, the major transplant antigen system in human beings (Festenstein and Demant, 1978). A variety of associations have been described both for schizophrenia and affective disorder (McGuffin, 1980). Unfortunately, the results have largely been inconsistent for these disorders as a whole. However, there has been agreement from a number of different centers of a weak but statistically highly significant association between one antigen, HLA A9, and the paranoid subtype of schizophrenia (McGuffin, Farmer, and Yonace, 1981).

Linkage studies present more practical difficulties, both in obtaining suitable samples and in analyzing the results. Essentially, the aim is to determine whether a particular genetic marker assorts with an illness within families. Where this occurs, it is possible to infer that there are two loci that are closely adjacent on the same chromosome. In psychiatric genetics the HLA region has again been a focus of interest. There have been claims of linkage between HLA and affective disorder (Weitkamp et al., 1981) and between HLA and "schizotaxia," i.e., schizophrenia plus schizophrenia spectrum disorder (Turner, 1979). Unfortunately, neither of these interesting findings have been confirmed by subsequent studies (Goldin et al., 1983; McGuffin, Farmer, and Yonace, 1981; McGuffin, Festenstein, and Murray, 1983).

Exciting prospects have been opened up by the revolutionary advances in "The genetics" (Weatherall, 1982). Techniques using recombinant DNA promise to provide many new markers, which will ensure that it is not long before the human genome is extensively mapped (Botstein et al., 1980). These new markers—which depend on normal variations in DNA sequences and are called *restriction fragment length polymorphisms*—have already allowed the mapping of the gene for Huntington's Chorea (Gusella et al., 1983). The finding was to some extent a stroke of luck, as must be all disease marker–linkage findings at this stage. Only 73 of the genes so far assigned to places in the human genome are polymorphic (American Journal of Human Genetics, 1983) and hence potentially useful as genetic markers. In current studies it is usually not practical to utilize more than a few of them. Thus, for example, a recent study at the Institute of Psychiatry, Maudsley Hospital in collaboration with other colleges of the University of London, utilized 21 genetic markers in a study of schizophrenia. The linkage results were entirely negative, but this would allow exclusion of a dominant gene for the condition from only 6 percent of the genome (McGuffin et al., 1983).

Preventive Strategies

We must now complete the circle and ask: What bearing does the burgeoning field of psychiatric genetics have on the policies for prevention? It is clear from all that we have discussed that old-fashioned, simplistic ideas about reducing mental illness by discouraging reproduction in the psychiatrically ill, or even by legislating it, are bound to fail. The patterns of transmission of psychiatric disorders are complex, and major gene effects, if they are present, are modified by other familial influences. Thus, for example, the majority of schizophrenics do not have schizophrenic parents. The vast majority of the offspring of schizophrenics, or nearly 90 percent, will not develop schizophrenia. Moreover, some forms of chronic mental illness interfere with the ability to find a suitable mate, settle down, and produce children. This is particularly true of schizophrenia. It has been estimated that the *biological fitness* of schizophrenics is only about 70 percent of that of the rest of the population, as judged by the number of children they produce and therefore their ability to pass on genes to subsequent generations (Slater and Cowie, 1972). This being so, a simple single gene theory will predict that the incidence of schizophrenia should be declining because spontaneous mutation could not account for the persistence of such a common disorder. Ingenious explanations for this have been devised, along the lines that the unaffected "carriers" of the schizophrenia gene might actually have greater fitness (Huxley et al., 1964). Such speculations, though intriguing, have not won general acceptance. Obsessive-compulsive neurosis has a similar adverse effect on fecundity (Hare, Price, and Slater, 1972), but it does not appear to be becoming less frequent. In both cases, multifactorial etiology cushioning against the effects of biological disadvantage would seem to be the most plausible explanation of persistence of these disorders in the population. Therefore the most important point for us here is that both disorders illustrate that any quasitotalitarian notions about enforced sterilization of the psychiatrically ill are not only morally reprehensible but are practically and scientifically flawed.

Currently, the principal preventive role for psychiatric genetics is in offering counseling and advice to psychiatric patients, their families, and prospective spouses. The role of the genetic counselor is, to a large extent, educational: It is to dispel mistaken beliefs, for example, that all offspring of a patient with serious mental illness are necessarily afflicted by "hereditary taint." This is untrue even for classical Mendelian traits. Furthermore, as we have already pointed out, 100 percent genetic influence in psychiatric disorders is the exception rather than the rule. It is also important to dispel the idea that genetic disorders are necessarily untreatable. Quite the opposite is true, and, as we have also discussed, the presence of genetic influences should encourage optimism in the development of biological methods of treatment for mental disorders. The inborn errors of metabolism, such as phenylketonuria, provide the most striking examples of how genetic knowledge may be put to preventive use. But it needs to be pointed out that chemical methods, such as the prescription of lithium carbonate or depot neuroleptics, have already proven efficacious in the secondary prevention of mental disorders.

Genetic counseling now correctly emphasizes that the counselee's personal autonomy and a noncoercive approach is the rule. However, as Tsuang (1978) has pointed out, it may be legitimate not only to lower anxiety by providing information and reassurance but also to raise the individual's anxiety and awareness of potential problems where this is appropriate. The counselor needs to help the counselee to assess the risk as accurately as possible and to understand the potential burden. However, the ultimate decision after assessing the *risk/burden ratio* must be that of the counselee.

The assessment of risk in genetic counseling can be derived from three sources (Murphy and Chase, 1975):

1. *Empirical information* comprises estimates based on actual research data.

2. *Modular information* is derived from a scientific understanding of the mode of inheritance of the disorder.

3. *Particular information* is a compilation of all the data which can be utilized in assessing the risks for a particular family.

To date most of the information of use in psychiatric genetic counseling is empirical information. Attempts to take a *modular* approach are likely to be misleading because different genetic models produce quite different risk estimates. To illustrate this point, we prepared Table 17. We utilized data from studies of schizophrenia in twins (Gottesman and Shields, 1982) to derive parameter estimates for a general, single, major-locus (SML) model (James, 1971) and for the sort of multifactorial (MF) model described earlier. (See Fig. 2.) We then used the parameter estimate to calculate the risk of disorder in various classes of relatives. Note that the observed risks differ from the expected risks under the two models, and the expected risks under the two models differ from each other.

TABLE 17

Comparison of expected and observed risks of schizophrenia for various types of relatives of schizophrenics

Type of Relative	Expected Risk (Percent Affected) SML Model	MF Model	Observed Risk (Percent Affected)
Siblings	14.0	14.0	10.1
Children	4.5	6.4	12.8
Children of two affected parents	29.6	23.5	46.3
Half-siblings raised together	2.8	7.2	6.0
Other second-degree relatives	2.8	2.8	2–3.7

There are occasions when particular information can be utilized in psychiatric genetic counseling so that, for example, the type of illness observed in relatives (i.e., chronic or acute, mild or severe) and the proportion of relatives already affected may influence the individual's assessment of risk.

These preventive strategies are at this stage a clinical art rather than an exact science. However, application of the new genetic technology to psychiatric disorders has already begun, and there is a high expectation that if there truly are major genes for the major psychoses they will be detected and isolated, probably by the end of this century. For nonpsychotic conditions, major gene effects seem more remote; indeed, the disorders in most cases differ from "normality" more in degree than in kind. However, the likely presence of polygenic mechanisms still implies a biological substrate and encourages continued research into central nervous system mechanisms (e.g. Gray, 1982). As we have mentioned in the discussion of some of our own current research, progress also depends on effective collaboration between social–environmental and biological schools of thought. Effective prevention can ultimately occur only when we understand the diathesis, comprehend the stress, and are able to usefully evaluate the ways in which the two coact and interact to produce mental disorder.

References

Abrams, R., and Taylor, M. A. (1983). The genetics of schizophrenia: A reassessment using modern criteria. *American Journal of Psychiatry, 140,* 171–175.

Allen, M. G., Cohen, S., Pollin, W., and Greenspan, S. I. (1974). Affective illness in veteran twins: A diagnostic review. *American Journal of Psychiatry, 131,* 1234–1239.

American Journal of Human Genetics (1983). The human gene map. *American Journal of Human Genetics, 35,* 134–156.

American Psychiatric Association (1980). *DSM-III: Diagnostic and statistical manual of mental disorders.* Washington, D.C.: The Association.

Angst, J., Frey, R., Lohmeyer, B., and Zerbin-Rudin, E. (1980). Bipolar manic depressive psychoses: Result of a genetic investigation. *Human Genetics, 55,* 237–254.

August, G. W., Stewart, M. A., and Tsai, L. (1981). The incidence of cognition disabilities in the siblings of autistic children. *British Journal of Psychiatry, 138,* 416–422.

Bertelsen, A., Harvald, B., and Hauge, M. (1977). A Danish twin study of manic depressive disorders. *British Journal of Psychiatry, 130,* 330–351.

Bleuler, M. (1978). The long term course of schizophrenic psychoses. In L. C. Wynne, R. L. Cromwell, and S. Matthysse (Eds.), The nature of schizophrenia: New approaches to research and treatment. New York: Wiley.

Bohman, M., Cloninger, C. R., Sigvardsson, S., and von Knorring, A. L. (1982). Predisposition to petty criminality in Swedish adoptees, I: Genetic and environmental heterogeneity. *Archives of General Psychiatry, 39,* 1233–1241.

Botstein, D., White, R. L., Skolnick, M., and Davis, R. W. (1980). Construction of a genetic linkage map in man using restriction fragment length polymorphisms. *American Journal of Human Genetics, 32,* 312–331.

Bouchard, R., and McGue, M. (1981). Familial studies of intelligence: A review, *Science, 212,* 1055–1059.

Brown, F. N. (1942). Heredity in the psychoneuroses. *Proceedings of the Royal Society of Medicine, 35,* 785–790.

Brown, G. W., and Harris, T. (1978). *The social origins of depression,* London: Tavistock.

Bucher, K. D., Elston, R. C., Green, R., Whybrow, P., Helzer, J., Reich, T., Clayton, R., and Winokur, G. (1981). The transmission of manic depressive illness, II: Segregation analysis of three sets of family data. *Journal of Psychiatric Research, 16,* 65–78.

Buglass, D., Clarke, J., Henderson, A. S., Kretiman, N., and Presley, A. S. (1977). A study of agorophobic housewives. *Psychological Medicine, 7,* 73–86.

Cadoret, R. J. (1978). Evidence for genetic inheritance of primary affective disorder in adoptees. *American Journal of Psychiatry, 135,* 463–466.

Cadoret, R. J., and Gath, A. (1978). Inheritance of alcoholism in adoptees. *British Journal of Psychiatry, 132,* 152.

Carey, G. (1978). A clinical-genetic study of obsessional and phobic states. Ph.D. Dissertation, University of Minnesota.

Carey, G. and Gottesman, I. I. (1981). Twin and family studies of anxiety, phobic and obsessive disorders. In D. F. Klein and J. Rabkin (Eds.), *Anxiety: New research and changing concepts* (pp. 117–136), New York: Raven Press.

Carroll, B. J. (1982). The dexamethasone suppression test for melancholia. *British Journal of Psychiatry, 140,* 292–304.

Carter, C. L., and Chung, C. S. (1980). Segregation analysis of schizophrenia under a mixed model. *Human Heredity, 30,* 350–356.

Christiansen, K. O. (1974). The genetics of aggressive criminality. Implications of a study of crime in a Danish twin study. In J. De Wit and W. W. Hartup (Eds.), *Determinants and origins of aggressive behaviour* (pp. 233–253). The Hague: Mouton.

Clifford, C. A., Fulker, D. W., Gurling, H. M. D., and Murray, R. M. (1981).

Preliminary findings from a twin study of alcohol use. In L. Gedda, P. Parisi, and W. E. Nance (Eds.), *Twin research* (pp. 47–52). New York: Alan Liss.

Clifford, C. A., Murray, R. M. and Fulker, D. W. (1984). Genetic and environmental influences on obsessional traits and symptoms. *Psychological Medicine, 14,* 791–800.

Cloninger, C. R., Bohman, M., and Sigvardsson, S. (1981). Inheritance of alcohol abuse. A cross fostering analysis of adopted men. *Archives of General Psychiatry, 38,* 861–868.

Cloninger, C. R., Martin, R. L., Clayton, P., and Guze, S. B. (1981a). A blind follow up and family study of anxiety neurosis: Preliminary analysis of the St. Louis 500. In D. F. Klein and J. Rabkin (Eds.), *Anxiety: New research and changing concepts* (pp. 137–154). New York: Raven Press.

Cloninger, C. R., Reich, T. and Guze, S. B. (1975). The multifactorial model of disease transmission, III: The familial relationship between sociopathy and hysteria (Briquet's syndrome). *British Journal of Psychiatry, 127,* 23–32.

Cloninger, C. R., Sigvardsson, S., Bohman, M., and von Knorring, A. L. (1982). Predisposition to petty criminality in Swedish adoptees, II: Cross fostering analysis of gene–environment interaction. *Archives of General Psychiatry, 39,* 1242–1247.

Cohen, M. E., Badel, D. W., Kilpatrick, A., Reed, E. W., and White, P. D. (1951). The high familial prevalence of neurocirculatory asthenia. *American Journal of Human Genetics, 3,* 126–158.

Crowe, R. R. (1974). An adoption study of antisocial personality. *Archives of General Psychiatry, 31,* 785–791.

Crowe, R. R., Pauls, D. L., Kerber, R. E., and Noyes, R. (1981). Panic disorders and mitral value prolapse. In D. F. Klein and J. Rabkin (Eds.), *Anxiety: New research and changing concepts* (pp. 103–116). New York: Raven Press.

Dalgaard, O. S., and Kringlen, E. (1976). A Norwegian twin study of criminality. *British Journal of Criminality, 16,* 213–232.

Eaves, L. J. and Young, P. A. (1981). How stable are personality traits? In L. Gedda, P. Parisi, and W. E. Nance (Eds.), *Twin research 3, Part B. Intelligence, personality and development* (pp. 87–98). New York: Alan R. Liss

Falconer, D. S. (1965). The inheritance of liability to certain diseases, estimated from the incidence among relatives. *Annals of Human Genetics, 29,* 51–76.

Feighner, J. P., Robins, E., Guze, S. B., Woodruff, R. A., Winokur, G. and Muñoz, R. (1972). Diagnostic Criteria for use in psychiatric research. *Archives of General Psychiatry, 26,* 57–63.

Festenstein, H., and Demant, P. (1978). *HLA and H2: Current topics in immunology, 9.* London: Edward Arnold.

Fischer, M. (1971). Psychoses in the offspring of schizophrenic monozygotic twins and their normal cotwins. *British Journal of Psychiatry, 115,* 981–990.

Fischer, M. (1973). Genetic and environmental factors in schizophrenia. *Acta Psychiatrica Scandinavica.* Supplement 238.

Fuller, J. L. and Thompson, W. R. (1978). *Foundations of behavior genetics.* St. Louis: C. V. Mosby.

Gershon, E. S., Bunney, W. F., Leckman, J. F., Van Eerdewegh, M., and Debauche, B. A. (1976). The inheritance of affective disorders: A review of data and hypotheses. *Behavior Genetics, 6,* 227–261.

Gershon, E. S., Hamovit, J., Guroff, J. J., et al. (1982). A family study of schizoaffective bipolar I, bipolar II, unipolar, and normal control probands. *Archives of General Psychiatry, 39,* 1157–1167.

Gershon, E. S., Mark, A., Cohen, N., Balizon, N., Baron, M., and Knobe, K. E. (1975). Transmitted factors in the morbid risk of affective disorders. *Journal of Psychiatric Research, 12,* 283–299.

Goetzl, U., Green, R., Whybrow, P., and Jackson, R. (1974). X linkage revisited. A further family study of manic depressive illness. *Archives of General Psychiatry, 31,* 274–288.

Goldin, L. R., Gershon, E. S., Targum, S. D., Sparkes, R. S., and McGuinniss, M. (1983). Segregation and linkage analyses in families of patients with bipolar, unipolar, and schizoaffective mood disorders. *American Journal of Human Genetics, 35,* 274–288.

Goodwin, D. W., Schulsinger, F., Hermansen, L., Guze, S. B., and Winokur, G. (1973). Alcohol problems in adoptees raised apart from alcoholic biological parents. *Archives of General Psychiatry, 28,* 238–243.

Gottesman, I. I. (1963). Heritability of personality: A demonstration. *Psychological Monograph, 77,* 1–21.

Gottesman, I. I. and Shields, J. (1982). *Schizophrenia, the epigenetic puzzle.* Cambridge, England: Cambridge University Press.

Gray, J. A. (1982). *The neuropsychology of anxiety: An enquiry into the functions of the septo-hippocampal system.* Oxford: Oxford University Press.

Gurling, H. M. D., Clifford, C. A., and Murray, R. M. (1981). Investigations into the genetics of alcohol dependence and into its effects on brain function. In L. Gedda, P. Parisi, and W. E. Nance (Eds.), *Twin research 3* (pp. 77–87). New York: Alan Liss.

Gusella, J. F., Wexler, N. S., Conneally, P. M., Naylor, S. L., Anderson, M. A., et al (1983). A polymorphic marker genetically linked to Huntington's Disease. *Nature, 306,* 234–238.

Guze, S. B., Cloninger, C. R., Martin, R. L., and Clayton, P. J. (1983). A follow up and family study of schizophrenia. *Archives of General Psychiatry, 40,* 1273–1276.

Hanson, D. R., and Gottesman, I. I. (1976). The genetics, if any, of infantile autism and childhood schizophrenia. *Journal of Autism and Childhood Schizophrenia, 6,* 209–234.

Hare, E., Price, J., and Slater, E. (1972). Fertility in obsessional neurosis. *British Journal of Psychiatry, 121,* 197–205.

Harvald, B., and Hauge, M. (1965). Hereditary factors elucidated by twin studies. In J. V. Neel, M. W. Shaw, and W. J. Schurr (Eds.), PHS Publication No. 1163, *Genetics and the epidemiology of chronic diseases* (pp. 61–76). Washington, D.C.: U.S. Department of Health, Education and Welfare.

Hayashi, S. (1967). A study of juvenile delinquency in twins. *Bull. Osaka Medical School,* XII, 373–378.

Helzer, J., and Winokur, G. (1974). A family interview study of male manic depressives. *Archives of General Psychiatry, 31,* 73–77.

Henderson, N. D. (1982). Human behavior genetics. *Annual Review of Psychology, 33,* 403–440.

Heston, L. L. (1966). Psychiatric disorders in foster home reared children of schizophrenic mothers. *British Journal of Psychiatry, 112,* 819–825.

Hutchings, B., and Mednick, S. A. (1974). Registered criminality in the adopted and biological parents of registered male adoptees. In S. A. Mednick, F. Schulsinger, J. Higgins, and B. Bell (Eds.), *Genetics environment and psychopathology* (pp. 105–116). Amsterdam: Elsevier.

Huxley, J., Mayr, E., Osmond, H., and Hoffer, A. (1964). Schizophrenia as a genetic morphism. *Nature, 204,* 220–221.

Jackson, D. P. (1960). A critique of the literature on the genetics of schizophrenia. In D. D. Jackson (Ed.), *The etiology of schizophrenia.* New York: Basic Books.

James, J. (1971). Frequency in relatives for an all-or-none trait. *Annals of Human Genetics, 35,* 47–49.

James, N. M., and Chapman, C. J. (1975). A genetic study of bipolar affective disorder. *British Journal of Psychiatry, 126,* 449–456.

Kaij, L. (1960). *Alcoholism in twins.* Stockholm: Almgvist and Stockholm.

Kallman, F. J. (1954). Genetics principles in manic depressive psychosis. In P. H. Hock, and J. Zubin (Eds.), *Depression* (pp. 1–24). New York: Grune and Stratton.

Kamin, L. J. (1974). *The science and politics of I.Q.* New York: Wiley.

Kendell, R. E. (1975). *The role of diagnosis in psychiatry,* Oxford: Blackwell Scientific Publications.

Kendler, K. S., Gruenberg, A. M., and Strauss, J. S. (1981). An independent analysis of the Copenhagen sample of the Danish adoption study of schizophrenia, II: The relationship between schizotypal personality disorder and schizophrenia. *Archives of General Psychiatry, 38,* 982–984.

Kety, S. S., Rosenthal, D., Wender, P. H., Schulsinger, F., and Jacobsen, B. (1976). Mental illness in the biological and adoptive families of individuals who have become schizophrenic. *Behaviour Genetics, 6,* 219–225.

Kranz, F., (1937). Untersuchungen an Zwillingen in Fursorgeerziehungsanstalten, *Z. Induktive Abstammungs-Vererbungslehre, 73,* 508–512.

Kringlen, E. (1967). *Heredity and environment in the functional psychoses.* London: Heinemann.

Kringlen, E. (1968). An epidemiological–clinical twin study on schizophrenia. In D. Rosenthal and S. S. Kety (Eds.), *The transmission of schizophrenia.* Oxford: Pergamon.

Lancet (1982). Editorial: The CT scan in schizophrenia. *Lancet* ii, 968.

Lange, J. (1931). *Crime as destiny.* Translated by C. Haldane. London: Allen and Unwin.

Leighton, A. H. (1959). *My name is legion.* New York: Basic Books.

Lewis, A. (1935). Problems of obsessional illness. *Proceedings of the Royal Society of Medicine,* 29, 325–336.

Lewis, A. (1974). Psychopathic personality: A most elusive category. *Psychological Medicine,* 4, 133–45.

Li, C. C. (1975). *Path analysis—A primer.* Pacific Grove, Calif.: Boxwood Press.

Loehlin, J. C., and Nichols, R. C. (1976). *Heredity, environment and personality: A study of 850 sets of twins.* Austin, Texas: University of Texas Press.

Lotter, V. (1966). Epidemiology of autistic conditions in young children, I: Prevalence. *Social Psychiatry, 1,* 123–137.

Luxenburger, H. (1930). Psychiatrisch-neurologische Zwillings-pathologie. *Zeitblatt fur die gesamte Neurologie und Psychiatrie, 56,* 145–180.

McGuffin, P. (1980). What have transplant antigens got to do with psychosis? *British Journal of Psychiatry, 136,* 510–11.

McGuffin, P. (1984). Biological markers and psychosis. *Psychological Medicine, 14*, 255–258.
McGuffin, P., Farmer, A. E., Gottesman, I. I., Murray, R. M., and Reveley, A. M. (1984). Twin concordance for operationally defined schizophrenia. Confirmation of familiality and heritability. *Archives of General Psychiatry, 41*, 541–545.
McGuffin, P., Farmer, A. E., and Yonace, A. H. (1981). HLA antigens and subtypes of schizophrenia. *Psychiatry Research, 5*, 115–122.
McGuffin, P., Festenstein, H., and Murray, R. (1983). A family study of HLA antigens and other genetic markers in schizophrenia. *Psychological Medicine, 13*, 31–43.
McGuffin, P., and Gottesman, I. I. (1984). Genetic influences on normal and abnormal development. In M. Rutter and L. Hersov (Eds.), *Child psychiatry: Modern approaches*, 2nd ed. (pp. 17–33). Oxford: Blackwell Scientific.
McGuffin, P., and Mawson, D. (1980). Obsessive compulsive neurosis: Two identical twin pairs. *British Journal of Psychiatry, 137*, 285–287.
McKeon, P., McGuffin, P., and Robinson, P. H. (1984). Obsessive compulsive neurosis following head injury: A report of four cases. *British Journal of Psychiatry, 144*, 190–193.
McKusick, V. A. (1983). *Mendelian inheritance in man*, 6th ed. Baltimore and London: Johns Hopkins University Press.
McKusick, V. A., and Ruddle, F. H. (1977). The status of the gene map of the human chromosomes. *Science, 196*, 390–405.
McNeil, T. F., and Kaij, L. (1978). Obstetric factors in the development of schizophrenia: Complications in the birth of preschizophrenics and in reproduction of schizophrenic parents. In L. C. Wynne, R. L. Cromwell, and S. Matthyse (Eds.), *The nature of schizophrenia* (pp. 401–429). Chichester, England: Wiley.
Mednick, S. A., Gabrielli, W., and Hutchings, B. (1984). Genetic influences in criminal convictions: Evidence from an adoption cohort. *Science, 224*, 891–894.
Mendelwicz, J., and Rainer, J. D. (1974). Morbidity risks and genetic transmission in manic depressive illness. *American Journal of Human Genetics, 26*, 692–701.
Mendelwicz, J., and Rainer, J. D. (1977). Adoption study supporting genetic transmission in manic depressive illness. *Nature, 268*, 326–329.
Morton, N. E. (1982). *An outline of genetic epidemiology*. Basel: Karger.
Murphy, E. A., and Chase, G. A. (1975). *Principles of genetic counselling*. Chicago: Year Book Publishers.
Murray, R. M., Clifford, C., Fulker, D. W., and Smith, A. (1981). Does heredity contribute to obsessional traits and symptoms? In M. T. Tsuang (Ed.), *Genetics issue: The psycho-social epidemiology monograph series, U.S. National Institute of Mental Health*. New York: Neale Watson Press.
Murray, R. M., and McGuffin, P. (1983). The genetics of mental illness. In R. E. Kendell and A. Zeally (Eds.), *Companion to psychiatric studies, 3rd Edition* (pp. 150–176). Edinburgh: Churchill Livinstone.
Noyes, R., Clancy, J., Crowe, R., Hoenk, P. R., and Slyman, D. J. (1978). The familial prevalence of anxiety neurosis. *Archives of General Psychiatry, 35*, 1057–1059.
O'Rourke, D. H., Gottesman, I. I., Suarez, B. K., Rice, J., and Reich, T.

(1982). Refutation in the single locus model in the etiology of schizophrenia. *American Journal of Human Genetics, 33,* 630–649.

O'Rourke, D. H., McGuffin, P., and Reich, T. (1983). Genetic analysis of manic depressive illness. *American Journal of Physical Anthropology, 62,* 51–59.

Partanen, J. K., Bruun, T., and Markanen, N. (1966). *Inheritance of drinking behaviour: A study on intelligence, personality and the use of alcohol in adult twins.* Helsinki: The Finnish Foundation for Alcohol Studies.

Perris, C. (1966). A study of bipolar, manic depressive and unipolar recurrent depressive psychoses. *Acta Psychiatrica et Neurologica Scandinavica Supplementum, 42.*

Perris, C., Perris, H., Ericsson, U., and von Knorring, A. L. (1983). The genetics of depression. A family study of unipolar and neurotic-reactive depressed patients. *Archiv Fur Psychiatrie und Nervenkranic Heiten* (Berlin), *232,* 137–155.

Pollin, W., and Stabenau, J. R. (1968). Biological, psychological and historical differences in a series of monozygotic twins discordant for schizophrenia. In D. Rosenthal and S. S. Kety (Eds.), *The transmission of schizophrenia* (pp. 317–332). Oxford: Pergamon.

Pollin, W., Allen, M. G., Hoffer, A., Stabenau, J. R., and Hrubec, Z. (1969). Psychopathology in 15,909 pairs of veteran twins: Evidence for a genetic factor in the pathogenesis of schizophrenia and its relative absence in psychoneurosis. *American Journal of Psychiatry, 126,* 597–610.

Pollitt, J. (1972). The relationship between genetic and precipitating factors in depressive illness. *British Journal of Psychiatry, 121,* 67–70.

Pope, H. G., Jonas, J., Cohen, B. A., and Lipinski, J. F. (1983). Heritability of schizophrenia. *American Journal of Psychiatry, 140,* 132–133.

Powell, G. E. (1984). Personality. In P. McGuffin, M. D. Shanks, and R. Hodgson, (Eds.), *Psychopathology* (pp. 409–446). London: Academic Press.

Reich, T., James, J. W., and Morris, C. A. (1972). The use of multiple thresholds in determining the mode of transmission of semi-continuous traits. *Annals of Human Genetics, 36,* 163–184.

Reveley, A. M., Reveley, M. A., and Murray, R. M. (1984). Cerebral ventricular enlargement in nongenetic schizophrenia: A controlled twin study. *British Journal of Psychiatry, 144,* 89–93.

Rieder, R. O., and Gershon, E. S. (1978). Genetic strategies in biological psychiatry. *Archives of General Psychiatry, 35,* 866–873.

Roe, A. (1944). The adult adjustment of children of alcoholic parents resident in foster homes. *Quarterly Journal of Studies on Alcohol, 5,* 378–393.

Rosanoff, A. J., Handy, L., and Plesset, I. R. (1935). The etiology of manic depressive syndromes with special reference to their occurrence in twins. *American Journal of Psychiatry, 91,* 725–762.

Rosanoff, A. J., Handy, L. M., and Plesset, I. R. (1941). The etiology of child behavior difficulties, juvenile delinquency and adult criminality with special reference to their occurrence in twins. *Psychiatric Monographs,* No. 1, Sacramento, Calif.: Department of Institutions, State of California.

Rose, R. J., Miller, J. Z., Pogue-Geile, M. F., and Cardwell, G. F. (1981). *Twin-family studies of common fears and phobias. Twin Research 3: Intelligence, personality and development* (pp. 169–174). New York: Alan R. Liss.

Rosenthal, D., Wender, P. H., Kety, S. S., Schulsinger, F., Welner, J., and Ostergaard, L. (1968). Schizophrenic's offspring reared in adoptive homes. In D.

Rosenthal and S. S. Kety (Eds.), *Transmission of schizophrenia* (pp. 337–391). Oxford: Pergamon.

Scarr, S., and Carter-Saltzman, L. (1979). Twin method: Defense of a critical assumption. *Behavior Genetics, 9,* 527–542.

Schneider, K. (1950). *Psychopathic personalities.* Translated by M. W. Hamilton, 1958. London: Cassell.

Shapiro, R. W. (1970). A twin study of non-endogenous depression. *Acta Jutlandica, XLII* (publications of the University of Aartus, Denmark.)

Shields, J. (1977). Polygenic influences. In M. Rutter and L. Hersov (Eds.), *Child psychiatry: Modern approaches* (pp. 22–46) Oxford: Blackwell Scientific Publications.

Slater, E. (1936). German eugenics in practice. *Eugenics Review, 27,* 285–295.

Slater, E. (1943). The neurotic constitution: A statistical study of two thousand soldiers. *Journal of Neurology and Psychiatry, 6,* 1–16.

Slater, E. (1953). *Psychotic and neurotic illness in twins.* Medical Research Council Special Report Series, No. 278. London: Her Majesty's Stationery Office.

Slater, E. (1961). The thirty-fifth Maudsley lecture: "Hysteria 311." *Journal of Mental Science, 107,* 359–81.

Slater, E., and Cowie, V. (1971). *The genetics of mental disorders.* Oxford: Oxford University Press.

Slater, E., and Shields, J. (1969). Genetical aspects of anxiety. In M. H. Lader (Ed.), *Studies of anxiety* (pp. 62–71), British Journal of Psychiatry Special Publication No. 3. Ashford: Headley Brothers.

Smeraldi, E., Negri, F., and Melil, A. M. (1977). A genetic study of affective disorders. *Acta Psychiatrica Scandinavica, 56,* 382–398.

Solyom, L., Beck, P., Solyom, C., and Hugel, R. (1974). Some etiological factors in phobic neurosis. *Canadian Psychiatric Association Journal, 19,* 69–78.

Spitzer, R. L., Endicott, J., and Robins, E. (1975). *Research Diagnostic Criteria, Instrument No. 58.* New York: Biometrics Research, New York State Psychiatric Institute.

Srole, L., Langner, T. S., Michael, S. T., Opler, M. K., and Rennie, T. A. C. (1962). *Mental Health in the metropolis.* New York: McGraw-Hill.

Stendstedt, A. (1966). Genetics of neurotic depression. *Acta Psychiatrica Scandinavica, 42,* 392–409.

Stumpfl, G. (1936). *Die Usprunge des Verbrechens am Lebenslaug von Zwillingen.* London: Thieme.

Tienari, P. (1968). Schizophrenia in monozygotic male twins. In D. Rosenthal, and S. S. Kety (Eds.), *The transmission of schizophrenia,* pp. 27–36. Oxford: Pergamon.

Tienari, P. (1971). Schizophrenia and monozygotic twins. *Psychiatrica Fennica,* 97–104.

Torgersen, S. (1978). The contribution of twin studies to psychiatric nosology. In L. Gedda, P. Parisi, and W. E. Nance (Eds.), *Twin research 3, Part A: Psychology and methodology.* New York: Allen R. Liss.

Torgersen, S. (1983). Genetic factors in anxiety disorders. *Archives of General Psychiatry, 40,* 1085–1089.

Torgersen, S. (1979). The nature and origin of common phobic fears. *British Journal of Psychiatry, 134,* 343–351.

Torgersen, S. (1981). Unpublished manuscript.

Tsuang, M. T. (1978). Genetic counselling for psychiatric patients and their families. *American Journal of Human Genetics, 135,* 1465–1476.

Tsuang, M., Winokur, G., and Crowe, R. (1980). Morbidity risks of schizophrenia and affective disorders among first degree relatives of patients with schizophrenia, mania, depression and surgical conditions. *British Journal of Psychiatry, 137,* 497–504.

Turner, W. D. (1979). Genetic markers for schizotaxia. *Biological Psychiatry, 14,* 177–205.

von Knorring, A., Cloninger, C. R., Bohman, M., and Sigvardsson, S. (1983). An adoption study of depressive disorders and substance abuse. *Archives of General Psychiatry, 40,* 943–950.

Weatherall, D. J. (1982). *The new genetics and clinical practice.* Nuffield Provincial Hospitals Trust.

Weissman, M. M., Gershon, E., Kidd, K. K., Prusoff, B. A., et al. (1984). Psychiatric disorders in the relatives of probands with affective disorders. *Archives of General Psychiatry, 41,* 13–21.

Weitkamp, L. R., Stancer, H. C., Persad, S., Flood, C., and Guttormsen, S. (1981). Depressive disorders and HLA: A gene on chromosome 6 that can affect behavior. *New England Journal of Medicine, 305,* 1301–1341.

Wender, P. H., Rosenthal, D., Kety, S. S., Schulsinger, F., and Welner, J. (1973). Social class and psychopathology in adoptees: A natural experimental method for separating the roles of genetic and environmental factors. *Archives of General Psychiatry, 28,* 318–325.

Wilson, R. S., Garron, D. C., and Klawans, H. L. (1978). Significance of genetic factors in Gilles de la Tourette Syndrome: A review. *Behavior Genetics, 8,* 503–510.

Winokur, G., and Clayton, P. (1967). Family history studies, I: Two types of affective disorders separated according to genetic and clinical factors. *Recent Advances in Biological Psychiatry, 9,* 35–50.

Winokur, G., Tsuang, M. T., and Crowe, R. R. (1982). Affective disorder in the relatives of manic and depressed patients. *American Journal of Psychiatry, 139,* 209–212.

Wright, A. F., Crichton, D. N., Loudon, J. B., Morten, J. E. N., and Steel, C. M. (1984). B-adrenoceptor binding defects in cell lines from families with manic depressive disorder. *Annals of Human Genetics, 80,* 201–214.

Wyatt, R. J., Plotkin, S. G., and Murphy, D. L. (1979). Platelet monoamine oxidase activity in schizophrenia: A review of the data. *American Journal of Psychiatry, 136,* 377–82.

Yoshimasu, S. (1961). The criminological significance of the family in the light of the studies of criminal twins. *Acta Criminal Medical Legal Japonica, 27,* 117–141.

Social Stress and Psychopathology

Bruce P. Dohrenwend

Much of the evidence that socioenvironmental factors in general and environmentally induced stress in particular are causally related to the occurrence and distribution of various types of psychopathology in communities is indirect. This evidence comes from three sources: (1) variation in rates of psychopathology in different cultural and subcultural settings; (2) the findings of genetic researchers using twin, adoption, and family studies; and (3) research on extreme situations.

The evidence is often vivid: the great variability in rates according to time and place of acting-out in types of personality disorder that involve antisocial behavior, alcohol abuse, and drug abuse (cf. Dohrenwend, 1983); the tendency for first admission cases of schizophrenia to vary inversely not only with social class but also with ethnic status, even with indicators of social class controlled (Dohrenwend and Dohrenwend, 1981); and the strong evidence that extreme situations, such as prolonged combat in wartime, produce a wide range and variety of psychopathology in previously normal persons (Dohrenwend, 1979; Dohrenwend and Egri, 1981). While such findings suggest that we look closely at life stress processes in the causation of psychopathology in community populations, some of them (such as the rate variations) are open to plausible alternative explanations, and none of them tells us much about how these processes may be operating in such settings.

My and my colleagues' assessment of most of this indirect evidence has been presented elsewhere (Dohrenwend, 1979; Dohrenwend and de Figueiredo, 1983; Dohrenwend and Dohrenwend, 1981; Dohrenwend, 1983). In this paper I will focus on more direct evidence from studies of stressful life events and other social and psychological variables in life stress processes. In doing so I will: (1) review what I regard as the most important studies; (2) refer to some preliminary results of our own research; (3) point to some of the methodological problems that stand in the way of needed future investigations; and (4) in the spirit of this con-

Some of the research reported in this chapter was supported by research grant MH 36208 from the National Institute of Mental Health, U.S. Public Health Service. My colleagues in this research are acknowledged at several points in the text.

ference, speculate on how past findings and the probable yield of future research could profitably inform and be informed by efforts at primary prevention.

Review of the Evidence

In reviewing the evidence I will emphasize the types of psychopathology in which I have been most interested: schizophrenia and schizophrenia-like disorders; major depression; the acting-out types of personality disorder that include antisocial personality and substance abuse; and a type of nonspecific distress that we think is best described by Jerome Frank's concept of *demoralization* (Frank, 1973). These include most of the major types of functional mental disorders, and they are the types of psychopathology that show the most interesting relations with gender and with social class.

The occurrence and distribution of the types of psychopathology to be explained

Taking the 80 or so epidemiological studies of current prevalence (i.e., prevalence usually during a few months to about a year) conducted since the turn of the century to about 1980, we have been able to calculate median rates for several of these types of psychopathology (Dohrenwend and Dohrenwend, 1969; Dohrenwend et al., 1980). Until a new generation of epidemiological studies, using far more rigorous methodology, produces a similar body of data, these provide interim hypotheses about the amounts of psychopathology in communities.

With a little more arithmetic, the figures in Table 1 would show that it would not be unusual to find 15 percent or so of the adults in a sample of communities suffering from a diagnosable mental disorder with no known organic basis. On average, we estimate that only about one-fourth of these cases have ever been in treatment with mental health professionals (Link and Dohrenwend, 1980).

Note that Table 1 shows 17 studies based on results secured with symptom scales of distress that, we think, are measures of demoralization. In these studies, about one-fourth of the adults showed distress as severe as that shown by psychiatric outpatients. We estimate that in about one-half of these cases the distress coincides with diagnosable mental disorders of the kinds shown in Table 1. Thus about 12 or 13 percent show severe distress unaccompanied by a major, diagnosable mental disorder.

When these 12 or 13 percent distressed are added to 15 percent or so with diagnosable disorders, it is evident that serious psychopathology is

TABLE I

Functional psychiatric disorders reported in epidemiological studies of "true" prevalence (published in 1950 or later)

Type of Disorder	Median (%)	Range (%)	Number of Studies
Schizophrenia	0.76	0.0023–1.96	17
Affective psychosis	0.43	0.0000–1.59	12
Neurosis	5.95	0.305–75.0*	25
Personality disorders	4.19	0.23–14.5*	19
Overall function disorders	14.05	1.25–63.5	27
"Demoralization"	27.5	3.4–69.0	17

*Includes Stirling County Study "symptom patterns" that are not necessarily considered "cases" in that study (D. C. Leighton et al., 1963).

Note: Percentages were adjusted for sex differences, except for rates of "Demoralization." Medians and ranges were calculated from detailed tables and bibliography prepared to supplement Dohrenwend, B. P. and Dohrenwend, B. S. (1974). Social and cultural influences on psychopathology. *Annual Review of Psychology, 25,* 417–452; Dohrenwend and Dohrenwend (1976) Sex differences and psychiatric disorders. *American Journal of Sociology, 81,* 1447–1454.

not rare in community populations; rather, it is shown by 25–30 percent of the adults on average. Note, however, that some of the important subtypes of psychopathology are extremely rare; the current prevalence of schizophrenia, for example, averages a bit less than one percent, as counted in these community studies. If we are to understand the role of life stress processes in the occurrence and distribution of psychopathology in communities, we have to deal with phenomena that, in the aggregate, are not rare but with some subtypes that are very rare.

All of the types of psychopathology with which we are concerned are inversely related to social class and therefore may be affected in common by certain stress factors, but there are also differences. Rates of depressive disorders, for example, are consistently much higher for women (Dohrenwend and Dohrenwend, 1976; Weissman and Klerman, 1977), whereas rates of the acting-out types of disorders are consistently higher in men (Dohrenwend and Dohrenwend, 1976). Such differences alone (and there are others from genetic research and treatment research) would suggest that we should also look for stress factors specific to the different disorders. When our concern is with specific disorders, we must of necessity become interested in case-control studies because most of the specific disorders (demoralization excepted) are too rare to be studied effectively in community samples. Therefore it is to case-control studies that we turn for detailed evidence on the role of life stress processes in psychopathology.

Our primary interest is in the role of stress factors at onset rather than in course. For this reason the case-control studies are retrospective in nature. Without advance, exact knowledge of the risk factors involving stress, prospective studies based on selection of cohorts exposed to the stress factors and followed through the risk period for developing the disorders have not yet been conducted.

Evidence mainly from case-control studies on the main elements of life stress processes: Recent life events, personal dispositions and ongoing social situations

Various investigators have listed criteria for adequate retrospective case-control studies of the role of environmentally induced stress in various types of psychopathology. We have been influenced by Brown (1974) and Hudgens (1974), for example, in developing the list shown in Table 2.

These criteria are probably essential if we are to have decisive findings. However, several of the criteria are extremely difficult to meet. Consider, by way of illustration, the problems that would be involved with some of the criteria in a case-control study of schizophrenia.

In an analysis of results from epidemiological studies of true prevalence, Link and Dohrenwend (1980) have found that substantial minori-

TABLE 2

Ideal criteria for a case-control study of life events and episodes of various types of psychopathology

- The cases should consist of a representative sample of individuals from the population being studied who have recently developed the episodes for the first time.
- The procedures for collecting the symptom data and the rules for combining these data into diagnoses of cases should be explicit and replicable.
- The controls should consist of a representative sample of the demographic counterparts of the cases in the population being studied.
- There should be similarly selected comparison groups of cases with other types of symptomatology.
- Data on life events should be gathered systematically from the subjects and their informants on fully enumerated lists of events rather than from patient charts where recording of the relevant information tends to be fragmented.
- Both the occurrence of the events and the occurrence of onsets and/or recurrences of the episodes should be dated accurately with respect to each other.
- Events that are likely to occur as consequences of the individual's mental state and behavior must be distinguished from events that occur independently of such personality factors.
- Data on alternative or complementary dispositional or risk factors should be secured.
- Repeated follow-ups should be conducted at suitable intervals of time to test whether the circumstances preceding recurrence are the same as the circumstances preceding onset and whether they can be made to differ in meaningful ways with the occurrence of intervening factors such as type and duration of treatment.

ties of the diagnosed schizophrenics in some communities have never been in inpatient or outpatient treatment. To obtain a representative sample of persons who develop schizophrenic episodes, therefore, we must be able not only to agree on and identify the important characteristics of these episodes but also to draw samples of those showing such characteristics—whether these individuals have been officially recognized (e.g., by admission to a mental hospital). And while it is clear that some fateful events, such as death of a loved one, are very likely to occur independently of the individual's mental condition or behavior—and others, such as being convicted of a crime, are not—most events are between these two extremes and require considerable additional information about the context in which they occur before we can even begin to make such a determination. The most widely used checklist approaches to measuring life events make no provision for doing this. Moreover, data on the most firmly established risk factor, a high rate of the schizophrenic symptomatology in first-degree relatives, are extremely difficult and expensive to secure.

It should not be surprising, therefore, that there is no single case-control study of life stress and schizophrenia that meets all of the above criteria. The fact of the matter is that very few of the retrospective case-control studies of life stress and psychopathology in the literature even came close. We have, in fact, to relax the criteria to obtain even a few studies to examine with this question in mind. Fortunately, these few are very much worth it.

I will organize the review of these studies around three main components of life stress processed: (1) recent life events; (2) personal dispositions; and (3) the ongoing social situation. Let me consider the evidence for each in turn, starting with the *pivotal* component of recent life events. I say pivotal because this component is the only one of the three that, in retrospective case-control or cross-sectional community studies, can be shown to be antecedent and proximal to the onset of disorder.

Recent Life Events

Recent life events can range from natural and manmade disasters to more usual occurrences, such as marriage, divorce, loss of a job, and death of a loved one. The concept can be stretched to include accumulations of small events that have recently been described as daily "hassles" (Kanner et al., 1981).

There is little doubt that natural and manmade disasters can produce severe psychopathology of a wide variety of types in previously normal persons (cf. Dohrenwend and Dohrenwend, 1969; Dohrenwend, 1979;

Dohrenwend and Egri, 1981). However, such extreme situations are rare and play little or no role in the occurrence and distribution of psychopathology in the epidemiological studies described previously. (Table 1). Therefore I will concentrate here on studies of more commonly occurring and less extreme life events that, when they accumulate in brief periods of time, may expose people to severe stress. It is even possible, for example, to envision a set of such events that, when they occur close together in a brief period of time, could approximate the conditions of extreme situations. These consist of fateful loss events such as death of loved ones that occur outside the person's control; events that exhaust the individual physically, especially those involving physical illness and injury that is life threatening; and, finally, events not previously classified in these two categories that are likely to disrupt social supports—events such as a move from one community to another, a change of job, or a marital separation. When events of each of these three types co-occur in a brief period of time, we have the presence of what we hypothesize to be a pathogenic triad approximating the stress conditions of extreme situations (Dohrenwend, 1979).

I will consider for the most part only those studies that come reasonably near to meeting four of the criteria in Table 2. The four constitute the irreducible minimum for providing useful results bearing on the problem of whether life events play a causal role, and they consist of adequate controls, replicable diagnostic criteria, attention to assessing which events occur independently of the subjects' prior mental state, and careful attention to dating of the occurrence of events in relation to the occurrence of the episodes of psychopathology. The failure of investigators to attend to these criteria make much of the published research difficult to interpret. With particular reference to life events, methodological problems (especially those related to the question of independence) have been particularly serious (cf. Dohrenwend et al., 1984).

A variety of definitions of *schizophrenia* have been used in case-control studies to date. I will discuss the occurrence of acute psychotic episodes rather than of schizophrenia as defined, for example, by DSM-III since operationally this is more nearly what was investigated in these studies.

Two case-control studies have shown that the number of life events reported by schizophrenics before onset of an episode was significantly greater than the number reported by controls for a comparable period. One of these studies (Jacobs and Myers, 1976), in New Haven, focused on a survey of 62 first admissions; the other (Brown and Birley, 1968), in London, was concerned with 50 patients admitted for acute episodes of schizophrenia. Although the consistent finding of these two studies was that there was a significantly higher rate of life events in their reporting periods—one year in the former and three months in the latter study—for patients compared to community controls, this excess was due mainly to events that could be dependent on the patient's mental condition. It is of considerable interest, therefore, that Brown and Birley, who dated the occurrence of events within one-week periods, found that events that were independent of a person's psychiatric condition occurred more frequently in the three-week period preceding episodes of schizophrenia than in a comparable period in the lives of their controls. Forty-six percent of the patients but only 12 percent of the controls experienced at least one independent event in this three-week period. This difference was not found in earlier three-week periods. Moreover, this finding is not an isolated one; Leff and colleagues (1973) found a relatively high frequency of events in the period just prior to relapse in a sample of schizophrenics being treated with phenothiazines in the community. In addition, Brown and Birley showed that their results held, regardless of first admission versus readmission status of the patient and also for patients experiencing first episodes versus those experiencing relapses.

How severe were the events that preceded the onset of schizophrenic episodes? Fortunately, Brown and Birley (1968) provide information on the actual events experienced in the 13-week period prior to onset or relapse. It is clear from this material that not one of the cases experienced events from all three elements of our hypothesized pathogenic triad. However, Brown, Harris, and Peto (1973) reported with regard to the same study that about 16 percent of the cases experienced events that the investigators judged to be markedly severe and that, moreover, this was three times the rate of such events among the controls.

Rogler and Hollinghead (1965) have provided additional relevant data from a study of 20 couples, with at least one person in each couple diagnosed as schizophrenic following their first contact with a mental health agency. They are compared to very carefully selected matched controls from a slum section of San Juan in Puerto Rico. The particular result of interest is that death of a child was a frequent antecedent to the onset of disorder. Of 12 child deaths in the 40 San Juan families, 11 were concentrated in 7 of the families containing one or more schizophrenic parents. I read the evidence from these studies as indicating that severely stressful life events play a causal role in the onset of acute schizophrenic disorder.

To date, case-control studies of *depression* have not been designed with current DSM-III, Feighner, or RDC criteria explicitly in mind. There are ambiguities in the best of the studies purporting to investigate depression: that by Brown and Harris (1978), centering on the problem of what the investigators are measuring as depression. Critics have, in fact, engaged Brown and Harris in a controversy about the extent to which clinical depression rather than some form of lesser distress has been identified in the community cases counted by Brown and colleagues (Wing et al., 1978; Brown and Harris, 1982).

On the basis of current evidence we really do not know very much about the relation of nonspecific distress or demoralization to major depression. There is no question that scores on scales of such distress vary with the occurrence of life events (e.g., Myers, Lindenthal, and Pepper, 1974). The role of life events in major depression, as currently defined by DSM-III criteria, however, requires some speculation on our part about the relation of demoralization to such disorder and our assessment of which is being counted in past studies of depression. It seems likely to me that a majority of the patient cases of depression studied by such researchers as Paykel (1974), and also included in the studies of Brown and colleagues, would meet criteria for major depression.

In his case-control studies of life events and clinical depression, Paykel (1974) found that an excessive number of undesirable events, but not of desirable events, were reported in the six months prior to the onset of depression. He also identified a class of events that he labeled *exits,* in which a person leaves the social field of the subject. The events that Paykel included in this category were death of close family member, marital separation, divorce, family member leaving home, child getting married, and son being drafted. Paykel found that the presence of one or more of these events was strongly associated with onsets of depression. While only 5 percent of controls reported one or more exits in the 6-month reporting period, 25 percent of the depressed patients reported at least one such event.

Brown and Harris (1978) also reported a difference in recent life events between depressed women, whether treated or untreated, and nondepressed community controls. They found that depressed women had experienced an excess of a class of events that Brown and Harris labeled *severe* in the period, on average, of 38 weeks before the onset of depression. Specifically, 61 percent of patient cases and 68 percent of community cases, but only 28 percent of community controls, had experienced at least one such event.

In general, comparisons with the results for schizophrenia suggest that life events play a considerably larger role in depression (Brown and Harris, 1978); however, considerably less attention has been given by Brown and colleagues and by Paykel to the problem of independence of the life events than in the studies of schizophrenia. Nevertheless, there are replications and related studies of their work that do pay attention to this problem.

For example, in an exploratory study of the difference in recent life events experienced by 34 diagnosed acute neurotic cases found in general practices (which probably included a substantial number of depressives) and in matched general-practice patients free from psychiatric disturbance, Cooper and Sylph (1973) adopted Brown and Harris's procedure for identifying severe events by means of ratings of long-term contextual threat. They found that 47 percent of their neurotic patients but only 6 percent of their controls had experienced at least one severe event during the three-month comparison period. Adopting another classification employed by Brown in his study of schizophrenics, but not in his study of depressed women, they did not find a significant difference in the number of events experienced by cases and controls who were independent of the illness. This statistical result may, however, be a function of the small number of subjects in the study because 53 percent of the cases and only 26 percent of controls reported at least one independent event. And Brown has stated (although the data are not provided) that the results of the London study hold for independent events (cf. Brown and Harris, 1978; Lloyd, 1980a).

The evidence on the role of recent life events in episodes of *antisocial behavior* and *substance abuse* is sparse. There is no group of case-control studies comparable, for example, to the work of Brown and colleagues on episodes of schizophrenia and depression. There are hints from several investigations, however, that recent life events may play a part in these types of deviant behaviors.

Antisocial personality as currently defined in DSM-III is a type of disorder or constellation of deviant behaviors with onset in the early teens. Vaux and Ruggiero's (1983) study of delinquent behavior among 531 school youths is of interest, therefore, in focusing on the kinds of early deviance that tends to predict the later development of antisocial personality. Using an adaptation of Coddington's (1972a, b) list of life events, Vaux and Ruggiero found that antecedent life events added significantly to age and background social class in predicting self-reported violence, theft, drug use, property damage, and several other, minor delinquent acts.

Although aware that some events can be consequences of personal dispositions to deviance, these authors do not present separate analyses for events that are clearly independent of such dispositions or of past deviant behavior. Other investigators (e.g., Masuda et al., 1978) also fail to pay attention to this problem. In addition, the Masuda et al. (1978) study put a tremendous burden on recall, going back five years prior to incarceration, in their study of the relation of life change to imprisonment among 176 male prisoners. They found an excess of events in the year preceding admission, but this could be a function of superior recall for this more recent period.

Drug use is one of the outcomes related to life events in the study by Vaux and Ruggiero (1983). There is little other publication of systematic research on life events and drug abuse (cf. Duncan, 1977; Vaux and Ruggiero, 1983) or on life events and alcohol abuse (cf. Morrissey and Schuckit, 1978; Morrissey, 1980).

Personal Dispositions

Personal dispositions include such factors as prior psychopathology, normal variations in directly measured personality characteristics that may affect coping, indirect measures of personality residues of remote events such as childhood bereavement, and genetic assets versus vulnerabilities.

Unlike life events, some variations in personal dispositions, when they take the form of directly measured personality characteristics, cannot be clearly established as antecedent to and/or independent of the psychopathology being investigated in retrospective case-control or cross-sectional community studies (Akiskal, Hirschfeld, and Yerevanian, 1983). Hence existing retrospective studies can provide only hints about which of these personality variables may be important. Particularly attractive, therefore, are personal dispositions that can be related to or inferred from remote events that are clearly both antecedent to and independent of the types of psychopathology being investigated.

Earlier, I focused on recent life events to the exclusion of more remote events. It should now be clear that I am not ignoring events that far precede the onset of disorder. I assume, however, that if these more remote events have a current impact it is via the incorporation of their effects into the personality. Even if we do not know enough to measure these personality characteristics, we want to assess the relation of the remote events themselves as risk factors. Such landmark events would include, loss of parents during childhood and serious physical illnesses or injuries to the subject throughout the life course up to the period for reporting recent events.

There are, for example, quite consistent findings that children of homes broken by divorce or separation tend to exhibit antisocial behavior later in life (cf. Rutter, 1974). The results of research on the later effects of the death of a child's parent or parents appear to be much less persuasive, and reviewers of this literature can reach quite opposite conclusions (Lloyd, 1980b; Tennant, Bebbington, and Hurry, 1980). There are, however, at least three studies with results that suggest that the death of one or both parents before the child reaches age 11 is associated with vulnerability to depression (Brown and Harris, 1978) and/or severe psychological distress (Dohrenwend and de Figueiredo, 1973; Langner and Michael, 1963, pp. 167–169) among adults in samples from the general population who experience stressful life events.

Much has been learned in the last two decades from observations in clinical and natural settings and from experimental studies about effective psychological defense and coping responses to stressful events (e.g., Hamburg and Adams, 1967; Horowitz, 1976; Lazarus, 1966). At the same time, hypotheses have been developed concerning the nature of individual differences in disposition that account for pathological outcomes related to stressful life events.

As one example, a hypothesis concerning individual differences in vulnerability to stress-related psychopathology grows out of Rotter's social learning theory and his concept that individuals have a generalized expectancy about the extent to which they control the rewards, punishments, and, in general, the events that occur in their lives. Rotter (1966) conceived this expectancy, which he labeled *locus of control,* as varying on a dimension from internal to external. Persons at the extreme internal end of the locus of control dimension expect to be in control of their life events to a high degree. In contrast, persons at the extreme external end of the locus of control dimension expect that their life events will generally be controlled by others or by fate. Although there is some controversy concerning the relation of locus of control expectancy to vulnerability to pathology, the hypothesis with the most extensive empirical support is that persons with an external locus of control expectancy have greater proneness to psychopathology than those with an internal locus of control expectancy (e.g., Lefcourt, 1976, Chapter 7). In fact, in some studies, internal locus of control expectancy has been equated with competence, coping ability, and relative invulnerability to debilitating effects of stressful events (Campbell, Converse, and Rodgers, 1976, pp. 59–60).

It is possible to envision a set of variations in normal personality ranging from attitudes of mastery at one pole to helplessness at the other. This basic dimension has interesting variants at each extreme, some of which lead to poor coping in certain stress situations. At the mastery end, for example, we can put extreme Type A personality reactions that may well lead to problems in coping (Matthews and Glass, 1980). At the helplessness end, we might consider denial that, under some circumstances, could be functional (Lazarus, 1981). And it is interesting to consider how closely attitudes of mastery appear to coincide with masculine personality characteristics and helplessness with feminine ones, as measured, for example, by the Spence–Helmreich scales (1978). This particular variant of the mastery–helplessness dimension may have implications for the development of depression, a disorder that is far more prevalent in women than in men.

Unfortunately, about all we can do, so far as the published literature on these personality characteristics is concerned, is speculate. With the exception of locus of control and related concepts such as fatalism, there are simply great gaps. With regard to locus of control and fatalism, there are a few studies (as mentioned earlier) suggesting that externality, a variant at the helplessness end, increases the likelihood of distress or demoralization (e.g., Husaini and Neff, 1981).

Ongoing Social Situations

Complementing efforts to find factors within the individual that affect his or her risk of psychopathology related to stressful life events are more recent attempts to identify social factors in the individual's environment that affect this risk. One of the most influential hypotheses in the recent literature on life stress states that social support mitigates the effects of stressful events (Caplan and Killilea, 1976). Secondary analyses of data not specifically designed to test this hypothesis have suggested that highly stressful events combined with low social support are significantly more pathogenic than highly stressful events combined with high social support or less stressful events with high or low social support (Gore, 1981). However, there is controversy about whether the effects of support are additive or interactive (cf. Gore, 1981) and how to measure support in ways that are not confounded with life events on the one hand and psychopathology on the other (e.g., Dohrenwend et al., 1984). Moreover, most of the research, with the possible and/or partial exception of Brown and colleagues in their work on depression, has focused on nonspecific distress or demoralization rather than depressive types of mental disorders.

What is the structure of the support systems available to an individual? Although early efforts to conceptualize social supports tended to focus on formal helping agencies, such as mental health centers (Caplan and Killilea, 1976), work has also been done on analysis of the structure of varied forms of informal support systems, particularly family, neighborhood, and friendship networks (Phillips and Fischer, 1980). What is needed now in measures to be used in stress research is objective information about social networks and their structures, unconfounded with the quality of an individual's participation in these networks. Without this separation the relative contribution to the life stress process of an individual's personality as opposed to his or her social situation cannot be assessed.

Another question is: What functions can be performed by the various structures in an individual's support systems? Although to date most studies of social support have, by implication, emphasized emotional support, some exploratory studies suggest that it is equally important to investigate the availability of instrumental support during life events (Carveth and Gottlieb, 1979). Financial support is probably an important type of instrumental support in many life events. For example, if there is illness in the family, is there adequate insurance available, or, if not, is there someone in the informal network or in a community agency who will help out? Other types of instrumental support may be specific to particular life events: In the case of serious illness, can the person obtain adequate medical care? Does the new mother have someone to turn to for advice about the care of her baby? Exploratory studies suggest that different functions may be served by different support structures (Litwak and Szelenyi, 1969). Thus friends and acquaintances may be able to do more than family about helping a person find a new job, but family may be a better source of help with problems in personal relationships.

Networks and social supports do not exhaust the important characteristics of ongoing social situations that may affect risk factors. Brown and Harris (1978) found that "ongoing difficulties," including having three or more children under age 14 in the home, increased the risk of onset of a depressive episode in the London women they studied. This list includes ongoing burdens such as having a chronically ill relative in the home, or an occupation that exposes a person to monotonous or hazardous working conditions. Once again, we know little about these possible risk factors in relation to recent life events and major types of psychopathology.

Preview of Results from One of Our Ongoing Studies of Life Stress and Psychopathology

We have several ongoing NIMH supported studies in the Social Psychiatry Research Unit of Columbia University that should add needed findings to those I have just presented. My colleagues in this research are Rochelle Kern, Lawrence Krasnoff, Itzhak Levav, Bruce Link, Michael Lyons, John Martin, Patrick Shrout, and Andrew Skodol.

While there are differences in emphasis and in some of the outcome variables in these studies, each has at its core a focus on five alternative models of how the three elements of the life stress process—recent life events, personal dispositions, and ongoing social situations—may contribute to adverse health changes that Barbara Dohrenwend and I have described in detail elsewhere (Dohrenwend and Dohrenwend, 1980;

1981a, 1981b). One of these studies is further along than the others, and preliminary analyses indicate that we will soon have striking findings to report in depth. Meanwhile, I would like to give you a few examples of the preliminary analyses.

In this study a retrospective case-control design is being used to investigate the occurrence of episodes of depression and of acute schizophrenic or schizophreniform disorder in adult subjects in New York City. The subjects consist of three groups. The first is made up of 121 persons diagnosed by DSM-III criteria as having a major depressive disorder; of these, 50 were in their first episode of major depression; the remainder were in a repeat episode; the large majority were psychiatric patients drawn mostly from an outpatient clinic at Columbia Presbyterian Hospital, but 24 were located in a community sample of adults in the Washington Heights section surrounding the medical center. The second group consists of 65 patients, mostly inpatients, with DSM-III diagnoses of schizophrenia, schizophreniform disorder, and other nonaffective, nonorganic psychotic disorders; of these, 21 were in their first acute psychotic episode; the remainder were in a repeat episode. The third group consists of 190 well controls. They were part of a larger community sample that we had screened to eliminate cases of severe psychopathology, i.e., the same sample that provided the 24 major depressives.

These samples of cases and controls are far from perfect in that they are not as representative as we would like. The cases are for the most part patients rather than untreated cases, and a substantial number of the patients we would have liked to interview were lost because they refused, were too ill at the time of their first contact, or could not be located and scheduled for interview once they left treatment. The controls were subsampled from a larger community sample, which was drawn for purposes of a methodological study comparing different symptom scales from a variety of instruments. In the methodological study, we did not give much attention to converting refusals or to rescheduling respondents who broke appointments or were otherwise difficult to reach.

Nevertheless, our case-control study of stress and disorder has unique strong points that are missing from previous studies of this kind. For example, previous studies have compared one type of case with controls or two types of cases without controls. In the present study, we are comparing two different types of cases together with a community control group in the same design and are investigating personality variables as well as recent life events and important aspects of the ongoing situation at the same time. Moreover, the cases were diagnosed according to explicit DSM-III criteria and the controls were carefully screened to exclude the types of cases in which we are interested and other types of severe disorder. This diagnostic work was supervised by Robert Spitzer, Andrew Skodal, Janet Williams, and Mimi Gibbon of Biometrics Research at the New York State Psychiatric Institute. All have been strongly involved in the construction of DSM-III and/or its revision. Until we are able to study truly representative samples of untreated as well as treated cases from the community, supplemented by treatment sources, it probably will not be possible to improve significantly the design of the present retrospective case-control study.

We have conducted several multivariate and univariate analyses of some of the data. Let me summarize briefly some of the differences among the major depressives, the persons with schizophrenia-like disorder, and the well controls on key variables in each of the three elements of the life stress process.

Recent Life Events

Let us consider first a comparison of recent life events in the one-year period prior to the episode of disorder for the depressive cases and the schizophrenia-like disorder cases with the one-year period to interview for the well controls. I will focus especially on events in each of the three categories of events in the pathogenic triad described earlier.

Fateful Loss Events

The events that we judged, a priori, as likely to involve fateful loss, which occurred directly to the subject and were included in the list our interviewers presented to respondents, are shown in Table 3. We probed

TABLE 3
Fateful loss

Event	Mag Score
Child died	1036
Spouse died	821
Unable to get treatment for an illness or injury	611
Lost home through fire, flood, or other disaster	580
Found out that they cannot have children	518
Family member other than spouse or child died	463
Miscarriage or stillbirth	457
Close friend died	457
Took a cut in wage or salary without a demotion	396
Assaulted	383
Did not get an expected wage or salary increase	343
Laid off from work	325

each of these and other events to elicit more details about what actually occurred. It is possible that we will subtract some of the events that do not prove to be fateful or involve substantial loss and add events from elsewhere that prove, on probing, to be fateful.

Based on a simple count of whether the subjects said the events in Table 3 were present or absent—and with controls on the demographic variables of gender, age, educational level (under 12, 12–15, and 16+ years), ethnic background (Black, Hispanic, and non-Hispanic White), and marital status—we found a significantly higher rate (at the .05 level or better) of fateful loss events for the major depressives than for the controls (means of .715 versus .457). Those with schizophrenia-like disorders (.365) did not differ significantly from the controls over the period of a year; we have not yet checked to see if these events nevertheless tended to build up in the 3–5 weeks prior to the psychotic episode, as occurred with independent events in the Brown and Birley (1968) and Leff et al. (1973) studies.

Physical Illness and Injury

The second category in the pathogenic triad consists of events that exhaust the individual physically—especially when they are life threatening. Among these, we expect physical illness and injury to be the most prominent. Again, we will know more about these matters when we analyze the detailed information elicited about each event. Until now, we have simply looked at the number of physical illnesses and injuries reported. These are significantly higher in both major depressives (mean of .317) and "schizophrenics" (.283) than in controls (.110), with the relevant demographic variables controlled.

Other Events Likely to Disrupt Usual Social Supports

The third and last category in the pathogenic triad consists of events, other than those involving fateful loss and serious physical illness or injury, that are highly likely to disrupt usual social supports.

Table 4 shows the events we put in this category, a priori, that is, prior to examining the detailed information elicited about each event. A higher rate of these events were reported by both major depressives and those with schizophrenia-like disorders than by well controls (.719, .859, and .304, respectively), holding relevant demographic variables constant.

In general, these differences held for both first-episode and repeat-episode cases. Thus the results have implications for both onset and recurrences of the two types of disorders. Moreover, the relationship was evident for these three categories of events in the pathogenic triad only. There was no relationship, for example, with total number of events.

TABLE 4
Objective loss in social network

Event	Mag Score
Divorce	633
Went to jail	566
Marital infidelity	558
Married couple separated	515
Retired	461
Stopped working (not retirement) for an extended period	456
Fired from job	407
Broke up with a friend	328
Person moved out of household	333
Engagement broken	309

Social Networks and Social Support

We followed the procedure developed by Claude Fischer and colleagues (1977) for eliciting the members of the social networks of our cases and controls. Briefly, this involved asking each person in the study to name those individuals with whom he or she had or could have had supportive exchanges during the past year in nine areas of activity, such as care of children, watching the house while he or she was away, discussion of decisions at work, discussion of personal problems, borrowing money, and social recreational activities.

We are now analyzing the network data for a variety of indications of three of their main characteristics, as shown in Fig. 1. With age, gender, educational level, marital status, and ethnic background statistically controlled, we have so far found differences such as:

- The networks of the controls are significantly larger than those for the cases, with the networks of the "schizophrenics" especially small (mean of 6.26 members in contrast with 9.99 for the controls).
- The schizophrenia-like cases have less extensive networks, as measured by number of areas of activity covered and depth of coverage in each (8.49), than either the depressed cases (9.50) or controls (9.92). The difference is pronounced for "schizophrenics" who are in their second or more episodes (8.19) in contrast with those in their first episode (9.11).
- All of the cases except the first-episode depressives have higher percentages of relatives in their network.

Some of these differences are undoubtedly a function of the personal characteristics and behaviors of the cases. We are conducting further analyses to see which network characteristics accompany differences in social

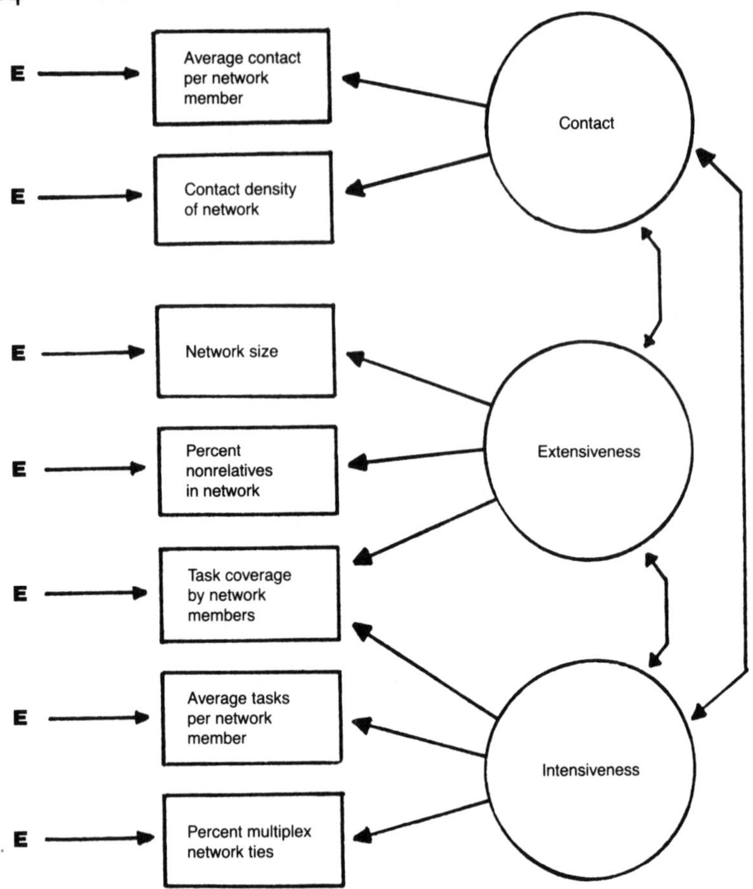

Figure 1. Possible model of the supportive social network with three main characteristics.

and cultural variables and hence are more likely to be environmental in origin. We are also investigating which characteristics lead to supportive responses of network members when particularly stressful events of various kinds occur.

Personality variables

Under the general heading of personal dispositions as the third major element of life stress processes, we are investigating a variety of personality variables. As might be expected from my earlier discussion, these include the following variables and measures:

- Locus of control.
- Mastery.
- Type A behavior pattern.
- Denial.

Controlling the same demographic variables as in the analyses of recent life events and network characteristics, we have found some strong differences:

- On the Rotter (1966) and Levenson Scales (1973) both depressive and schizophrenia-like cases show greater external locus of control orientation than controls.
- Depressives endorse more negative femininity items on the Spence–Helmreich masculinity–femininity measure than "schizophrenics" or controls. Examples of these negative femininity items are "very emotional," "highly needful of others' approval," "feelings easily hurt," and "cries very easily."
- Depressives score higher than both "schizophrenics" and controls on subsets of items from Jenkins (1967), which we grouped to measure "hostility" and "speed" dimensions of the Type A behavior pattern.
- Both depressives and "schizophrenics" endorse fewer positive items that we have selected from the Spence–Helmreich masculinity scale to indicate an orientation characterized by mastery.
- Both depressives and "schizophrenics" show more denial than controls on a subset of Crowne–Marlowe (1960) negative items, which we selected to measure this variable.

As was the case with network characteristics and some of the recent life events, some of these personality variables could be reactive to psychopathology or indicators of the insidious onset of psychopathology. Their causal status is less clear in retrospective case-control studies of this kind than, say, fateful loss events or some kinds of physical illness and injury. We hope to be able to investigate the extent to which these personality variables are state-dependent in a follow-up of cases at a time when they are not in an episode of disorder (cf. Hirschfeld et al., 1983). The variables will also be investigated in the set of theoretical models of interrelations among the three elements of the life stress process, as they determine how events are perceived and reacted to (coped with), and in relation to the various types of psychopathology in which we are interested. Taken together with other results on class and ethnic differences in rates of disorders that are inversely related to social class, tests of these models may, indeed, contribute to causal interpretation (Dohrenwend and Dohrenwend, 1981; Dohrenwend and Dohrenwend, 1981b).

As they stand, then, these preliminary results do not demonstrate, but are consistent with, the following picture of social and psychological risk factors for episodes of major depression and of schizophrenia-like psychosis: that of recent environmentally induced stress impinging on persons with problematic personality characteristics in the context of relatively weak networks of potential social support. Moreover, some differences in the types of events, personality characteristics, and social supports involved for the two different types of disorders, themselves, appear intriguing. These differences include, for example, the greater role of fateful loss for the depressives and their stronger tendency to score high on hostility and speed dimensions of the Type A behavior pattern, and the relatively smaller and less extensive networks of the cases with schizophrenia-like disorders.

Next Steps in the Study

Barbara Dohrenwend and I have extracted from the theoretical and empirical literature five alternative models, referred to earlier, about the nature of life stress processes. We have called them *victimization, vulnerability, additive burden, chronic burden,* and *event proneness* and published several articles and chapters in books about them, with Barbara as senior author (e.g., Dohrenwend and Dohrenwend, 1981a; 1981b). Further analyses of the data from our study will include an investigation of the applicability of these models.

I will describe the models primarily in terms of my interest in various types of psychopathology, but they could also be referenced to other adverse health changes thought to be related to stress. They are summarized in Figure 2.

The first model, *victimization,* indicates that cumulations of stressful life events cause psychopathology. This model was developed empirically in studies of extreme situations, such as combat and concentration camps. I have generalized it to normal civil life in terms of the pathogenic triad of concommitant events and conditions mentioned earlier (Dohrenwend, 1979).

The second model, *vulnerability,* describes how preexisting personal dispositions and social conditions moderate the causal relation between stressful life events and psychopathology. This hypothesis underlies the literature on vulnerability, involving concepts of coping ability and social support.

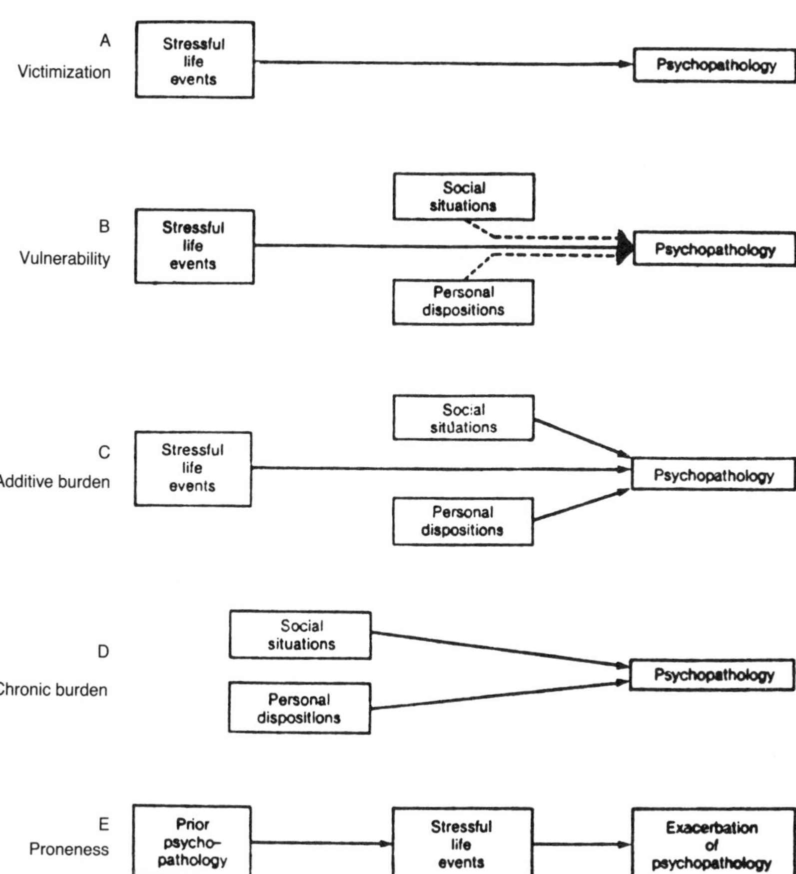

Figure 2. Five hypotheses about the life stress process.
Dohrenwend and Dohrenwend, 1981b.

The third model, *additive burden,* contrasts with the second in that, rather than moderating the impact of stressful life events, personal dispositions and social conditions are portrayed as making independent causal contributions to the occurrence of psychopathology.

The fourth model, *chronic burden,* is another and further modification of the second. It denies any role to recent life events, suggesting instead that stable personal dispositions and social conditions alone cause adverse health changes.

The final model, *proneness,* enables us to confront directly the crucial issue of the direction of the causal relation between life events and psychopathology. It indicates that the presence of a disorder leads to stressful life events which, in turn, exacerbate the disorder. Proneness to stressful events is the central mechanism posited.

These models are neither exhaustive nor mutually exclusive. Nevertheless, they provide a framework for designing research to advance our understanding of relations between life stress and psychopathology.

In investigating these models, there is an underlying theme or issue that has implications for the measurement strategies to be employed. This is the problem of determining the extent to which personal dispositions and social circumstances predict ways that people will cope with life events. In the context of our focus on social and psychological factors, the ways of coping to be predicted include perceptions of various dimensions of an event and the situation related to it (e.g., whether occurrence of the event is seen as within or outside the control of the individual). The key question we ask is whether these perceptions are determined by the objective characteristics of the event and situation in contrast with personal dispositions (e.g., locus of control as a personality variable) or some complex interaction of the two. These distinctions require that we be able to designate and measure the important objective characteristics of the events and the social situations related to them; the individual's perceptions of these events and situations; and the relevant personality variables. We presented our approach in some detail in a symposium held at the 1983 Annual Meeting of the American Psychological Association (Dohrenwend, 1983). Suffice it to note now that this approach involves collecting a great deal more information about events and changes related to them than is provided for in the usual life events lists, and it also focuses on social supports or hindrances *in specific relation* to reported events. Also involved is attention to personality variables such as locus of control, denial, masculinity–femininity, and Type A behavior pattern, which I mentioned earlier, and some others, such as sensation seeking.

Methodological Problems

As is so often the case in the behavioral sciences, research in this area is severely hampered by the lack of adequate solutions to key measurement problems. These problems have made many of the results from much previous research on stress and psychopathology difficult to interpret. The problems are especially severe when we deal with events that, unlike natural and manmade disasters, have occurrences that are not clearly outside the control of the individuals affected. It is all too easy to confound measures of events, personal dispositions, enduring social conditions, and psychopathology with each other. For example, is the stressful life event of divorce independent of a vulnerable personal disposition to psychopathology? Does failure to obtain social support result from a priori defects in the external social situation, or is the failure a consequence of the individual's psychopathology? Such confounding guarantees results that at best are uninterpretable and, at worst, can lead to erroneous conclusions. Enough progress has been made in the clarification of these measurement ambiguities that there is no need to repeat past mistakes (cf. Dohrenwend et al., 1984). These mistakes include, for example, failure to distinguish between life events that are independent of a subject's mental condition and those that are not, between the structure of objective social networks and their effectiveness, or between these networks and personal dispositions related to having friends or not having them.

Future Research

It is probably not surprising that the future research I will recommend has strong similarities to my own program, but there are some differences, as well, which I think are especially relevant to the theme of this conference. With regard to the similarities, the need that I see is for designs that combine large-scale epidemiological investigations with carefully constructed retrospective case-control studies.

The epidemiological studies, if carefully designed, will provide two ingredients that are important to adequate case-control studies: (1) a representative sample of well controls; and (2) samples of untreated cases to supplement samples of treated or officially recognized cases. The addition of the untreated cases will make it possible for us to secure more nearly representative samples of the types of psychopathology being investigated.

Prospective features need to be added to these designs for two purposes. First, if we are fortunate enough to secure a sample of first episode cases for the retrospective portion of the study, we can use the prospective portion to test whether the factors at onset are similar to or different from the factors in relapse. In addition, the prospective study can provide evidence on the temporal sequence of variables, which is difficult to assess in retrospective case-control studies.

When enough is known about the relevant risk factors from combined retrospective and prospective case-control studies, we can design the epidemiological stage of the study not so much to isolate persons exposed to various risk factors who can then be studied within the framework of purely prospective designs.

Even then, however, the research designs will not be experimental, and there will be ambiguities about the nature of the relations among the variables in the life stress process. It is at this point, I think, that preventive interventions can be justified not only on practical and humanitarian grounds but, in some cases, on grounds of being the next logical research step in increasing our knowledge of the nature of life stress processes. We can learn things about the nature of key relationships among variables in the life stress process by manipulating key risk factors that we cannot either learn or be sure of in nonexperimental studies.

Clues to Preventive Strategies from Past and Present Research on Life Stress

Even now, I think there are some strong clues as to where prevention intervention strategies might focus. However, there is some major missing information that we very much need if we are to pursue them with confidence.

Recall from Table 1 that the single most frequent type of psychopathology observed in community populations is a set of symptoms of nonspecific distress for which we are using Frank's (1973) term *demoralization*. About one-fourth of the adults at any given time in an average community are likely to be demoralized in this sense and, in about one-half the cases, there is no accompanying major mental disorder. We do not know whether demoralization in and of itself puts the individual at risk for mental disorders such as major depression, schizophrenia, or substance abuse, although we know that it frequently coincides with episodes of such disorders.

Frank (1973) argues on the basis of his clinical observations that demoralization not only leads people to seek social support—frequently in the form of psychotherapy—but it also is something that is helped almost immediately by such social support. Of all the important factors in the life stress process, social networks and the nature and types of support they provide are probably the most amenable to modification through planned intervention.

If demoralization itself is often a function of environmentally induced stress, if it is a risk factor for important diagnosable disorders such as major depression and substance abuse, and if it can be effectively reduced by provision of social support, then a whole set of preventive strategies can be developed and evaluated within an epidemiological framework. One strategy would be to focus on locating demoralized individuals who had not yet developed full-blown disorders, with the aim of reversing the demoralization by providing social supports. Another strategy would focus on reversing modifiable risk factors leading to demoralization. In the process, both types of intervention should tell us a great deal about the nature of life stress processes as they are related to various types of psychopathology in community populations.

References

Akiskal, H. S., Hirschfeld, R. M. A., and Yerevanian, B. I. (1983). The relationship of personality to affective disorders. *Archives of General Psychiatry, 40,* 801–810.

Brown, G. W. (1974). Meaning, measurement, and stressful life events. In B. S. Dohrenwend and B. P. Dohrenwend (Eds.), *Stressful life events: Their nature and effects* (pp. 217–243). New York: Wiley.

Brown, G. W., and Birley, J. L. T. (1968). Crises and life changes and the onset of schizophrenia. *Journal of Health and Social Behavior, 9,* 203–214.

Brown, G. W., and Harris, T. (1978). *Social origins of depression: A study of psychiatric disorder in women.* New York: Free Press.

Brown, G. W., and Harris, T. (1982). Disease, distress and depression. *Journal of Affective Disorders, 4,* 1–8.

Brown, G. W., Harris, T. O., and Peto, J. (1973). Life events and psychiatric disorders. Part 2: Nature of the causal link. *Psychological Medicine, 3,* 159–176.

Campbell, A., Converse, P. E., and Rodgers, W. L. (1976). *The quality of American life.* New York: Russell Sage Foundation.

Caplan, G., and Killilea, M. (Eds.). (1976). *Support systems and mutual help: Multidisciplinary explorations.* New York: Grune and Stratton.

Carveth, W. B., and Gottlieb, G. H. (1973). The measurement of social support and its relation to stress. *Canadian Journal of Behavioral Sciences, 11*(3), 179–188.

Coddington, R. D. (1972a). The significance of life events as etiologic factors in the diseases of children: 2. A survey of professional workers. *Journal of Psychosomatic Research, 16,* 7–18.

Coddington, R. D. (1972b). The significance of life events as etiologic factors in the diseases of children: 2. A study of a normal population. *Journal of Psychosomatic Research, 16,* 205–213.

Cooper, B., and Sylph, J. (1973). Life events and the onset of neurotic illness: An investigation in general practice. *Psychological Medicine, 3,* 421–435.

Crowne, D. P., and Marlowe, D. (1960). A new scale of social desirability independent of psychopathology. *Journal of Consulting Psychology, 24,* 349–354.

Dohrenwend, B. P. (1979). Stressful life events and psychopathology: Some issues of theory and method. In J. F. Barrett, R. M. Rose, and G. L. Klerman (Eds.), *Stress and mental disorder* (pp. 1–16). New York: Raven Press.

Dohrenwend, B. P. (Chair.). (1983, August). *Measurement innovations in the study of life stress processes.* Symposium conducted at the meeting of the American Psychological Association, Anaheim, California.

Dohrenwend, B. P. (1983). The epidemiology of mental disorder. In D. Mechanic (Ed.), *Handbook of health, health care, and the health professions* (pp. 157–194). New York: Free Press.

Dohrenwend, B. P., and Dohrenwend, B. S. (1969). *Social status and psychological disorder: A causal inquiry.* New York: Wiley.

Dohrenwend, B. P., and Dohrenwend, B. S. (1976). Sex differences and psychiatric disorders. *American Journal of Sociology, 81,* 1447–1454.

Dohrenwend, B. P., and Dohrenwend, B. S. (1981). Socioenvironmental factors, stress and psychopathology—Part 1: Quasi-experimental evidence on the social causation–social section issue posed by class differences. *American Journal of Community Psychology, 9*(2), 129–146.

Dohrenwend, B. P., Dohrenwend, B. S., Gould, M. S., Link, B., Neugebauer, R., and Wunsch-Hitzig, R. (1980). *Mental illness in the United States: Epidemiologic estimates.* New York: Praeger.

Dohrenwend, B. P., and Egri, G. (1981). Recent stressful life events and episodes of schizophrenia. *Schizophrenia Bulletin, 7,* 12–23.

Dohrenwend, B. P., and de Figueiredo, J. M. (1983). Remote and recent life events and psychopathology. In D. F. Ricks and B. S. Dohrenwend (Eds.), *Origins of psychopathology: Problems in research and public policy* (pp. 91–106). New York: Cambridge University Press.

Dohrenwend, B. S., and Dohrenwend, B. P. (Eds.). (1974). *Stressful life events: Their nature and effects.* New York: Wiley.

Dohrenwend, B. S., and Dohrenwend, B. P. (1981a). *Life stress and illness: Formulation of the issues.* In B. S. Dohrenwend and B. P. Dohrenwend (Eds.), *Stressful life events and their contexts* (pp. 1–27). New Brunswick, N.J.: Rutgers University Press.

Dohrenwend, B. S., and Dohrenwend, B. P. (1981b). Socioenvironmental factors, stress and psychopathology—Part 2: Hypotheses about stress processes linking social class to various types of psychopathology. *American Journal of Community Psychology, 9*(2), 146–155.

Dohrenwend, B. S., Dohrenwend, B. P., Dodson, M., and Shrout, P. E. (1984). Symptoms, hassles, social supports, and life events: Problem of confounded measures. *Journal of Abnormal Psychology, 93*(2), 222–230.

Duncan, D. F. (1977). Life stress as a precursor to adolescent drug dependence. *The International Journal of the Addictions, 12*(8), 1047–1056.

Fischer, C. S., Jackson, R. M., Stueve, C. A., Gerson, K., Jones, L. Mc., and Baldassare, M. (1977). *Networks and places: Social relations in the urban setting.* New York: Free Press.

Frank, J. D. (1973). *Persuasion and healing.* Baltimore: Johns Hopkins University Press.

Gore, S. (1981). Stress-buffering functions of social supports: An appraisal and clarification of research models. In B. S. Dohrenwend and B. P. Dohrenwend (Eds.), *Stressful life events and their contexts* (pp. 202–222). New Brunswick, N.J.: Rutgers University Press.

Hamburg, D., and Adams, J. (1967). A perspective on coping behavior: Seeking and utilizing information in major transitions. *Archives of General Psychiatry, 17,* 277–284.

Hirschfeld, R. M. A., Klerman, G. L., Clayton, P. J., Keller, M. B., McDonald-Scott, P., and Larkin, B. H. (1983). Assessing personality: effects of the depressive state on trait measurement. *American Journal of Psychiatry, 140,* 695–699.

Horowitz, M. J. (1976). *Stress response syndrome.* New York: Jason Aronson.

Hudgens, R. W. (1974). Personal catastrophe and depression: A consideration of the subject with respect to medically ill adolescents, and a requiem for retrospective life event studies. In B. S. Dohrenwend and B. P. Dohrenwend

(Eds.), *Stressful life events: Their nature and effects* (pp. 110–134). New York: Wiley.
Husaini, B. A., and Neff, J. A. (1981). Social class and depressive symptomatology: The role of life change events and locus of control. *Journal of Nervous and Mental Disease, 169,* 638–647.
Jacobs, S., and Meyers, J. (1976). Recent life events and schizophrenic psychosis: A controlled study. *Journal of Nervous and Mental Disease, 162,* 75–87.
Jenkins, C. D., Rosenman, R. H., and Friedman, M. (1967). Development of an objective psychological test for the determination of the coronary-prone behavior pattern. *Journal of Chronic Diseases, 20,* 371–379.
Kanner, A. D., Coyne, J. C., Schaefer, C., and Lazarus, R. S. (1981). Comparison of two modes of stress measurement: Daily hassles and uplifts versus major life events. *Journal of Behavioral Medicine, 4,* 1–39.
Langner, T. S., and Michael, S. T. (1963). *Life stress and mental health.* New York: Free Press of Glencoe.
Lazarus, R. S. (1966). *Psychological stress and the coping process.* New York: McGraw-Hill.
Lazarus, R. S. (1981). The costs and benefits of denial. In B. S. Dohrenwend and B. P. Dohrenwend (Eds.), *Stressful life events and their contexts* (pp. 131–156). New Brunswick, N.J.: Rutgers University Press.
Lefcourt, H. M. (1976). *Locus of control: Current trends on theory and research.* New York: Lawrence Erlbaum Associates.
Leff, J. P., Hirsch, S. R., Gaind, R., Rohde, P. D., and Stevens, B. S. (1973). Life events and maintenance therapy in schizophrenic relapse. *British Journal of Psychiatry, 123,* 659–660.
Levenson, H. (1973). Multidimensional locus of control in psychiatric patients. *Journal of Consulting and Clinical Psychology, 41,* 397–404.
Link, B., and Dohrenwend, B. P. (1980). Formulation of hypotheses about the ratio of untreated to treated cases in the true prevalence studies of functional psychiatric disorders in adults in the United States. In B. P. Dohrenwend, B. S. Dohrenwend, M. S. Gould, B. Link, R. Neugebauer, and R. Wunsch-Hitzig (Eds.), *Mental illness in the United States: Epidemiologic estimates* (pp. 133–149). New York: Praeger.
Litwak, E., and Szelenyi, I. (1969). Primary group structures and their functions: Kin, neighbors, and friends. *American Sociological Review, 34,* 465–481.
Lloyd, C. (1980a). Life events and depressive disorder reviewed: II. Events as precipitating factors. *Archives of General Psychiatry, 37,* 529–535.
Lloyd, C. (1980b). Life events and depressive disorder reviewed: I. Events as predisposing factors. *Archives of General Psychiatry, 37,* 541–548.
Masuda, M., Cutler, D. L., Hein, L., and Holmes, T. H. (1978). Life events and prisoners. *Archives of General Psychiatry, 35,* 197–203.
Matthews, K. A., and Glass, D. C. (1981). Type A behavior, stressful life events, and coronary heart disease. In B. S. Dohrenwend and B. P. Dohrenwend (Eds.), *Stressful life events and their contexts* (pp. 167–177). New Brunswick, N.J.: Rutgers University Press.
Morrissey, E. R. (1980). *The role of life change in the development of alcohol-related problems: An investigation of gender differences.* Unpublished Ph.D. dissertation, University of Washington. Ann Arbor, Mich.: University Microfilms International.
Morrissey, E. R., and Schuckit, M. A. (1978). Stressful life events and alcohol

problems among women seen at a detoxification center. *Journal of Studies on Alcohol, 39*(9), 1559–1576.

Myers, J., Lindenthal, J. J., and Pepper, M. P. (1974). Social class, life events and psychiatric symptoms: A longitudinal study. In B. S. Dohrenwend and B. P. Dohrenwend (Eds.), *Stressful life events: Their nature and effects* (pp. 191–205). New York: Wiley.

Paykel, E. S. (1974). Life stress and psychiatric disorder: Applications of the clinical approach. In B. S. Dohrenwend and B. P. Dohrenwend (Eds.), *Stressful life events: Their nature and effects* (pp. 119–134). New York: Wiley.

Paykel, E. S. (1982). Life events and early environment. In E. S. Paykel (Ed.), *Handbook of Affective Disorders* (pp. 146–161). New York: Guilford Press.

Phillips, S. L., and Fischer, C. S. (1981). Measuring social support networks in general populations. In B. S. Dohrenwend and B. P. Dohrenwend (Eds.), *Stressful life events and their contexts* (pp. 223–233). New Brunswick, N.J.: Rutgers University Press.

Rogler, L. H., and Hollingshead, A. B. (1965). *Trapped: Families and schizophrenia.* New York: Wiley.

Rotter, J. B. (1966). Generalized expectancies of internal versus external control of reinforcement. *Psychological Monographs, 80* (monograph no. 609).

Rutter, M. (1974). *The qualities of mothering: Maternal deprivation reassessed.* New York: Jason Aronson.

Spence, J. T., and Helmreich, R. (1978). *Masculinity and femininity: Their psychological dimensions, correlates and antecedents.* Austin: University of Texas Press.

Tennant, C., Bebbington, P., and Hurry, J. (1980). Parental death in childhood and risk of adult depressive disorders: A review. *Psychological Medicine, 10,* 289–299.

Vaux, A., and Ruggiero, M. (1983). Stressful life change and delinquent behavior. *American Journal of Community Psychology, 11,* 169–183.

Weissman, M. M., and Klerman, G. L. (1977). Sex differences and the epidemiology of depression. *Archives of General Psychiatry, 34,* 98–111.

Wing, J. K., Mann, S. A., Leff, J. P., and Nixon, J. M. (1978). The concept of a "case" in psychiatric population surveys. *Psychological Medicine, 8,* 203–217.

Risk Research in Schizophrenia and Other Major Psychological Disorders

Norman F. Watt

The focus for this review is to summarize the advances in our knowledge about risk factors for schizophrenia and other major psychological disorders made during the last decade. Eaton (1981) defines a *risk factor* as any characteristic associated with increased probability of becoming mentally disordered. In this definition, *risk* does not necessarily imply that the factor causes the disorder, whereas a *causal factor* is known to have a causal effect on the disorder. Typically, causal analysis begins with retrospective study of afflicted people in order to identify (preferably distinctive) precursors or antecedents of the disorder that may eventually serve as guideposts or markers for early identification and/or preventive intervention. Subsequent research then targets those markers for systematic prospective or high-risk investigation to test their relationship to the disorder in question, confirm their temporal priority and elaborate the *nomological network* (Cronbach and Meehl, 1955) that encompasses their relationship to the disorder. This requires careful observation of the longitudinal process of development from the premorbid phase through the precipitant phase to symptom onset and outcome (Garmezy, 1970).

Risk research in the major psychoses is a field of investigation still in its infancy, so it is much too soon to present definitive evidence about the causal implications of risk factors. However, a growing body of research literature is emerging, with promising findings about potential precursors that will be reviewed here. To illustrate the sequence of investigation just described, I will begin with a synopsis of retrospective studies of mental patients by myself and my students that concentrated on childhood behavioral development and provided leads for subsequent prospective investigations that are now in progress. Then I will summarize the interim progress reports of more than a dozen current projects studying children at high risk for schizophrenia and other psychological disorders.

A Retrospective Study of Psychiatric Patients in West Germany

For her master's thesis, Eva Schoenfeld (1974) analyzed retrospectively the childhood antecedents of psychosis, utilizing research data I collected on sabbatical leave at the University of Göttingen Psychiatric Clinic in West Germany. The Clinic is a small (120-bed), public inpatient facility serving a population of 100,000 in the Göttingen region. It is a training hospital that specializes in biological treatment modes for acute psychiatric disorders but also includes a small unit for psychotherapeutic treatment. At that time patients stayed, on average, one to three months for residential treatment. Cases requiring long-term treatment were usually referred to a state hospital after a brief period of evaluation.

Subjects

Subjects for this study were all functionally disordered patients admitted in Fiscal Year 1967. Diagnostic classifications were made by Schoenfeld and myself, drawing on photocopies and extensive abstracts of the case records and thus relying primarily on diagnoses by the clinic's staff. Our classifications followed customary American usage according to DSM-II (American Psychiatric Association, 1968) but were applied very conservatively. For example, the Germans employed a diagnostic spectrum for schizophrenia that was narrower than the norm used in the United States, but we accepted only 90 of 102 schizophrenic diagnoses by the staff as unequivocally correct. Similarly, we accepted only 120 of their 135 diagnoses of depressive psychosis for this study. It seems reasonable to conclude that the stringency of diagnosis we employed then came close to the level now required in DSM-III (APA, 1980), with the possible exception that a few of the schizophrenics might not have met the criterion of six months of continuous symptom expression. The convergence of classifications by Schoenfeld and myself yielded high reliability coefficients for the major diagnostic groups: .96 for schizophrenia, .91 for depressive psychosis, .84 for neuroses, and .91 for other disorders.

From the original sample of 465 patients, 21 were eliminated for substantial organic involvement or primary mental retardation, and 57 patients suffering from various forms of psychosomatic disturbances or anorexia nervosa were dropped from the analysis because of the small number who could be classified in coherent diagnostic groups. Schoenfeld's final sample comprised 387 patients, about one-half from each sex: 90 schizophrenics, 120 psychotic depressives, 130 "neurotics" (including 66 neurotic depressives and 76 with varying forms of symptom neurosis or personality disorder), and 47 drug abusers (including 37 achoholics). No comparable data were available for nonpsychiatric controls.

Age at first mental hospital admission ranged from 16–65, with the median at 39 years, so these patients were substantially older than is typical nowadays in the United States. Because of training and research interests, the Chief of Medicine at the clinic gave some priority to admission for depressive disorders that occurred in the middle adult years. Education ranged from 4–21 years, with a median of 10 years, which is approximately equivalent to a completed high school education in the United States. Social class of the father was measured on a 7-point scale from 1–7 (high–low). The median score of 4 was labeled lower-middle class, so the patients in this sample represented a broad cross-section of the populace around Göttingen, although the privileged upper classes may have been slightly underrepresented.

Measures and Procedure

The clinic's records included extensive psychiatric interviews with the patients and members of their families and assessed family background, childhood and adolescent development, period of onset of psychiatric disturbance, current psychiatric condition, and brief accounts of the course of illness and outcome, when available. Descriptive and demographic data were extracted from the records by medical students, serving as research assistants, who were not acquainted with the theoretical rationale of the research. Three of the assistants read only those portions of the record concerned with premorbid history and rated each case on 14 personality traits and 6 aspects of family relations. Coding reliability was tested by Pearson correlations for variables that met parametric assumptions and by contingency coefficients, otherwise. The range for the reliability coefficients was from .31 to .79, with a median of .61. These values were disappointing, but acceptable, because almost all the variables of primary interest showed coefficients above the median.

A fourth assistant read only the portions of the records that reported on the present psychiatric condition and course of illness, filled out a checklist of 29 psychiatric symptoms (indicating secondarily their salience), and transcribed the psychiatric diagnosis rendered by the staff. These clinical data were useful to us primarily for classifying the subjects in diagnostic groups.

Ratings of premorbid variables were pooled over two or three judges in order to create the most stable estimates for each score. Average scores on each variable were compared among the four diagnostic groups, with primary interest focused on the two psychotic groups.

Rationale

Following the published literature, Schoenfeld hypothesized that the premorbid histories of schizophrenics would be characterized by isolation from the outside world and by alienation from peers and family, with distinct evidence of impairment in social competence. By contrast, psychotic depressives were expected to show a strong internalizing orientation in their psychological development, superior development of social competence, and close relations with morally strict parents.

Results

The hypothesized differences were tested by comparing the premorbid characteristics of the two psychotic groups, using the neurotic patients and the drug abusers as further contrast groups. The findings are presented briefly in the following paragraphs.*

Late Development

This refers to the usual childhood milestones, such as sitting, walking, talking, and physical growth, as well as late social maturation, excessive dependency on parents, and retarded psychomotor development. More schizophrenics (10%) and neurotics (17%) were later in developing than depressives (3%) or drug abusers (3%). The proportions differed between the depressives and schizophrenics, $\chi^2(1\ df) = 3.52$, $p < .05$ (one-tailed), and between the depressives and neurotics, $\chi^2(1\ df) = 10.75$, $p < .005$.

Childhood Neurotic Symptoms

This refers to nail-biting, thumb-sucking, finicky eating, and night terrors. Slightly more of these signs were reported for the schizophrenics than for the depressives, $\chi^2(1\ df) = 2.85$, $p < .10$, but the neurotics exhibited more of these symptoms than either psychotic group.

Orderliness

Schizophrenics were less orderly than the depressives $\chi^2(1\ df) = 6.40$, $p < .025$ (one-tailed), and the neurotics $\chi^2(1\ df) = 4.04$, $p < .05$, but there were no differences between the depressives and the neurotics. Within the neurotic group, orderliness was most prominent in the neurotic depressives. The drug abusers were also less orderly than those two

*Only degrees of freedom are reported. The numbers in each group were as indicated on pp. 116–117.

groups, so the trait appears to be most closely associated with depression, whether at the neurotic or psychotic level.

Liveliness

Depressives were more lively as children than the schizophrenics, χ^2(1 df) = 3.89, $p < .025$ (one-tailed), and the neurotics, χ^2(1 df) = 3.85, $p < .05$, but not different from the drug abusers.

Oppositionalism

Depressives were less oppositional in childhood than the schizophrenics, χ^2(1 df) = 12.43, $p < .001$ (one-tailed), the neurotics χ^2(1 df) = 12.48, $p < .001$, and the drug abusers, χ^2(1 df) = 7.33, $p < .01$.

Sensitivity

This refers to physical weakness, emotional brittleness, oversensitivity, and interpersonal vulnerability. There were no differences between the psychotic groups. The neurotics were the most sensitive of all four groups.

Persistence

This characterization refers to assertiveness, goal orientation, and determination. Depressives were more persistent than the schizophrenics, χ^2(4 df) = 13.74, $p < .005$ (one-tailed), and both other groups.

Social Relations

This construct refers to extraversion, as measured by openness to peer relationships, orientation to new situations, quality of friendships, and adolescent experience with the opposite sex. Depressives were more sociable than the schizophrenics, χ^2(4 df) = 17.80, $p < .001$ (one-tailed), and the neurotics.

Social Initiative

This trait refers to interpersonal leadership qualities, resourcefulness, and enterprise. Depressives showed more childhood initiative than the schizophrenics, χ^2(4 df) = 19.79, $p < .001$ (one-tailed), and the neurotics but not significantly more than the drug abusers.

Capacity for Relationship

This refers to the capacity for attachment to others, especially in long-term relationships. Depressives were rated higher than schizophrenics, χ^2(4 df) = 10.40, $p < .05$, and both other groups.

Competence

This concept refers to diligence, resourcefulness, capability, and versatility in work. Depressives were judged to be much more competent as children than the schizophrenics $\chi^2(4\ df) = 18.49$, $p < .001$ (one-tailed), and both other groups, but the schizophrenics were not less competent than either the neurotics or the drug abusers. There was a significant interaction on this variable involving sex: the diagnostic group differences were much greater among the males than among the females, $\chi^2(2\ df) = 6.01$, $p < .01$.

Marital Status

More depressives (81%) had married than schizophrenics (31%), $\chi^2(1\ df) = 56.82$, $p < .001$ (one-tailed), or neurotics (53%), $\chi^2(1\ df) = 21.96$, $p < .001$, but not more than the drug abusers (89%). The differences were clearest among patients first admitted before 39 years of age; among the older patients, the marriage rates were not significantly different.

Intelligence

This was rated intuitively by intake psychiatrists, as inferred from comments about the patients' school work as children, general level of sophistication, and social awareness. Depressives were judged to have higher premorbid intelligence than the schizophrenics, $\chi^2(4\ df) = 9.18$, $p < .05$ (one-tailed), and both other groups. The schizophrenics were judged equivalent to the other two groups.

School Failure

The neurotics and the schizophrenics failed in school the most often, but the rates for the two psychotic groups did not differ from each other. Nor did the psychotic groups differ in the proportions of those who completed a vocational apprenticeship successfully.

Years of Education

Schizophrenics had completed *more* years of schooling than the depressives, $\chi^2(2\ df) = 6.00$, $p < .05$, and the neurotics, but not more than the drug abusers. This result could not be attributed to differential age sampling of the diagnostic groups. The proportions of patients in the four groups who had completed a college education did not differ.

Self-Ratings

Schizophrenics viewed themselves as significantly more shy, dependent, and unassertive in childhood than did the depressives, but not as more quiet, oppositional, delicate, or sensitive. However, self-characterizations of schizophrenics differed from those of neurotics only on one scale: claiming greater dependency. Self-portraits of depressives differed from those of drug abusers on only two scales: claiming greater independence but less assertiveness.

Relations with Father

Schizophrenics had encountered more conflict as children with their fathers than had the depressives, $\chi^2(2\ df) = 10.41$, $p < .005$ (one-tailed), but not more than the neurotics. Schizophrenics were also more distant from their fathers than were the depressives, $\chi^2(2\ df) = 4.96$, $p < .05$ (one-tailed).

Relations with Mother

There were no differences between the psychotic groups in conflict with mothers, but, when extreme conflict with the mother *was* reported, schizophrenics simultaneously reported greater distance from the mother than did the depressives, $\chi^2(2\ df) = 9.39$, $p < .01$). Therefore conflicted symbiotic attachments with mothers were not more common among schizophrenics than among depressives, but distant conflictual maternal relationships were. Otherwise, there were no significant group differences in which parent was preferred by the patient, in the personality characteristics of the parents (as rated by the patients), or in the strictness of the child-rearing practices in the home.

Summary of Findings

Compared to the psychotic depressives, the schizophrenics

(a) were later in developing as children;

(b) were more oppositional;

(c) were more isolated and less active socially;

(d) saw themselves as more shy, dependent, and unassertive;

(e) had significantly more years of schooling;

(f) exhibited slightly more childhood neurotic symptoms;

(g) experienced more conflict and distance in relation to their fathers; and

(h) if they encountered great conflict with their mothers, the conflicts were also more distant (time).

By contrast to the schizophrenics, the depressives

(a) were more orderly as children;

(b) were more persistent;

(c) were more competent;

(d) exhibited greater social initiative;

(e) were more likely to marry;

(f) were more intelligent; and

(g) showed greater capacity for relationship.

There were no significant differences between the psychotic groups in

(a) sensitivity;

(b) parental personality traits;

(c) preference for mother or father;

(d) conflict with mothers;

(e) frequency of school failures;

(f) proportions with college degrees;

(g) proportions with successfully completed vocational apprenticeship; and

(h) strictness of childhood upbringing.

Discussion

Results supported the conclusion that schizophrenics and psychotic depressives are descriptively very different in their premorbid behavior. However, the hypotheses implicating differential parenting in the two psychotic groups were, for the most part, not supported by the data.

Although never entirely explicit in the rationale offered for the study, it was generally presumed that behavioral deviations distinguishing one psychotic group from another would distinguish it likewise from the nonpsychotic groups. However, the results included several striking exceptions, mostly involving the group broadly labeled here as "neurotic." There were clusters of antecedent traits that linked the neurotics closely with the schizophrenics and other clusters that linked the neurotics closely with the psychotic depressives. Psychotic depressives and neurotic depressives were both more orderly and less oppositional than the schizophrenics (or drug abusers). This confirms the view expressed by

Phillips (1968) that, under stress, a characterological inclination to conscientiousness and conformity lends itself to depressive and neurotic symptoms. On the other hand, schizophrenics and "other" neurotics were alike in showing characteristics of social passivity, sensitivity, late development, interpersonal isolation, school failure, and childhood neurotic symptoms. This cluster of findings might be summarized as showing that schizophrenics and nondepressive neurotics share in common a generalized insufficiency or retardation in social development or social competence.

In childhood the depressives were lively, orderly, competent, persistent, socially active, intelligent, and conforming (rather than oppositional)—and exhibited a large capacity for human relationship. They describe themselves retrospectively as gregarious, independent, and assertive. Clearly they are highly socialized and *engaged* socially. We can easily imagine that their childhood experiences with friends and family and in school—and later at work—would be quite positive and ego-enhancing. Their behavior as children could be differentiated from that of normals in the more conforming attitudes of the predepressives, perhaps even suggesting excessive conformity. Extending the longitudinal perspective to the adult years, Phillips (1968) argues that, because depressives achieve a high level of social competence and incorporate society's values to a great extent, they experience much guilt and anxiety about not meeting these values under stress. Hence they manifest psychiatric symptoms that signify "self-deprivation and turning against self", e.g., suicidal ideas, anorexia, self-depreciation, bodily complaints, depressed mood, obsessions, and fear of their own hostile impulses. Pathological solutions to life's problems, such as being crazy or indolent or dependent on society, are unacceptable to depressives. This, in combination with the high level of social competence achieved prior to breakdown, accounts for the well-established fact that, among psychotics, the prognosis for recovery is best for depressives (Vaillant, 1962).

It is important to emphasize that the premorbid functioning of the psychotic depressives was far superior in most respects to that of *both* the schizophrenics and the neurotics. About one-half of the childhood inadequacies manifested by the schizophrenics were shared with the neurotics. We should keep in mind the sharp behavioral differences found between the neurotic and psychotic depressives, for they raise an important theoretical issue to which I will return.

A Retrospective Study of Psychiatric Patients in the United States

A parallel program of archival research in this country provided more robust and more precise descriptions of the childhood development of adult psychiatric patients by analyzing systematically the content of their cumulative school records and their subsequent hospital records. To conserve space, I will not present the methodological details of the research because they have been published elsewhere (Watt et al., 1979). Let it suffice to report here that the sample comprised 59 schizophrenics, 41 patients with personality disorders, 31 neurotics, and 14 psychotic depressives drawn from the entire social class spectrum in a suburb of Boston. Their ages at first admission to a hospital ranged from 16–35, with a median of 27 years. Childhood control records were drawn from the school files of classmates, who were carefully matched individually with the index subjects for sex, age, race, and parental social class. Follow-up study of hospital records provided extensive information about the clinical disorders and psychiatric outcome of the patients six years after first admission. The principal findings of the research and some key conceptual implications will be reviewed concisely here.

Childhood Behavior of Psychiatric Patients in General

Except for early signs of emotional insecurity among the male patients, the psychiatric patients in general were not behaviorally distinguishable from normals in early childhood. Future psychiatric patients began to differ substantially from peers only in early adolescence. The differences centered on emotional instability and disagreeable interpersonal style rather than on scholastic performance or attitudes toward school work. Girls were especially praised for their scholastic motivation in the early school years, and they were more favorably characterized than boys in the later school years for every aspect of school behavior except social participation. The most notable behavioral change over time was the progressively inconsiderate behavior of the psychiatric patients. We concluded from these data that people destined for psychiatric hospitalization are characterized by slowly evolving patterns of social and emotional maladjustment. These patterns center on emotional insecurity and interpersonal abrasiveness but are neither very extreme nor highly differentiated in childhood. The developmental changes suggest that the psychiatric patients gradually fall behind their peers in emotional and interpersonal maturation.

Precursors of Schizophrenic Disorders

As a group, children destined to become schizophrenic adults behaved differently in school than other children. From one-third to one-half of them were obviously deviant in childhood before they showed any clear indication of psychotic disorganization. Behavioral deviations were obvious enough that teachers commented on them spontaneously in cumulative school records. The patterns of maladjustment differed for boys and girls: The boys were *negativistic, egocentric, unpleasant,* and *antisocial,* whereas the girls were primarily *quiet* and *introverted,* though also *egocentric;* in addition, the boys were *scholastic underachievers.* Both sexes were *emotionally unstable,* but even here the boys and girls differed qualitatively: The boys were *cheerless, emotional,* and *actively maladjusted,* whereas the girls were *calm, immature,* and *quiety maladjusted.* The pattern of *introversion* for the preschizophrenic girls was manifest in the early school years and continued through the later school years, although the comments about *passivity* dropped off.

The preschizophrenic boys, on the other hand, were not characterized differently from other boys during the first seven years of school, and as a group they were not more introverted than other boys during either period in school, which casts doubt on the classical notion that the "shut-in" personality is the most common premorbid type in schizophrenics of both sexes (Wittman, 1948; Bower et al., 1960; Barthell and Holmes, 1968). With age, the preschizophrenic boys became quite *unpleasant, aggressive, self-centered,* and *defiant of authority.* In short, they became adolescent behavior problems rather than wallflowers. It may be that they did deviate behaviorally in the early years, but this behavior was not salient enough to warrant abundant comment by their teachers.

The premorbid intelligence of the schizophrenics fell within the normal range and was stable over time. As a group, they had significantly lower intelligence scores than their matched controls, but there was no significant difference in intelligence scores between the preschizophrenics and their own siblings. On this basis, we could certainly not classify the preschizophrenics as extremely deficient intellectually. Childhood intelligence was not significantly related to length of hospitalization, which challenges the value of premorbid intelligence as a prognostic sign. The analysis of school marks permits us to locate their limited intellectual handicap more precisely in mathematical performance rather than in English. The absence of a relationship between childhood intelligence and schizophrenic outcome (length of hospitalization) is consistent with Astrup and Noreik's (1966) findings. Furthermore, *intelligence rating* in adulthood was the only one of the five social competence variables (the others being age of onset, social class, working capacity, marital status) that was *not* significantly associated with recovery or improvement following a schizophrenic episode (Fryer, 1974).

Among the psychiatric patients, premature parental death was distinctively associated with schizophrenic (especially paranoid schizophrenic) disorder in adulthood. Among psychiatric patients bereaved in childhood, parental death occurred somewhat earlier, on average, in the lives of schizophrenics.

Finally, the school records indicated that the preschizophrenic children were more subject to organic handicaps and to internal conflict in the family during childhood.

Childhood Functioning of Psychotic Depressives

In contrast to the negative picture for preschizophrenics, children eventually hospitalized for psychotic depression were seen as *more* independent (independent, mature, and leader) than their matched controls. In this finding we have longitudinal evidence for the theory that depression is associated with high levels of maturity and development (Phillips, 1968). Otherwise, neither the psychotic depressives nor the neurotics were behaviorally different than normals as children.

Longitudinal Patterns of Social Competence and Behavior Style

As children, the psychiatric patients had lower than normal social competence in terms of work skills and interpersonal skills. The patients were also more oriented than controls to act against others. Role orientations, as a matter of individual style, remained constant from childhood through adult psychiatric hospitalization. A child competent in work skills and interpersonal relations was more inclined to turn against the self and to express disturbance in the affective sphere if hospitalized as an adult. On the other hand, a child with poor work skills was likely to turn against others and to express disturbance in the form of action if hospitalized as an adult, and a child with low interpersonal competence was likely to avoid others and to express disturbance in the thought sphere as an adult psychiatric patient. The socially competent child, particularly in the interpersonal sphere, got better after psychiatric hospitalization, whereas the child who avoided others had the poorest prognosis.

Viewed theoretically, these results generally confirm Phillips's (1968) maturational model of psychopathology with regard to role orientation and social competence. Social competence in childhood was a favorable prognostic indicator of vulnerability to, and outcome of, psychiatric disorder in adulthood. The maturational model offers a significant advantage for conceptualizing the ontogenesis of psychiatric symptoms; i.e., as integral manifestations of character, with traceable history and predictable future. It is interesting to note that, with the exception of social competence and role orientation, there was very little correlation between childhood behavior and adult psychiatric symptoms.

Social Competence and Clinical Symptoms

The longitudinal analysis of social competence was primarily of interest because it showed that psychiatric symptoms are strongly correlated with contemporary social competence but not at all related to childhood social competence. This may be related to the distinction between *positive symptoms* (delusions, hallucinations, and other "active" processes) and *negative symptoms* (blunting of affect, apathy, and formal thought disorder, such as blocking). Strauss, Carpenter, and Bartko (1974) found that positive symptoms are frequently nonspecific responses to a variety of conditions and seem to have little prognostic value. On the other hand, negative symptoms are related to chronicity, although it is not clear whether chronicity is, or negative symptoms are, primary in the causal sense. The association we found between low levels of longitudinal social competence and a cluster of schizoid symptoms is consistent with that distinction. The positive symptoms appear not to be part of a long-standing or longitudinal process, but the negative symptoms included in the withdrawal cluster show at least some association with childhood behavior and a distinct association with poor outcome. It is intriguing to note that thought disorder and cognitive dysfunction in general showed limited historical continuity in either direction, whereas interpersonal style and social withdrawal, in particular, were obviously continuous in both directions. For this reason the latter may prove to be more profitable for prognostic study than the former.

Postdiction of Psychiatric Outcome

The presence of hallucinations at initial hospitalization was the surest indicator of poor long-term outcome. Withdrawal in men and perplexity or confusion in women were about equally reliable postdictors. We may generalize from this that symptoms of thought disorder and extreme social disengagement are the most stable signs of malignancy in psychiatric disorder. The length of hospitalization required is easily foretold by the level of social competence attained prior to breakdown. We might infer that highly competent individuals require less hospitalization because they are the most self-sufficient and vocationally viable.

It is striking that six of the ten variables which survived all three steps in the regression analyses of outcome concerned school behavior or childhood experience, whereas only two specific clinical symptoms (hallucinations and perplexity) appeared in the final analyses. Family disruption, in the form of premature parental death or conflict in the childhood family, was a common forerunner of poor outcome, especially in women, presumably because of its damaging effect on childhood socialization and identity development.

We may summarize these findings by offering a list of indicators for poor prognosis: thought disorder, social withdrawal or low social competence at the time of first hospital admission, a history of family conflict or early parental death, and a childhood profile of retiring and conforming behavior or one of unreliable behavior.

Discussion

At the heart of the description of the preschizophrenic children is *emotional immaturity*. There were frequent references to "crying with slight provocation," "being overshadowed by older siblings," "insensitivity to the feelings of others," "late development in physical and scholastic skills," "temper outbursts," and "self-consciousness." The introversion of the girls and the extreme alienation of the boys, especially in later childhood, seemed to be natural outgrowths of a history of retarded emotional development.

The early characterizations of the preschizophrenic girls as quiet, passive, immature, and socially introverted suggest that they lacked the emotional strength and confidence to meet the requirements of assertive action and interpersonal engagement that school work and social intercourse entail. The pattern of introversion continued through the later school years, although the comments about passivity dropped off. Grade-school teachers were especially attentive to these signs of emotional vulnerability, but the volume of commentary on them for all groups diminished in junior- and senior-high school, perhaps because the increasing emphasis on scholastic performance took precedence over demands for action and confident self-presentation. Therefore we cannot conclude definitely whether the preschizophrenic girls actually gained slightly in self-confidence and emotional adjustment with age or the signs of continuing vulnerability in these areas merely escaped the teachers' attention because of the changed nature of the school situation. The demands for social engagement do not diminish in the later school years, however; on the contrary, they expand, to include more interaction with members of the opposite sex. Hence the social aloofness of the preschizophrenic girls was even more apparent during this period than before.

The oppositional behavior of the preschizophrenic boys increased as they approached adolescence, with expanding size and independence and the additional stresses associated with conflicts over control and social reciprocity. Therefore it is plausible to reason that the longitudinal changes found here represent primarily increments in degree of deviation rather than fundamental changes in modes of adjustment in school. This interpretation also conforms with impressions from reading the records: The continuity of adjustment styles over time was much more impressive than the evidence of dramatic changes. Mildly oppositional boys became more blatantly negativistic and belligerent as they grew older, just as moderately introverted girls became more aloof with age. Thus it appears that the social deviations that culminate in hospitalization (at least among boys) are progressive over time, becoming more apparent in adolescence and presumably still more extreme just prior to hospitalization.

From a theoretical point of view, it seems that a major developmental task for boys is to establish control over their own hostility, so as to avoid social and affective isolation and make possible the kind of intimacy and public acceptance that mature social intercourse requires. On the other hand, girls must acquire independence and learn to approach their social experiences assertively, with confidence and self-respect. (We may even wonder to what extent social conditioning to a submissive role in life, typical of the years prior to the women's liberation movement, might actively dispose some women to schizophrenic dysfunction.) Failure or retardation in these developmental tasks characterizes preschizophrenic children in general, but cannot be related specifically to prognosis on the basis of these data.

In the main, the cognitive variables in the study differentiated schizophrenics from their controls much less clearly than did the emotional and interpersonal measures. This may be interpreted in at least three ways. First, the measures of social development based on teachers' comments may be stronger than the cognitive measures, and hence more revealing. Second, emotional and interpersonal deviance may be a more explicit indication of incipient schizophrenia than cognitive disturbance is. Third, interpersonal and emotional alienation may precede thought disorder in the development of schizophrenia. The last interpretation is especially provocative because it implies that thought disorder, which is the most distinctive clinical feature of schizophrenic disorder, may be ontogenetically discontinuous with premorbid behavior. We might speculate that emotional distress, social alienation, and interpersonal isolation reach a peak that exceeds a threshhold for tolerance before the florid symptoms of schizophrenic thought disorder are manifest during the acute phase of breakdown. This hypothetical pattern of development deserves further consideration in future longitudinal studies.

Our results indicate that abnormally aggressive behavior, rather than withdrawal, in childhood is the more crucial variable for predicting subsequent psychiatric hospitalization. However, within the group of children destined for future psychiatric hospitalization, withdrawal rather than externalization of aggression is the more ominous prognostic indicator. Thus, we may have to choose different prognostic measures for different purposes, depending on whether the aim is early identification of persons vulnerable to mental disorder or differential prognosis within this vulnerable group.

Comparing the childhood behavior of the patient groups with matched controls, schizophrenics clearly stand out as the most deviant group. Five of the seven significant patient-control comparisons involved the schizophrenic group, who were described as less secure, personable, and considerate of others and more introverted and submissive than their matched controls. Disagreeable personal traits in childhood were almost as common for personality disorders as for schizophrenia and distinguished both of these groups from neurotics and psychotic depressives. These results are consistent with other reports that schizophrenics (Garmezy, 1974) and patients with personality disorders (Woerner et al., 1972) already show signs of emotional and interpersonal deviance in childhood long before the presence of overt disorder. Consequently, it is appropriate to expand our concepts of adult psychiatric disorder to include social and work relationships, as has been done in recent revisions of diagnostic procedure (Strauss, 1975; Strauss and Carpenter, 1974; APA, 1980).

Parental Bereavement

How might we understand a causal relation between bereavement in childhood and schizophrenic breakdown in adulthood? Obviously, having a parent die may be quite traumatic emotionally, causing a sudden loss of emotional support and potentially increased hardship for the family members. Phillips (1968) points out that the disorientation (disintegration) caused by a parent's death is related to the degree of that person's previous integration in the family. Disorganization of a child's social matrix is likely to lead to adaptive failure in some form, and schizophrenia is a plausible result if Arieti (1959) is correct in characterizing schizophrenia as "the psychopathology of social disintegration" (in contrast with depression: "the psychopathology of social overintegration").

Phillips (1968) offers an extensive discussion of the implications of bereavement for a child's moral and social development. Moral development is centrally dependent on internalization of "law-giving" parental figures, especially viewed in the sense of ego ideals. Parents serve as role models for authority, accountability for one's actions and their consequences, obligation for the welfare of others, and reciprocity in one's conduct with others. Especially important for social development is stability in interpersonal relations, with the allied quality of intimacy or involvement in those relationships. A child learns, chiefly from parents, to differentiate among the roles adopted by the child or complementary others. These are all crucial aspects of character development, and clearly a bereaved child may be handicapped in some of these elements of social apprenticeship.

A child's sense of identity is normally anchored in the recognition that he or she is a member of a family group, with a particular place in it and a particular history and future associated with it. Identity distortion is a common sign of schizophrenic disorder that is plausibly traceable, at least in part, to childhood bereavement. Identity confusion is a major element in Cameron's (1959) classical account of the psychological etiology of paranoid thinking, which we may relate to the high frequency of bereavement among the paranoid subgroup in the Göttingen study and in this study. The adoption studies in Copenhagen (Kety, 1978) indicate that the process and borderline forms of schizophrenia may be genetically transmitted to a significant extent from one generation to the next. Less impressive evidence shows an appreciable genetic link in schizoaffective schizophrenia (McCabe et al., 1971). All of these subgroups have modest rates of parental death in childhood. We might infer that such psychological stressors play a lesser role in the etiology of these forms of schizophrenia than in the paranoid form. Cameron emphasizes that interpersonal insecurity and self-doubts about identity contribute to paranoid transformations in thinking. We might speculate that childhood bereavement is therefore especially likely to lead to a paranoid form of schizophrenia.

Prediction of Outcome

We might draw the simple conclusion that poor outcome is best predicted by the signs of schizophrenic disorder, i.e., thought disorder, social withdrawal, low social competence, a history of family conflict or early parental death, and a childhood profile of unreliable or retiring and conforming behavior. However, it would be a mistake to equate schizophrenic diagnosis with poor outcome, because one-fourth of the patients in the poorest outcome group were *not* schizophrenic and one-fourth of the patients in the best outcome group *were* schizophrenic. The behavioral precursors of schizophrenic disorder and poor long-term outcome also differed sharply in some respects. The childhood behaviors most closely related to poor outcome were introversion and generally inadequate adjustment but also included positive features such as conformity and conscientiousness. On the other hand, in addition to introversion, schizophrenia was distinguished in childhood (especially in the boys) by emotional instability and disagreeable behavior, although neither variable survived the regression studies to predict outcome. It is important therefore to caution that schizophrenic diagnosis is not synonymous with poor outcome.

Childhood Differences between Schizophrenics and Psychotic Depressives

Sparse research published more recently has characterized the premorbid personality of depressives more pejoratively than reported here. A review of Hirschfeld and Cross (1981) featured findings of low self-esteem, low frustration tolerance, high dependency on others for support, neuroticism, introversion, obsessionality, and guilt. This suggests that depressives are worrisome, socially inept, insecure, sensitive, and vulnerable to breakdown under stress. They also cited research on the home environment of depressed children and (retrospectively) of depressed adults that suggested family discord, parental rejection, and a generally disruptive, negative atmosphere in the home. Most of these recent studies, especially community surveys, have employed operationalized diagnostic criteria (e.g., the SADS and RDC of Spitzer, Endicott, and Robins, 1978; and the PSE of Wing, Cooper, and Sartorius, 1975), which do not draw sharp differentiations among depressed subjects regarding the severity of impairment in social and ego functions. Thus it is possible that the recent research analyzes a broader and more diverse spectrum of depressive disorders, with smaller proportions of psychotics, whereas earlier studies (including the two summarized here) sampled clinical populations primarily comprised of severely psychotic and/or chronic hospitalized patients.

Klerman (1978) estimates that only about 10 percent of depressed patients in current clinical practice are psychotic. The recent studies deemphasized the differences between neurotic and psychotic levels of depression, so differentiation of premorbid development in the two major psychoses remains ambiguous.

Prospective Research on Children at High Risk for Schizophrenia and Other Major Disorders

I have reviewed two types of retrospective archival research on the antecedents of major psychological disorders, one utilizing hospital records exclusively and the other employing both cumulative school records and hospital files. The next logical step in a longitudinal program of risk research is to study prospectively children at high risk for disorder, relying on the foregoing retrospective findings for empirical and conceptual leads to pursue in identifying subjects and developing causal theory. The prospective approach offers an important advantage over the retrospective approach, namely, the possibility of determining whether abnormalities observed reflect a cause or a consequence of the disorder. To coordinate these efforts, a cadre of enterprising investigators with a common interest in the study of schizophrenic disorders organized formally in May 1973, creating the Risk Research Consortium. With financial support from the Grant Foundation and NIMH, the Consortium has sponsored one or two research meetings each year, usually small and limited in attendance, in order to promote active interchange among the 16 research groups participating.

Most of the prospective projects were launched in the early 1970s and are now maturing, as are the research subjects they have studied in childhood and adolescence. Children at risk for schizophrenia have now been followed from a variety of points in development for periods of up to 20 years. The aggregate number of subjects at risk that have been studied by members of the Consortium approximates 1200, with 1400 normal controls and about 750 children of parents with other (mostly depressive) psychiatric disorders. It was therefore considered timely, at this important midpoint in the lives of the research subjects, to organize a plenary conference of Consortium members for the purpose of presenting comprehensive progress reports of the research projects conducted thus far. That conference was held in 1980, and most of the papers presented there were carefully edited and published in the recently released book, *Children at Risk for Schizophrenia: A Longitudinal Perspective* (Watt et al., 1984).

The present overview is a highly condensed distillation of the summary chapter from that book, entitled *In a Nutshell: The First Two Decades of High-Risk Research in Schizophrenia*. Most of the references will be to chapters in that volume, since it contains more than 1000 citations of literature in the field and is most up-to-date. Except for a few observations about method, I will focus on research findings and their significance.

Issues of Method and Inference

The basic logic of the high-risk approach has been to study prospectively children believed to have greater risk for schizophrenia than the average person. The question of whether to use broadly or narrowly defined risk groups for this purpose has clearly been answered in favor of the narrowly defined. The Mauritius project (Mednick et al., 1984) is the only large-scale attempt to study a whole population of children by any criterion of risk. There have been no population surveys with follow-up that have *not* selected research subjects by some specific criterion of risk. Hence we have not followed the suggestion of sociologist to pursue large stratified samples in order to offset the scientific restrictions imposed by studying narrowly defined risk groups. The overwhelming majority in the Consortium has concentrated on children of schizophrenic parents, reflecting, perhaps, the urgent need felt by most to exceed population base rates for schizophrenic prevalence in our research samples. Except for the UCLA and Mauritius programs (and to a lesser extent the Minneapolis program), selection criteria other than genetic ones have been neglected.

We have paid a strategic price for that preference. Lewine, Watt, and Grubb (1984) remind us that we have concentrated on quite unrepresentative samples, in effect targeting only 10–15 percent of the ultimate spectrum of schizophrenic adults, namely, those with schizophrenic parents. Moreover, our samples contain an overwhelming predominance of schizophrenic mothers over fathers and selective sampling of the fathers because schizophrenic men usually do not marry and have families. It is also likely that the schizophrenic parents we have studied are unrepresentative of schizophrenics generally (for example, being less chronic or tending more toward schizo-affective forms of the disorder). We must be circumspect about these sampling restrictions, recognizing that we may learn a great deal about some schizophrenic people that does not apply to others.

Sex differences have been studied by some research groups, but the salience of those differences has not been impressive. Most of the sex differences observed in the samples at risk have paralleled differences found in the control groups, thus offering little leverage to advance our knowledge in this area of psychopathology.

Most of the research groups have included appropriate contrast groups for study, comprised frequently of children of psychiatrically hospitalized (but not schizophrenic) parents. Intelligence and social class have proven to be pervasive and troublesome sources of confusion in interpreting research results. Should they be controlled as "sources of contamination" in analyzing statistical results, or should they be considered as important precursors of schizophrenic disorders worthy of study in their own right? Social class plays a powerful role in the family lives and in the individual functioning of both children and their parents and, indeed, a greater role in Sameroff's project (Sameroff, Barocas, and Seifer, 1984) than parental diagnosis. We should confess that social class has received inadequate attention, either methodologically or conceptually, from most Consortium teams. It remains a continuing source of ambiguity in interpreting our data.

Teachers and parents clearly have been entrusted with a great deal of responsibility for evaluating children's behavior, notwithstanding the heavy skepticism from decades past regarding the reliability and validity of their judgments. The breadth of their employment as referees in Copenhagen, New York, Stony Brook, Rochester, Minneapolis, Waterloo, and St. Louis speaks both for the confidence in them as observers and for the lack of alternative sources of observation. More than was envisioned in 1972, peers have been similarly employed, especially in Stony Brook, Minneapolis, and Waterloo.

There has been an appreciable swing during the last decade from linear analyses of group differences to more diversified searches for "outliers" that may plausibly include the subjects most likely to become schizophrenic. This may, in part, reflect some frustration in seeking monolithic markers that distinguish high-risk samples from controls, for such have decidedly *not* been found. It also reflects increasing sophistication and appropriate disillusionment with simplistic conceptions about very complex disorders. It is unrealistic to expect breakthroughs in treatment and etiological theory along the lines of the Salk vaccine for polio and the discovery of chromosomal damage in Down's Syndrome. The adjustments in statistical approach take account of the subtlety and complexity of the disorders under study.

Research on Pregnancy and Delivery of Schizophrenic Mothers

Most of the reports published in *Children at Risk for Schizophrenia* were written by several authors. For simplicity, the ideas and findings featured in this review will cite only the first author unless further detail is required to indicate which chapter is intended. When abbreviations are used, HR stands for High Risk, or children of a schizophrenic parent; PC for Psychiatric Controls, or children of a nonschizophrenic psychiatric patient; NC for Normal Controls, or children of two normal parents; and RRC for Risk Research Consortium.

The studies of pregnancy and delivery present a grim picture of schizophrenic mothers, but one that hardly differs from the plight of mothers with other psychiatric disturbance. Wrede et al. (1984) found that the deliveries of schizophrenic women, most of which occurred *before* the onset of psychosis, were attended by more difficulties than average. Similarly, Sameroff found more prenatal complications and lower birth weight in HR infants than in NCs, but these were attributed to chronic antipsychotic medications. (This implies that most of Sameroff's deliveries occurred *after* the onset of psychosis.) According to McNeil (1984), mothers with previous psychiatric disturbances of *all* kinds reported more stressful pregnancies than average, as visibly reflected by their psychological status during the pregnancy interviews.

Severity and chronicity of psychiatric disability were strongly associated with socioeconomic deprivation in Wrede's and Sameroff's samples. We cannot clearly relate social class to reproductive problems, however, because of conflicting findings. Sameroff found that reproductive abnormalities of many kinds were associated with socioeconomic deprivation, but Wrede reported that they were not. Wrede found that chronic schizophrenics experienced the most pregnancy complications but that mild schizophrenics registered the most severe complications at delivery. She also reported that reproductive complications were most frequent among winter deliveries and least frequent among summer deliveries. This may be related in some way to the replicated finding (Dalen, 1975; Kety and Kinney, 1981) that a higher percentage of schizophrenics are born during the winter or spring months than is true for the general population. It has been speculated that this reflects some causal factor that varies with the seasons rather than the calendar year, such as perinatal viral infections or neonatal hemorrhaging, which might be associated with birth complications.

It is not surprising that many schizophrenic mothers give up their babies for adoption or foster-home placement, and Sameroff studied them closely. Those who gave up their babies were older and from lower class backgrounds than those who kept their babies; they were also more likely to be unmarried currently, socially incompetent, anxious, severely disturbed, and to have longer histories of emotional disturbance. The course of the pregnancy and the condition of the infants were also worse, which indicates that schizophrenic mothers who relinquish their babies are not a random sample of schizophrenic mothers in general. On the contrary, they were severely and chronically disturbed, older, poorer, and so forth. Hence their offspring might be expected to have a more malignant disposition for emotional disorder. A higher degree of pathology has likewise been suspected in the Danish adoption studies (Wender et al., 1974).

Infancy and Early Development

In an Israeli study, Marcus (1984) found that about two-thirds of the HR infants performed motor and sensorimotor tasks poorly during the first year of life (with two extreme outliers) and discounted the potential explanation of causation by reproductive complications. He speculated that the findings may reflect some genetically determined neurointegrative defect, which is consistent with the findings and formulations of Fish (1984) regarding "pandevelopmental retardation." However, Marcus's theory glides over a parsimonious interpretation of his results, namely, that low birth weight per se may account for most of the sensorimotor deficiencies observed, independently of any genetic mediation.

The HR infants observed by McNeil (1984) showed slightly more evidence of neurological abnormality, which corroborates results of both Marcus and Fish, but temperamentally they differed very little from controls. The babies of cycloid and schizophrenic psychotics, especially, displayed little reaction to separation from their mothers and no sign of stranger anxiety, which suggests early disturbance in the emotional bonding of these babies.

Sameroff found no behavioral abnormalities at birth among HR infants, and the only deficiencies observed at 4 months and 12 months were in psychomotor development. At 30 months the HR infants were only "less reactive" than NC infants, which seems consistent with McNeil's finding of a possible disturbance of emotional bonding at about the same age. Sameroff departs sharply from Fish and Marcus in interpreting the significance of his findings. He concludes that HR children have many developmental problems, but these problems do not appear to be the simple result of schizophrenic parentage. Social class and severity and chronicity of the mother's psychiatric condition accounted for most of these differences, not schizophrenia per se.

Sameroff reinforces this viewpoint in interpreting the findings for HR babies given up for adoption. Placement infants were more premature and had more physical problems than the home-reared sample, which challenges the assumption that such HR babies bring nothing unique to their new families other than "schizophrenic genes." The extra caretaking demands for prematurity, as well as predictable temperamental abnormalities, may contribute to a negative chain of interpersonal transactions that could produce a deviant outcome regardless of the infant's genetic inheritance.

From the studies of pregnancy, birth, and infant development we can draw several general conclusions. Schizophrenic mothers have unusually frequent and serious complications of pregnancy and delivery, which may threaten the development of their children. Such complications are more extreme if the mother's psychiatric disturbance is severe and chronic, and in such cases the mothers are more likely to give up their babies for adoption or foster-home placement. It is not clear whether reproductive complications are specific to schizophrenic disorders or characteristic of psychiatric disorders generally. Infants of schizophrenic mothers are not extremely deviant in most respects, but they do show deficiencies in psychomotor development early and in emotional attachment later in the preschool period. Again it is problematic to attribute these developmental abnormalities to a genetically inherited diathesis for schizophrenia because they could plausibly result from socioeconomic deprivation and/or the damaging effects of reproductive complications.

Later Childhood Development

The studies of school-aged children have focused mainly on competence, interpersonal style, and temperament. The picture of early childhood in children at risk is not very distinctive. Rolf (1984) reports that, as preschoolers, the children of psychotic parents in Vermont did not show signs of severe behavior problems. Worland (1984a) found that the St. Louis groups did not differ behaviorally in elementary school. Weintraub's (1984b) overall impression of the HR children in the Stony Brook project was that they were not grossly deviant as young children.

Behavioral differences did begin to emerge in the middle childhood years. Rolf's (1972) results in Minneapolis generally showed that teachers and peers rated competence lowest in externalizing, HR, and internalizing children, whereas PC children were considered to be the most competent. Reaction time performance of the HR children was the poorest of the four groups, which brings to mind the findings of retarded psychomotor development in infancy reported by Fish, Marcus, McNeil, and Sameroff. Externalizing children displayed the poorest citizenship in school and HR children the best. All target groups except the HR group had poorer intermediate outcomes than their controls, although the high migration rate for HR children may have masked negative outcomes for them. Externalizing children generally showed the poorest outcomes.

Fisher (1984) developed an interesting profile of school behavior by combining teacher and peer ratings in the Rochester project. Initial comparisons showed teachers and peers in close agreement, judging sons of affective psychotics strikingly above average in competence, sons of schizophrenics even more than that *below* average, and sons of nonpsychotic psychiatric controls slightly below average. On the other hand, children of depressed parents in Stony Brook (Weintraub, 1984a and b) resembled HR offspring in most respects, including that of both groups being less competent than their respective control groups. In contrast to both the Rochester and Stony Brook patterns, Worland (1984a) found that offspring of manic-depressives in St. Louis were rated lowest on social competence and total competence in high school, whereas HR offspring were not different from normal controls. The teacher ratings of competence remained stable over time in St. Louis, which implies temporal constancy throughout development.

Janes (1984) found that scholastic motivation and emotional stability were lower among HR adolescents in St. Louis than among NC adolescents. Watt (1982) corroborated these findings in the New York sample but was not able, definitively, to rule out social class or intelligence as explanations for his findings.

Greater uniformity emerges in the descriptions of interpersonal style. The HR children in Stony Brook (Weintraub, 1984a, b) were rated by teachers as more aggressive/disruptive, less cognitively competent, and less socially competent than NC children but not significantly different from PC children, who were rated less socially competent and less anxious about achievement than NC children. Peer ratings showed HR children to be more aggressive and more unhappy/withdrawn than NC children. HR girls were less likeable than NC girls. The Stony Brook results showed no differences in social behavior among the offspring of the two patient groups. School assessments of the New York sample reported by Watt, Grubb, and Erlenmeyer-Kimling (1982) showed strong evidence of interpersonal disharmony but little indication of introversion among HR subjects at about age 15. Similarly, Rolf (1972) found children of schizophrenic mothers in Minneapolis to resemble externalizing children the most and in Vermont (Rolf et al., 1984) to be *less* withdrawn, shy, and socially unresponsive than children of depressed parents. Convergent results were found in Rodnick's (1984) follow-up of four adolescent risk groups. Among the eight subjects classified in the schizophrenic spectrum outcome group in young adulthood, only three had been characterized as passive/negative or withdrawn and socially isolated adolescents, whereas five had been antisocially aggressive or had active family conflict.

The follow-up study of the Danish HR sample (Rodnick, 1984a) located 15 eventual schizophrenics, who had been described by school teachers as prone to be angered and upset, disturbing in class with inappropriate behavior, violent, aggressive, and frequently subject to disciplinary action. Clearly, the results of all of these studies conform more to Arieti's (1975) characterization of the "stormy" prepsychotic personality than of the "introverted" type.

Intellectual Functions

Neale (1984) found lower verbal and performance IQs among HR subjects in the Stony Brook sample than among NC subjects. This lower verbal intelligence replicates findings of Mednick in the Danish project and of Erlenmeyer-Kimling (1984a) in the New York study. However, the IQs of the Stony Brook HR group (Weintraub, 1984a) did not differ from the PC group's. In the St. Louis sample Worland (1984b) found that HR and PC children also had lower verbal IQs than NC subjects, but there were no performance IQ differences. Relative to those of the controls, the IQs of the HR children were lower in adolescence than in early childhood. Worland implies that the drop in intelligence may be attributed to the cumulative *psychological* impact of parental psychosis on their children, but the change observed could reflect just as plausibly an intrinsic intellectual deterioration that is not mediated by the psychological relationship with an ill parent. (The decline was not found in the PC group.)

On the basis of extensive analysis of the St. Louis data, Worland (1984b) concluded that preadolescent children of psychotic parents are not noticeably impaired in either cognitive or intellectual development. By adolescence, children of both schizophrenic and depressed parents showed lower than average verbal intelligence, with the greatest decline in the former group.

In an object-sorting task, HR children at Stony Brook (Neale, 1984) made fewer superordinate responses than the NC group (thought not more than the PC group), but more "complexive" responses than either control group, which implies more disjointed conceptualization in HR children. Except for "cognitive slippage," deficits in most areas of cognitive functioning among HR children were matched in the offspring of depressed parents, raising doubts about whether the findings are specific to risk for schizophrenic disorder.

Studies of attention have been featured prominently in Consortium projects in New York, Minneapolis, and Waterloo. Cornblatt (1984) found deficits in sustained and focused attention and greater susceptibility to distraction among HR subjects. Early attentional dysfunction was correlated with behavioral deviance in adolescence, which was interpreted to support the hypothesis that attentional deviance is a precursor of later psychopathology. However, it was not shown that attention is a *discriminantly* better predictor than other (e.g., behavioral) indicators. Some corroboration was provided by Steffy's (1984) project in Waterloo, which was unique in sampling HR children raised in foster homes. Steffy reported an association between extreme attentional deficits and significant elevations on the MMPI Schizophrenia Scale. HR children with both attentional problems and high MMPI scores for schizophrenia and Psychasthenia also showed role difficulties as students in school, some social isolation, and difficulty in modulating anger.

The experimental studies of attention, learning, and reaction time in Minneapolis (Garmezy, 1984) yielded largely negative findings, which led to the conclusion that there was no broad attentional dysfunction in those HR children.

In his overview of the attentional, intellectual, and cognitive research presented, Lewine (1984) draws appropriately conservative conclusions. Among children at risk for schizophrenia, only a modest subset (11–44%) stands out as deviant. Almost without exception, the significant deviance found in HR children is likewise found in psychiatric controls. A parsimonious inference to draw from this is that a general vulnerability to psychosis may be transmitted genetically, with the specific form of the psychosis largely determined environmentally (Zubin and Spring, 1978). Further, Lewine makes an excellent observation about *instability of deviance*. Early markers for schizophrenia may be more distinguished by variability than by constancy. Hence we may be mistaken to expect future schizophrenics to be permanently branded by visible and stable stigmata that announce their vulnerability. The early evidence may be much more subtle, fluctuating, and erratic. That possibility behooves us to search as patiently and persistently for patterns of variation and change as for constant, structural precursors of psychopathology.

Family Relations and Communication

Wynne (1984) points out that even the most ardent genetic theorists concede that environmental experience plays a significant role in determining the occurrence, course, and outcome of schizophrenic disorder. As a consequence, the unafflicted spouses of schizophrenic mothers or fathers are pivotal persons who exert important formative influence on their children. The family must be regarded as an integrated system, not as a collection of independent individuals that interact occasionally. Mednick's (1984a) path analysis suggests that separation from parents may affect HR children significantly, e.g., augmenting antisocial tendencies, and subsequent institutionalization may exacerbate that disturbance further.

In Stony Brook (Weintraub, 1984a) marital adjustment was found to be better in the PC families than in the HR families and best in the NC families. Marital discord was reflected in parental disagreements over demonstrations of affection, sex relations, and propriety of conduct. Compared with the normal controls, spouses in both patient groups were less conciliatory toward one another, less happy, less engaged in mutual outside interests, and less inclined to confide in their mates or to marry the same partner again. Depressives rated their marriages even less happy than schizophrenics. These extremely negative marital evaluations, especially among the depressives, reveal emphatically how conflictual their marriages must be.

Family functioning in the Stony Brook sample was also more disturbed among the two patient groups in several areas: family solidarity, children's relations, household facilities, and financial circumstances. The two patient groups did not differ from one another in these respects. The parenting characteristics, as viewed by their children, are instructive. Schizophrenic mothers were considered to be more accepting and child-centered and depressed mothers more child-centered than were normal mothers. Schizophrenic mothers were more lax in discipline than depressive mothers. Schizophrenic fathers were perceived more negatively (i.e., unaccepting and uninvolved) than normal fathers, whereas depressed fathers were not different from the normals. Husbands of schizophrenic and depressed mothers covertly controlled their offspring through inducing anxiety or guilt. (It should be remembered that *lack* of control by these mothers was criticized by the offspring.)

From a methodological viewpoint the most impressive work in this area is the research on free play among families, inspired mainly by Clara and Al Baldwin (1984). Not surprisingly, interactions between a child and a parent are reciprocal: Frequent actions directed to one person are matched by frequent actions in return. Interestingly, a hydraulic principle seems to apply to the general family ecology: Initiatives directed to one person in the family are "subtracted" from initiatives to another. Hence we can surmise that the relationship to a nonpatient parent has important compensating potential for healthy development of the offspring.

It is important to observe that expressive warmth is contagious within the family. Affection expressed by one family member is generally shared among others in the family. Rochester patients interacted less with their children than healthy spouses did, presumably reflecting a depletion in the patients' emotional resources for family living that can be attributed to their illness. As expected, schizophrenic parents were the least active in free-play participation and nonpsychotic patients were the most active, with affectively disordered patients in between. Also as predicted, patients rated as most disturbed psychiatrically interacted least with their children, and their families displayed the least warmth.

What are the effects on children of relating to, and communicating with, psychiatrically disturbed parents? Worland (1984a) reported that there was some evidence that family skew was predictive of later need for psychological treatment in the offspring.

Reporting on the Rochester sample, Cole (1984) found that transactional style and warmth of family interaction were positively correlated with teacher and peer ratings of children's competence at school. Active, warm, and balanced communication among family members in the Family Rorschach Test likewise related positively to teacher ratings (in one sample) and to peer ratings of children's competence.

The UCLA Family Project yielded results that were quite independent but highly convergent with the Rochester findings. Rodnick (1984) found that level of parental communication deviance (CD) was strongly related to *schizophrenia spectrum* disorders in the offspring. Similarly, rejecting style in parental affective expression toward the offspring was also significantly related to later schizophrenic outcome. Parents of later schizophrenics seemed disinclined to acknowledge their children in direct interactions, implying either indifference or hostility. They also did not impose the required structure when discussions drifted off target. When both parents were high in CD, they exerted a dominant force in the family interaction, which might explain their apparent pathogenic impact on the development of their children. High CD in parents was associated with avoidance of eye contact and with unchanging facial expression, which obviously could lead to a sense of disconfirmation in the children.

Doane (1984) pursued Rodnick's research with configural analysis of parental styles, concluding that families who are *not* affectively rejecting in either what they say or how they say it produce offspring with benign outcomes. Conversely, if parents say harshly negative things and deliver them in a hostile, angry, or challenging tone of voice, the result is often (eight of nine cases!) an outcome in the schizophrenic spectrum.

The rationale gradually emerging from these two projects is that the transactional style of children is shaped (for better or worse) by the transactional style of the family's interactions. Children reared in families with active, warm, and responsive interpersonal style are likely to be outgoing and friendly and successful in engaging their social environment outside the home. By contrast, children reared in rejecting or detached family environments are likely to reflect this style in their approach to others outside the home and thus be seriously handicapped. For this reason, accurate assessment of the modal pattern of interaction within the family may help to identify those children with the highest risk for serious behavioral or emotional disorders.

The Premorbid Picture in Cases of Early Breakdown

Mednick's 1967 follow-up found that HR children with poor intermediate outcomes (the "Sick" group) experienced frequent pregnancy and birth complications, were separated from their mothers early in life, showed volatile electrodermal patterns and attentional drift in their associative functioning, and were disruptive at school rather than retiring (Mednick, 1984a). His 1972 follow-up yielded 15 diagnosed schizophrenics who also had experienced perinatal problems, were placed early in children's homes, recorded volatile autonomic functions, and were disruptive in school—nothing was reported about attentional drift—and whose mothers experienced severe courses of illness. Mothers of borderline schizophrenics, on the other hand, showed late onset of schizophrenic disorder and relatively good social, vocational, and personal adjustment, providing therefore a comparatively stable rearing environment for their children. Mednick suggests that there may be a gradient of potency in the genetically transmitted disposition for psychopathology, the diathesis for chronic schizophrenia being the strongest, for borderline disorders weaker, and for normal or neurotic conditions weakest of all. However, by his own reasoning, the severity of the maternal syndrome also shapes the quality of the home environment, which in turn influences the development of the child *psychologically.* Both patterns of causation may be important.

By an average age of 17.5 years, five of Erlenmeyer-Kimling's (1984b) HR subjects, two PC subjects, and one normal control were hospitalized for psychiatric disorders, most of them with hospital-diagnosed schizophrenias. Fifteen others required some form of psychological treatment outside the hospital. Global assessments by psychiatrists at 7–12 years of age were lowest for those subsequently hospitalized, highest for those that functioned well, and intermediate for the treated subjects, indicating that early clinical appraisals *can* identify the most vulnerable youngsters. Reviewing the early performance deficits of the hospitalized HR children, she found significantly lower IQs (mean of 93 versus 104 for other HR subjects) and a relative deficit in verbal IQ (mean of 88 versus 99 for performance IQ). This suggests that low (especially verbal) intelligence may be an early marker for clinical breakdown or for early onset of psychiatric disorder. In contrast, the hospitalized PC subjects both achieved high IQs (117 and 109). The hospitalized HR group also performed poorly on the Bender–Gestalt Test, the Lincoln–Oseretsky Test of motor impairment, and on several attentional measures, but their electrodermal responding was not deviant.

Worland (1984a) examined the *precursors* of schizophrenia and borderline schizophrenia, primarily in terms of interpersonal style and temperament. Among the boys, preschizophrenics were anxious, lonely, and restrained, having discipline problems at school (the latter corroborating Mednick's results). The preborderline boys were simply described as isolated and distant. Both groups of girls were anhedonic, withdrawn, disengaged, and isolated; the preschizophrenic girls were poorly controlled, whereas the preborderline girls were overly restrained. Contrary to

Mednick's finding, the precursors of schizophrenia did *not* include verbal associative disturbance. Childhood intelligence was *not* lower than average overall, and verbal IQ was higher than performance IQ, contradicting Erlenmeyer-Kimling's results.

It is noteworthy that few of the findings reported in this area by one research group have been replicated by other groups. This might be attributed to the very small samples that have had detectable clinical outcomes thus far. However, it is also consistent with Cudeck's (1984) observation that the early patterns of clinical symptoms that emerge among high-risk subjects in young adulthood are extremely diverse, including a broad range of familiar syndromes: psychosis, personality disorders, psychopathy, antisocial disorders, depression, and various (rather poorly defined) neurotic disorders.

Neglected Research Issues

Several concepts have received theoretical attention in the risk research field but either have been neglected empirically or yielded confusing results. They merit further consideration in future research. Methodological difficulties in psychophysiological techniques have precluded effective testing of research hypotheses in some projects and failed to replicate research findings across laboratories. Some promising leads reported in the areas of cortical evoked-potential response and neuromotor functioning may take on significance mainly as evidence accumulates regarding outcomes. For the most part, the evidence and conclusions about biopsychological functioning are ambiguous, at best.

Adaptive Strengths of Children at Risk

There has been much speculation and enthusiastic support for studying adaptive strengths in children of schizophrenic parents but little programmatic pursuit of this intriguing idea. Many have paid lip service to the concept of the *invulnerable* or *resistant* child at risk. Bleuler (1984) found that 84 percent of his HR subjects who married had successful marriages, and the great majority achieved higher social status than their parents, which implies adaptive and relationship skills. A strong new emphasis on stress and coping in the theoretical literature and in research funding programs (e.g., the Grant Foundation's new program direction) promises some headway along these lines in the near future.

Early Intervention

There is an obvious natural alliance between high-risk research and practical efforts at preventive intervention. All of the research groups in the

Consortium have been conscious of this connection and many have taken concrete steps to offer treatment referral services for their subjects and/or their families. However, the only systematic intervention research project took place on the island of Mauritius, off the coast of southern Africa (Mednick, 1984b). Children were selected on the basis of deviant skin conductance patterns and placed in nursery schools for special enrichment in their learning experience. Follow-up studies after three years showed that the nursery school training channeled the children into constructive modes of play, displacing watching behavior with more positive interactions of a social nature. An 11-year follow-up of their school progress since that time is currently underway.

The dilemma for investigations of early intervention is plain to see. It is difficult to know what to treat in children at risk until we know what is "wrong" or abnormal about them. The primary objective of this first phase of risk research is precisely to determine how such children differ from others. Until the answers to this question are well established, we will have to continue to grope in the dark with our intervention efforts.

Discussion

A wide variety of theoretical convictions is represented in the Risk Research Consortium, covering the entire spectrum from extreme genetic and biological views of etiology to clear psychodynamic conceptions that feature the potential causal primacy of distortions in family communication and relationship. Along the latter lines there is a broad consensus of support for *transactional* modes of development that emphasize relationship and coping procedures. Transactional conceptions represent an important advance beyond traditional disease models based on epigenetic principles, which tend to stereotype developmental processes. The early results from these projects do not resoundingly confirm our wishful (and plausible) hypothesizing along such traditional lines. For example, Mednick (1984a) found that malignant parental schizophrenia does *not* yield a high frequency of schizophrenia (at least with early onset) among offspring. Hence we must look toward more complex and less monolithic models to explain the transmission and development of schizophrenic disorders.

There is an interesting contrast in the conceptual treatment of developmental events. Environmentalists look for *pathogenic* life experiences to explain schizophrenic vulnerability, whereas geneticists look for *buffering* life experiences to explain the suppression of such vulnerability.

A diathesis-stress model of etiology (Gottesman and Shields, 1982) clearly offers the most popular approach. Weintraub (1984a) argues that it is unjustified to search for a single cause, in view of the obvious heterogeneity of the disorders. Research is therefore focussed primarily on a wide variety of factors that may "potentiate" the diathesis, i.e., trigger the manifest disorder. For this reason, much of the Stony Brook work attempts to describe the general ecology of the HR children and their families. The project has been quite successful in providing many such provocative descriptions.

Sameroff is the most outspoken about etiological theory, frankly doubting that a *specific* deficit can account for the predisposition to schizophrenia. He concedes that some latent constitutional deficit might emerge later in development or that the wrong variables were measured to reveal such a deficit. On the basis of the published research thus far, he concludes that *risk* in the offspring of schizophrenic mothers can be attributed more to prolonged emotional disturbance in the mothers, unstable family organization, poor economic circumstance, and low social status than to the schizophrenic disorders of the mothers per se. He also doubts that many of the HR children will become schizophrenic, which may be correct; Bleuler (1978) found, after all, that only 9 percent of the HR offspring in his sample became schizophrenic in their lifetimes. Sameroff concludes that social milieu at least matches the effects of maternal psychopathology on the social and emotional development of children—and overpowers it in the cognitive sphere. This leads him to question theories that posit a unique constitutional deficit, usually inferred to be transmitted genetically, as the cause of schizophrenia. Caretaking environments with high levels of stress, whether because of economic or emotional instability of the caregivers, produce young children with high levels of incompetent behavior. Hence they deserve primary attention as potential causes of schizophrenic disorders.

The Question of Specificity

Hundreds of significant findings have been reported pertaining to children at risk for schizophrenia. This usually means that they differ in some respects from children of normal parents or from children otherwise considered unlikely to become schizophrenic adults. It is vitally important to know whether such findings signal specific precursors of schizophrenic disorders or markers for psychopathology in general. The answer to this question has been complicated by recent advances in the DSM-III diagnostic system, which have virtually dictated changes in the sampling of the schizophrenic spectrum and in the combinations of genetic loading studied. For example, many subjects previously diagnosed as schizophrenic are now considered schizo-affectives or affective psychotics. Lewine (1984b) concludes that the evidence thus far weighs against specificity because most findings that distinguish HR subjects from normal controls also characterize psychiatric controls as well. High-risk samples, of course, include relatively few future schizophrenics, so the conceptual significance of findings may change as psychological outcomes unfold. For the present, Mednick (1984a) concludes that there may be no monolithic schizophrenic disorder that followed predictable rules of genetic transmission, as phenylketonuria and Huntington's chorea do. Consequently, he recommends that we look for "degrees of schizophrenicity" or schizophrenic vulnerability, which obviously calls for subtle and complex conceptions of the disorder.

Behavioral Continuity

A thorny problem confronts any longitudinal investigation covering an extensive period of time. It is obviously advantageous for purposes of prediction to establish developmental continuities in the behavior of subjects being studied, but how should that be tested and proved if the concrete performance and actions that reflect psychological constructs are expected to change with age? Most teams in the Consortium seem to operate on the assumption that broad continuities in behavior over time can be found. Children with early attentional deficits are expected to have problems deploying attention later, and abrasive, antisocial children are expected to have conduct problems in adolescence. For the most part, these theoretical expectations are accommodated by making *operational* adjustments in measurement to account for age differences. For example, the behavior defined as competent at 4 years of age may differ from the actions considered competent at 13, but it is generally assumed that a child's *relative* position in a sample on the competence dimension will not change substantially in the interim. In point of fact, some rather large changes have been observed, leading Lewine et al. (1984) to conclude that change or process may be a more important focus than stable traits for future research and conceptual formulation. However, enough evidence of modest temporal stability has emerged to sustain the general expectation that stable traits can be found.

A special problem in this regard arises in longitudinal research on psychoses. Considering that typical signs and symptoms of schizophrenic and affective disorders seldom occur prior to adolescence, even in those destined to be afflicted as adults, what are the logical precursors to look for in childhood? We have looked for early aberrations in thinking, interpersonal style, mood, intelligence, temperament, psychophysiological functions, and competence, but we have also studied pregnancy and birth complications, parental communication deviance, socioeconomic deprivation, and family relations, which might contribute to such aberrations. And we still do not know what the key variables are. We do know that children at risk are different from normal children in many respects, some of which seem to be associated with the earliest signs of psychological disruption in adolescence or young adulthood. But we cannot yet judge how much developmental continuity will be found ultimately.

It seems fair to conclude that risk research in schizophrenia is a field of endeavor that promises much but has delivered little that is definite thus far. Risk research in affective disorders is much further behind, but also shows signs of awakening. The consensus of experts (Regier and Allen, 1981) is that systematic research to intervene preventively is premature at present because of the lack of definitive knowledge about the precursors of the major disorders. We look forward to such developments in the not-too-distant future as the next step in the advancement of our knowledge.

References

American Psychiatric Association. (1968). *Diagnostic and statistical manual of mental disorders,* 2nd ed. Washington, D.C.: The Association.

American Psychiatric Association. (1980). *Diagnostic and statistical manual of mental disorders,* 3rd ed. Washington, D.C.: The Association.

Arieti, S. (Ed.). (1959). *American handbook of psychiatry.* New York: Basic Books.

Arieti, S. (1975). *Interpretation of schizophrenia.* New York: Basic Books.

Astrup, C., and Noreik, K. (1966). *Functional psychoses.* Springfield, Ill.: Charles C Thomas.

Baldwin, C. P., Baldwin, A. L., Cole, R. E., and Kokes, R. F. (1984). Free Play family interaction and the behavior of the patient in Free Play. In N. F. Watt, E. J. Anthony, L. C. Wynne, and J. E. Rolf (Eds.), *Children at risk for schizophrenia: A longitudinal perspective* (pp. 376–387). New York: Cambridge University Press.

Barthell, C., and Holmes, D. (1968). High school yearbooks: A non-reactive measure of social isolation in graduates who later became schizophrenic. *Journal of Abnormal Psychology, 73,* 313–316.

Bleuler, M. (1978). *The schizophrenic disorders: Long-term patients and family studies.* New Haven, Conn.: Yale University Press.

Bleuler, M. (1984). Different forms of childhood stress and patterns of adult psychiatric outcome. In Watt et al., op. cit. (pp. 537–542).

Bower, E. M., Schellhammer, T., Daily, J. A., and Bower, M. (1960). High school students who later became schizophrenic. *Bulletin of the California State Department of Education, 29,* 1–158.

Cameron, N. (1959). The paranoid pseudo-community revisited. *American Journal of Sociology, 65,* 52–58.

Cole, R. E., Al-Khayyal, M., Baldwin, A. L., Baldwin, C. P., Fisher, L., and

Wynne, L. C. (1984). A cross-setting assessment of family interaction and the prediction of school competence in children at risk. In Watt et al., (pp. 388–392).

Cornblatt, B., and Erlenmeyer-Kimling, L. (1984). Early attentional predictors of adolescent behavioral disturbances in children at risk for schizophrenia. In Watt et al., op. cit. (pp. 198–211).

Cronbach, L. J., and Meehl, P. E. (1955). Construct validity in psychological tests. *Psychological Bulletin, 52,* 281–302.

Cudeck, R., Mednick, S. A., Schulsinger, F., and Schulsinger, H. (1984). A multidimensional approach to the identification of schizophrenia. In Watt et al. op. cit. (pp. 43–70).

Dalen, P. (1975). *Season of birth: A study of schizophrenia and other mental disorders.* Amsterdam: North-Holland Publishing.

Doane, J. A., and Lewis, J. M. (1984). Measurement strategies in family interaction research: A profile approach. In Watt et al., op. cit. (pp. 93–101).

Eaton, W. W. (1981). Demographic and social-ecologic risk factors for mental disorders. In D. A. Regier and G. Allen (Eds.), *Risk factor research in the major mental disorders* (pp. 111–129). Department of Health and Human Services Publication No. (ADM) 81-1068. Washington, D.C.: U.S. Government Printing Office.

Erlenmeyer-Kimling, L., Marcuse, Y., Cornblatt, B., Friedman, D., Rainer, J. D., and Rutschmann, J. (1984a). The New York High-Risk Project. In Watt et al., op. cit. (pp. 169–189).

Erlenmeyer-Kimling, L., Kestenbaum, C., Bird, H., and Hilldoff, U. (1984b). Assessment of the New York High-Risk Project subjects in Sample A who are now clinically deviant. In Watt et al., op. cit. (pp. 227–239).

Fish, B. (1984). Characteristics and sequelae of the neurointegrative disorder in infants at risk for schizophrenia. In Watt et al., op. cit. (pp. 423–439).

Fisher, L., Schwartzman, P., Harder, D., and Kokes, R. F. (1984). A strategy and methodology for assessing school competence in high-risk children. In Watt et al., op. cit. (pp. 355–359).

Fryer, J. H. (1974). Childhood social competence, behavior style, and adult mental disorder. Unpublished Ph.D. dissertation, Harvard University.

Garmezy, N. (1970). Process and reactive schizophrenia: Some conceptions and issues. *Schizophrenia Bulletin, 2,* 30–74.

Garmezy, N. (1974). The study of competence in children at risk for severe psychopathology. In E. J. Anthony and C. Koupernik (Eds.), *The child in his family: Children at psychiatric risk* (pp. 77–97). New York: Wiley.

Garmezy, N., and Devine, V. (1984). Project competence: The Minnesota studies of children vulnerable to psychopathology. In Watt et al., op. cit. pp. 289–303.

Gottesman, I. I., and Shields, J. (1982). *Schizophrenia: The epigenetic puzzle.* New York: Cambridge University Press.

Hirschfeld, R. M. A., and Cross, C. K. (1981). Psychosocial risk factors for depression. In D. A. Regier and G. Allen (Eds.), *Risk factor research in the major mental disorders* (pp. 55–67). Washington, D.C.: U.S. Government Printing Office.

Janes, C. L., Worland, J., Weeks, D. G., and Konen, P. M. (1984). Interrelationships among possible predictors of schizophrenia. In Watt et al., op. cit. (pp. 160–166).

Kety, S. S. (1978). Heredity and environment. In J. C. Shershow (Ed.), *Schizophrenia: Science and practice* (pp. 47–68). Cambridge, Mass.: Harvard University Press.

Kety, S. S., and Kinney, D. K. (1981). Biological risk factors in schizophrenia. In D. A. Regier and G. Allen (Eds.), *Risk factor research in the major mental disorders* (pp. 41–54). Washington, D.C.: U.S. Government Printing Office.

Klerman, G. L. (1978). Affective disorders. In A. M. Nicholi, Jr. (Ed.), *The Harvard guide to modern psychiatry* (pp. 253–281). Cambridge, Mass.: Harvard University Press.

Lewine, R. R. J. (1984). Stalking the schizophrenia marker: Evidence for a general vulnerability model of psychopathology. In Watt et al., op. cit. (pp. 545–550).

Lewine, R. R. J., Watt, N. F., and Grubb, T. W. (1984). High-risk-for-schizophrenia research: Sampling bias and its implications. In Watt et al., op. cit. (pp. 557–564).

McCabe, M. S., Fowler, R. C., Cadoret, R. J., and Winokur, G. (1971). Familial differences in schizophrenia with good and poor prognosis. *Psychological Medicine, 1,* 326–332.

McNeil, T. F., and Kaij, L. (1984). Offspring of women with non-organic psychoses. In Watt et al., op. cit. (pp. 465–481).

Marcus, J., Auerbach, J., Wilkinson, L., and Burack, C. M. (1984). Infants at risk for schizophrenia: The Jerusalem Infant Development Study. In Watt et al., op. cit. (pp. 440–464).

Mednick, S. A., Cudeck, R., Griffith, J. J., Talovic, S. A., and Schulsinger, F. (1984a). The Danish High-Risk Project: Recent methods and findings. In Watt et al., op. cit. (pp. 21–42).

Mednick, S. A., Venables, P. H., Schulsinger, F., Dalais, C., and Van Dusen, K. (1984b). A controlled study of primary prevention: The Mauritius Project. In Watt et al., op. cit. (pp. 71–78).

Neale, J. M., Winters, K. C., and Weintraub, S. (1984). Information processing deficits in children at high risk for schizophrenia. In Watt et al., op. cit. (pp. 264–278).

Phillips, L. (1968). *Human adaptation and its failures.* New York: Academic Press.

Regier, D. A., and Allen, G. (Eds.). (1981). *Risk factor research in the major mental disorders.* Department of Health and Human Services Publication No. (ADM) 81-1068. Washington, D.C.: U.S. Government Printing Office.

Rodnick, E. H., Goldstein, M. J., Lewis, J. M., and Doane, J. A. (1984). Parental communication style, affect, and role as precursors of offspring schizophrenia-spectrum disorders. In Watt et al., op. cit. (pp. 81–92).

Rolf, J. E. (1972). The social and academic competence of children vulnerable to schizophrenia and other behavior pathologies. *Journal of Abnormal Psychology, 80,* 225–243.

Rolf, J. E., Crowther, J., Teri, L., and Bond, L. (1984). Contrasting developmental risks in preschool children of psychiatrically hospitalized parents. In Watt et al., op. cit. (pp. 526–534).

Sameroff, A. J., Barocas, R., and Seifer, R. (1984). The early development of children born to mentally ill women. In Watt et al., op. cit. (pp. 482–514).

Schoenfeld, E. (1974). Descriptive and behavioral childhood antecedents of psychosis. Unpublished master's thesis. University of Massachusetts.

Spitzer, R. L., Endicott, J., and Robins, E. (1978). *Research diagnostic criteria.*

New York: Biometrics Research, Evaluation Section, New York State Psychiatric Institute.

Steffy, R. A., Asarnow, R. F., Asarnow, J. R., MacCrimmon, D. J., and Cleghorn, J. H. (1984). The McMaster-Waterloo High-Risk Project: Multi-faceted strategy for high-risk research. In Watt et al., op. cit. (pp. 401–413).

Strauss, J. (1975). A comprehensive approach to psychiatric diagnosis. *American Journal of Psychiatry, 132,* 1193–1197.

Strauss, J., and Carpenter, W. T. (1974). The prediction of outcome in schizophrenia, II: Relationships between predictor and outcome variables. A report from the WHO International Pilot Study of Schizophrenia. *Archives of General Psychiatry, 31,* 37–41.

Strauss, J., Carpenter, W. T., and Bartko, J. J. (1974). Schizophrenic signs and symptoms. *Schizophrenia Bulletin, 2,* 61–69.

Vaillant, G. E. (1962). The prediction of recovery in schizophrenia. *Journal of Nervous and Mental Disease, 135,* 534–543.

Watt, N. F., Anthony, E. J., Wynne, L. C., and Rolf, J. E. (Eds.). (1984). *Children at risk for schizophrenia: A longitudinal perspective.* New York: Cambridge University Press.

Watt, N. F., Fryer, J. H., Lewine, R. R. J., and Prentky, R. A. (1979). Toward longitudinal conceptions of psychiatric disorder. In B. A. Maher (Ed.), *Progress in experimental personality research,* Vol. 9. New York: Academic Press (pp. 199–283).

Watt, N. F., Grubb, T. W., and Erlenmeyer-Kimling, L. (1982). Social, emotional, and intellectual behavior at school among children at high risk for schizophrenia. *Journal of Consulting and Clinical Psychology, 50,* 171–181.

Weintraub, S., and Neale, J. M. (1984a). The Stony Brook High-Risk Project. In Watt et al., op. cit. (pp. 243–263).

Weintraub, S., and Neale, J. M. (1984b). Social behavior of children at risk for schizophrenia. In Watt et al., op. cit. (pp. 279–285).

Wender, P. H., Rosenthal, D., Kety, S. S., Schulsinger, F., and Welner, J. (1974). Cross-fostering: A research strategy for clarifying the role of genetic and experiential factors in the etiology of schizophrenia. *Archives of General Psychiatry, 30,* 121–128.

Wing, J., Cooper, J., and Sartorius, N. (1975). *The measurement and classification of psychiatric symptoms.* Cambridge, England: Cambridge University Press.

Wittman, P. (1948). Diagnostic and prognostic significance of the shut-in personality type as a prodromal factor in schizophrenia. *Journal of Clinical Psychology, 4,* 211–214.

Woerner, M., Pollack, M., Rogalski, C., Pollack, Y., and Klein, D. (1972). A comparison of the school records of personality disorders, schizophrenics, and their sibs. In M. Roff, L. Robins, and M. Pollack (Eds.), *Life history research in psychopathology,* Vol. 2. Minneapolis: University of Minnesota Press (pp. 47–65).

Worland, J., Janes, C. L., Anthony, E. J., McGinnis, M., and Cass, L. (1984a). St. Louis Risk Research Project: Comprehensive progress report of experimental studies. In Watt et al., op. cit. (pp. 105–147).

Worland, J., Edenhart-Pepe, R., Weeks, D. G., and Konen, P. M. (1984b). Cognitive evaluation of children at risk: IQ, differentation, and egocentricity. In Watt et al., op. cit. (pp. 148–159).

Wrede, G., Mednick, S. A., Huttunen, M. O, and Nilsson, C. G. (1984). Pregnancy and delivery complications in the births of an unselecteed series of Finnish children with schizophrenic mothers. In Watt et al., op. cit. (pp. 515–525).

Wynne, L. C. (1984). The University of Rochester Child and Family Study: Overview of research plan. In Watt et al., op. cit. (pp. 335–347).

Zubin, J., and Spring, B. (1978). Vulnerability—A new view of schizophrenia. *Journal of Abnormal Psychology, 86,* 103–126.

Developmental Epidemiology

A Basis for Prevention

Sheppard G. Kellam and Lisa Werthamer-Larsson

Introduction

Effective primary prevention in mental health may be feasible by intervening in the developmental paths leading to specific outcomes (Kellam, Ensminger, and Turner, 1977). This approach implies that a preventive strategy will be more effective if the developmental path can be specified well in terms of external and internal environmental characteristics and the features of their interaction. This requires that we identify groups of children vulnerable to later mental health problems by identifying specific problem antecedents and determining the functions of these antecedents along the adverse developmental path or paths leading to the problem. Research in the last decade provides a fairly strong empirical basis for optimism and points to important prevention research trials that can rest on well-developed theory. In this chapter we will explore the empirical basis, theoretical premises, and other necessary parameters of such prevention research.

Developmental epidemiology, which integrates community epidemiologic and life-span developmental orientations, is well-suited as a key component in the theoretical foundation for such prevention research. It has considerable utility for identifying, in defined populations, early antecedents of later mental health problems, which are the potential targets for specific preventive interventions. We will therefore use a developmental epidemiological perspective to discuss selected childhood antecedents of later mental health problems; theoretically and empirically based preventive interventions already attempted by others and ourselves; and the basic structure and new trials now under way at The Johns Hopkins Prevention Research Center in the School of Hygiene, Department of Mental Hygiene.

Developmental Epidemiology: An Integration of Community Epidemiologic and Life-span Developmental Orientations

Demographic epidemiology comprises the accurate measurement of incidence and prevalence rates of illness or disorder in large populations that are defined by criteria such as region, ethnicity, or national identity. It also includes the study of conditions or groups across which rates will vary, thereby suggesting where to look more closely for causes.

Serving complementary but more analytic functions, community epidemiology holds the macrocharacteristics of a smaller but more closely definable community population constant and examines variation in conditions and rates within the population, thus searching for causes at a more specific level. Variation in the characteristics of families, classrooms, peer groups, work places, and other environments that may enhance or inhibit mental health are emphasized. The distribution of illness, disorders, or behaviors of interest is examined within small social fields such as the communities' various types of families or classrooms. Community epidemiology thus involves research in particular types of communities that must then be replicated in similar and dissimilar communities (Kellam et al., 1975). It allows microanalysis of the causes of health or disorder, thus providing a foundation for preventive trials based on causal models. Such trials allow tests of the function of the antecedent targeted by the preventive trial. If we shift the antecedent, we can then determine whether we have shifted the outcome.

This strategy, however, requires repeated epidemiological measures of the same cohort to determine both the baseline and outcomes. A life-span developmental orientation is necessary to complement community epidemiology by focusing on the developmental paths that lead to disease or disorder or adaptive or maladaptive behavioral outcomes. Three perspectives comprise such an orientation: (1) the contribution of normative socialization and development to the individual's behavior; (2) normative cohort effects including the influence of evolving societal values and patterns of behavior on the behavior of individuals (for example, the current greater acceptance of drug use); and, (3) idiosyncratic non-normative events that influence an individual's behavior, such as loss of a loved one or being in a poor work situation by chance (Baltes, Reese, and Lipsitt, 1980).

Developmental epidemiology is therefore derived from both community epidemiological and life-span developmental orientations. It involves longitudinal epidemiologic study of the developmental paths leading to the distributions of adaptive or maladaptive behavior or of psychologically well or disordered individuals in the social fields of the community. It employs causal modeling to hypothesize and test the antecedents and evolution of these paths. Such modeling permits the definition of potential targets for early prevention trials. Causal modeling may specify both the locus and the nature of possible preventive interventions. These interventions can be directed either at the subgroups of high-risk individuals, at social and physical environmental risk conditions, or at the interaction between individuals and their immediate environment.

Preventive interventions have been differentiated by Gordon (1983) into universal, selected, and indicated interventions. Universal interventions are not specific as to populations at risk. Much of the effort to reduce cigarette and substance use are of this type. Selected interventions are directed at epidemiologically defined high-risk subgroups. Indicated interventions are directed at individuals and are actually treatments focused on prodromal symptomatology.

Developmental epidemiology is especially suited for selected or indicated preventive interventions that are directed at specifically identified subgroups of children who are vulnerable to later mental health problems. By specifying risk factors, we can specify targets for preventive trials, and the intervention itself can be better specified so as to address the defined antecedent. In summary, integration of community epidemiologic and life-span developmental orientations may be used to identify childhood antecedents of later mental health problems. These antecedents identify epidemiologically defined high-risk groups and point to specific loci and specific kinds of preventive interventions.

Selected Childhood Antecedents of Later Mental Health Problems and Related Preventive Interventions

During the last ten years, research on the identification of childhood antecedents of later mental health problems has followed three major strategies. One involves retrospectively following populations of adolescents and adults and comparing histories of cases to noncases. The second involves prospectively following populations of children into adolescence and adulthood. The third involves prospectively following populations at high risk, such as children in families with an ill member. The last strategy has been used where incidence and prevalence are low in order to enhance the number of cases (see, for example, Mednick and McNeil, 1968). The last two strategies avoid the bias of retrospective studies, especially with respect to representativeness of the sample.

The antecedents of later mental health problems found thus far may be classified into four domains: (1) characteristics of social fields; (2) characteristics of the social task demands and behavioral responses in specific social fields (we have named this process *social adaptation*); (3) psychological status; and (4) biological variables. We will discuss specific antecedents and preventive interventions in each of these domains.

The review is drawn from an annotated bibliography on the prevention of child and adolescent mental health problems by Werthamer-Larsson (1985). It includes prospective and retrospective high-risk studies and focuses particularly on the childhood antecedents and related school-based interventions that are within the theoretical framework guiding The Johns Hopkins University Prevention Research Center.

Social Field Characteristics as Antecedents

At each stage in life, individuals are involved in specific social fields such as the family, the school, the peer group, and the workplace (Kellam et al., 1975). In any one field, social task demands are defined and the adequacy of performance in that field is judged by natural raters, such as parents in the home, teachers at school, significant peers in the peer group, spouse in the marriage, and supervisors at work. Fairly prototypical stages of life, social fields, and natural raters throughout the life course are shown in Fig. 1. The changes in size of each bar signify the ebb and flow of importance of each social field at each stage of life. The social fields important to the child are first the family, then the school, and soon the peer group.

Childhood social field risk factors, for example, are certain family settings such as mothers who alone are raising their children. Another closely related factor is level of family income. Federal income programs have been directed at the latter and should be classified as major prevention programs, even if poorly designed. Great opportunity exists for further specifying such programs so that they have a better chance for success. Rather than merely mailing a mother welfare money at her home, she could receive the income as a salary at school for a real job with far less stigma. Her job might include helping a teacher, home visits to other mothers, or increasing her own skills with groups of mothers for handling problems such as coping with difficult child behavior.

The school itself has been reported to have antecedent characteristics predictive of long-term outcome (Rutter, 1978). The validity of such findings and of postulated mechanisms of how risk conditions operate continues to warrant study. Interventions in curriculum and classroom organization are proceeding and fairly recent research gives reason to be

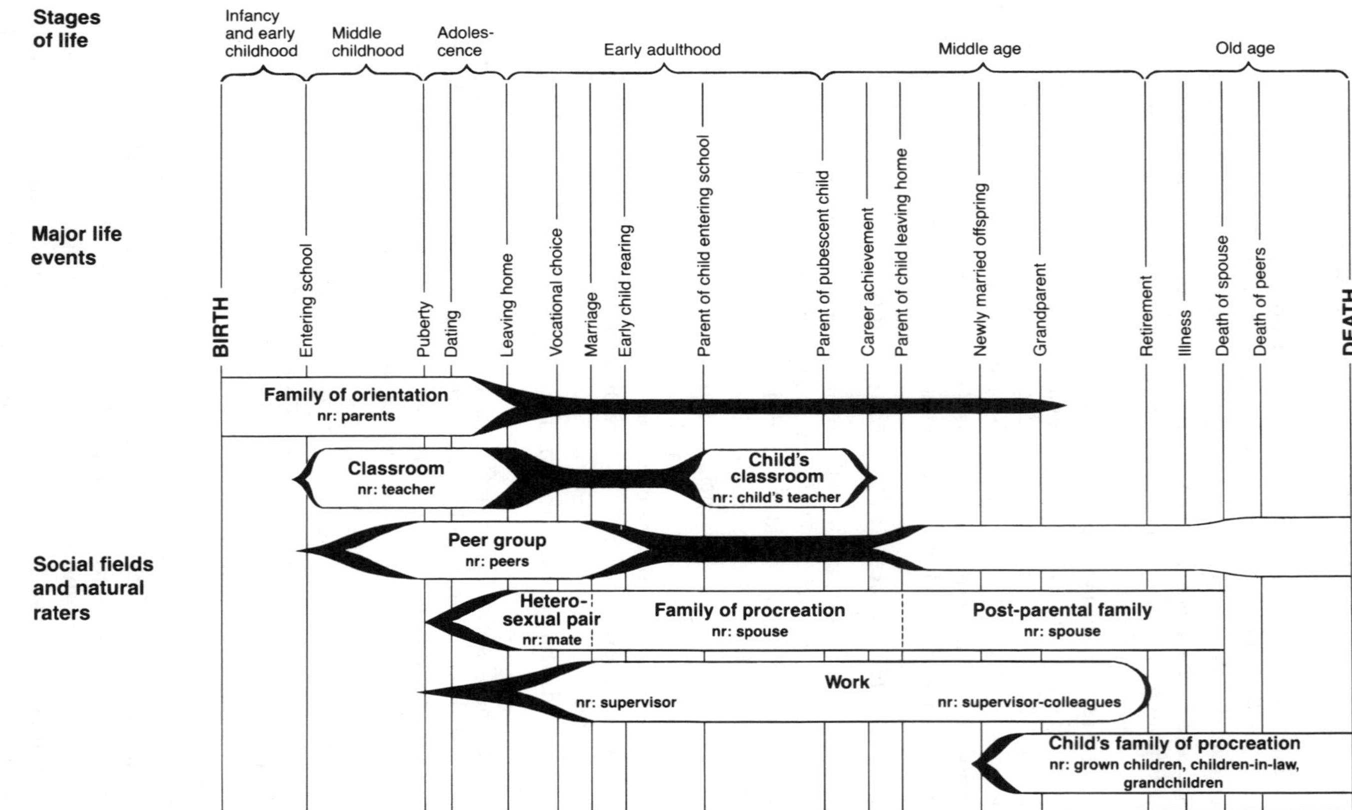

Figure 1. Life course–social field concept.

optimistic (Abt Associates, 1976, 1977; Harris and Sherman, 1973; Block and Burns, 1977).

Single-parent families have been related to a child's later psychological status (Lynn, 1974) and cognitive performance (Trotter, 1976). However, the relationship between a child's family composition and the child's later mental health problems has usually been studied using a dichotomous independent variable such as intact versus nonintact or father absent versus present (Herzog and Sudia, 1973). Such contrasts do not take into account the variety of family types that may result from illegitimacy or divorce.

The variation in types of family has been studied extensively in Woodlawn (a poor Chicago community) by Kellam, Ensminger, and Turner (1977), who developed a family taxonomy through community epidemiological methods that defines the family types raising children in a community by specifying the adult combinations in the home. Using this method, 86 different combinations of adults were found to be raising the total cohort of roughly 1400 first-grade children in one school year, with very similar results in another cohort. Ten major family types were classified, e.g., mother alone, mother/father, mother/grandmother, mother/aunt. Mother alone and mother/stepfather families had the highest risk of psychological and behavioral problems for the child, while mother/father and mother/grandmother families had the lowest risk. Mother/aunt families were almost as effective as mother/grandmother and mother/father families in minimizing risk to the child. We concluded that the absence of a father was not as critical as the aloneness of the mother. Mother and certain second adults appeared to be comparably effective to mother/father families.

Investigation of the effects of family variables such as these on the child's later mental health is a crucial issue in the design of preventive trials. Family variables that are probably explanatory are age at parental loss, parental mental disorder and resulting distortion of role, marital discord, affection, rule setting and enforcing, and values regarding education and social role and control. An example of the importance of investigating family risk variables was the Cambridge–Somerville project, which related the single-parent family to subsequent delinquency (Glueck and Glueck, 1950). Later analyses by McCord, McCord, and Thurber (1962) showed that family conflict and parental criminal behavior mediated the prediction of delinquency, thus partially explaining the earlier result and pointing to potential targets for prevention. Family conflict is at least conceivably amenable to change.

The timing and longevity of family effects is another issue in the investigation of the family and the child's later mental health. Wallerstein's

10-year follow-up of 131 children who were 2.5–6 years of age when their parents divorced indicated that the youngest children at that time had better mental health outcomes than the older children (Wallerstein, 1984). This is an elaboration of Wallerstein and Kelly's (1975, 1980) earlier, less age-specific inferences, which showed that preschool children in general were severely distressed by family crises. Again, further specification resulted in identification of high-risk children for prevention trials.

Low family SES has been associated with later mental health problems, including cognitive performance. The Berkeley Guidance Study—designed to investigate general personality development—assessed children from infancy to age 18 with a focus on the preschool years. Family SES and the child's performance on intelligence tests were directly related, at least until age 18 (Honzik, 1967).

Guidubaldi et al. (1983) distinguished social from academic competence in 699 children from divorced and intact families and found that children of intact families performed better socially than children of divorced families. Guidubaldi and Perry's (1984) later study concluded that although social class was associated with both intellectual and social measures, family intactness was associated only with social competencies. The differentiation of the dependent variable into social behavior and academic performance, if it is replicable, further points to different potential subgroups for different preventive trials.

Social Adaptational Status Antecedents

Considerable opportunity for preventive trials lies in the social task demands and the adequacy of the individual's behavioral responses in specific social fields. In fact, much of the recent research on prediction of outcomes at later stages of life has been in this area (Kellam, Brown, and Fleming, 1983; Kellam, Simon, and Ensminger, 1983; Kellam et al., 1983; Ensminger, Kellam, and Rubin, 1983). The concept of social adaptational process postulates that an individual is involved in specific social fields at each stage of his or her life. Natural raters within each social field define the social tasks to be performed and assess an individual's adequacy of performance. We have named the individual's behavioral responses to social task demands *social adaptation*. *Social adaptational status* (SAS) is the rating or grade given by the natural rater to the individual's adequacy of performance in a particular social field at a particular stage of life (Kellam et al., 1975; Kellam and Ensminger, 1980). Chance, idiosyncracy, and the fit of the individual with the natural rater and others in the social field all play a role in the SAS of the individual. We consider social adaptation and SAS to be the basic interface between individuals and their environments, representing the integration of biological, social, and psychological processes.

Examples of childhood antecedents in this domain include poor school achievement, shyness (i.e., sitting alone, not participating), and what we have called aggressive behavior (i.e., fighting, truancy, breaking rules). Many school-based preventive interventions have been tried, and we will discuss examples of them for each of these antecedents.

Poor School Achievement

Early learning problems are highly predictive of later psychiatric symptoms. Kellam and colleagues (Kellam, Simon, and Ensminger, 1983; Kellam et al., 1983) periodically assessed four total cohorts of first-grade schoolchildren in an urban poor community. They assessed these children again in third grade and then reassessed one cohort during adolescence ten years later. Early learning problems predicted adolescent depression and other symptoms of distress. Whether measured by teacher ratings, readiness-for-school test scores, or IQ, the results showed markedly increased risk of psychiatric symptoms later in life. Robins (1966) compared adults who had been child-guidance clinic patients to adults who had no such history and found that early learning problems predicted depression in men and paranoid feelings in women.

School-based interventions directed at learning problems include *Mastery Learning, DISTAR, Class Teams, Positive Behavior Reinforcement,* and *Family Problem-Solving*. Mastery Learning is a group-based approach in which students learn cooperatively with their classmates (Bloom, 1964). It is based on the assumption that virtually all students can master the material taught if given sufficient time and instruction. Block and Burns (1977) reviewed Mastery Learning research and found that it more or less consistently demonstrated a positive effect in greater student achievement and in higher order learning, both in terms of abstraction and problem solving.

DISTAR is an intervention directed at the school performance decrement associated with low family SES. It is a direct instructional program using a highly structured curriculum and teaching methods based on behavioral principles (Englemann and Carnine, 1982). In a national evaluation (Project Follow Through), DISTAR showed consistent positive effects on measures of basic skills, cognitive achievement, and psychological well-being (Abt Associates, 1976, 1977).

DISTAR is an application of a carefully drawn theory of instruction for small groups of students. Material is presented at a rapid pace through a well-designed sequence of curriculum, with the content and mode of instruction specified in advance. Follow-up of students participating in programs using this method at four evaluation sites indicated that after one year of intervention, children who had been expected to perform at the 20th percentile level in reading performed instead at the 43rd, 66th, 39th, and 52nd percentile levels at the different sites (Becker and Gersten, 1982).

Another preventive intervention aimed at learning consists of the formation of heterogeneous classroom teams that compete against each other in academic contests. Team members help to score worksheets and formative tests and provide coaching for other members of the team who are working at a lower level. These strategies have been subjected to empirical evaluation (summarized by Slavin, 1983) and have been shown to increase academic performance, liking for school, and cross-race and cross-sex friendships. However, their effect on psychological well-being needs further study.

Many school-based learning interventions use positive behavior reinforcement. Lysakowski and Walberg (1981) examined 89 studies involving 4842 students in 202 classes and concluded that significant improvements in school performance are achieved through the use of positive rewards. These effects appear from kindergarten through college and across socioeconomic levels, race, private and public schools, and types of community. Tangible reinforcers were associated with slightly larger efforts than were intangible ones.

Another preventive intervention focused on school and family articulation. Blechman, Taylor, and Schrader (1981) randomly assigned 335 elementary-school children who had been identified by the unevenness of their math-class work to a home-note, Family Problem-Solving, or untreated control condition. In the home-note intervention, families received notes on their child's math and were asked to reward the child for a "good news" note (achievement of 80 percent or more). In the Family Problem-Solving intervention, families additionally wrote a contingency contract with their child concerning rewards for a "good news" note and were instructed each week by phone to provide the reward regularly. Both forms of intervention significantly reduced inconsistency in class work compared to the control condition. However, only the children in the Family Problem-Solving intervention maintained their performance as the difficulty of the work increased. This study highlights the involvement of the family with the school for improved classroom performance of students.

Aggressiveness

Although learning problems appeared to predict substance use in many studies (Jessor and Jessor, 1978; Kandel, Kessler, and Margulies, 1978; Smith and Fogg, 1978), this may in fact reflect an association between early learning problems and early aggression. We studied models in the Woodlawn analyses that included both learning problems and aggression, measured separately. The results indicated that learning problems in first grade predicted psychiatric symptoms, while aggression in first grade predicted delinquency and heavy substance use later (Kellam et al., 1983; Kellam, Simon, and Ensminger, 1983; Ensminger, Kellam, and Rubin, 1983).

Disobedience, poor conduct, fighting, and truancy predict many later problems. Robins et al. (1966, 1967, 1977, 1978) showed that early antisocial behavior strongly predicted drug and alcohol abuse, schizophrenia for men, and sociopathic personality for both sexes. Lefkowitz and colleagues (1977) found in a country population of third graders and their parents that early aggression predicted adult antisocial behavior.

Kellam and colleagues found that aggressiveness as early as first grade strongly predicted adolescent substance use and delinquency 10 years later, but only for boys (Kellam, Ensminger, and Simon, 1980; Ensminger, Brown, and Kellam, 1982; Kellam et al., 1983; Kellam, Brown, and Fleming, 1983). Ensminger, Kellam, and Rubin (1983) found early social adaptational and family antecedents interacting with each other to predict teenage delinquency. The prediction was much stronger in lower risk families, where fewer aggressive children were found, but those few had a higher risk of later delinquency. Children from high-risk families were more frequently aggressive first graders, but were not much different in risk than children who were not aggressive. The difference appeared to stem from the strength of social control exerted by the two kinds of families.

As mentioned before, when we included learning problems in the analyses of childhood aggression and later mental health problems, learning problems predicted later symptoms of distress, and aggressiveness in boys predicted delinquency and heavy substance use but did not predict psychiatric symptoms (Kellam, Ensminger, and Simon, 1980; Kellam et al., 1983). The combination of shyness with aggression (loners who are also disobedient) is even more highly predictive of later heavy drug use and antisocial behavior (Ledingham, 1981; Kellam et al, 1983).

School-based interventions directed at early aggression include the *Good Behavior Game, Interpersonal Cognitive Problem-Solving,* and *Empathy Training*. The Good Behavior Game (Barrish, Saunders, and Wolf, 1969) is an example of classroom management through contingency manipulations. The researchers divided a fourth-grade classroom into two teams, then clearly defined rules, targeted behaviors, and group consequences in order to reduce "talking out" and "out of seat" behaviors in the class.

The Good Behavior Game reduced such target behaviors in several small studies. Medland and Stachnik (1972) describe its implementation in a fifth-grade reading class. The game reduced the frequency of target behaviors by more than 95 percent in both groups. Harris and Sherman (1973) introduced the Good Behavior Game in a sixth-grade class and, again, it markedly reduced disruptive behavior. Further, the removal of certain rewards adversely affected such reduction. Importantly, the investigators found no consistent relationship between academic performance and the reduction in disruptive behavior.

Interpersonal Cognitive Problem-Solving was designed originally for children in a Head Start program who had behavior problems (Shure, Spivack, and Gordon, 1972). The test group received instruction in alternative ways of responding to interpersonal problems, while the comparison group received either no instruction or were instructed in activities to stimulate adult–child interaction. Those who received the experimental intervention improved most in problem solving and also improved significantly in classroom behavior.

Another school-based intervention for aggression is Empathy Training, a psychoeducational program to train aggressive children in empathic skills (Feshbach, 1984). Training procedures and curricula were developed to foster personal growth and enhance development of positive social behavior. Empathy training was directed at the capacity to discriminate the emotional state of another child, to react with empathy toward others' joy or anger, and to identify the level of the child's own effectiveness. Results indicated that the intervention decreased aggressiveness.

Shyness

Shyness in boys appears to predict psychiatric symptoms, especially anxiety (Kellam et al., 1983) and also seems to predict inhibition of adolescent delinquency and heavy substance use (Smith and Fogg, 1978; Kellam, Ensminger, and Simon, 1980; Kellam et al., 1983). The meaning of *shyness* varies across studies. In our earlier work in Woodlawn we meant the child's actual lack of participation with teacher and classmates (not raising hand, sitting alone, not speaking up when called on by teacher). Other studies have considered shyness from an affective perspective, e.g., fear of social participation.

Gottman (1977) makes still another distinction: that low frequency of peer interaction and low peer acceptance are not equivalent concepts. Using behavioral and sociometric data, he found no relationship between frequency of peer interaction and peer acceptance.

Kohlberg, Ricks, and Snarey (1984), in a broad review of the behavioral, cognitive, and emotional antecedents of adult adaptation, note the distinction between actual social isolation and shyness, which they prefer to restrict to psychological discomfort or passivity about initiating social interaction. They present evidence, including ours from Woodlawn, that actual social isolation is the real predictor of later mental health problems. In the Woodlawn studies social isolation might have been a better choice of terms than shyness, but we meant the social *behavior* of isolation rather than a feeling.

A school-based preventive intervention directed at shyness is Peer Socialization, with mixed-age and same-age peers. Furman, Rahe, and Hartup (1979) observed preschool children who were enrolled in day-care centers and identified those who were socially isolated. They were assigned either to groups socializing with another child during ten play sessions or to no group. Assignment to a group increased the sociability of the child.

Psychological Well-Being Antecedents

Many investigators report that early symptoms predict later psychiatric symptoms and disorders. However, these relationships are not always strong and sex differences may be important (Kellam et al., 1983). Feelings of depression predict schizophrenia for men (Robins, 1966; Watt, 1974). Anxiety, worrying, and specific fears seem to predict a number of later outcomes, including adult anxiety in both sexes (Pritchard and Graham, 1966), schizophrenia among men (Robins, 1966; Fleming and Ricks, 1969), and anxiety and depression in women (Kellam, Simon, and Ensminger, 1983). The combination of anxiety and poor achievement is also related to later psychiatric problems (Cowen, 1973). Early psychological distress also has been found to predict substance use (Smith and Fogg, 1978; Paton, Kessler, and Kandel, 1977; Kaplan, 1975), but whether this is due to the presence of early aggression remains unclear. Our work in Woodlawn suggests this to be the case (Kellam et al., 1983).

It is important to note sex differences in predicting later outcomes from early psychological symptoms. When boys and girls were analyzed separately, early symptoms did not predict outcome in men in the Woodlawn analyses. However, there was a powerful effect for women, whose psychological symptoms at age 6 or 7 were associated with adolescent anxiety and depression and weakly associated with inhibition of substance use (Kellam, Simon, and Ensminger, 1983; Kellam et al., 1983).

A potentially intriguing set of variables in the relationship of early psychological symptoms and later mental health problems is child attributions concerning academic and social success or failure. This variable may explain the sex difference in the predictive effect of early psychological symptoms. Among children of equivalent ability, girls are more likely to attribute failure on cognitive tasks to lack of ability than are boys (Dweck and Bush, 1976). Those who attribute failure to a presumed ability deficit are more likely to give up and feel hopeless than those who attribute failure to lack of motivation (Diener and Dweck, 1980).

The Multi-Session Tandem Program, a school-based intervention developed by Cary and Reveal (1967), consisted of children and mothers who received group-based services to promote the child's healthy ego development, improve the mother's knowledge of childhood emotional growth, and provide therapeutic intervention for those children in need. Program results included improvement in children, improvement in mothers' insights, and detection of children in need of further help.

Group Anticipatory Guidance, another school-based intervention, was directed at parents of children eligible for entry into kindergarten (Signell, 1972). Group discussions of projected fears, loss, and anxiety were held repeatedly, the first being held ten days before the kindergarten began and continuing regularly thereafter. Parents who participated became more aware of how to respond to crises and childhood anxiety.

Biological Antecedents

While genetics has been a major focus of interest in the last two decades, it is only one of a set of biological antecedents, none of which is totally independent of environment, which interact very strongly with the kinds of antecedents described in social field characteristics, social adaptational antecedents, and psychological antecedents. We will focus here not on genetic antecedents, which are reported extensively in the current literature, but rather on a wide variety of other biological antecedents that clearly are amenable to preventive trials and other research.

Antecedents in the Physical Environment

The biological parameters of interest include nutritional aspects related to psychological and physiological functioning of children in general and, of course, in regard to their learning and behavior in the classroom and their psychological well-being. The Women, Infants, and Children (WIC) Program is an effort to prevent the consequences of malnutrition in both the mother and the child during the prenatal period. Evaluations of the WIC Program have just begun to be reported and the results will be of considerable interest.

Pioneering studies of birth trauma were carried out by Pasamanick, Rogers, and Lilienfeld (1956). This early research was done at The Johns

Hopkins School of Hygiene and gave rise to great interest in obstetrical, prenatal, and postnatal biological influences on subsequent behavior.

Lead and carbon monoxide exposure in the form of air pollutants has been shown in recent years to have a marked influence on subsequent behavior and learning. The epidemiology of lead exposure has barely begun, however, following the important earlier work of Needleman and colleagues (1979). Likewise, work on many aspects of air pollution has barely begun, but, based on earlier knowledge regarding lead, it is probable that other pollutants will be shown to have important effects on the outcomes and interests of this review.

There are two important conclusions about biological factors. The first is that developmental epidemiology is fundamentally important to an understanding of the relative power of genetic and other biological factors. The second is that almost all biological factors, with the possible exception of genetics, lend themselves to rather clear and high probabilities for prevention. It is possible to hypothesize an important effect of a WIC program on malnutrition. Reduction of lead in gasoline has already been shown, at least tentatively, to affect lead levels. Birth trauma can be reasonably well controlled with an understanding of the results of improper prenatal care and of obstetrical procedures that have more rather than less risk of birth injury. Mechanical injury and hypoxia due to improper anesthetic and other invasive treatments can be avoided in many cases.

Prevention trials related to these targets will provide opportunities to test the function of early events and conditions on the outcomes of classroom behavior and psychological status. If we can reduce air pollution and decrease blood and intracellular lead levels, and such reduction improves behavior, we will have demonstrated a developmental relationship.

Infectious Diseases

The consequences of measles and other infectious diseases on brain development and consequent behavior, including learning and psychiatric symptoms, are well-known. We often accept without question that these potential antecedents of behavioral problems, as well as psychiatric symptoms, have been largely eliminated as a result of immunization. However, infectious diseases still require study in regard to behavioral and psychiatric consequences, and the whole issue of the immune response of children to classroom stress, particularly experiences of success and failure, has barely begun to be conceptualized, let alone investigated.

The problem of vaccines themselves is an important area of investigation because these agents are not without risk in regard to behavioral and psychiatric consequences. Developmental epidemiology coupled with a community epidemiology orientation is a potent way of studying these outcomes. Without following the same children periodically over a significant portion of their lives, we are forced to use data that do not fully explore the developmental significance of early trauma or exposure.

Even more important is the opportunity to study, through preventive trials, the reversibility of the effects of injuries, environmental exposures, or disease sequelae. By measuring biological antecedents such as prior lead exposure in children, we will be able to determine whether changes in learning, shyness and aggressiveness, and psychiatric symptoms are random across children or occur more or less with particular kinds of antecedents. The use of the preventive trial as a field experiment has value not only in terms of developing effective prevention programs, but has equal value in developing an understanding of the etiology of maladaptive behavior and psychiatric symptoms.

The conclusions regarding the preventability or reversibility of lead exposure or birth trauma are also warranted in regard to aspects of social field characteristics, social adaptational antecedents, and psychological characteristics. While poverty may not be any more amenable to change than genetic structure, infectious disease and almost all the other antecedents that we have discussed here are amenable to prevention trials and related research. The next issue is how to organize this prevention research so that it will include the necessary components.

In the following section of this chapter, we address issues relating to the structure of prevention research in its next stage. We also discuss the strategy we have chosen in beginning preventive trials directed at social maladaptive behaviors in the classroom.

Prevention Research Based on Developmental Epidemiology

As we have pointed out, specific antecedents early in life can be identified; their functions and paths leading to identified outcomes can be determined by preventive trials aimed at those antecedents. Longitudinal developmental epidemiology studies are the most promising approach because such studies are based on total, defined populations and constitute a major and promising advance over studies that examine only hospital or clinic populations.

The trials serve two basic and related purposes. First, they add to the empirical basis for theory construction by assessing the effect on the outcome of changing the antecedent. Second, they test the hypothesis that reducing the earlier risk factor reduces the risk of the outcome. If successful, both approaches result in increasingly effective prevention programs and identification of directions for further prevention research.

Entrance into first grade is a major transition in the life of the child and brings together children from the child-rearing families of the community served by the school. The social task demands on the child and the child's behavioral responses represent the interface between society and the biopsychosocial capacities and limitations of the child for successful social adaptation. We chose this site and stage of life for the first focus of The Johns Hopkins Prevention Research Center. By periodically measuring the behavioral and psychological responses of the child to classroom demands, we can conduct baseline studies of the effectiveness of specific preventive trials. Multivariate models that include social, psychological, and biological risk factors can guide the next stages of preventive trials.

Poor conduct and disobedience in school have been shown repeatedly to be antecedent to later delinquency and heavy substance use. If preventive trials reduce aggressive behavior in first-grade children and if the consequences of this early reduction include a reduction in later delinquency and substance use, then the preventive trial will have revealed that early classroom aggressive behavior has a functional role in the developmental path leading to delinquency. Similar reasoning regarding shyness and learning problems guide our planning. In addition, these trials will have provided information regarding the degree of change or reversal of specific antecedent risk factors that can be obtained under specific conditions of intervention and over a range of other variables in the child's background. Finally, preventive trials that change specific social task demands and/or specific behavioral responses and have a significant effect on developmental outcomes can be used to test explanatory models of development and socialization.

The central public-health role of preventive trials is their utility in providing a basis for large-scale prevention programs. They serve to establish the efficacy of interventions and thereby (1) permit the development and refinement of prevention efforts in the field setting; (2) allow systematic estimates of costs and benefits; and (3) make available research for policy setting in public health. There is considerable logic to concentrating prevention efforts in the early years of the life cycle for both theory-building and utilitarian reasons.

We will now illustrate these aspects of prevention research by reference to the structure and initial research program of the recently established Prevention Research Center at The Johns Hopkins School of Hygiene and Public Health.

Structure of the Prevention Research Center

The structure of the Center reflects its main focus on research, which is guided by the perspectives outlined in the preceding paragraphs. Two complementary preventive interventions in two total first-grade cohorts constitute the field trials in the first five years. These school-based trials will be complemented in incidence and prevalence studies of risk behaviors, symptoms, and disorders in order to obtain the baseline data for periodic outcome evaluations and related methodological research. These measures will be coupled with classroom monitoring of implementation of the interventions. Risk behaviors and conditions in the family will draw on our prior work and on data from the NIMH Epidemiological Catchment Areas studies that have been carried out by the Department of Mental Hygiene at Johns Hopkins University over the last eight years. The development of statistical methods for large, community-based prevention trials is an equally important aspect of the effort, as are the incorporation of health services research and operations research perspectives. The interdisciplinary orientation required by this approach is reflected in the work groups formed to meet program objectives:

- A *Steering Committee* sets policy, its membership includes research-work group leaders and leaders from the Baltimore City Public Schools.
- A *Data Center* provides a central resource for data storage and retrieval and for continued monitoring of the quality of new data and documentation as analyses proceed.
- An *Epidemiologic Assessment and Monitoring Group* develops instruments for the periodic measurement of early risk behaviors and symptoms, risk conditions, and later outcomes in the domains of psychopathology and well-being (PWB) and social adaptational status (SAS); and develops, tests, and supervises the use of classroom monitoring instruments and methods for measuring the implementation of preventive interventions.
- A *Data Analysis Group* will design, test, and refine statistical methods for prevention trial research and will conduct effectiveness analyses of prevention trials.
- An *Operations Research Group* will develop cost/benefit models and methods for integrating prevention programs of demonstrated efficacy into large institutions, such as the public schools.
- A *Health Services Research Group* will evaluate changes in patterns of service referral and treatment for children identified as having behav-

ioral, learning, or psychological problems, both prior to and after the classroom intervention.

• The *Community Sanction Group* is to develop the necessary theory and methods for and to carry out sanction development and maintenance.

Integration of the Prevention Center with the larger academic and public-agency communities is provided by a *Preceptee Program in Prevention Research,* which will offer interdepartmental and interinstitutional teaching programs and supervised field experience. Based at the Center and the Department of Mental Hygiene, the program's goal is to educate professionals and policy makers in mental health prevention research.

In view of the methodological and substantive importance of prevention trials, structured and integrated *dissemination of information* must receive special attention beyond the traditional publication of research papers and reports—and must involve not only researchers but also program designers and implementers, public officials and agency administrators, and community representatives. We recognize that prevention research and programming must involve the public to foster acceptance of intervention trials and to develop community support for implementing programs.

From the beginning, this effort has involved input from the community and particularly from those whose schools are in areas where the trials will take place. The rationale underlying the special emphasis on public sanction and support is that highly visible and intrusive programs in schools or community settings require careful attention to community values and aspirations. The Woodlawn experience (Kellam and Branch, 1971; Kellam et al., 1972) provided one successful model of community engagement and support for psychiatric, general health, and human-services programs in urban neighborhoods. Others need to be developed, and this area must become a core part of the curriculum for students of prevention research.

We have described in some detail the structure of the Center and its relationship to the community to emphasize the importance of an approach that not only integrates academic disciplines into prevention research on a large, developmental epidemiology basis but also draws on the support and sanction of the community that is the focus of its work.

The First Prevention Trials

The Mastery Learning Trial

The relationships among learning problems, shyness, aggressiveness, and psychiatric symptoms in first graders may well hinge on mastery of the basic learning tasks in the classroom. We postulate that experience of failing to master basic tasks leads to shyness (withdrawing or remaining aloof) or aggression (lashing out at the authorities that impose the tasks) or both. Psychiatric symptoms may also be a response to the experience of failure; their reduction consequent to mastery appears to be a particularly cogent hypothesis for girls. Psychiatric symptoms that result from failure to master learning could represent an internalizing response, as opposed to the social behavioral responses of boys.

The first trial is therefore directed at mastery of learning tasks, based on the hypothetical model that failure to learn leads to poor psychological well-being, shy behavior, and conduct problems. Hypotheses to be tested by this intervention trial are as follows:

- The direct-effect hypothesis states that improvement in mastery of basic learning tasks in first and second grade will ameliorate psychiatric symptoms and possibly the short-term risk of mental disorders in children and later in life. The relationship of learning problems to later outcomes is illustrated in Fig. (2).
- The indirect-effect hypothesis reflects the possible relationship of mastery of learning tasks to shyness and aggressiveness. It states that improved mastery of basic learning tasks will result in a reduction of aggressive behavior, shy behavior, and the combination of shyness and aggressiveness. This will, in turn, bring about reduced delinquency and substance use. In other words, by reducing the failure to learn we reduce not only the consequent psychiatric distress but also aggression and shy-

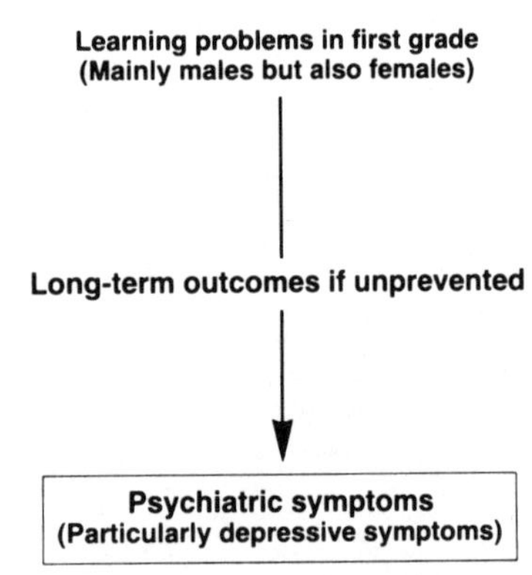

Figure 2. Empirical basis for a preventive trial with mastery learning.

ness and, in turn, the longer-term consequences of these risk behaviors as well.

The Good Behavior Game Trial

The second major trial complements the first and is based on a different model of the relationships among the risk behaviors. In this model, aggression and shyness are not responses to failure but are behavioral predispositions antecedent to the new classroom/school environment generally. The second trial therefore directly addresses the reduction of shyness and aggressiveness, using a behavior–analytic approach to classroom management. Hypotheses to be tested are as follows:

- The direct-effect hypothesis is that reduction of shyness will result in the reduction of later anxiety; that reduction of aggression and of the combination of shyness and aggression will result in reduced risk of later delinquency and substance use. This relationship is illustrated in Fig. 3.
- The indirect-effect hypothesis states that by reducing shyness and aggressiveness, learning will be improved, resulting in greater psychological well-being, which, in turn, will reduce later psychiatric symptoms and possibly mental disorders.

Epidemiologic Research on Behaviors, Symptoms, and Disorders

This research will provide a bridge between the ratings of socially maladaptive behavior and psychiatric symptoms, as measured by periodic assessments based on teacher ratings and observation of symptoms and psychiatric diagnoses. In particular, our aims are to estimate the preva-

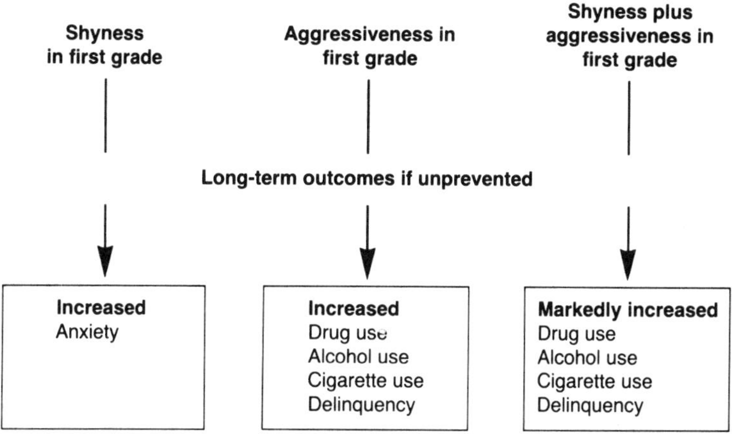

Figure 3. Empirical basis for a preventive trial with good behavior game.

lence of specific behavioral responses, symptoms, and disorders among first-grade children in eastern Baltimore. A related goal is to study the interrelationships among behavioral responses, symptoms, and disorders, thereby improving nosology. The research will be carried out as a two-phase mental morbidity survey, with probability sampling of the participating first-grade children. First-stage measurement will be by teacher ratings and classroom observations of risk behaviors and symptoms. Second-stage measurement will be a standardized psychiatric diagnosis in terms of DSM-III criteria.

The sample for the two-phase survey will consist of a subsample of the children in the classrooms who are assigned to intervention and control groups in the Mastery Learning and the Good Behavior Game preventive trials. A probability sampling plan, with strata based on teacher ratings, will be used to draw a sample for the second-phase psychiatric inquiry.

The Family Project

A retrospective case-control study of the effect of parental mental disorder and family composition on child social adaptational process and status in the first-grade classroom will complement these studies. While the two prevention trials will modify curriculum and classroom behavior management, it is highly probable that the targeted risk behaviors have family determinants that are also amenable to preventive trials. Parental mental status interacting with family composition represents a probable risk to the child and is the focus of this part of the study. Data will be used from the Johns Hopkins Epidemiological Catchment Area Project (one of the five NIMH/ECA sites).

This linkage of ECA and preventive intervention trial data will be the foundation for a field trial of family-based interventions directed at parental mental disorders in order to reduce the incidence and duration of offspring social maladaptive behaviors and their later sequelae. Other family intervention trials are planned, with the protocols of Blechman, Taylor, and Schrader (1981) and Patterson, Chamberlain, and Reid (1982) being considered. Both protocols have a strong evaluation history and are directed at high-risk aggressive behavior in children. The results of the Good Behavior Game and Mastery Learning, along with the results of related research, will provide a basis for sample selection and integration of these protocols into the overall preventive intervention program.

Research on New Statistical Methods for Prevention Trials

Prevention research faces numerous methodologic problems. Many arise from constraints that render efficient designs logistically, ethically, or financially unsuitable. For example, it is not always possible to randomize assignment to treatment. Typically, even the best prevention trials cannot achieve control or balance with respect to all potentially confounding variables. Interventions themselves often change the social structure of institutions and networks, and these changes can make treatment comparisons difficult. Our objectives are to develop new methods for making valid statistical inferences in preventive trial research in order to obtain as much scientific information as possible. This involves developing new procedures for analyzing the types of data typically encountered in preventive trials.

In recent years, the international emphasis on cancer research has enormously stimulated methodologic development relevant to analysis of survival data (Kalbfleisch and Prentice, 1980; Cox, 1975). This applied statistical research has greatly benefited cancer studies and has been used in widely diverse fields. Mental health prevention research can also provide a focal point for important new developments in statistics and data analysis. Guided by the conceptual framework of community epidemiology with a lifespan developmental orientation, our prevention research will involve analyses of experimental or quasiexperimental data in which time-dependent processes are critical to the analysis, and in which there are large numbers of subjects. New statistical methods will be developed in the following areas: longitudinal analysis with missing data; longitudinal analysis with ordinal data; analysis of time series with multiple binary observations; and certain exploratory-data analytic techniques.

Five Year Research Plan

Prevention trials are being planned that will examine the use of the pediatrician's office in the preschool physical examination for extended assessment of the child's needs. The assessment now being tested will allow the linking of the child and family to appropriate agencies and to the school and teacher for follow-up. Such a preventive method, based on developmental epidemiological principles, holds promise for intervening prior to the child's maladaptive behavioral responses to the classroom. An intended consequence of early epidemiological assessment is the conversion of back-up social agencies into providers of prevention instead of crisis response.

Once studies of the incidence and prevalence of mental disorders and their relationships to behavioral responses in the classroom and to psychiatric symptoms have been completed, child psychiatric treatment research protocols are also being planned for those children diagnosed as having mental disorders. Studies of lead exposure and the reversibility of its effects are being designed. Nutrition and infectious disease designs are also being considered. The prevention trial offers the opportunity to test the function and reversibility of these antecedents.

Summary

Developmental epidemiology comprises community epidemiologic and lifespan developmental orientations. Applied to prevention research, it requires empirical data on the antecedents of child and adolescent mental health problems in order to identify specific subgroups at risk for later problems. Preventive trials aimed at the early antecedents can then be designed. Periodic epidemiologic assessment allows evaluation and strengthening of cost/benefit analysis.

Community epidemiology holds macropopulation characteristics constant and focuses attention on variation in small environments within the community, thus enabling microanalytic studies of causes of disease or disorder. A lifespan developmental orientation easily complements that of epidemiology, focusing on the course that precedes and follows onset of disease or disorder. Knowledge of specific social field, social adaptational, psychological, and biological antecedents provide targets for preventive interventions. A prevention research center oriented to concepts of developmental epidemiology thus defined illustrates current prevention research in child and adolescent mental health problems.

References

Abt Associates. (1976). *Education as experimentation: A planned variation model,* Vol. III. Cambridge, Mass.: Abt Associates.

Abt Associates. (1977). *Education as experimentation: A planned variation model,* Vol. IV. Cambridge, Mass.: Abt Associates.

Baltes, P. B., Reese, H. W., and Lipsitt, L. P. (1980). Life-span developmental psychology. In M. R. Rosenzweig and L. W. Porter (Eds.), *Annual Review of Psychology, 31:* 65–110.

Barrish, H. H., Saunders, M., and Wolf, M. M. (1969). Good behavior game: Effects of individual contingencies for group consequences on disruptive behavior in a classroom. *Journal of Applied Behavior Analysis, 2:* 119–124.

Becker, W. C., and Gersten, R. (1982). A follow-up of Follow Through: The later effects of the direct instruction model on children in fifth and sixth grades. *American Education Research Journal, 19:* 75–92.

Blechman, E. A., Taylor, C. I., and Schrader, S. M. (1981). Family problem solving versus home notes as early intervention with high-risk children. *Journal of Consulting and Clinical Psychology, 49:* 919–926.

Block, J. H., and Burns, R. B. (1976). In L. Shulman (Ed.), Mastery Learning, *Review of research in education* (pp. 3–49). Itasca, Ill.: Peacock.

Bloom, B. S. (1964). *Stability and changes in human characteristics*. New York: Wiley.

Cary, A. O., and Reveal, M. T. (1967). Prevention and detection of emotional disturbances in preschool children. *American Journal of Orthopsychiatry, 37,* 719–723.

Cowen, E. L., Babigian, H., Izzo, L. D., Pederson, A., and Trost, M. A. (1973). Long-term follow-up of early detected vulnerable children. *Journal of Consulting and Clinical Psychology, 41*(3), 438–446.

Cox, D. R. (1975). Partial likelihood. *Biometrika, 62,* 269–276.

Diener, C. L., and Dweck, C. S. (1980). An analysis of learned helplessness: II. The processing of success. *Journal of Personality and Social Psychology, 39*(5), 940–952.

Dweck, C. S., and Bush, E. S. (1976). Sex differences in learned helplessness: I. Differential debilitation with peer and adult evaluators. *Developmental Psychology, 12,* 147–156.

Englemann, S., and Carnine, D. (1982). *Theory of instruction: Principles and applications*. New York: Irvington.

Ensminger, M. E., Brown, C. H., and Kellam, S. G. (1982). Sex differences in antecedents of substance use among adolescents. *Journal of Social Issues, 38,* 25–42.

Ensminger, M. E., Kellam, S. G., and Rubin, B. R. (1983). School and family origins of delinquency: Comparisons by sex. In K. T. Van Dusen and S. Mednick (Eds.), *Prospective studies of crime and delinquency*. Boston: Kluwer-Nijhoff.

Feshbach, N. D. (1984). Empathy, empathy training and the regulation of aggression in elementary school children. In R. M. Kaplan, V. J. Konecni, and R. W. Novaco (Eds.), *Aggression in children and youth* (pp. 192–208). The Hague: Martinus Nijhoff Publishers.

Fleming, P., and Ricks, D. F. (1969). Emotions of children before schizophrenia and character disorders. In M. Roff and D. F. Ricks (Eds.), *Life history studies in psychopathology*. Minneapolis: University of Minnesota Press.

Furman, W., Rahe, D. F., and Hartup, W. W. (1979). Rehabilitation of socially withdrawn preschool children through mixed-age and same-age socialization. *Child Development, 50,* 915–922.

Glueck, S., and Glueck, E. (1950). *Unraveling juvenile delinquency*. Cambridge, Mass.: Harvard University Press.

Gordon, R. S. (1983). An operational classification of disease prevention. *Public Health Reports, 98,* 107–109.

Gottman, J. M. (1977). Toward a definition of social isolation in children. *Child Development, 48,* 513–517.

Guidubaldi, J., and Perry, J. D. (1984). Divorce, socioeconomic status and children's cognitive–social competence at school entry. *American Journal of Orthopsychiatry, 54,* 459–468.

Guidubaldi, J., Clemshaw, H. K., Perry, J. D., and McLoughlin, C. S. (1983). The impact of parental divorce on children: Report of the nationwide NASP study. *School Psychological Review, 12,* 300–323.

Harris, V. W., and Sherman, J. A. (1973). Use and analysis of the "good behavior game" to reduce disruptive classroom behavior. *Journal of Applied Behavior Analysis, 3,* 405–417.

Herzog, E., and Sudia, C. E. (1973). Children in fatherless families. In B. M.

Caldwell and H. N. Ricciuti (Eds.), *Review of child development research, Vol. 3*. Chicago: The University of Chicago Press.

Honzik, M. P. (1967). Environmental correlates of mental growth: Prediction from the family setting at 21 months. *Child Development, 38*, 337–363.

Jessor, R., and Jessor, S. L. (1978). Theory testing in longitudinal research on marijuana use. In D. Kandel (Ed.), *Longitudinal research on drug use: Empirical findings and methodological issues* (pp. 41–71). Washington, D.C.: Hemisphere–John Wiley.

Kalbfleisch, J. D., and Prentice, R. L. (1980). *The statistical analysis of failure time data*. New York: Wiley.

Kandel, D. B., Kessler, R. C., and Margulies, R. Z. (1978). Antecedents of adolescent initiation into stages of drug use: A developmental analysis. In D. Kandel (Ed.), *Longitudinal research on drug use: Empirical findings and methodological issues*. Washington, D.C.: Hemisphere–John Wiley.

Kaplan, H. B. (1975). Increase in self-rejection as an antecedent of deviant responses. *Journal of Youth and Adolescence, 4*, 281–292.

Kellam, S. G., and Branch, J. D. (1971). An approach to community mental health: An analysis of basic problems. *Seminars in Psychiatry, 3*, 207–225.

Kellam, S. G., Branch, J. D., Agrawal, K. C., and Ensminger, M. E. (1975). *Mental health and going to school: The Woodlawn Program of assessment, early intervention, and evaluation*. Chicago: University of Chicago Press.

Kellam, S. G., Branch, J. D., Agrawal, K. C., and Grabill, M. E. (1972). Strategies in urban mental health. In S. E. Golann and C. Eisdorfer (Eds.), *Handbook of community mental health*. New York: Appleton-Century-Crofts.

Kellam, S. G., Brown, C. H., and Fleming, J. P. (1983). The prevention of teenage substance use: Longitudinal research and strategy. In T. J. Coates, A. C. Petersen, and C. Perry (Eds.), *Promoting adolescent health: A dialogue on research and practices*. New York: Academic Press.

Kellam, S. G., Brown, C. H., Rubin, B. R., and Ensminger, M. E. (1983). Paths leading to teenage psychiatric symptoms and substance use: Developmental epidemiological studies in Woodlawn. In S. B. Guze, F. Earls, and J. E. Barrett (Eds.), *Childhood psychopathology and development*. New York: Raven Press.

Kellam, S. G., and Ensminger, M. E. (1980). Theory and method in child psychiatric epidemiology. In F. Earls (Ed.), *Studying children epidemiologically, Vol. 1* (pp. 145–180); International monograph series in psychosocial epidemiology (B. Z. Locke and A. E. Slaby, series Eds.). New York: Neale Watson.

Kellam, S. G., Ensminger, M. E., and Simon, M. B. (1980). Mental health in first grade and teenage drug, alcohol, and cigarette use. *Drug and Alcohol Dependence, 5*, 273–304.

Kellam, S. G., Ensminger, M. E., and Turner, R. J. (1977). Family structure and the mental health of children: Concurrent and longitudinal community-wide studies. *Archives of General Psychiatry, 34*, 1012–1022.

Kellam, S. G., Simon, M. B., and Ensminger, M. E. (1983). Antecedents in first grade of teenage drug use and psychological well-being: A ten-year community-wide perspective study. In D. Ricks and B. Dohrenwend (Eds.), *Origins of psychopathology: Research and public policy*. New York: Cambridge University Press.

Kitagawa, E. M., and Tauber, K. E. (1963). *Local community fact book, Chicago metropolitan area 1960*. Chicago: Chicago Community Inventory.

Kohlberg, L., Ricks, D., and Snarey, J. (1984). Childhood development as a predictor of adaptation in adulthood. *Genetic Psychology Monographs, 110.*

Ledingham, J. E. (1981). Developmental patterns of aggressive and withdrawn behavior in childhood: A possible method for identifying Preschizophrenics. *Journal of Abnormal Child Psychology, 9,* 1–22.

Lefkowitz, M. M., Eron, L. D., Walder, L. O., and Huesman, L. R. (1977). *Growing up to be violent: A longitudinal study of the development of aggression.* New York: Pergamon.

Lynn, D. B. (1974). *The father: His role in child development.* Monterey, Calif.: Brooks/Cole.

Lysakowski, R., and Walberg, H. (1981). Classroom reinforcement and learning: a quantitative synthesis. *Journal of Educational Research, 75,* 69–77.

McCord, J., McCord, W., and Thurber, E. (1962). Some effects of paternal absence on male children. *Journal of Abnormal and Social Psychology, 64,* 361–369.

Medland, M. B., and Stachnick, T. J. (1972). Good behavior game: A replication and systematic analysis. *Journal of Applied Behavior Analysis, 5,* 45–51.

Mednick, S. A., and McNeil, P. S. (1968). Current methodology in research in etiology of schizophrenia: Serious difficulties which suggest the use of the highline approach. *Psychological Bulletin, 70,* 681–693.

Mosteller, F., and Tukey, J. W. (1977). *Data analyses and regression.* Reading, Mass.: Addison-Wesley.

Needleman, H. L., Gunnod, C., Leviton, A., Reeder, R., Peresie, H., Maher, C., and Barrett, P. (1979). Deficits in psychologic and classroom performance of children with elevated dentine lead levels. *The New England Journal of Medicine, 300*(13), 689–695.

Pasamanick, B., Rogers, M. E., and Lilienfeld, A. M. (1956). Pregnancy experience and the development of behavior disorder in children. *American Journal of Psychiatry, 112,* 613–618.

Paton, S., Kessler, R., and Kandel, D. (1977). Depressive mood and adolescent illicit drug use: A longitudinal analysis. *Journal of Genetic Psychology, 131,* 267–289.

Patterson, G. R., Chamberlain, P., and Reid, J. B. (1982). A comparative evaluation of a parent-training program. *Behavior Therapy, 13,* 638–650.

Pritchard, M., and Graham, P. (1966). An investigation of a group of patients who have attended both the child and adult departments of the same psychiatric hospital. *British Journal of Psychiatry, 112,* 603–12.

Robins, L. N. (1966). *Deviant children grow up: A sociological and psychiatric study of sociopathic personality.* Baltimore: Williams and Wilkins. Reprinted and published by Krieger, Huntington, New York.

Robins, L. N. (1978). *Sturdy childhood predictors of adult outcomes: Replications from longitudinal studies.* Paper presented at Paul Hoch Award lecture, American Psychopathological Association Meeting, Boston.

Robins, L. N., Davis, D. H., and Wish, E. (1977). Detecting predictors of rare events: Demographic, family, and personal deviance as predictors of stages in the progression toward narcotic addiction. In J. S. Strauss, H. Babigian, and M. Roff (Eds.), *The origins and course of psychopathology: Methods of longitudinal research.* New York: Plenum.

Robins, L. N., and Murphy, G. E. (1967). Drug use in a normal population of young Negro men. *American Journal of Public Health, 57,* 1580–1596.

Rutter, M. (1978). Family, area and school influences in the genesis of conduct disorders. In L. A. Hersov, M. Berger, and D. Shaffer (Eds.), *Aggression and anti-social behavior in childhood and adolescence.* Oxford: Pergamon.

Shure, M. S., Spivack, G., and Gordon, R. (1972). Problem solving thinking: A preventive mental health program for preschool children. *Reading World, 11,* 259–273.

Signell, K. A. (1972). Kindergarten entry: A preventive approach to community mental health. *Community Mental Health Journal, 8,* 60–70.

Slavin, R. E. (1983). *Cooperative Learning.* New York: Sonograms.

Smith, G. M., and Fogg, C. P. (1978). Psychological predictors of early use, late use, and nonuse of marijuana among teenage students. In D. B. Kandel (Ed.), *Longitudinal research on drug use: Empirical findings and methodological issues* (pp. 101–113). Washington, D.C.: Hemisphere–John Wiley.

Trotter, S. (1976). Zajonc defuses IQ debate: Birth order working prize. *APA Monitor,* May, 1–10.

Tukey, J. W. (1977). *Exploring data analysis.* Reading, Mass.: Addison-Wesley.

Wallerstein, J. S., and Kelly, J. (1975). The effects of parental divorce: The experience of the preschool child. *Journal of American Academy of Child Psychiatry, 14,* 600–616.

Wallerstein, J., and Kelly, J. (1980). *Surviving the break up: How children and parents cope with divorce.* New York: Basic Books.

Wallerstein, J. S. (1984). Children of divorce: Preliminary report of a ten-year follow-up of young children. *American Journal of Orthopsychiatry, 54*(3), 444–458.

Watt, N. F. (1974). Childhood and adolescent routes to schizophrenia. In D. F. Ricks, A. Thomas, and M. Roff (Eds.), *Life history research in psychopathology: Vol. 3* (pp. 194–211). Minneapolis: University of Minnesota Press.

Werthamer-Larsson, L. A. (1985). An annotated bibliography of the prevention of child and adolescent mental health problems through the use of school-based intervention strategies. Prepared for NIMH, Center for Prevention Research.

Perspectives on Infant Mental Health

Joy D. Osofsky

In presenting a perspective on infant mental health by reviewing major theoretical, research, and prevention efforts over the last ten years, I will focus on two main areas that are extremely important to an understanding of this field. First, I will discuss issues in infant mental health that have been studied by theoreticians and researchers and that have important implications for prevention. Second, I will discuss prevention, providing an overview on early developmental risk (including infant vulnerabilities) and reciprocal influences within the family, which are important factors in the identification of developmental risk. Then I will review briefly common themes for intervention approaches. Finally, I will present information about my current longitudinal preventive intervention study with adolescent mothers and their infants as an example of an approach to prevention.

Clinical and Research Issues in Infant Mental Health

Several major issues have emerged in the last ten years and have been the focus of theory and research in infant psychiatry. In this section, I will first present a theoretical perspective within which to consider the issues and then describe developments related to affective or emotional development, continuities and discontinuities in development, and nosology and diagnosis.

Perspective

In attempting to understand the developing infant–parent relationship, a fruitful approach is to use a transactional perspective, proposed by Sameroff and Chandler (1975) and further elaborated by Belsky (1984) and others, which assumes that each individual in the dyad affects and is, in turn, affected by the other. The model is not static but proposes that the child actively reorganizes the environment and develops through changes

Preparation of this manuscript was assisted by Grant MH 36895-03 from the National Institute of Mental Health Center for Preventive Research, Division of Prevention and Special Mental Health Programs.

involving transactions between the organism and the environment. The clinician involved in understanding the developing family system will also become a part of the system that is being evaluated. In order for interventions to make a difference, it is important to understand the complexity and transactional nature of the process. Some past and current theoretical positions provide a perspective for understanding this approach.

Donald Winnicott (1960), the British pediatrician–psychoanalyst made an extremely perceptive, if at first surprising, remark that "there is no such thing as a baby." He elaborated by pointing out the important and crucial impact of the family and environment on the developing infant and the "vital reciprocity between mother and infant," which we accept now as a dynamic interaction process that is ongoing and changing throughout development. It should be pointed out, however, that the recognition of this dynamic interactional or transactional process is one that has developed recently and that only a few years ago the infant was generally viewed as a passive recipient of stimulation and the parent as the primary actor upon the infant. Some of the newest and most exciting research developments in the area have reflected the growing awareness of this reciprocal dynamic interactive process. Winnicott's extreme sensitivity to the mother–infant relationship, which emerged from his clinical perspective, has provided a framework for research that takes into account the contributions of *both* the infant and the mother to the interactive process from a very early stage. Winnicott was one of the first observers to state clearly that infant care and, by implication, infant psychiatry has a great deal to contribute to an understanding of adult development and psychiatry.

In pursuing these ideas further, Anthony (1983) in his foreword to the first volume of *Frontiers of Infant Psychiatry,* reviewed Middlemore's work—including her concept of the *nursing couple*—which influenced Winnicott and others. According to Middlemore, the mutual adaptation of mother and baby during breast feeding is fundamental to the future adjustment of the individual throughout the life cycle. It is useful to note Middlemore's work in relation to the theories of Winnicott (1960), Bowlby (1969), and Spitz (1965), which call attention to a very important tenet of infant psychiatry, i.e., the relationship between maternal and infant disorder. Some of their perspectives appear to be forerunners of the more sophisticated research currently being carried out that focus on concepts such as *intersubjectivity, reciprocity,* and *affect attunement* (Stern, 1983; Trevarthen, 1980; Emde, 1980; Brazelton, Koslowski, and Main, 1974; Sameroff and Chandler, 1975). Their perspectives are also applicable to intervention research in the area of infant mental health with high-risk mothers and infants; i.e., we must attempt to effect changes in the mother as well as the infant in order to influence the reciprocal system and impact on the infant's development.

Affective, or Emotional, Development

One of the most exciting new areas of clinical and research study related to infant mental health is that of *affective, or emotional, development.* Currently ongoing research in several laboratories (Stern, Emde, Osofsky, Zahn-Waxler, Stechler, and Demos) is allowing a greater objectification of some of the sensitive perceptions about the development of infant emotions that have emerged from careful clinical observations.

One of the theoretical underpinnings for recent advances in the study of affective development is the work of Rene Spitz, whose classic observations of deprived infants presented graphic illustrations of the suffering and depression that can result from separation and loss. Spitz's (1946) observations indicated that the experience of institutionalized infants, leading to developmental and physical retardation, had to do with deficits in mothering and separation and resulted, in extreme cases, in what he called *anaclitic depression.* The disturbances described by Spitz can have major impact on the later psychosocial development of the child. As Emde (1983) points out in his introduction to the recent compilation of Spitz's writings, we have become increasingly aware that Spitz was writing not just about babies and their mothers but about the *mothering process* in an attempt to identify essential factors that lead to early ego development. Thus we see the precursors of more recent work on the importance of affective reciprocity in relationship to early infant development (Stern, 1983).

From a clinical perspective, investigators such as Provence (1983) have described affective responses that focus on normal development and aberrations in the infant's development during the first year of life; these descriptions provide a fascinating perspective, which parallels recent research on affective development. Many clinician–researchers who are trained to understand patterns of abnormality in development maintain that changes and problems in affective development are key indicators of difficulties both in the developing infant and in the relationship.

There is also a major and growing interest in the attachment process. John Bowlby (1969), the British psychiatrist and psychoanalyst, has contributed theoretically and influenced research considerably in the area of infant development. Attempting to bridge disciplinary concepts, he took an ethological perspective to attachment theory, integrating ideas about the development of object relations (a psychoanalytic notion) with more traditional developmental psychological theories of cognitive and social–

emotional development. Bowlby's theoretical position was very much influenced by the time that he spent in a school for disturbed children, before completing his medical training, where he observed and was impressed by the impact of real-life experiences on outcomes for children and adults. He made careful observations about infants undergoing traumatic separations or institutionalization and was concerned about the effects of separation and loss on outcomes for the infants. Out of his early observations came a fruitful and productive theoretical and research perspective on the importance of the emotional attachment of an infant or child to his or her parent, with the attachment having a major impact on the early developmental process as well as subsequently influencing successes or failures in the establishment of relationships later in life. Bowlby's theoretical system has had a significant impact on the area of infant mental health; it also has stimulated major research led by Ainsworth and students in developing a broad perspective on attachment theory. (See Bretherton and Waters, 1984).

Studies of attachment are linked closely with those of affect because it is not discrete behaviors but the patterns of behavioral organization, i.e., the quality of the attachment or the affective bond, that endure. Therefore, in studying the developmental literature on attachment behavior, it is important to consider attachment in relation to specific patterns of affective development. Sroufe and Waters (1977) have demonstrated that it is possible to show stable individual differences in attachment and consistencies or inconsistencies in security of attachment over time. Recent research and theoretical writings in this area include Sroufe (1979); Ainsworth et al. (1978); Bretherton and Waters (1984); and Campos et al. (1984).

Clinicians have long found emotions to be crucial to their everyday work. Researchers have recently pointed out that the role of emotions for infants may be even greater than at other ages because emotional signals serve as the language of the baby who cannot talk and are essential for caregiving. Thus crying, or smiling, or a bright, alert look relay to the caregiver feelings, emotions, and readiness for interaction that the infant cannot communicate in any other way. Expressions of fear, anger, and sadness also communicate compelling messages. From a clinical point of view, emotions in infancy are used as a way of determining whether development, particularly social and emotional development, is proceeding as it should. If sustained pleasure or smiling between parent and infant or a range of expressed emotions in the infant are not present, the clinician may worry about the developmental course and the future for the parenting process and the parent–infant relationship.

Stern (1984) goes further in talking about the interchange between infant and parent, describing a process occurring between them that allows the infant to perceive how he or she is perceived. In the process, parents nonverbally reflect back to the infant his or her own experiences. Stern notes that this process, which he describes as affect attunement, has been observed by developmental psychologists, child psychiatrists, and psychoanalysts who have all agreed on the need for such a process and have offered a number of terms to label the phenomena. For example, the term *mirroring* has been used by Kohut (1977) and Mahler, Pine, and Bergman (1975); *affect matching* by Malatesta and Izard (1984); *affect contagion* by Sagi and Hoffman (1976); and *intersubjectivity* by Trevarthan (1980). These terms indicate, to some extent, two sequential acts of social perception. First, the parent must be able to read the infant's mental state or inner experience from the infant's overt behavior, and the parent must perform some corresponding responsive behavior. Second, the infant must be able to read this overt parental response as reflecting back his or her original experience. The concern can be broadened to include empathy and intimacy in relationships (Hinde, 1976; Zahn-Waxler, and Radker-Yarrow, 1982). Stern (1983) feels that affect attunement, i.e., being able to capture the quality of another's internal feeling state, is an extremely important concept for understanding the developing infant and parent–infant relationship.

Another important concept related to emotional development that has generated a growing body of research is that of *emotional availability.* Emde (1980) has described emotional availability as providing a reciprocal reward system for infants and parents. This notion is particularly useful in attempts to understand and prevent psychopathology and psychosocial disorders. Emotional availability involves an emphatic sensitivity that allows resonance with a variety of feelings that may be uniquely individual and commonly human. Emde proposes it as a developmental principle, i.e., an ability that may facilitate and foster security, exploration, and learning. The notion of emotional availability assumes a biologically based reward system for infants and parents that influences the developing relationship. Based on the longitudinal research of Emde, Gaensbauer, and Harmon (1976) and that of others, emotional development can be understood in relation to three phases of social interaction during the first year of infant life. These phases include: (1) the newborn period, extending through the first two months of life; (2) the awakening of sociability (two to seven months); and (3) the onset of focused attachment (eight months through the end of the first year). Research has been carried out on the rewarding dimensions of emotions, the clarification of discrete emotions, and assessment of emotional availability and emotional signaling. Implications of this work can be related to conditions that may interfere with emotional availability and can provide a framework for intervention. The notion of emotional availability and its effect on the reciprocal reward system between parent and infant holds much promise for future understanding of the developing parent–infant relationship and specific preventive interventions in relation to infant psychopathology.

In sum, there have been important new developments related to the study of affects and the transactions that occur between infant and caregiver, which are mediated through the primary role of affects. Before the child is old enough to use language or other symbolic forms of representation, affective expressions are the only reliable and valid indicators of the saliency of events for the infant and constitute the primary medium of communication and meaning (Stechler and Carpenter, 1967; Demos, 1982; Sroufe, 1979). The role of affective development has been studied in relation to changes in cognitive capacities (Kagan, 1971; Sroufe and Wunsch, 1972; Ricciuti, 1972) and in relation to their value as signaling major neurological and developmental reorganization (Emde et al., 1976; Spitz, 1959, 1965; Stern, 1985). In addition, as mentioned previously, the quality of attachment and adequacy of caregiving often depend on affective factors such as sensitivity to the infant's affective signals, his or her expression of positive affect, and the reciprocity that develops between infant and parent (Ainsworth, Bell, and Stayton, 1974).

Development of procedures for measuring early affective responses is proceeding in a number of laboratories (Emde and Easterbrooks, 1984; Osofsky and Culp, 1984; Stern, 1983; and Zahn-Waxler et al., 1984). Ekman and Friesen (1975) and Izard (1971) have provided microanalytic approaches to the rating of affects, based on a comprehensive view of facial movements. Other approaches to measurement include molar ratings of affective expressions, such as those dealing with the reciprocity or the lack of reciprocity that may be occurring within the parent–infant dyad. Theoretical and research developments in this area hold great promise for providing more understanding of the complexities of early emotional development and increased knowledge about factors that may contribute to aberrations in the early parent–infant interactive system, which may lead to maladaptive and pathological relationships at a later time.

Continuities and Discontinuities: Issue of Predictability

The notion of *continuities and discontinuities,* or *predictability,* from earlier to later behaviors is extremely important in the area of infant mental health, particularly as it relates to prevention. Until recently, a general assumption in developmental psychology was that we could expect significant continuities from earlier to later development. It was assumed that infants would grow and develop in a predictable and continuous manner. However, as more focus has been placed on expectable changes, shifts, and discontinuities that seem to occur quite naturally, the fascinating idea has emerged that discontinuous rather than continuous patterns of development are often an expectable part of the normal process. (See, for example, McCall, 1979.) Spitz (1959), Emde et al. (1976), and Sroufe (1979) have pointed out significant biobehavioral shifts that take place at various points in development and lead to logical patterns of discontinuities. Some of these factors may contribute to the consistent finding that, except for individuals at the extreme lower end of the distribution, it is very difficult to predict later from earlier patterns.

Development is marked by change, and it is difficult to determine at an early stage how this change will manifest itself within individuals and groups. Some researchers maintain that we have not yet found consistent continuities in development because our methods of measurement are not well enough refined; others believe that, in general, we should not expect continuities. Sameroff (1978) has discussed this issue in some depth in a monograph devoted to the Brazelton Neonatal Behavioral Assessment Scale. The notion of continuities and discontinuities is particularly interesting clinically in that we often observe apparent continuities in an individual from infancy to adulthood, and yet within groups of individuals we have a great deal of difficulty specifying these consistent patterns. (See Thomas et al., 1963; Murphy and Moriarty, 1976.)

New perspectives and research strategies include those that focus on continuities while at the same time taking into account discontinuities or periods of developmental transition. Kagan (1984) notes that older views about the cumulative value of early experience and about its linearity are now thought to be distorted; with this newer perspective early development can be understood as an aspect of a multidimensional life course. Early behavioral change processes that occur may or may not be connected with later behavioral changes, and novel behavioral systems can emerge not only in early childhood but in later childhood, adulthood, and old age (Baltes, 1983).

A consideration of continuities and discontinuities in socioemotional development places the focus on possible mechanisms that may underlie continuities (Rutter, 1984). The understanding of such mechanisms may help in the identification of research approaches to the study of continuities. Rutter notes the following important mechanisms:

1. Continuities in the environment.
2. The availability of opportunities.

3. Effects on the environment.

4. Vulnerability, resilience, and coping skills.

5. Habits, attitudes, and self-concept.

6. The effects of experiences in altering somatic structures and functioning.

7. Imprinting of rapid forms of early learning.

8. Adverse early experiences leading to lasting interference with the structure of personality development.

Based on these possible mechanisms, we come to expect discontinuities; however, despite dramatic transformations, continuities may also result. As Rutter says, ". . . continuities stem from a multitude of links over time. Because each link is incomplete, subjected to marked individual variation and open to modification, there are many opportunities to break the chain. Such opportunities continue right into adult life." (p. 63) It is interesting to note the longitudinal work of Sroufe and colleagues, who have focused on specific patterns of behavior (notably attachment) and found some continuities over time (Erickson, Sroufe, and Egeland, 1984). In these studies the investigators have been able to define and study parallel behavioral processes over time and have found evidence for patterns of continuity (Sroufe, 1983). This is an important area of study, which links theoretical notions with practical considerations in relation to infant mental health, psychopathology, and possibilities for change, prevention, and intervention.

Nosology and Diagnosis in Infancy

The problem of developing a nosology or diagnostic scheme continues to be an important one for the area of infant mental health and has been elaborated by a number of clinician–researchers (Call, 1983; Emde, Harmon, and Mrazek, 1984; Greenspan, 1981). Several groups have been established recently to deal with the difficult problem of attempting to diagnose or label disorders of infancy. However, as noted earlier in Winnicott's sensitive statement that "there is no such thing as a baby," the problem of diagnosis is complicated because infants exist in families, and their development proceeds through reciprocal interactive patterns. In the foreword to *Frontiers of Infant Psychiatry, Vol. II,* Emde points out that "infancy presents major dilemmas for diagnosis and it often seems difficult, if not impossible, to apply our traditional medical model." Parenting difficulties or marital problems may result in the infant developing a "symptom," often a sleep or eating disorder, which is usually quickly alleviated when the stress within the family is reduced. Call (1983) has proposed a multiaxial system that is appropriate for multidimensional diagnosis in infancy. The system includes clinical psychiatric syndromes, medical disorders, and developmental assessments that specify:

1. The highest level of present functioning.
2. Particular defects or immaturities.
3. Unusual capacities or sensitivities in sensory and motor development, cognitive development, psychosocial development, psychosexual functioning, and overall level of functioning.
4. Degree of regression.
5. Degree of risk and vulnerability.

As stated by Call and reiterated by others working in the infancy area, progress in defining infant psychiatric disorders or precursors of later psychopathology will depend on broadly based efforts carried out with a multidisciplinary perspective. The intensive deliberations of the British Working Group, carried on over several years, indicate that an understanding of the clinical syndrome, intellectual level, etiological factors, and associated cultural and social factors are of considerable importance.

Provence and Greenspan (1984) have recently been working on another multiaxial system to understand infancy and early childhood developmental and emotional disturbances. Their system is based on a comprehensive integrated approach for infants and young children and their families and environment. It includes attention to physical, emotional, cognitive, interactive, and environmental factors. The development of various systems for understanding diagnosis in infancy is still very much in process but prospects for enhancing our future understanding appear promising.

Clinical Intervention Approaches

Clinical approaches range from individual work with parents (based on their past histories) to work with infants directly to prospective intervention with multirisk families—or a combination of all three approaches.

One of the pioneers in the field of infant mental health, Selma Fraiberg, was courageous enough to attempt to intervene clinically with very disturbed infants and parents. Her book *Clinical Studies in Infant Mental Health* (1980) and her numerous and frequently cited articles (e.g., Fraiberg, Adelson, and Shapiro, 1975) have provided a framework for learning more about clinical intervention approaches with extremely disturbed infants and families. Fraiberg developed treatment approaches requiring much effort and persistence with highly disturbed families, where the mothers often needed extensive treatment before efforts could be started with the children. She had confidence that, even in the most dire environmental circumstances with multirisk, significantly emotionally disturbed, and handicapped families, much could be done to help the infant and family. Noting the press for developmental growth and the gains that could be made under the most difficult circumstances, she stated in her book, "It's a little bit like having God on your side."

In a similar vein, Wolkind and Hall (1979) described a longitudinal investigation, still in progress, of later maternal behavior of women who had been disadvantaged in their own childhood. The research question is whether the mothers' disadvantaged childhoods would affect their behavior with their children and whether there might be long-term effects on the children. They found that mothers who had been severely deprived in early childhood did not necessarily cope ineffectively with their own children. In addition, they found that separations starting before the age of 5 were no more likely to be associated with difficulties than those occurring after that age and that separation, per se, did not seem to have lasting deleterious effects. In the study, children admitted to children's homes before the age of 3 showed a persistent quality of disinhibition or lack of awareness of appropriate social boundaries.

Although on clinical grounds it has been assumed that early separation will inevitably be associated with an inability to maintain a one-to-one relationship, Tizard's (1977) work with adopted children has shown that this assumption is not necessarily true. As a result, Tizard suggests that there is a need for an alternative model. While a woman's early family experience appears to relate to her mothering behavior, the process that leads to difficulty in parenting is complex and is influenced by a number of factors, such as economic difficulties, low involvement of spouse, a limited support system, and unplanned pregnancy. Thus it is necessary to take a multidimensional approach to understanding the effects of early deprivation or difficulty on later outcomes. Emphasis must be placed on the infant, the family, and the overall system rather than focused on any one individual in the family in order to understand fully the interactive processes that may occur.

Greenspan's (1981) longitudinal research program proposes such a multidimensional perspective as part of a developmental structuralist approach to assessment and intervention. His system requires an examination of the demand characteristics of each subphase of infancy and early childhood. The infant and mother (or other caregiver) are evaluated separately within a system that requires a high level of integration for optimal functioning. Within this system, high risk exists when the parent–infant integration is poor in terms of stage-specific demands. Greenspan delineates key stage-specific tasks for each phase of development during infancy and early childhood that allow for the interaction of constitutional, maturational, environmental, and parenting patterns. The results to date indicate that the effects of negative early experiences can be reversed to some extent, depending on many factors. These factors include: (1) the age of the child at the time of intervention; (2) the ability of the infant and the family to work with an outreach- or center-based program; and (3) the staff's expertise in developing an appropriate intervention program related to the maladaptive condition at a particular stage.

Two recent sets of clinical reports provide illustrative examples of case studies having different diagnostic and therapeutic issues for which a variety of intervention strategies have been attempted (Provence, 1983; Tyson, 1984). In the Provence reports, the settings, treatment approaches, and infants' presenting problems vary from case to case. However, the approaches share the beliefs and attitudes that: (1) diagnosis and treatment can best be carried out when parents have an opportunity to become involved in a therapeutic alliance with those who offer help; (2) there is no substitute for the careful individualization of each infant and parent in clinical work; and (3) parents and their infants must be encouraged to work actively on their own behalf and that helping them to do so is part of the function of the clinician for an infant–parent system. These case reports emphasize that, even with much effort, some infants and parents will not improve as much as desired. However, Provence maintains the conviction that we must mobilize our best resources for each infant and meet the challenge to build better services for infants and families.

Tyson (1984) in a chapter based on a panel discussion at the Second World Congress on Infant Psychiatry considers several important issues regarding clinical intervention. The panelists discussed the dynamic interaction between mother and infant in cases where more points of developmental vulnerability are identified than had originally been recognized. The panelists indicated that the implications of observed disturbance at various points in development need to be reassessed and that criteria to evaluate emotional difficulties need to be reevaluated. The panelists also emphasized that the issue of predictability is extremely important; i.e., the clinician needs to determine whether the existence of a current disturbance implies a continuing disturbance of development, whether subsequent development will be changed in some way to amplify vulnerability, or whether there will be a self-righting tendency, with developmental plasticity being sufficiently positive to allow normal development to occur. The panelists presented case material dealing with the following clinical issues: (1) Do manifestations of disturbance in infancy result in definable psychopathology in later life? (2) Will developmental plasticity and discontinuities inherent in the process of development obscure observation of normal developmental pathways? and (3) Are we much better at explaining deviant development and psychopathology than at explaining health?

Other issues considered in the paper include the concern that, in many cases, it is difficult to define risk and potential outcome and that, in order to decide whether intervention is necessary, it is important to have predictive criteria such as the presence or type of affective expression, quality of play, reciprocity, consistency or inconsistency in mothering activity, and the degree of support available from the family or outside of the family.

From a clinical perspective, we should neither concentrate exclusively on inner conflict nor on the environment because either can obscure important aspects of the other. With prevention, it is important to determine what is being prevented and what prevention activities are involved or required. Perhaps it is appropriate in concluding this section on clinical intervention to remind ourselves of Solnit's (1974) sensitive observation, "care for your children as you wish them to care for your grandchildren."

A Preventive Intervention Program for Adolescent Mothers and Their Infants

Approximately 600,000 babies are born each year to women younger than 20 years of age in the United States, and about 95 percent of those children remain with their families. These young families are at risk for various psychosocial reasons, including socioeconomic disadvantage, poor education and vocational opportunities, frequent subsequent pregnancies, and less ability to cope with parenthood. Within this group there is also a greater incidence of infant medical and developmental difficulties. Research studies carried out during the last decade have indicated some strengths and considerable weaknesses in the patterns of interaction between adolescent mothers and their infants. An important issue for both health-care providers and researchers is whether an adolescent has completed enough of her psychological, social, and emotional adjustment to be able to parent effectively. Studies that have examined adolescent mother–infant relationships point consistently to the poor potential for both mother and child. Adolescent development may be severely strained by the early assumption of parenting responsibilities, and the outcomes for the infants are often compromised.

In our longitudinal project (initiated in 1982) we have been studying the early interactive environment of the adolescent and infant, which forms the foundation of the mother–infant emotional tie for future parenting. This evaluation and intervention program for mothers, aged 17 and under, is presented as an example of a preventive intervention approach for high-risk mothers and infants.

Program Design

The program is designed to follow 200 adolescent mothers, aged 17 and younger, and their infants, carrying out developmental and psychosocial evaluations for the first 30 months of life. Our goals are to identify infants, mothers, and families who are at risk to develop problems, to provide appropriate interventions, to evaluate outcomes and the impact of interventions, and to lessen the incidence of problems.

Since the program was initiated in April 1982, 130 adolescent mothers have been identified. Of those, 107 have since given birth and have been placed in three different groups. Intervention Group 1 is composed of mothers who are in the Maternal and Infant (M&I) project of the Topeka-Shawnee County Health Department and the AIM (Aid for Infants and Mothers) program of the Menninger Foundation. Intervention Group 2 is composed of M&I mothers not in the AIM program. The Control group consists of mothers who are not in an organized intervention program.

Services Provided to Participants

As indicated, Groups I and II include mothers who are enrolled in the M&I program. In the M&I program, they receive prenatal medical care, nutritional guidance, social service support, and home visitation and clinical follow-up by nurses and social workers until their infants are 15 months old.

Intervention Group I mothers are also enrolled in the AIM program. As part of the AIM program, a carefully supervised nonprofessional home visitor initiated contact with the mother during the prenatal period and visits the mother in her home on a weekly basis for the first few months of the infant's life. The frequency of these visits decreases as the baby grows older; however, the home visitor remains available to the mother for the first 2½ years of the infant's life. During the visits, the home visitor may help the mother both in taking care of the baby's needs and in reviewing her own situation. The home visitor also brings sample sheets describing various activities that are appropriate to the infant's developmental level, which the mother then carries out during the home visitor's absence. In this way it is hoped that the mothers will gain in awareness and enjoyment of the different developmental abilities of their infants and will encourage their infants' developmental growth. The AIM program also provides a 24-hour "Warm Line" staffed by project professionals whom the mothers can call to receive information, advice, or help regarding problems or concerns that they may have about their infants. A weekly Drop-In Center is available where the mothers can either visit with their babies or leave their babies for a few hours. At the Drop-In Center, mothers have the opportunity to learn more about ways to take care of themselves and establish a household, as well as different activities that they may participate in with their infants. Another portion of the AIM program is a component for the fathers who continue to be involved with their infants or who initiate contact with the mothers and want greater participation.

Characteristics of Participants

The characteristics of the participants assessed to date during the prenatal period are presented in Table 1. The mean age of the mothers is a little over 16 years; the mean level of education is 9½ years, the mean age of

TABLE 1
Characteristics of participants

Variable	*N*	*Mean*	*Range*	*s**
Mother's age	131	16.4	13.4–17.7	1.0
Mother's education	131	9.5	6–13	1.3
Father's age	126	19.8	15–33	3.3
Father's education	107	10.9	7–14	1.3
Total risk (excludes control group)	131	2.2	1–3 (high)	.71

Mother's race	64% Caucasian; 24% black; 7% Hispanic; and 5% mixed.
Marital status	13% married and living with husband. 87% single, of whom 70% live with parents; 12% live with grandparents, aunts; 7% live with boyfriend, father of child; 7% live with boyfriend and his parents; and 4% live alone.
First pregnancy (prima-gravida) = 76%	26% previously pregnant, of whom 26% report therapeutic abortions, and 41% report spontaneous abortions.
Parity	First child, 88%; second child, 12%.
PPVT score	Mean = 81.98, *s.* = 11.7, and median = 80.
Age equivalent	Mean = 13.4 years and Median = 12.7 years.

**s* = Standard deviation.

the fathers is almost 20 years; and the racial composition is 64 percent Caucasian, 24 percent black, 7 percent Hispanic, and 5 percent mixed. Most of the young women are single, and, although they live in a variety of types of family situations, the majority live with their own mothers. Of the sample, 88 percent were pregnant for the first time; 12 percent were having their second child. Of some note, the mean of the young women's scores on the Peabody Picture Vocabulary Test is 82; the median is 80. The age equivalents for these scores are 13.4 and 12.7 years, respectively. Thus, using this general measure of cognitive functioning, the young women are functioning considerably below their age level.

Table 2 presents descriptive statistics on the first 107 babies at and shortly after birth. To date there are no significant differences on any of these variables across the three groups. Let me emphasize that this is a sample at high risk for prematurity, but the mean gestational age of the infants at birth is a little over 39 weeks, the mean birth weight is 3226 grams, and the total number of premature infants born to date is only 14; of the premature infants, 6 are less than 36 weeks gestational age, and only 1 is less than 33 weeks. These data are consistent with data from other studies, indicating that, with good prenatal care, the incidence of complications can be significantly reduced within this risk population.

Although the number of subjects assessed at the various follow-up

TABLE 2

Descriptive statistics for newborns

Total	Group 1	Group 2	Group 3
N = 107	N = 47	N = 37	N = 23
Measurement*	*Mean*	*s*†	
Gestational age	39.3 weeks	1.7 weeks	
Birth weight	3226 grams	517 grams	
Apgar 1 minute	7.5	1.2	
Apgar 5 minutes	8.7	.67	
Days in hospital	2.8 days	1.03 days	
Number of premature infants	= 1 ≤ 33 weeks; 5 ≤ 36 weeks; 8 ≤ 37 weeks.		
Sex of infant	Female = 49%	Male = 51%	
Delivery	Vaginal, 74%; forceps, 10%; and C-section 16%		
Feeding	Breast, 44%; Bottle 56%		
Brazelton–Lester Scores*	*Mean*	*s*†	*Range*
Orientation: Best	5.94	1.43	1–9 (best score)
Orientation: Modal	5.18	1.69	1–9

*No significant differences across the three groups.
†*s* = Standard deviation.

times are not yet large enough to draw comparisons between the intervention and control groups, findings from 43 completed six-month evaluations are quite interesting. An attachment paradigm based on a modification of the Ainsworth Strange Situation, is carried out at age six months. This is not usually done with infants as young as six months, but it has been included in order to be consistent with data to be collected at a later time. According to Ainsworth classifications, 53 percent of the infants in this group were rated secure, 47 percent were rated as insecure–avoidant, and 5 percent were rated as insecure–resistant. Although this differential may be related to the early time that the assessments were done, the findings are particularly interesting for a group of infants known to be at psychosocial developmental risk. The findings are consistent with other studies of infants at risk (Crittenden and Bonvillian, 1984), where there is evidence of a higher percentage of insecurely attached infants, as well as indications of a somewhat different developmental course. Because most of the studies of attachment with atypical groups have focused on those who have been abused or neglected, much less is known about other risk groups. Another interesting finding at six months concerned mother–stranger differential scores measured during a give-and-take play situation and while the mother was holding the baby. During this situation, 58 percent of the infants showed no preference for mother over stranger, an unexpectedly high percentage; 19 percent were wary and 16 percent were fearful of the stranger; and 7 percent were mother avoidant. These findings will be related to concurrent and later security-of-attachment classifications. The scores on the Bayley Scales of Infant Development done at six months showed that most of the infants were functioning at an average level. It will be interesting to evaluate possible changes that occur as infants grow older; emerging data suggest a relative cognitive decline in some at-risk groups at 2–3 years of age.

We have also carried out a preliminary analysis of the data on the relationship between the cluster scores on the Brazelton Neonatal Behavioral Assessment Scale and six-month observational ratings of interaction between mother and infant during feeding. The Brazelton cluster measuring newborn orientation related positively and significantly to several of the feeding variables at six months. For example, the better the baby's orientation responses during the newborn period, the more often the mother looked at the baby during feeding at six months; the more she handled her baby during functional activities, the more synchrony she had with her baby; and the better the quality of verbal interaction, the better the quality of physical contact and the more overall sensitivity the mother demonstrated toward the baby. The better the infant's orientation responses during the newborn period, the more the mother also seemed to take more delight in feeding at six months. These findings have held up consistently during our analysis of the first 43 subjects on whom we have newborn and six-month data and may be important in relation to potential early and later reciprocity during the mother–infant interaction process.

Our impressionistic or clinically oriented findings taken from the interaction observations carried out when the infants were 6, 13, and 20 months of age are of some interest. In general, although some of the adolescent mothers are quite warm toward their infants, they tend to encourage developmentally inappropriate behaviors at all ages. We are also struck with the frequent teasing episodes and the sending of double messages. This is an area that we are studying in more depth.

Conclusion

In conclusion, I would like to emphasize several important directions for future research in the area of infant mental health:

- The clinical research perspective that combines sensitive observations of infants and the infant–parent relationship with objective assessments of the interaction process promises to be an important direction for exciting new developments in this area.
- Research on affective, or emotional, development may provide more objective indications of potential psychopathological development at an early stage.
- New developments related to diagnosis and nosology will provide information and definitions of early problems and at-risk interaction patterns to allow preventive interventions to be initiated as early as possible.
- Preventive intervention research and evaluations with at-risk populations (such as our study) will provide important information in helping to evaluate different strategies of intervention and their effectiveness.
- Prospective studies of risk factors in parents and infants should contribute in a meaningful manner to increase understanding of the development of psychopathology. I have demonstrated the importance of recognizing—and considering seriously—early developmental patterns that may be, at the least, problematic and, possibly, place infants at risk for the development of later psychopathology. Much more information is needed in this important area.

From the work that has been carried out during the last decade, we are now able to recognize and deal with at-risk behavior in infancy. Although there is much more to be learned, we must consider and use the most effective ways we have currently to intervene at an early point to ameliorate early patterns that can lead to later more serious problems.

References

Ainsworth, M. D. S., Bell, S. M., and Stayton, D. J. (1974). Infant–mother attachment and social development: "Socialization" as a product of reciprocal responsiveness to signals. In M. P. M. Richards (Ed.), *The integration of a child into a social world* (pp. 99–135). London: Cambridge University Press.

Ainsworth, M. S., Blehar, M. C., Waters, E., and Wall, S. (1978). *Patterns of attachment: A psychological study of the strange situation.* Hillsdale, N.J.: Lawrence Erlbaum.

Anthony, E. J. (1983). Foreword in J. Call, E. Galenson, and R. Tyson (Eds.), *Frontiers of infant psychiatry,* Vol. 1. New York: Basic Books.

Baltes, P. B. (1983). Life-span developmental psychology: Observations on history and theory revisited. In R. M. Lerner (Ed.), *Developmental psychology: Historical and philosophical perspectives.* Hillsdale, N.J.: Lawerence Erlbaum.

Belsky, J. (1984). The determinants of parenting: A process model. *Child Development, 55,* 83–96.

Bowlby, J. (1969). *Attachment and loss, I: Attachment.* New York: Basic Books.

Brazelton, T. B., Koslowski, B., and Main, M. (1974). The origins of reciprocity: The early mother–infant interaction. In M. Lewis and L. Rosenblum (Eds.), *The effect of the infant on its caregiver.* New York: Wiley.

Bretherton, I., and Waters, E. (1984). Growing points in attachment theory and research. *Monographs of the Society for Research in Child Development, 50* (monograph no. 209).

Call, J. D. (1983). Toward a nosology of psychiatric disorders in infancy. In J. Call, E. Galenson, and R. Tyson (Eds.), *Frontiers of infant psychiatry,* Vol. 1. New York: Basic Books.

Campos, J. J., Barrett, K. C., Lamb, M. E., Goldsmith, H. H., and Stenberg, C. (1983). Socioemotional development. In P. H. Mussen (Ed.), *Handbook of child psychology,* Vol. II. M. M. Haith and J. J. Campos (Vol. Eds.), Infancy and developmental psychobiology. New York: Wiley.

Crittenden, P. M., and Bonvillian, J. D. (1984). The relationship between maternal risk status and maternal sensitivity. *American Journal of Orthopsychiatry, 54,* 250–262.

Demos, V. (1982). Affect in early infancy. *Psychoanalytic Inquiry, 1,* 533–574.

Ekman, P., and Friesen, W. (1975). *Unmasking the face.* Englewood Cliffs, N.J.: Prentice-Hall.

Emde, R. N. (1980). Emotional availability: A reciprocal reward system for infants and parents with implications for prevention of psychosocial disorders. In P. M. Taylor (Ed.), *Parent–infant relationships.* New York: Grune and Stratton, 1980.

Emde, R. N. (Ed.) (1983). *Rene Spitz: Dialogues from infancy.* New York: International Universities Press.

Emde, R. N. (1984). Foreword in R. Tyson, J. Call, and E. Galenson (Eds.), *Frontiers of infant psychiatry,* Vol. 2. New York: Basic Books.

Emde, R. N., and Easterbrooks, M. A. (1984). Assessing emotional availability in early development. Unpublished manuscript. Boulder: University of Colorado Health Sciences Center.

Emde, R. N., Gaensbauer, T. J., and Harmon, R. J. (1976). Emotional expression in infancy: A biobehavioral study. *Psychological Issues,* Monograph 10. New York: International Universities Press.

Emde, R. N., Harmon, R. J., and Mrazek, D. (1984). A proposed multi-axial scheme for infancy diagnosis. Unpublished manuscript. Boulder: University of Colorado Health Sciences Center.

Erickson, M. F., Sroufe, L. A., and Egeland, B. (1984). The relationship between quality of attachment and behavior problems in preschool in a high-risk sample. In I. Bretherton and E. Waters (Eds.), Growing points in attachment theory and research. *Monographs of the Society for Research in Child Development, 50,* (monograph no. 209).

Fraiberg, S. (Ed.) (1980). *Clinical studies in infant mental health.* New York: Basic Books.

Fraiberg, S., Adelson, E., and Shapiro, V. (1975). Ghosts in the nursery: A psychoanalytic approach to the problems of impaired infant–mother relationships. *Journal of the American Academy of Child Psychiatry, 14,* 387–422.

Greenspan, S. I. (1981). *Psychopathology and adaptation in infancy and early childhood.* New York: International Universities Press.

Hinde, R. (1976). On describing relationships. *Journal of Child Psychology and Psychiatry, 17,* 1–19.

Izard, C. (1971). *The face of emotion.* New York: Appelton-Century-Crofts.

Kagan, J. (1971). *Change and continuity in infancy.* New York: Wiley.

Kagan, J. (1984). Continuity and change in the opening years of life. In R. N. Emde and R. J. Harmon (Eds.), *Continuities and discontinuities in development.* New York: Plenum.

Kohut, H. (1977). *The restoration of the self.* New York: International Universities Press.

Mahler, M. S., Pine, F., and Bergman, A. (1975). *The psychological birth of the human infant.* New York: Basic Books.

Malatesta, C., and Izard, C. E. (1984). The ontogenesis of human social signals: From biological imperative to symbol utilization. In N. Fox and R. Davidson (Eds.), *The psychobiology of affective development.* Hillsdale, N.J.: Lawrence Erlbaum.

McCall, R. B. (1979). The development of intellectual functioning in infancy and the prediction of later I.Q. In J. D. Osofsky (Ed.), *Handbook of Infant Development.* New York: Wiley.

Murphy, L. B., and Moriarty, A. E. (1976). *Vulnerability, coping, and growth: From infancy to adolescence.* New Haven, Conn.: Yale University Press.

Osofsky, J. D., and Culp, A. M. (1984). Affective responses of adolescent mothers and their infants. Unpublished manuscript. Topeka, Kans.: The Menninger Foundation.

Provence, S. (1983). *Infants and parents: Clinical case reports.* New York: International Universities Press.

Provence, S., and Greenspan, S. (1984). Schematic overview of multiaxial approach to the diagnosis of emotional and developmental disturbances in infancy and early childhood. Unpublished manuscript; National Center for Infant Programs, Washington, D.C.

Ricciuti, H. N. (1972). Emotional behavior and development in the first year of life: An analysis of arousal, approach–withdrawal and affective responses. In A. D. Pick (Ed.), *Minnesota symposium on child psychology,* Vol. 6. Minneapolis: University of Minnesota Press.

Rutter, M. (1984). Continuities and discontinuities in socioemotional development. In R. N. Emde and R. J. Harmon (Eds.), *Continuities and discontinuities in development.* New York: Plenum.

Sagi, A., and Hoffman, M. (1976). Empathic distress in the newborn. *Developmental Psychology, 12,* 175–176.

Sameroff, A. (1978). Organization and stability of newborn behavior: A commentary on the Brazelton Neonatal Behavior Assessment Scale. *Monographs of the Society for Research in Child Development, 43,* (5–6, Serial No. 177).

Sameroff, A., and Chandler, M. (1975). Reproductive risk and the continuation of caretaking casualty. In F. Horowitz, E. M. Hetherington, S. Scarr-Salapatek, and G. Siegel (Eds.), *Review of child development research,* Vol. 4. Chicago: University of Chicago Press.

Solnit, A. A. (1974). A summing up of the Dakar conference. In E. J. Anthony and C. Koupernik (Eds.), *The child in his family: Children at psychiatric risk.* New York: Wiley.

Spitz, R. (1946). Anaclitic depression. *Psychoanalytic Study of the Child, 2,* 313–342.

Spitz, R. (1959). *A genetic field theory of ego formation: Its implications for pathology.* New York: International Universities Press.

Spitz, R. (1965). *The first year of life: A psychoanalytic study of normal and deviant objective relations.* New York: International Universities Press.

Sroufe, L. A. (1979). Socioemotional development. In J. Osofsky (Ed.), *Handbook of infant development.* New York: Wiley.

Sroufe, L. A. (1983). Infant–caregiver attachment and patterns of adaptation in preschool: The roots of maladaptation and competence. In M. Perlmutter (Ed.), *Minnesota symposium on child psychology,* Vol. 16. Hillsdale, N.J.: Lawrence Erlbaum.

Sroufe, L. A., and Waters, E. (1977). Attachment as an organizational construct. *Child Development, 48,* 1184–1199.

Sroufe, L. A., and Wunsch, J. (1972). The development of laughter in the first year of life. *Child Development, 43,* 1326–1344.

Stechler, G., and Carpenter, G. (1967). A viewpoint on early affective development. In J. Hellmuth (Ed.), *The exceptional infant. Vol. 1: The normal infant.* Seattle: Special Child Publications.

Stern, D. (1984). Affect attunement: The sharing of feeling states between mother and infant by means of inter-modal fluency. In T. Field and N. Fox (Eds.), *Social perception in infants.* Norwood, N.J.: Ablex.

Stern, D. N. (1985). *The interpersonal world of the infant.* New York: Basic Books.

Thomas, A., Chess, S., Birch, H., Hertzig, M., and Korn, S. (1963). *Behavioral individuality in early childhood.* New York: New York University Press.

Tizard, B. (1977). *The adoption of children from institutions after infancy in child adoption.* London: Association of British Adoption and Fostering Agencies.

Trevarthen, C. (1980). The foundations of intersubjectivity: Development of interpersonal and cooperative understanding in infants. In D. R. Olson (Ed.), *The social foundation of language and thought—Essays in honor of Jerome S. Bruner.* New York: Norton.

Tyson, R. (1984). The origins and fates of psychopathology in infancy: A panel discussion. In E. Galenson and J. Call (Eds.), *Frontiers of infant psychiatry,* Vol. II (pp. 480–489). New York: Basic Books.

Winnicott, D. W. (1965). *The maturational processes and the facilitating environment.* New York: International Universities Press.

Wolkind, S., and Hall, F. (1979). Disadvantaged infants as parents. In J. Howells (Ed.), *Modern perspectives in the psychiatry of infancy.* New York: Brunner/Mazel.

Zahn-Waxler, C., and Radke-Yarrow, M. (1982). The development of altruism: Alternative research strategies. In N. Eisenberg (Ed.), *The development of prosocial behaviors.* New York: Academic Press.

Zahn-Waxler, C., Cummings, E. M., Ianotti, R. J., and Radke-Yarrow, M. (1984). Young offspring of depressed parents: A population at risk for affective problems. In D. Cicchetti and K. Schneider-Rosen (Eds.), *Childhood depression.* New York: Jossey-Bass.

PART III

Perspectives on Prevention Programs

Translating Research into Practice

Marshall S. Swift and Kathryn N. Healey

A Retrospective Analysis

Preparing this analysis forced us to examine the foundations of our work over the past 10 years. It required organizing our thinking about the many influences on those activities and the experiences we have had in building preventive intervention services within the structure of a treatment-oriented community mental health center located in an impoverished, urban catchment area.

In this process two key axioms emerged and are the focus of our discussion: (1) preventive interventions must have a foundation based on good research, and this occurs only when practitioners understand the research methods and findings; and (2) prevention practitioners must build constituencies for a program if it is to survive beyond field trials, regardless of the quality of its research or the skills of those providing the service.

The goal of this chapter is to provide a guided tour, tracing our thinking and experience as these two issues merged: Making a research base usable for practitioners, and building broad-based constituent validation for prevention programs.

To guide our prevention activities we created a working model to foster communication between practitioners and researchers—and among them and their potential constituent users and supporters. Only when these two bridges are established and used does prevention gain its place as an important element in the continuum of mental health services.

In retrospect we must acknowledge that there have been many who made us conceptualize, for practitioners are doers. We must recognize those who shared our early failures and those who supported us as we developed a working model for translating research into successful preventive interventions. Since 1974, major support for these efforts has come from NIMH through Consultation and Education, and Child Mental Health Service grants, and from contracts and funding from schools, community-based medical clinics, social welfare agencies, foundations, the Office of Prevention at NIMH, and the Philadelphia City government and its Department of Mental Health. In 1983, we and our colleagues, George Spivack (principal investigator) and Myrna Shure, established a Preventive Intervention Research Center (PIRC) at Hahnemann, funded by the Center for Prevention Research of NIMH and further supported by the PEW Memorial Trust and the Philadelphia School District. Each of these sources of support, whether funders or community-based field settings, offered both significant assistance and demanding challenges. Each had its own view of prevention and outcome expectations. The wide array of systems within which and with whom we were required to work necessitated the creation of generalizable guiding principles. These principles were essential to enable successful communication about the evolving nature of prevention concepts in general and the programs we were being commissioned to do specifically. To build and sustain a prevention-focused program within a treatment-oriented mental health setting, our staff quickly learned that as preventionists we all had to broaden our thinking from our roots in clinical psychology, psychiatry, education, and social work into child development, anthropology and sociology, adult education and program evaluation, and beyond into marketing, organizational development and behavior, political action and community organizing, as well as fund-raising, budgeting, and cost accounting.

In the beginning we initiated a process that started slowly but carried us far—a continuing search of the literature about research with potential for preventive interventions of value to mental health. It was our view that such interventions without a research base would ultimately fulfill the prophecies of many of our clinical and administrative colleagues: that there is no justification for such activities in mental health (Perlmutter, 1976). This viewpoint was ultimately summarized by Lamb and Zusman (1979) who asserted: "Mental illness is in large part probably genetically determined and it is therefore not preventable, at most only modifiable. Even that it can be modified is questioned by many and there is little hard evidence one way or the other" (p. 13). While this was the prevailing view in traditional mental health, we found that educators, public welfare personnel, and community residents typically did not share that conviction.

Nevertheless, by 1975 there were some research studies and some effort to translate them into practical programs (Caplan, 1961; Caplan and Gruenbaum, 1967; Swift and Spivack, 1974; Bloom, 1975), but little of significance had penetrated mental health practice. A review of practitioner-oriented literature at that time further revealed that research findings in key areas were virtually ignored (Warren, 1967). Rothman (1974) lamented about the "failure of scholars (in the social sciences) to translate social science findings into fully usable knowledge for practitioners."

Undeterred, but with cautious optimism, we entered settings where we were known and our professional skills recognized. Although somewhat uncomfortable about our own foundation in prevention, we believed that we could enhance our limited base by selecting staff who could engage varied communities and agencies in the problem-identification and problem-solving process. We hired people who knew, and were known and well-respected by those communities. Our staff, a former principal and ex-teachers trained through advanced degrees in mental health and developmental psychology, worked in schools; our psychiatrist, mental health nurse, and pediatrician adopted neighborhood clinics and small hospitals; our social workers and indigenous paraprofessionals were located in social service and family-care systems and community centers, and our anthropologist and psychologists (who were later to resonate to Sarason's, (1976), *Mr. Everyman* concept), went everywhere they were welcomed—and some places where they were not.

Unlike others who knew little about the field settings they had used for research studies, and then left without apparent concern about the future adoption of their study methods into ongoing programs, we were selecting personnel who would have intimate knowledge of the needs and problems of those settings. They also were strong in their understanding of the foundations of mental health and were not enamored with the notion that treatment of the mentally ill was the best use of their talents. We shared attitudes, concepts, and skills with which, we were convinced, we were going to provide successfully new methods of essential value to those who worked or lived in the particular organization or community. With our methods we were going to openly share our collective wisdom and thereby optimize continued utilization of whatever programs emerged.

We decided to follow William Hollister's advice and "start humble." The first step was to examine the question, "What can we prevent?" In 1976 Hollister told us:

> Humility is the keynote in setting the goals of prevention programs. Someday, we hope we shall learn how to prevent the major psychoses, neuroses and the character disorders, but until that day we must settle for more humble objectives. Those of us in psychological fields can wisely borrow from the experience gained in preventing physical disorders. Even in physical medicine the first preventive efforts were not to prevent serious disease processes like heart disease, cancer or arthritis. Their first efforts were to prevent injuries, hemorrhages, debilitation

from fever, wound infections and disabilities. Instead of rejecting prevention in the mental health field because we cannot yet for sure prevent schizophrenia, let us, like physical medicine has done, start humbly with today's knowledge and gain experience step by step. (Hollister, 1977, p. 41)

Basic Strategies in Designing Prevention Programs

With these ideas in mind we began by testing some interventions that met our early understanding of our criteria: Have a basis in research and make sense to practitioners and constituent users. Three examples of early thinking and programs provide a picture of the experience we gained as we learned about applying preventive interventions.

One example involved a program for babies at risk due to lack of regular stimulation while still in the hospital because of very low birth weight. We wanted to provide training to nursing staff and the new mothers using what we knew about the importance of early infant stimulation. This process was based on research by Powell (1974), which indicated that—when low birth weight/low SES newborns were regularly handled by nursery personnel or by their own mothers—the babies thrived in a manner superior to those not given this added and specific attention. Those who received this added stimulation, compared to less engaged controls, gained weight faster and had higher Bayley mental and motor scores at four months, and performed better on the Bayley Behavior Record at six months. From these results we were convinced of the potential for long-range benefits of such an early stimulation program for all high-risk newborns and their mothers (Masterpasqua and Swift, 1984).

A second example involved providing poorly educated, impoverished single mothers specialized training to enable them to participate skillfully in the process of fostering growth and development of their four-year-old children, as well as to decrease feelings of alienation, loneliness, and depression for themselves (Swift, 1976a). The project was stimulated by the number of similar women who were making use of the community mental health center's outpatient treatment facilities (Harakel and Furey, 1971; Turner and Spivack, 1973), and by the ambivalent sentiments echoed by several of them about the community's preschool. "My child loves the school. He comes home saying 'the teacher said this, the teacher said that; the teacher knows more than you do.' It used to be that they took your children away from you when they were 5; now it's 3." To many of the mothers, participation of their children in the preschool program was reinforcing their feelings of inadequacy, loneliness, and depression. We recognized the implications of these perceptions for continued pregnancies, child abuse and neglect, and later school failure for the children.

With these needs in mind, we based the program, in part, on the research of Hess, Shipman, and Jackson (1965) and Hess and Shipman (1966), which related maternal teaching behavior to children's learning. These studies revealed that the typical impoverished mother's verbal explanations frequently did not give her child instructions, which, if followed, would lead to successful responses (which the teacher was doing!). One example from among many, occurred in discussion with a mother who was angry at her daughter for "disobeying." The mother related that in the morning she had told her 4 year old to "put four potatoes on the stove for supper." When she arrived home that evening there were four potatoes on the stove—not in a pot of water. Examining the issue with the group of mothers, we found that they typically reacted to their children's questions with commands to "just do it! Do what I told you. Don't think ahead of me." The mothers agreed that they did this because "no matter how much you tell them they don't listen."

We also based this mother- and child-focused program on the work of Chilman (1966), which suggested that the life style of many lower-class mothers is characterized by "constant and overpowering frustrations which make achievement an untenable goal and seriously weaken the ego or self-esteem" of both mothers and their children. In the program, story-telling with preschool books was demonstrated and taught to the mothers, so that they could be skillful with their children. The story content provided the basis for discussion of child development issues (e.g., "Who's smarter, the curious monkey or the monkey who never asks questions or does things he's not supposed to?"). In the end both children and mothers made significant social and emotional gains.

In a third program we provided teachers with behavior-rating scales that measured achievement-related classroom behaviors and provided a practical profile of behavior for each child (Spivack and Swift, 1971, 1975) and with easily readable books created by Swift and Spivack (1974, 1975), which translated researched alternatives into methods for promoting productive classroom behavior and mental health as part of the regular teaching process. Here we based our program on our knowledge of the nature and extent of maladaptive behavior in urban schools and the implications of these data for later mental health and social problems (Kellam and Schiff, 1968; Swift et al., 1972).

By a variety of criteria each of these interventions was a success: The babies were more viable than their counterparts; the preschool children of the trained mothers learned better, and their mothers indicated a greater sense of social support, competence, and self-confidence, as well as greater ability to use native intellect; and the teachers using our methods were observed to be better and to promote effective adaptation to class demands.

Remember, these were not intended to be research studies. Yet they were designed to test the effectiveness of specific interventions that, on the face of things, had solid rationale; and by most standards, they worked. As Glasscote (1980) later reported in the results of a study of six community mental health center programs (including ours):

> We are inclined to be impressed by having observed that they were responding to important problems experienced by distressed people; that the participants frequently expressed the feeling that their participation had been "beneficial" and that support was being provided to "vulnerable people in their efforts to cope." [The report concluded with the following statement:] A specific purpose of this study was to develop information that would justify encouraging community mental health centers to expand their prevention activities. On the basis of what we learned at these selected facilities, we have no problem at all in doing so. (p. 135)

Pleased with ourselves, we prepared to replicate our programs in another of the many settings within which at-risk groups gathered—only to find that as we were packing our extra infant stimulation manuals, our surplus preschool books for mothers, and our teaching strategy materials, the staff of the organizations within which we had demonstrated the value of our programs were returning to business as usual. We found that the hospital could see no reason for doing things with newborns any differently than they had done in the past, in spite of the project results; that the nursery school teachers and administrators did not see the time spent training the mothers as of value to their program and that changing teaching styles requires more than mere demonstration of another way, no matter how successful. We had demonstrated that we could translate research into effective and understandable programs and that those programs promoted or prevented. But we sadly learned that sustaining even the most effective preventive intervention in a community-based setting required far more than mere application of effective methods and positive translation of mental health concepts into understandable language or programs.

What We Learned

Examining these experiences we recognized that we had been faithful to our professional and scientific foundations, but we had treated the interventions as extensions of our work and had not acted to have them become integral to the settings in which we had sincerely but artificially placed them. Unfortunately, our carefully planned programs were like most professional applications: They were viewed as separate from, not part of, the systems into which we had placed them. In spite of their apparent acceptance, they did not address what the nurses, parents, teachers, or administrators were having to contend with. This was true even though it was evident that we had provided a valid means for promoting mental health and preventing dysfunction.

Thus the need for a guide for our actions became more clearly focused. We needed a means to enable researchers, practitioners, and community-based personnel to plan together to identify goals and target groups, develop methods, and evaluate outcomes beyond those directed to the at-risk group in question. More specifically, we had to articulate the many needs that had to be met because we now knew that the answer was not simply to teach prevention practitioners to better use research methods to target at-risk populations. While essential, this is only part of the preventive intervention process. We had repeatedly demonstrated that to target only the vulnerable individual would result in showing only that we could directly implement a program in almost any setting where we could gain entry.

Sustaining a program, we learned, bore less relationship to the qualifications of our staff or to our knowledge of a particular methodology than to our understanding of the dynamics of the systems within which we worked. And we had been warned because an NIMH report in 1973 had told us that

> The underlying basis for this problem often is the inability of mental health specialists to understand the internal dynamics of the systems—the moral dilemmas educators face on a daily basis, the political pressures with which they must constantly deal, the conflicts among staff related to differences in philosophy, and the conflicting demands and pressures from parents and state codes. In short, failure to understand the social dynamics often is the single most significant determinant of success or failure. (p. 5)

Building a Guiding Model for Prevention

From these experiences we drew two conclusions: (1) that preventive interventions with a good research foundation could be demonstrated to have positive outcomes of importance to mental health; and (2) that validation for prevention must come from recipients outside the mental health profession. In the first instance, the successful programs had scientific validity. We had been certain to replicate or intervene in a carefully controlled manner and to evaluate attitudinal, knowledge, or behavioral change. To accomplish the second, we learned that we had to gain constituent validity. Without community constituents the most scientifically valid intervention would have little chance for ongoing success.

Although we were providing services in a manner different from our treatment-oriented colleagues by reaching out to other settings to identify at-risk populations before the fact of emotional disturbance, we were still primarily focusing on the at-risk individual. By reviewing our experiences we identified six constituent levels within the community that had to be addressed (Swift, 1980):

1. *At-risk individuals,* through the promotion of their individual competence.

2. *Potential community supports* (i.e., parents, foster parents, other local residents), by the promotion and development of a "repertoire of possibilities and alternatives" gained from programs that increased knowledge and skills (Iscoe, 1974).

3. *Nonmental health caregivers* (i.e., teachers, nurses, social caseworkers), by enhancing their ability to more effectively identify and meet client/student social–emotional needs in the context of the regular work environment.

4. *Organizational leaders* (i.e., school principals, social welfare agency directors), by engaging them directly in the process of identifying new alternatives to solve old problems.

5. *Policymakers* (i.e., superintendents of schools and their boards, government officials, welfare commissioners), by increasing their awareness of the potential for prevention services and the impact of social policies.

6. *Interagency coalitions* (i.e., mental health agencies, schools, and social agencies), by demonstrating how to extend services and resources through collaborative programs.

Most prevention practitioners focus their attention primarily on the individual, community, *or* caregiver level by providing resources for at-risk individuals *or* through community-based self-help programs *or* by training caregivers. We learned that successfully sustained programs involve, as a significant part of the working plan, specific interventions to be carried out at two or more ecological levels simultaneously; that we optimize success as we increase the number of levels involved. Furthermore, although practitioners are hesitant to engage organizational leaders (e.g., the school principal) intimately in a prevention program, this failure undermines program maintenance. Officials at the state level (i.e.,

Directors of Offices of Prevention) on the other hand, focus their attention on the interagency, policy, and organization decisionmaker levels. To accomplish state goals in ways that have positive impact on the practice of prevention, they need to have a means of understanding and collaborating with practitioners who have experience at policy and decisionmaking levels as well as at individual and caregiver levels (Tableman, 1980).

A display of the working model for integrating scientific- and constituent-validity criteria is presented in Fig. 1. This model is designed, and has been used, to plan and analyze preventive interventions in an ongoing fashion, along two dimensions: scientific and constituent.

The *scientific concerns* are listed down the vertical axis and the *constituent levels* to be engaged along the horizontal. We have found it necessary to identify concrete targets and goals across each constituent level and to articulate the methods and outcomes desired for each level. Although most programs do not require action at all of the levels simultaneously, or even that action be taken beyond two or three of the levels, it is essential to think through potential methods that might be needed and the outcomes desired for all of the constituent levels. As we will show in the following case-study examples, such actions and outcomes often become apparent only after an intervention has run into problems. However, careful attention to the issues raised in each of the boxes, or "cells," while creating an intervention, prevents many problems and furthers attainment of preventive intervention goals. Experience also indicates that, if you have a particular preventive intervention in mind as you read the rest of this material, the utility of the model becomes evident.

In the first case study we show how we used the model to "save" a project that was in trouble; in the second case study we provide a sample of how the model can be used to optimize the acceptance, adoption, and incorporation of an intervention by ensuring (insofar as possible) that both scientific and multiple constituent validity are attained.

Before presenting these examples of the use of the model, however, we need to make a brief statement about model building. There are a number of different models that can be of value to those who wish to bridge research and practice. Furthermore, Glazer and his group at the Human Interaction Research Institute (1976) examined a number of such guides and concluded:

> It is true that the term "model" is used in a number of different senses, and that the model-building enterprise is in a fluid state. In attempting to put models to work, it is well to remember that they do not necessarily represent established laws. Ordinarily the model builder draws upon theory, experience, and, to a

FIGURE I

Working model for integrating scientific and constituent-validity criteria.

Scientific Concern	Constituent Level					
	Individuals	Community	Caregivers	Organization	Policymakers	Inter-Organization
Target group and goal						
Methods (action taken)						
Impact: Attitudes						
Impact: Knowledge						
Direct behavioral outcomes (feasible, short-term)						
Ultimate outcomes						
Ideal outcomes						

degree, validated evidence concerning relationships of one kind or another; but the model itself is to be judged in terms of its fruitfulness in leading to useful knowledge and dependable outcomes, and it is not in any way, a priori, offered as reflecting truth itself. (p. 65)

While all models oversimplify very complex sets of variables, they do provide a valuable framework for engaging the relevant parties in the planning, multiple goal-setting, and implementation/evaluation processes of programs. We use the plural, *processes,* because, as we have noted, our model requires consideration of two or more constituent target levels and a variety of outcomes. These outcomes include changes in attitudes, knowledge, and behaviors (which are directly measured and short-term), as well as "ultimate" or long-term outcomes (say, six months or two years after the specific preventive intervention was completed). The "ideal" is included to allow for brainstorming about an outcome beyond reach at the present time (e.g., the establishment of day-care centers for all families who desire one, a full-employment policy, all foster-care children adopted). Nonetheless, we consider it important for those who work in prevention to be able to identify and articulate such ideals.

Case Study 1: Retrospective Analysis (Prevention in Foster Care)

The model crystalized as we struggled with the response of preadoptive foster parents who were participating in a program designed to enhance the cognitive development, and thus the "adoptability," of newborns "temporarily" placed in their care. In theory, the children were to be placed with these parents for only a brief period of time; they were to be moved to permanent adoptive homes as soon as possible. Armed with a long line of research demonstrating that early intervention is most effective when parents are actively involved (see Bronfenbrenner, 1975), we began a program designed to teach preadoptive parents how best to enrich the cognitive development of their infants. We began by asking foster parents when they acquired custody of their infants. The norm was for the children to be placed with the preadoptive parents soon after birth, and the plan was for them to remain there until they were 6–13 months old. Knowing a little about early child development, we realized immediately that this was precisely the worst possible time for a parent–child separation, inasmuch as strong attachments are formed during this sensitive period. So how were we to instruct the foster parents? Should or could we ethically provide these parents with enrichment techniques that would serve only to strengthen an attachment that would inevitably lead to a terribly timed separation?

But we were not the only ones in an untenable situation. How could anyone be expected to invest emotionally in newborns who they know would be taken from them once an attachment was formed? Indeed, the problem appeared to rest not with the foster parents but with a foster-care policy that did not appear to recognize the basic "developmental rights" (Masterpasqua, 1981) of both the child and the foster parents.

In order to sustain this intervention, which was designed to integrate research findings about emotional development of infants with practice, we now understood that it was essential to draw the system directly into the prevention process—and we now had a model to guide our thinking and actions. We used the model to organize this intervention as shown in Fig. 2.

From the experiences described earlier, we knew that a preventive intervention would be adapted and sustained only if we engaged the organization's leadership and those designated as its caregivers. This process of involvement required as much thought and planning as the original intervention program. Although they believed in us—that was how we were invited to train the foster parents in the first place—it was more important to involve each constituent level in ways that enabled understanding of how current organizational policies and practices impeded (or aided) the attainment of the goal for the infants, i.e., to increase the psychological viability of the foster infants by enhancing the bonding process with community-based foster parents. We met with organization leaders and caregivers to review the instructions given to the foster parents and the social service system's rationale for discouraging emotional ties. We learned that some foster parents become attached to the babies and have great difficulty with giving them up. However, we were able to bring to the surface the fact that all too few of the babies would actually be adopted or return to natural homes, now or in the future. Thus the practice required of the foster parents (i.e., give good parenting but at an emotional distance) was based on the notion that the system would work and the babies would be adopted—a process that too rarely happened for this population.

Without a bonding experience many of these children would start life without reasonable mothering, which the foster parents could and wanted to give. Together with the foster parents, caseworkers, and social service organization leaders, we reasoned that, although we could not change the entire system, we could make the system more responsive to the mental health needs of the infants—that it would be in the child's (and society's) best interest to encourage the attachment process between

FIGURE 2

Case study 1: Prevention in foster care.

	Constituent Level					
Scientific Concern	Individuals	Community	Caregivers	Organization	Policymakers	Inter-Organization
arget group and goal	Foster infants Increase emotional viability and ability to maintain attachments.	Foster parents Increase understanding of child's need for verbal, physical, contact.	Caseworkers Support foster parents in aiding emotional development of infants.	Supervisors, Executives Modify policy to bring it in line with infant's developmental needs.		
ethods (action taken)	Foster parents hold gaze at eyes and talk to babies on regular basis. Give verbal feedback when baby verbalizes.	Methods modeled, discussed, feedback from babies (e.g., smiling, cooing) analyzed.	Meetings to review their needs, values and practices and to share information about emotional development in foster care.	Discuss foster care in light of research and real-world issues.		
pact: Attitudes	——	It is appropriate to provide special "mothering."	Foster parent's closeness not detrimental; will encourage attachment.	Willingness to examine practices and effect of emotional development.		
pact: Knowledge	——	How to encourage infant emotional growth.	How infant growth can be enhanced during foster-care period and beyond with simple methods; process of attachment is good.	Positive emotional growth can be fostered by specific parenting.		
rect behavioral utcomes (feasible, hort-term)	More smiling, eye contact, reaching.	More comfortable contact with infants, talking.	Active encouragement of foster parents.	Set time for all staff and foster parents to learn to promote mental health of infants.		
timate outcomes	Trusting toddlers/children, comfortable with adults.	Continued use of knowledge with other babies.	Encouragement and training of new foster parents by caseworkers.	Ongoing program established.		
eal outcomes	Adoption.	——	Work with and encourage own supervisor at welfare dept. to examine other foster care practices.	More effective adoption system.		

foster parents and infants. In this case the targets of our mental health preventive intervention were neither merely the babies nor even just the babies and their community-based foster caregivers. Rather, it was necessary for us to include in our design for the intervention a means for translating prevention research in ways that would have an impact on the social service system's policies and practices. We had to translate research knowledge into concepts and principles that would be understandable and of real value both to the social service leadership and their designated caregivers. Then, in order to sustain a successful preventive intervention and effect a positive outcome, we needed to change attitudes and behaviors of social case workers and their supervisors. We had refined our notions about preventive interventions to: (1) include those in the system who are potential and necessary targets of an intervention (in addition to the children and their foster parents); (2) optimize the use of research methods, in order to attain scientific validity; (3) blend research criteria and the needs of people at the levels where interventions are to occur in order to significantly enhance the prevention process.

As we will demonstrate in the next case study, we are ready to conceptualize goals, actions, impacts, and short- and long-term outcomes across all constituent levels. The model enhances researcher, practitioner, and constituent users' communication about how best to operationalize a mental health promotion/prevention program for the particular setting(s) and populations in question.

Case Study 2: Prospective Analysis (Interpersonal Cognitive Problem Solving Program)

This case study is presented to provide a complete example of the thinking and methods behind a large-scale preventive intervention involving the dissemination of the Interpersonal Cognitive Problem Solving (ICPS) Program (Spivack, Platt, and Shure, 1976). This particular project is set in kindergartens in a public school system; our model provided a guiding framework for this prevention program.

We are in the midst of an extensive and expanding project to demonstrate that (1) a prevention program can be effectively integrated and sustained in a major system; and (2) this system-wide application will prevent psychological dysfunction by helping children develop healthy social adjustment and interpersonal competencies. Our goal is to demonstrate that the well-researched and validated ICPS program can be adapted for and adopted by a host system and thus have an impact on large numbers of at-risk children in a cost-effective way—not just during the research and/or project's intervention years but also in the years to follow.

Integration and incorporation is expected to take three years. In Year 1, four resource teachers learned the program and cotrained 6 kindergarten teachers and their classroom (community-resident) teaching aides. A total of 360 children received one of two kinds of training: (1) formal direct lessons, plus in-the-classroom follow-up through the use of semistructured dialoguing when real interpersonal problems occur; or (2) the semistructured dialoguing only.

This intervention immediately involves all six of the constituent levels in the model. Successful incorporation of this program requires the formulation of goals at the organization level (resource teachers), caregiver level (teacher), and the community level (local-resident aides), as well as at the individual level (at-risk children), which is typically addressed in research. In addition, successful incorporation requires a focus on interorganizational issues (mental health and education systems) and school policy. We know that the questions for which we seek answers must consider, but go beyond, those asked during the research phase. The earlier research questions were: "What are the problems to be prevented?" (What can we prevent with at-risk children?); "How can we intervene?" (What works for that specific population?); "How can we intervene successfully in a complex field setting?" (How do we maintain control of the variables of importance to our research?); "Whose support do we need to do research?" (How do we protect the research design?).

As translators of prevention research, practitioners are faced with the additional goals of incorporation and maintenance, which involve a greater number of people at all levels in the model. The questions now are: "How do we engage a system in the process of change from a reactive to a proactive stance regarding the promotion of mental health and the prevention of dysfunction for all children?" (What policy and organization level goals do we have?); "Who must participate and how will they be involved?" (What target groups in the system do we need to focus on and what methods will be used?); "What outcomes across the system do we want to achieve?" (What attitude, knowledge, behavioral changes are desired at each level?).

Examining the model we used for this project, presented as Fig. 3, you can see that one goal, for example, is to involve a growing number of caregivers (teachers) in learning and continuing to use the program in successive years (6 in the Year 1, 12 in Year 2, and 24 in Year 3). However, there has been a barrier to this process. We know from past experience that a mental health promotion program is perceived as an add-on to

FIGURE 3

Case study 2: ICPS program for a school system.

Scientific Concern	Constituent Level		
	Individuals	Community	Caregivers
Target group and goal	Enhance interperson. competence and preven. beh./emot. malad.; at risk for behav./emot. problems; Yr 1, N = 360, Yr 2, N = 720, Yr 3, N = 1440.	Increase understanding/use of program by community-based personnel: teachers' aides and parent-scholars.	Enhance teachers' ability to foster mh at-risk child engage aids as team with the RT; Yr 1 N = 6, Yr 2 N = 12, Yr 3 N = 24 teachers.
Methods (action taken)	Lessons teaching thinking skills to solve interperson. problems; use skills in real prob. solv. thru dialoguing.	Only teachers and resource teachers (RT) trained; reconsidered; engage teachers' aides directly in w'shops; assist teacher doing review lessons.	Train to do ICPS in reg. classroom prog. and to engage aides and parent-scholars; train in use of informal dialoguing.
Impact: Attitudes	Create view within child that "I *can* problem solve" when faced with interpers. problems.	Apprec. import. of helping child think and solve interp. probs. themselves; see program as help in their community.	Apprec. import. of helping child think and solve interp. problems themselves; see program as re evant to learning.
Impact: Knowledge	Children acquire thinking skills in problem solving.	Learn ICPS concepts; how to present lessons and dialogue when children having interpers. difficulties.	Learn ICPS; how to present lessons and dialogue when children have interp. diffic.; learn to engage aides.
Direct behavioral outcomes (feasible, short-term)	Reduce/prevent impulsive aggressive shy/timid beh. prodromal to emot.; academic dysfunction; maint./improve prosocial behavior.	Provide classroom lessons, use dialoguing in real life; decrease solving problems for children.	Regular use of curr. dialog. provides opportunity for aides to work with children in new ways; feedback to us and RTs.
Ultimate outcomes	"I *can* problem solve"; decrease incidence of maladaptive beh.; in all kindergartens; N = 2800 children.	Use new skills in subsequent years to aid new groups.	Dialoguing part of natura teaching style; reg. and consist. use of prog. wit new groups of children.
Ideal outcomes	Mentally healthier children in spite of adverse life situations; decrease special class (emot. disturb.) placements.	Generalize skills; be broader commun.; be better interpersonal problem solvers themselves.	Teachers become disseminators of program on their own for all childrer over entire system.

FIGURE 3
(continued)

Organization	Policymakers	Inter-Organization
Establish mechan. for implemen. across classrooms and schools; Yr 1 in 6 schools, Yr 2 in 12, Yr 3 in 24.	Prev. beh. emot. dysfunction in schools is goal and promo. of interpers. comp. is policy; board, super., dept. head sanction ICPS.	Dev. common goals to promote inter. comp. and prev. emot./beh. dysfunct. in children; planners, foundation, research, and practitioners.
Train RTs. feedback progress; mon. further prog. in org. policy-level update; facil. cont. use across system.	Prog. solid res. base; demo. relevence of syst. at all levels (not just dir. involve demo); willing to work thru stresses together.	Focus ICPS prog. dev. plan for collab., analysis/ evaluation/support from each system
Develop belief in value prog. educat. process; that work toward change worthwhile; that mh and educ. goals are compatible.	Develop belief in value prog. educat. process; that work toward change worthwhile; that mh and educ. goals compatible, in promot. mh and prev.	Establ. syst. share view of importance of interp. comp. prev. emot./beh. dysfunc. prior to need for mh treatment sch. discip./spec.
RTs know how to teach ICPS; princ./dept. staff underst. principles (adult guide children in how to think vs. solve probl. for).	Import of struc'd. meth. guide children to think/ teachers' beh. related to beh./emot./learn. progress, potential of prevention.	How each system contrib. to promo. mh of at-risk children and how might be achieved collectively with shared resources.
RTs integr. into job; demo. leader to maint. and train others; be spokesperson; inform us of ways to disseminate/further incorporat.	Meet reg. place prev./ ICPS on agenda and in curric., allocate funds, other resources; attend when staff present program.	Share resources under umbrella, active participation in eval.; look for opportun. to integrate in other settings.
Develop mechanisms, to aid maintenance continuation and integrity of prog. across schools.	Integrate ICPS into official, standard curriculum, across schools/up grades, decrease need for spec. classes.	Systematic, ongoing multisystem support for prev. interv. as part of shared mission; prog. reach many children; new research.
Schools with program excel in increased interpers. competence and decr. in incidence of beh./emot. dysfunct.	System be proud of innovation, maint.; save $ and increase productivity and mh of children in 6th year.	Cost savings in terms of $ and increase of productive, mentally healthy children successful in school.

regular requirements for teachers. Each year, pressure to meet other system demands (generated at the policy and organization levels), interfered with even the motivated teacher's ability to use the ICPS program. Therefore, as practitioners, we had to identify mechanisms (methods) to help organization and policy leaders support and encourage such activities rather than add them to the burden of already overwhelmed administrative (organization level) (Johnston, Healey, and Swift, 1981) and teaching (caregiver) staffs. These issues are summarized in Fig. 3 and amplified for each level in the following sections.

Interventions at the Policy Level

Clearly these systemwide barriers to prevention point to the need to establish policy-level goals, target populations, and methods *before* any new program is included as an integral part of the system's core curriculum (i.e., policy-level decisions). Action is required with policymakers (e.g., the superintendent and department head) to gain sanction and establish methods to integrate ICPS into the educational curriculum so that time allocated is legitimized for its use in lesson plans. To accomplish this end we had to interpret the research data to provide evidence of the solid research bases and to establish the program's relevance to solving problems faced by the system. To optimize the likelihood that integration would occur, we needed to articulate carefully the methods we would use to affect the attitudes, knowledge, and behaviors from the policy makers. In our thinking, as reflected in the model, they became both constituents and targets of the intervention.

In every instance the practitioner has to demonstrate the relevance of the program to the host's system (i.e., gain constituent validity). We have to identify shared goals and methods for communicating appropriately with policymakers and their staffs and engaging them in the program's processes; we have to demonstrate a willingness to work through the inevitable stresses of change with them, using our mental health consultation skills. Thus components of any prevention program in mental health must have practical utility (in this case, educational meaning) to the host system if its policymakers are to be expected to act on program incorporation.

In the ICPS program we engaged them by offering means for incorporating mental health promotion and problem prevention into the standardized curriculum. This involved clearly addressing the relevance of the program to areas of concern identified by the system (i.e., decreasing behavioral/emotional problems that interfere with learning, increasing the number of children who can be retained in the less costly regular classroom). To accomplish this, we needed to know about and relate our program to their curriculum. In that curriculum, development of "human values" was identified as the educational area where the ICPS program could be included. Thus the existing curriculum already allowed for *passive* inclusion of our mental health/preventive intervention. However, further steps were necessary if we were to achieve the ultimate goal of integrating ICPS into the official standard curriculum. (See Fig. 3, policymakers level.) Our goal was to gain *active* participation in the process of prevention from those at each constituent level. Only after active involvement (at any level) is obtained can constituent validation be attained. Attainment of this end required that we negotiate for the opportunity to participate in the writing of the school system's curriculum for the coming year. Collaborating with the appropriate department head and staff, we integrated the principles of the ICPS with the curriculum as a guide to program philosophy and practice.

This policy-level directive will lead the ultimate users of the guide—the teachers—to seek out interpersonal problem-solving training materials to meet curriculum requirements. Furthermore, this affords us a large-scale opportunity to evaluate the program over time. While this will require a number of years, the stage is now set for increasingly greater opportunities to test the program's impact at a variety of levels and provide feedback to policymakers.

Achievement of this policy-level goal is only one of the many necessary for active incorporation and maintenance. Beyond engaging policymakers intimately in the prevention program incorporation process, focus on the organization level is essential because this is where policy is carried out and operational problems surface.

Engaging the Organization Level

In order to optimize integration into the organization's practices each step in the process is closely coordinated with those at the department (policy) level. Invitations to planning meetings, first for district superintendents (with geographic area authority), and later through them for their principals, are initiated directly by policy-level staff. Meetings such as these establish the importance of the prevention intervention program, emphasize its inclusion in the school's curriculum, and underscore the need to support and encourage full participation by teachers. Examining Fig. 3, you can see that this led us to identify, with school personnel, another set of targets of our intervention, i.e., those who interpret policy and put it into practice, and to develop methods to ensure their involvement. These organization-level leaders include principals, who have responsibility for individual schools, and resource teachers, who cross boundaries to help maintain quality control across schools.

Critically important to accomplishing the outcomes identified at the caregiver (teacher) level are those who consult with teachers in several schools, the resource teachers. They are organization-level personnel who are best suited to negotiate and maintain the ICPS program across the system. These individuals are identified by policy-level personnel, and methods for their involvement are carefully developed with those personnel. Just as those at the caregiver level learn of the importance of the prevention/mental health/ICPS program through its inclusion in the curriculum, so too do organization-level personnel need to know from their superiors that this is a legitimate part of their role (i.e., that it is in concert with the policies and practices of the system). Thus interaction among the levels is needed to accomplish the systemwide incorporation and maintenance goal. Those at the policy level must directly sanction organization-level involvement, as well as convey a message of commitment and support to the caregiver level.

In practice, our methods required that regular weekly meetings be held with the resource teachers to: (1) sharpen their skills as ICPS consultants and trainers with the teachers and teachers' aides; and (2) collaborate with us in the process of identifying goals and defining methods to foster integration of the program with the system. (See Fig. 3, organization level.)

These meetings emphasize the specific elements of the approach and generalizable strategies for assisting with classroom implementation of the program. We convey to them that retention of the specific researched methods are *required* for program success, and we emphasize that there must be creative partnerships if the program is to be successful. In this way scientific- and constituent-validity criteria are again carefully addressed and the ICPS material is incorporated into the resource teacher's major role as classroom consultant. These meetings also serve to engage the resource teachers as advocates for the program and partners in its widespread dissemination in Year 1 and subsequent years. Because of their position at the organization level, resource teachers also are encouraged to identify necessary steps to be taken at the other levels in order to further the prevention incorporation goal.

In all systems there are those who operate to implement policy. They must be identified as targets of the prevention program and engaged in its dissemination. In this manner these personnel function as identifiers and translators of system messages that we, as outsiders, could not perceive or understand. For example, when the newly developing standardized curriculum was discussed, organization-level staff quickly saw the implications at the caregiver level: "If you're not in the guide, you can just forget it. The teachers will say to us, 'It's not part of the standard curriculum and therefore we don't have time for it.'" As key internal staff in the system organization-level personnel often serve as alarm raisers and challenge us to rethink the actions to be taken at each level. Fostering this behavior is one of our model-dictated goals. (See organization level, direct behavioral outcomes.)

When a school agrees to participate (and we initially accept only a limited number of schools in a system), we plan methods to ensure continual engagement of the principals. Note in Fig. 3 that the goal for the principals is for them to communicate their view of the relevance of the program within their school to teachers, to parents, and to their colleagues across the system—and to gain feedback about program validity. Although direct contact between practitioners and organizational leaders is always limited, the importance of identifying ways to keep these leaders engaged cannot be underestimated. This can be accomplished in a variety of ways, as noted in the model:

1. We (the prevention team) guide teachers to report on the program during regular faculty meetings.

2. We encourage resource teachers to provide verbal feedback to their department head and to school principals.

3. We routinely stop by the principal's office to "check in" and to build working relationships.

4. We are always available to "trouble shoot."

5. We hold wrap-up meetings with the principals at the close of each school year.

These methods are designed to help organization leaders feel involved and to solidify their ongoing and active understanding of the program, so that it becomes *theirs* in subsequent years.

Engaging the Caregivers and Their Community-Based Aides

In a school system the caregivers are the teachers. (Nurses, social services caseworkers, and on-the-street police officers play this role in other systems.) They are in the position to implement new practices and to expand their role to include the promotion of mental health and the prevention of emotional/behavioral dysfunction.

Even with careful involvement of policy- and organization-level personnel, crucial new issues emerge at the caregiver level that are significant for both constituent and scientific validity. For example, at the first training session the teachers requested that their classroom aides be included in the workshops. The original researched methods (scientific validity) called for the resource teachers to train directly only the classroom teachers—then, for teachers to give their aides opportunities to learn the program by watching and reading about it. It was clear, however, that not including the aides in the group training sessions would have several negative effects on the program (i.e., on its constituent validation). Non-invitation, it was noted, would have a practical, interpersonal impact (the caregiver system would be disrupted) and might adversely affect community understanding and commitment (through the lack of engagement of a community resident, the teacher's aide). Furthermore, since the program is used to facilitate daily problem solving with children when real problems occur, both teachers and aides need to use the same constituent process to support each other. Thus it was apparent that the aides were needed as active participants from the outset. Perhaps even more important were the views that the aides would feel left out and that, if the program really is important and of value to the growth of the children, then the aides, too, should participate in the training sessions.

In addition to providing support to the teacher, one aspect of community-level validation is addressed through the direct involvement of the classroom aide. These aides are parents of children in the school and members of the parents' organization. They are sensitive to the needs expressed by the community. Their appreciation of children's ability to solve problems and their generalization of ICPS skills to the broader community are elements already recognized as important at the community level (see Fig. 3, target group and goal.) Furthermore, principals and classroom personnel emphasized their need for community support and raised questions about how we might expand this level of the intervention by including as a target the children's parents. An earlier research project (Shure and Spivack, 1978) reported that parents were successful ICPS trainers for their children. With this clear merging of scientific and constituent validity, expansion of individual-level implementation (methods) to include parents is being explored.

Intervention at the Individual Level

Goals at the individual level are closely tied to the extensive scientific knowledge base developed by Spivack, Platt, and Shure (1976). Based on this research we anticipate that the ICPS intervention will: (1) reduce the incidence of socially maladjusted behaviors prodromal to interpersonal and emotional disturbance in children; and (2) prevent such behaviors from occurring. Children showing signs of adjustive failure have repeatedly been found to have poorly developed interpersonal cognitive problem-solving (ICPS) skills in comparison to their better adjusted peers. Shure and Spivack (1982) have demonstrated that an identifiable set of ICPS skills mediates healthy functioning and that training in these skills can therefore improve adjustment. The ICPS program was developed to teach the cognitive skills that are most predictive of interpersonal competence: alternative solution thinking and consequential thinking. This program has been demonstrated to enhance skills as early as age 4, thereby preventing the development of adjustment problems in normal children and improving the adjustment of those children displaying excessively inhibited or overly impulsive behaviors and poor prosocial skills.

The ICPS program teaches a set of skills necessary for thinking through and effectively solving interpersonal problems. The emphasis is on *how* to think, not *what* to think or do. When successfully implemented, the program has been shown to prevent and/or reduce the incidence of overtly timid, impulsive, and/or aggressive behaviors in children from populations at risk for adjustive failure—and to have lasting effects over a two-year follow-up period (Shure and Spivack, 1982).

The intervention is a group process, which is taught in sequential daily lessons (Shure and Spivack, 1974a) that help guide children to think more effectively about interpersonal problems and encourage them to take action based on such thinking.

Key elements in the ICPS program for kindergarten and first-grade children include:

1. Prerequisite skills.
   (a) Problem-solving language and feelings.
   Learning to use key words such as why–because, now–later, same–different.
   Identifying feelings of happy-sad-mad.
   (b) Problem identification.
   Ability to see that a problem exists and to focus on the interpersonal components that may have led to the problem.
   (c) Perspective-taking.
   "What might others be thinking and feeling?"
   (d) Understanding how to stop and think.
   "What do I need to think about to handle this situation?"
2. Problem-solving skills.
   (a) Alternative solutions.
   Capacity to generate alternative ways of solving interpersonal problems.
   "That's one solution; can I think of others?"
   (b) Consequential thinking.
   Capacity to consider the consequences before acting.
   "What might happen next?"

In addition to use of the formal lessons, teachers and aides are taught how to dialogue with children when actual personal problems arise. Research evidence indicates that the use of problem-solving methods whenever problems occur has a significant effect on ICPS program success (Weissberg and Gesten, 1982; Weissberg et al., 1981). All of the children in a classroom gain when they see the problem-solving method used for resolving specific interpersonal problems among their peers.

As the model suggests, evaluation of impact is done at each level, either informally or formally. Because of the need to demonstrate the effectiveness of the program with data, evaluation at the individual level is typically more formal and extensive than at the other levels, although this need not be the case. Other options include environmental assessment (Moos, 1979; Felner, Ginter, and Primavera, 1982). In this instance we want to know whether children who participate in the ICPS program acquire problem-solving–thinking skills and the attitude that "I *can* problem solve" (the children's version of ICPS), as well as show reductions in the incidence of impulsive, aggressive, shy, or timid behaviors. While research support for such findings is now extensive (Shure and Spivack, 1982), we feel that it is essential for prevention practitioners to be concerned with scientific validity. Therefore careful assessment is done to ensure that the inevitable environmental pressures on such an intervention have not decreased the impact of the program (Shure, 1982).

Interorganization Coordination

While rarely considered in the planning of prevention services, we have found it useful to conceptualize the interplay between mental health and other systems during the intervention process. The model guides our thinking at the interorganization level by examining what needs to transpire in order to evolve common goals between, in this case, mental health and education, for which commonality of language is critical. A central issue is the uniting of the educator's orientation (toward improving achievement-related behavior) with that of the mental health specialist (concerned with the prevention of emotional problems). From our earlier experiences we knew that mental health specialists approach other settings from an egocentric perspective (Swift, 1976b, c). As the model suggests, at each stage of the process mental health specialists wishing to integrate prevention programs must work with educators to understand the different perspectives and develop shared goals. This process requires the establishment of *balanced partnerships* of personnel in different fields (Litwak, 1971). It requires that participants consciously identify the multiple methodologies to be used and the numerous outcomes desired. Such a method conveys respect for and allows response to the diversity of goals and attitudes of each participating system (Muñoz, Snowden, and Kelly, 1979). We have learned that the achievement of desired change, i.e., to incorporate a mental health promotion program, is greatly enhanced if that change increases the validation of the host organization's ideology as well (Brager and Holloway, 1978).

Conclusion

Analyses of prevention programs in a array of settings, with a variety of populations, reveal the existence of at least two basic elements essential (although not sufficient) to ensure successful implementation and maintenance: (1) a serious effort is made to use researched methods to establish scientific validity; and (2) constituent validation is considered a significant variable and goal to attain.

We have used case study examples to convey how one model is being used to guide preventive intervention planning, development, and integration. While we view this process to be essential, we recognize that this method of model building is but one among many. Furthermore, modifications of the model have already begun (Hall, 1983; Swift and Weirich, in press). Hall, for example, has added a timetable to the model and suggested differentiating *targets* at each ecological (constituent) level from *change agents*, in a plan for a statewide application in Connecticut. Such a model provides the means to depict how, with whom, where, and when prevention practitioners will work and what their multiple goals are.

Because these services are not provided within controlled mental health settings, any approach to guiding action must attend to the means of fostering collaboration among prevention researchers, practitioner-disseminators, and those intimately involved in the intervention/change process (e.g., principals, teachers, foster parents, social services caseworkers, to name only a few of the intervention targets). It is essential that we integrate the needs and values of those potential prevention constituents with the scientific requirements by which prevention will be measured. This is done to: "(a) optimize the prevention program acceptance, (b) increase the likelihood that a program will reach the ultimate target population in a manner as close [as possible] to that intended in the original research, and (c) assure that a program is adopted and sustained," according to Swift (1983).

Although most prevention research has been focused primarily on one of the constituent levels—the individual level—analysis of "examplary" programs reveals that the multiple-level approach is gaining widespread use (see Cowen, 1982).

The model provides readily usable guidelines for those who wish to adopt and use research knowledge in service settings. As with most models, application in the real world reveals limitations, needs for modification, and missing elements. For example, we have found it necessary to consider new constituent issues during the current ICPS integration project (Case Study 2), while maintaining the basic aspects of the original research. We recognize that it is almost "axiomatic that programs as implemented, are never the same as programs designed." (Morell, 1983). This is due in large part to the emphasis placed on gaining constituent validation at so many levels. The practitioner must recognize, however, that true adoption requires replication based on original methods and not merely on attainment of an outcome desired by a host institution. Studies of interventions within organizations reveal that there is strong pressure to change a program in ways that may even be contradictory to that of the originators (Rappaport, Seidman, and Davidson, 1979).

Because of the large number of pressures created at each constituency level, there is great tendency by practitioners to make changes to accommodate and gain support. It is essential therefore that issues such as how to determine what might be added or left out be examined and reviewed carefully. Simply put, we must ask how much change a program can stand and still be the same research-based intervention. Then we must think beyond whether a program can be demonstrated to work or was adopted. We must examine results and ask, "How and where did the intervention change the organization?"

Based on our experience, we have identified six constituent levels that prevention research users must address:

1. *Individuals at risk*—through direct promotion of individual competence and, in particular, to anticipate and deal with normal and transitional stages; and, further, to prevent the damaging affects of stressful conditions and life events.

2. *Community members*—by increasing their knowledge of and commitment to the prevention of mental health problems, enhancing their skills to recognize risk, and encouraging them to become active participants in the mental health promotion process.

3. *Caregivers*—by enhancing their ability to identify effectively and meet needs before the display of pathology and increasing their knowledge about how to implement appropriate prevention strategies as part of their regular activities.

4. *Organization Decisionmakers*—who must translate policy into program actions and set the tone and course for staff and community and

who must defend the program, identify problems early, and know what to do to intervene appropriately.

5. *Policymakers*—who must formulate a policy that sanctions the program and ultimately justify the cost of sustaining the program.

6. *Interagency coalitions*—by engaging all of the constituent levels in interagency and interdisciplinary efforts and by overcoming the differences in values, concepts, and language brought to the effort by educators, social workers, community residents, and others at every level.

Planning interventions at these six levels is a limited and arbitrary notion, as there may be other subunits within any setting that deserve consideration. Intervention practitioners should become familiar enough with a setting to be able to provide appropriate interventions—and at each of the levels engaged. Nevertheless, experience leads us to conclude that the six levels do encompass the major elements of a community and its organizations.

Finally, it takes more than good research or dissemination programs to "popularize" even the most effective preventive intervention. Furthermore, acceptance of a program by a constituency does not guarantee its longevity. The existence of a number of useful prevention methods wedded to a means of integration for an array of constituent levels makes for an exciting and challenging addition to the potential for research-based prevention services in community settings.

References

Bloom, B. B. (1975). *Community mental health: A general introduction*. Monterey, Calif.: Brooks/Cole.

Brager, G., and Holloway, S. (1978). *Changing human service organizations: Politics and practice*. New York: Free Press.

Bronfenbrenner, U. (1975). Is early intervention effective? In B. Z. Friedlander, G. M. Sterritt, and G. E. Rink (Eds.), *Exceptional infant 3: Assessment and intervention*. New York: Brunner/Mazel.

Caplan, G. (1961). *Prevention of mental disorders in children*. New York: Basic Books.

Caplan, G., and Gruenbaum, H. (1967). Perspectives on primary prevention: A review. *Archives of General Psychiatry, 17*, 331–346.

Chilman, C. S. (1966). *Growing up poor*. U.S. Department of Health, Education and Welfare, Division of Research. Welfare Administration Publication No. 13.

Cowen, E. L. (1982). Special issue: Research in primary prevention in mental health. *American Journal of Community Psychology, 10*, 239–250.

Felner, R. D., Ginter, M., and Primavera, J. (1982). Primary prevention during school transitions. *American Journal of Community Psychology, 10*, 277–290.

Glasscote, R. M. (1980). *Preventing mental illness: Efforts and attitudes.* Washington, D.C.: American Psychiatric Association Joint Information Service.

Glazer, E. (1976). *Putting knowledge to use.* Los Angeles: Human Interaction Research Institute.

Hall, C. H. (1983). *Prevention goals and program development: A model for prevention planning.* State of Connecticut, Office of the State-Wide Coordinator for Prevention.

Harakel, C., and Furey, F. (1971). *Patients served by the Hahnemann Community Mental Health Center,* Report No. 1. Philadelphia: Hahnemann Community Mental Health Center.

Hess, R. D., and Shipman, V. (1966). *Cognitive elements in maternal behavior.* Mimeo., Research Grant No. 34. Rockville, Md.: Children's Bureau, Department of Health, Education, and Welfare.

Hess, R. D., Shipman, V., and Jackson, D. (1965). Early experience and the socialization of cognitive modes in children. *Child Development, 36,* 869–886.

Hollister, W. G. (1976). Basic strategies in designing primary prevention programs. In D. C. Klein and S. E. Goldston (Eds.), *Primary Prevention: An Idea Whose Time Has Come* (pp. 41–47). Department of Health, Education and Welfare Publication No. ADM 77-447. Washington, D.C.: U.S. Government Printing Office.

Iscoe, I. (1974). Community psychology and the competent community. *American Psychologist, 29,* 607–613.

Johnston, J. C., Healey, K. N., and Swift, M. (1981). Burnout prevention training for school administrators. *Stress, 2,* 15–19.

Kellam, S., and Schiff, S. K. (1968). *Adaptation and mental illness in the first grade classrooms of an urban community.* Psychiatric Research Report No. 21 (pp. 79–81). Washington, D.C.: American Psychiatric Association.

Lamb, H. R., and Zusman, J. (1979). Primary prevention in perspective. *American Journal of Psychiatry, 136,* 12–17.

Litwak, E. (1971). An approach to linkage in grass roots community organization. In F. Cox, J. Rothman, and J. Tropman (Eds.), *Strategies of community organization* (pp. 126–138). Itasca, Ill.: Peacock.

Masterpasqua, F. (1981). Toward a synergism of developmental and community psychology. *American Psychologist, 36,* 782–786.

Masterpasqua, F., and Swift, M. (1984). Prevention of mental health problems on a community-wide basis. In M. C. Roberts, and L. Peterson (Eds.), *Prevention of problems in childhood: Psychological research and applications.* New York: Wiley.

Masterpasqua, F., Swift, M., and Weirich, T. (1983). *Integrating research on high-risk infants into mental health services: A primer.* Rockville, Md.: National Institute of Mental Health Technical Report.

Moos, R. H. (1979). Improving social settings by social climate measurement and feedback. In R. F. Muñoz, L. R. Snowden, and J. G. Kelly (Eds.), *Social and psychological research in community settings* (pp. 145–182). San Francisco: Jossey-Bass.

Morell, J. A. (1981). Evaluation in prevention: Implications from a general model. *Evaluation and Prevention in Human Services, 1,* 7–40.

Muñoz, R. F., Snowden, L. R., and Kelly, J. G. (Eds.) (1979). *Social and psychological research in community settings.* San Francisco: Jossey-Bass.

National Institute of Mental Health. (1973). *Evaluation of the impact of community mental health center. Consultation center services on school systems.* Department of Health, Education, and Welfare, Division of Mental Health Services Program (BASICO No. 645-01. Washington, D.C.: U.S. Government Printing Office.

Perlmutter, F. D. (1976). *Primary prevention as a source of conflict in community mental health centers.* Presented at the Annual Meeting of the Society for the Study of Social Problems, New York.

Powell, L. R. (1974). The effect of extra stimulation and maternal involvement on the development of low birth weight infants and on maternal behavior. *Child Development, 45,* 106–113.

Rappaport, J., Seidman, E., and Davidson, W. S. (1979). Demonstration research and manifest versus time adoption: The natural history of a research project to divert adolescents from the legal system. In R. F. Muñoz, L. R. Snowden, and J. G. Kelly (Eds.), *Social and psychological research in community settings* (pp. 132–144). San Francisco: Jossey-Bass.

Rothman, J. (1974). *Planning and organizing for social change.* New York: Columbia University Press.

Sarason, S. B. (1976). *Community psychology networks and Mr. Everyman. American Psychologist, 31,* 317–328.

Shure, M. (1982). *Prevention research, evaluation and application: Reflections on a cognitive approach.* Paper presented at the National Institute of Mental Health Conference on Primary Prevention, Austin, Texas.

Shure, M. B., and Spivack, G. (1974a). *ICPS: A mental health program for kindergarten and first-grade children.* Philadelphia: Hahnemann University Publication.

Shure, M. B., and Spivack, G. (1982). Interpersonal problem-solving in young children: A cognitive approach to prevention. *American Journal of Community Psychology, 10,* 341–356.

Spivack, G., Platt, J. J., and Shure, M. B. (1976). *The problem-solving approach to adjustment.* San Francisco: Jossey-Bass.

Spivack, G., and Swift, M. (1971). *The Hahnemann High School Behavior (HHSB) Rating Scale.* Philadelphia: Hahnemann University Publication.

Spivak, G., and Swift, M. (1975). *The Hahnemann Elementary School Behavior Rating Scale and Manual.* Philadelphia: Hahnemann University Publication.

Swift, M. (1976a). *Language style of the lower class mother: A preliminary study of a prevention technique.* Unpublished manuscript, Hahnemann Medical College, Philadelphia.

Swift, M. (1976b). *Some significant issues in training mental health clinicians in consultation and education.* Philadelphia: Hahnemann Community Mental Health/Mental Retardation Center.

Swift, M. (1976c). *Education for prevention in a community mental health setting: Creating a Part F program.* Philadelphia: Hahnemann Community Mental Health/Mental Retardation Center.

Swift, M. (1980). *A working model for primary prevention.* Paper presented at Annual Meeting of the National Committee for Mental Health Education, Virginia Beach, Va.

Swift, M. (1983). *The interpersonal problem-solving program: Prevention from research to adoption in real-life settings.* Paper presented at National Institute of Mental Health Workshop on Interpersonal Problem Solving, Rockville, Md.

Swift, M., and Spivack, G. (1974). Therapeutic teaching: A review of teaching methods for behaviorally troubled children. *The Journal of Special Education,* Monograph No. 4 (pp. 259–289).

Swift, M., and Spivack, G. (1975). *Alternative teaching strategies: A guide for teachers and psychologists*. Champagne, Ill.: Research Press.

Swift, M., and Weirich, T. (in press). Prevention planning as social and organizational change. In J. A. Hermalin and J. A. Morell (Eds.). *Prevention planning for mental health*. Beverly Hills, Calif.: Sage.

Swift, M., Spivack, G., Danset, L. J., and Winneykamen, F. (1972). Classroom behavior and academic success of French and American elementary school children. *International Review of Applied Psychology, 21*, 1–11.

Tableman, B. (1980). Prevention activities at the state level. In R. Price, R. Ketterer, B. Bader, and J. Monahan (Eds.), *Prevention in mental health: Research policy and practice*. Beverly Hills, Calif.: Sage.

Turner, C. O., and Spivack, G. (1973). *Conceptions of mental illness among low income, urban women*, Report No. 13. Philadelphia: Hahnemann Community Mental Health Center.

Warren, R. (1967). Application of social science knowledge to the community organization field. *Journal of Education for Social Work, 3*, 60–72.

Weissberg, R. P., and Gesten, E. L. (1982). Considerations for developing effective school-based social problem-solving (SPS) training programs. *School Psychology Review, 11*, 56–63.

Weissberg, R. P., Gesten, E. L., Carnrike, C. L., Toro, P. R., Rapkin, B. D., Davidson, E., and Cowen, E. (1981). Social problem skills training: A competence-building intervention with second-to-fourth-grade children. *American Journal of Community Psychology, 9*, 411–423.

Recent Developments in Crisis Intervention and in the Promotion of Support Services

Gerald Caplan

Overview

In this chapter I describe and discuss the following developments, which have occurred in primary prevention during the past ten years:

1. A comprehensive model of primary prevention has been developed that articulates past risk factors, mental health outcome, and intermediate variables of competence, teaching of competence, reaction to current stress, and social supports.
2. Methods of crisis intervention—anticipatory guidance and preventive intervention—have been explicated in detail.
3. Similar explication has occurred in several methods of support systems practice.

I conclude the chapter by predicting likely future developments, which include: (1) focus of research on populations exposed to specific stressors; (2) focus on explicating and measuring proximal and distal outcome variables; and (3) development of standard research instruments for widespread use.

Introduction

Twenty years ago when I wrote my book, *Principles of Preventive Psychiatry* (1964), the main goal of our model building was to adapt traditional

The research on which this chapter is based was supported by a grant from the Israel Cancer Association and by grants from the Shainberg Fellowship Fund of New York, which are gratefully acknowledged. The preventive work with children and their parents has been conducted by the staff of the Hadassah Department of Child and Adolescent Psychiatry in collaboration with Professor Zvi Fuks, Professor Shoshanna Biran, and their colleagues of the Hadassah Department of Radiation and Clinical Oncology, and with Professor Israel Tamir and his colleagues of the Hadassah Department of Pediatrics, Ein Kerem.

public health theories and practices for use in the mental health field. We focused in those days on two issues: (1) developing a list of past biopsychosocial stressful events and processes that were thought to increase the risk of future mental disorder in an exposed population; and (2) studying so-called life crises, namely, limited time periods of upset in the psychosocial functioning of individuals, precipitated by current exposure to environmental stressors, which appeared to be turning points in the development of mental disorder. Methods of primary prevention were directed toward influencing decisionmakers to change conditions of community life so as to reduce the occurrence or intensity of biopsychosocial hazards; toward modifying health, education, and welfare services so that community caregivers would intervene preventively during life crises provoked by stress; and toward developing and disseminating techniques of preventive intervention for use with individuals in crisis and their families. Much of this crisis intervention was directed at helping target individuals and their families reduce the intensity and incapacitating effects of their crisis-induced emotional upset and at offering them guidance and material help in grappling with their predicaments.

Another goal was to develop viable roles for mental health specialists as energizers of primary prevention programs that would be implemented mainly by community decisionmakers and caregiving professionals. Our approach was to use the limited number of mental health specialists as consultants and educators to the network of community key workers, who in turn would influence high-risk groups on a widespread scale in the population they served. In my second book on preventive psychiatry, *Theory and Practice of Mental Health Consultation,* (1970), I described the techniques we had worked out over the previous decade to accomplish this goal.

During the past ten years the two elements of the original model have been supplemented by postulating: (a) *competence* as an internal constitutional and acquired quality of individuals that enables them to withstand the harmful effects of hazardous circumstances; and (b) *social supports* as an external mechanism that protects individuals against the damage that might be caused by environmental stressors.

Figure 1 summarizes how these elements articulate and reverberate with each other, in the manner of the themes of a musical composition. For example, the hazardous circumstances of past risk factors reappear as the current stressor that precipitates a crisis; the elements of competence that enable an individual to master both a past hazard and a current stress recur in a modified form in the outcome of the individual's reaction to current stress as changed vulnerability to mental disorder that may predispose eventually to actual psychopathology; and adequate social

FIGURE 1

Recurrent themes model of primary prevention.

Past risk factors	Intermediate variables				Outcome
Bio-psycho-social hazards (episodes or continuing)	Teaching of competence	Competence (constitutional and acquired)	Reaction to recent or current stress (**crisis**)	Social supports	
Examples Genetic defects Pregnancy problems Birth trauma Prematurity Congenital anomaly Developmental problems Accidents Illness Hospitalization Poverty Cultural deprivation School failure Family discord Family disruption Parental mental or physical illness Sibling illness	Parents and teachers provide opportunities for child to learn self-efficacy and problem-solving skills. Exposure to increasing stress while providing guidance, emotional support, and teaching skills.	Self-efficacy Quality of self-image and identity. Expect mastery by self and support by others. Tolerance of frustration and confusion. Problem-solving skills Social and material.	Bio-psycho-social hazard Bodily damage. Current or recent life change events: loss, threat, or challenge. Adaptation by *Active Mastery* versus *Passive Surrender.* Hopeful perseverance despite cognitive erosion and fatigue. Containment of feelings. Enlisting support.	Cognitive, emotional, and material Supplement ego strength in problem solving. Validate identity. Maintain hope. Help with tasks. Contain feelings. Counteract fatigue.	Sense of wellbeing. Capacity to study, work, love, and play. Enhanced or eroded competence. Actual psychopathology (D.S.M. III)
Types of Intervention					
Social action in health, education, welfare, and legal services **Consultation collaboration, and education** for professionals	**Education** of parents and child-care professionals	**Education** of children and parents	**Crisis intervention** by anticipatory guidance and preventive intervention **Preventive intervention** to target populations (highest risk groups)	**Promote supports** Convene network. Convene mutual-help couple. Help mutual-help organizations. Support the supporters.	

supports not only buffer reaction to current stress but also were probably a crucial element in determining whether a past risk factor led to a current unhealthy outcome, as well as being a central element in the mediated learning process whereby children acquire self-efficacy and problem-solving skills that form the core of competence. Because of these reverberations, I have given to the overall conceptual structure the name of the *recurring themes model of primary prevention*. Figure 1 provides a summary of present day conceptualizations of the field, and I believe that it shows how crisis intervention and the promotion of support systems articulate with the other elements in a comprehensive primary prevention program.

Models of Crisis and Support Systems

Twenty-five years of experience with the crisis model indicates that it has fostered two significant developments in community mental health practice. First, it has emphasized the importance of a short time framework in dealing with persons exposed to hazardous life circumstances. It has provided a catalyst for changing agency policies and professional practices to ensure that time-limited help would be made available on an immediate and intensive basis during the first few days and weeks following the upsetting life event—and, wherever possible for predictable hazards, even ahead of time in the form of anticipatory guidance.

Second, the model defines crisis as a period of *opportunity* as well as *danger,* and links the chance for improved mental health with the quality of the individual's immediate coping and problem-solving reactions. This approach has impelled us to explore the details of successful coping patterns that enable some individuals to emerge from a crisis episode with better mental health than previously and unsuccessful coping patterns that may lead to a poor outcome. On the basis of such findings, specialists have developed methods of crisis intervention that aim to turn poor copers into effective copers during the crisis experience; this approach has led us to the realization that our focus in these efforts must always encompass not only the individuals in crisis, but also their families and their close social contacts. We can help these people to assist the individual in crisis to deal more successfully with the challenges and burdens of the crisis predicament and thereby promote an improved mental health outcome.

This model has proved most attractive, and has gained widespread acceptance among community mental health practitioners. It conforms with their clinical experience and particularly with anamnestic data, which repeatedly indicate that life predicaments appear to be turning points of lasting significance for mental health. Moreover, the emphasis of the model on the increased openness to offers of outside help by individuals in crisis, and their heightened suggestibility because of raised dependency needs during the period of their upset, provides a rationale for developing techniques of short-term psychotherapy. Many psychotherapists prefer to operate during crises and to restrict the focus of their treatment to the segment of the patient's problems that is activated at those times.

Unfortunately, although many mental health workers are satisfied with the success of this approach, little research evidence has accumulated to validate it, as in the case of evaluating more traditional types of psychotherapy. For crisis intervention this lack of evidence is related to the intrinsic difficulties of developing a research design that deals adequately with issues such as a retrospective measure of precrisis mental health to enable us to evaluate our postcrisis findings; the precise explication and replication of intervention techniques; and the circumscription of the individual's coping and problem-solving responses during crisis to those being generically evoked by the crisis predicament and associated interventions (excluding those derived fundamentally from personality idiosyncracies).

And so, a model that has proved very powerful as a guide to intervention philosophy, policy, and methodology has turned out to be rather weak as a stimulus to hypothesis-testing research. That is one reason why crisis concepts must still be called models and cannot claim to have advanced to the level of a scientific theory. The situation is more promising when we turn our attention to a newer model: that of support systems. It, in part, is a derivative of the crisis model and, in part, has emerged from the field of animal and human stress research. Here the issues are more clear-cut and amenable to precise definition and measurement. The basic thesis is that individuals exposed to a particular level of stress, who concomitantly benefit from a high level of social support, have less risk of subsequent mental and physical illness than do similar individuals exposed to similar stress who do not have such support. The implications for research design are relatively simple: All we have to do is define a population exposed to a particular stress and measure the incidence of subsequent illness in two matched subsamples of those who receive a defined type of support and those who do not. Such a design lends itself both to a natural history approach and an experimental approach.

It is significant that the work of Lindemann (1944), Eliott (1930), and others, myself included (Caplan, 1954, 1955, 1956, 1959, 1961), going back more than 30 years, usually emphasized that the outcome of crisis was greatly influenced by the intervention of key individuals—the so-called formal and informal caregivers. However, it was not until 5–10 years ago that we began to write about support systems and to focus on explicating the details of such social patterns as a basis for developing new approaches to mental health practice (Caplan, 1974; Caplan and Killilea, 1976). The reason is that support systems theory grew out of previous empirical research, which only recently has been seen to have implications for our practice, and was not entirely grounded, as was the crisis model, in clinical experience.

What then are the empirical roots of support systems theory? They are two-fold (Caplan, 1981), arising from research on stress both in animals and in human beings.

Studies of Stress in Animals

A significant body of experimental research (Cassel, 1974a and 1976; Cobb, 1976) with animals such as rats and mice shows that induced population-oriented stress conditions (e.g., colony overcrowding) result in increased rates of certain bodily diseases, such as arteriosclerosis, high blood pressure, increased susceptibility to pathogenic microorganisms, and various types of neoplasia. Not all members of a population exposed to such stress are equally affected. Certain subpopulations seem to be protected because they are members of regularly interacting groups or networks. Apparently, it is not overcrowding per se that is the harmful factor. Rather, it is the resultant increased exposure of the animals to contact with strangers, so that they can never relax but must be in a continuing, autonomically depleting state of alert to ward off possible attacks and to compete for scarce essential resources. High-status animals, who can rely on their signs of dominance to prevent strangers from attacking them or competing with them, are also relatively immune from increased morbidity due to overcrowding.

Apparently, those animals who move around in social subgroups are less exposed to contacts with strangers and can rely on the protection of familiar animals if they should be attacked. Membership in the subgroup thus buffers them not only by reducing the stress, but also by providing added protection, either actual or imagined. The last possibility is corroborated by experimental research on individual animals. For example, unanticipated electric shocks in rats who have been conditioned to avoid them produce high rates of peptic ulcers in isolated animals but low ulcer rates in those animals shocked in the presence of litter mates (Cassel, 1974b). Similarly, experiments that promote territorial conflict by placing mice in intercommunicating boxes produce hypertension if the animals are strangers but not when the mice are litter mates (Cassel, 1974b).

What emerges from such research—and also from epidemiological studies in human beings, which show that diseases such as tuberculosis and mental illness occur more frequently in people who for various reasons are deprived of meaningful social contacts (Cobb, 1976; Cassel, 1974b)—is the postulate that membership in a social group is in some way a protection against increased vulnerability to disease consequent on experience of stress. Cassel (1974a) believes that a major contribution of the protective social matrix is that it provides a pool of information, which enables its members to understand feedback cues. They are therefore able to determine when it is safe to relax, instead of becoming exhausted by needless vigilence. Autonomic depletion and exhaustion may also be reduced by concrete help in protecting the individual when attacked or by its reliance on the promise of this protection.

Studies of Stress in Human Beings

The second body of research consists of studies that focus on a variety of acute and chronic stress situations in human beings. These situations include pregnancy, major life difficulties, old age, job loss, severe asthma, cardiac infarction, and battle stress. The studies compare the incidence of disease complications and consequences in those who are supported during the stress experience by having a friend, an intimate, or a cohesive social group or network, with those who have little or no such support (Caplan, 1981). The findings are strikingly uniform. If the stress level is high, the poorly supported individuals have about 3–10 times the incidence of subsequent physical or mental illness found in the well-supported individuals. These studies were not set up to test the hypothesis that social support protects against the harmful effects of acute and chronic stress. This conclusion emerges serendipitously from analyzing their findings. But the results can also be interpreted as showing that those individuals who have a capacity to attract and keep supportive relationships are less vulnerable to stress than are individuals who do not have such a personality trait (Henderson, 1981).

The only way to clarify this issue is by carrying through a planned experimental design. Five recent studies have accomplished this by assigning matched subjects to experimental and control groups exposed to high stress with and without specific social support.

Two of the studies compared matched subsamples of adult patients undergoing elective major surgery with and without anticipatory guidance or training in selective inattention that could be interpreted by the patients as forms of intensive interpersonal support. The supported patients needed significantly less pain killers after the operation and had a shorter hospital stay than the unsupported patients (Egbert, Battit, and Welch, 1964; Langer, Janis, and Wolfer, 1975).

The third study investigated the incidence of postoperative impotence in patients after prostatectomy for benign hyperplasia of the prostate (Zohar, Meiraz, Maoz, and Durst, 1976). One subsample received a seven-minute session of anticipatory guidance before the operation, and a matched subsample did not. In no case did postoperative impotence occur in the supported patients, whereas it did occur in 70 percent of the unsupported patients.

In the fourth study children undergoing tonsillectomy were randomly assigned to an experimental and a control group. In the former, a special nurse provided guidance to the mothers on how to support the children while they were in the hospital. Postoperatively, this group had significantly less fever, vomiting, and signs of emotional disturbance than the control group and had less fears, crying, and disturbed sleep during their first week at home (Skipper and Leonard, 1968).

In the fifth study a random sample of unselected men hospitalized for major trauma resulting from road accidents were given 2–10 hours of practical advice and emotional and social support and guidance by social workers (Bordow and Porritt, 1979). Of this group 70 percent received high social support following discharge, compared to 20 percent of a matched control group; the experimental group did significantly better on a series of adjustment measures than the control group.

How does social support achieve these results?

In a recent article in the *American Journal of Psychiatry* (Caplan, 1981) I showed that exposure to acute or chronic stress may increase vulnerability to future physical and mental illness. This may occur if the individual fails to deal effectively with the immediate threats or long-term privations and is therefore forced to seek relief from an inevitable rise of tension by unhealthy bodily or mental mechanisms. Such a maladaptive course is fostered by dysphoric emotional arousal stimulated by awareness of threat or loss and by the frustration of fundamental needs for love, social status, self-respect, and security. This emotional arousal with its associated neuro-endocrine manifestations interferes with the work of adaptation by eroding in characteristic ways the individual's cognitive and volitional level of functioning. In particular, the individual commonly experiences a disorder of attention, scanning, information collection, access to relevant memories that associate significant meaning to perceptions, judgment, planning, and the capacity to implement plans and evaluate feedback. The individual's usual orderly process of externally oriented instrumental ego functioning is upset precisely when operating at maximum effectiveness is needed for grappling constructively with current problems.

In addition to the disorder in externally directed cognitive functioning, a person under stress also characteristically manifests a deterioration in the clarity of self-concept. The individual loses orderly access not only to memories that lend meaning to perceptions of the outer world, but also to those memories that help the person evaluate his or her own identity.

Capacity for effective problem-solving action is greatly influenced by an individual's expectation of likely success in at least partially achieving personal goals; this in turn will depend on the memory of success in the past in situations of similar difficulty by exhibiting the fortitude to overcome the obstacles involved. On this basis the person can go forward. The drive to go forward is buttressed by the person's memory of identifying with certain values and the support and approbation received from likeminded significant others, which helped the individual to persevere. These are among the factors that make a clear and positive concept of enduring self-identity a major impetus for an individual to press forward with problem-solving in a situation of stress—a situation that creates marked frustration, overburdens current capabilities, and demands novel approaches in the face of cognitive confusion and uncertainty about the future. Perseverance in problem solving also depends on the individual's expectation that a certain level of pain and discomfort is likely to be involved and the belief that other people are capable of tolerating such unpleasantness.

Supportive individuals, networks, groups, and institutions increase an individual's chances of mastering stress, helping to hold emotional upset below the level that it interferes unduly with the person's cognition and volition. At the same time they assist with problem-solving efforts by making up for the person's eroded capacities in collecting and appraising information and planning and carrying out needed action. The supporters remind the person of prestress self-identity and help maintain the hope that, with their help, he or she will have the strength to persevere in adaptational efforts despite confusion, frustration, and discomfort. They also play an active part, whenever needed, in helping the person act or taking direct, effective action themselves to accomplish the concrete tasks necessary to change the environmental situation. The supporters monitor the individual's current capacity to confront difficulties; they help the person to withdraw and construct defenses until he or she feels capable of dealing with the difficulties. The supporters also monitor the individual's fatigue level and urge rest as needed, until he or she has recuperated sufficiently to be able to return to the struggle.

In all these ways the supporters act as *auxiliary ego figures* in making up for capacities of the individual that have been weakened by the stress. They also extend the person's ego functions by additional strengths of their own, as well as making concrete contributions of knowledge, skills, and resources in enabling the individual to overcome the difficulties confronted.

Who are the Supporters?

Over the past ten years we have come to realize that few individuals struggle with stress on their own. In most instances, a variety of supporters are readily available and are spontaneously activated when a member of their community runs into difficulties.

There are two main categories of support systems: (1) the system of formal professional caregivers and community caregiving agencies in health, welfare, and education; and (2) the informal and natural helping individuals, networks, groups, and organizations—family, friends, neighbors; volunteer, charitable, fraternal, ethnic, and *landsmanschaften* organizations and mutual-help groups. In addition to these two main categories there is a third, which has in some measure the characteristics of each, namely, religious denominations. These are formal institutions, but their formal character relates mainly to the worship and service of God. They also have an explicit and implicit set of informal support-system functions that resemble those of the natural support system. They provide an organized framework within which operate the supports of families, neighbors, and mutual-help groups and networks, which are actively fostered as manifestations of religious piety (Caplan, 1974; Caplan and Killilea, 1976).

Methods of Preventive Intervention

The following methods of intervention were developed on the basis of the models discussed. I have molded them during the past seven years by daily clinical interactions in a university teaching hospital with child patients suffering from major bodily illnesses and their families, for whom I have accepted a preventive psychiatric responsibility. During the past three years, I supplemented this service to a population at high mental health risk with a preventive service to the children of parents suffering from cancer. The latter children are also thought to be at risk of increased vulnerability to psychological disorder because of possible maladaptation to the high intrafamily stress often associated with the illness of a parent.

I have made an attempt to specify my intervention techniques with precision in order to facilitate replication and to provide a basis for systematic evaluation.

Crisis Intervention

Anticipatory Guidance and Emotional Inoculation

This method may be employed if a crisis can be predicted, as in a planned admission of a child to the hospital. The essential techniques used are as follows:

1. *Individual or group method,* preferably with a group of children and families, who support each other.
2. *Intervene close in time and place to crisis.*
3. *Arouse anticipatory distress* by describing expectable stresses in evocative detail.
4. *Predict boundaries* of intensity and duration of likely pain and discomfort.
5. *Urge active self-help and help from others* to reduce discomfort.
6. *Arouse hope* that such activity will lead to mastery.
7. *Guide family members in helping each other.*
8. *Emphasize normality* of expectable cognitive and emotional disorganization and *counteract fear of psychological illness.*

The closer in time and place the intervention is to the crisis, the better the response. For example, it is best to do the intervention with a group of children and their families in the hospital ward shortly after admission, so that the authenticity of the message is buttressed by the sights, sounds, and smells of the hospital environment.

The central element of the method is the communication of details of expectable burdensome events and of the normative emotional reactions to them (anxiety, anger, confusion, helplessness, etc.). The intervenor aims to arouse anticipatory feelings at an optimal level. The intervenor must be sensitive to the effects of his or her words on the audience. If there appears to be little response, the intervenor increases the intensity of predictions of burden; if the children and their parents seem to become too anxious, the intervenor tones down the warnings.

As soon as anticipatory distress has been evoked, the intervenor helps the participants work out ways to master the expected burdens. The intervenor aids cognitive mastery by emphasizing the time-limited nature of the discomforts, so that when they occur the sufferers will remember that they have been told that the discomforts are temporary. The intervenor tells participants what they will be able to do themselves to gain relief and how they can get help from others, and thus prepares them to be active participants in the crisis rather than passive sufferers. The intervenor counteracts the fear that seeking help during the crisis will be perceived as a sign of weakness. And the intervenor arouses the hope that activity, as well as the natural unfolding of events over a relatively short period of time, will lead to a successful outcome.

Finally, the intervenor defines the expectable confusion and distress of the crisis upset as a normal response of healthy individuals exposed to an inescapable predicament. The intervenor emphasizes that they are not a sign of incipient psychological disorder, which might provoke fear or shame.

Preventive Intervention

In this method the intervenors operate during the crisis as supplementary ego figures who make up for expectable cognitive erosion; they also help reduce and contain negative emotional arousal and extend material assistance in mastering the predicament. The essential techniques used are as follows:

1. *Repeated short contacts during crisis* to satisfy increased dependency needs.

2. *Support strategic withdrawal* at height of crisis.

3. Then *support active confrontation* of problems. Impart information. Help find meanings. Help focus on present. Help plan what to do.

4. Help *family members communicate with each other.*

5. *Help plan activities* to solve crisis problems. Take part in implementing plans.

6. Help them bear the *frustration of unknown outcome* and urge perseverance despite confusion.

7. Warn them about *danger of expectable fatigue*. Encourage division of labor to prevent fatigue. Organize monitoring of fatigue level and rest periods for recuperation.

8. *Maintain hope. Encourage activity* to achieve mastery.

9. *Encourage invoking outside help* and counteract shame that this means weakness.

10. *Remind them of their precrisis identity.* Do not validate crisis-eroded identity of weak helplessness.

11. *Urge family members to express negative feelings* and help each other master them. *Emphasize normality of expectable upset.*

12. *Counteract blaming of self or others* to relieve tension.

These techniques focus on the *here-and-now.* They do not involve identifying past reasons why individuals may not be grappling effectively with the crisis problems. Rather, they use the personal influence of the intervenor to modify current behavior. Therefore no specialized psychological training or sophistication is necessary, and this approach may be quite adequately used by lay persons in the form of offering an ordinary human helping hand to individuals in crisis.

Support System Methods

The focus in these methods is on (1) monitoring the adequacy of social supports experienced by individuals during the period when they are burdened by stressors; and (2) on offering or organizing appropriate supportive intervention if the stressed individual does not ask for help, receive help when asked for, or accept needed help when it is offered. The type of support that buffers the harmful effect of stressors appears to be that which is *actually received* when the stress is operating and is felt by the recipient to be helpful. It should include cognitive guidance, help in reducing the intensity of negative emotional upset, and concrete assistance in implementing plans for dealing with the stressful predicament.

Intervention consists of convening individual supporters and groups or networks of supporters and ensuring that these persons provide help in ways that are acceptable to the stressed individuals. Such help should include the essential elements for bolstering adaptive efforts (with particular reference to current level of competence) and overcoming the negative effects of stress-induced emotional arousal, cognitive erosion, and possible faltering of will to master their predicament in a reality-based way.

Because of the relative novelty of these methods, the following explication includes some anecdotal illustrations.

Providing and Orchestrating Professional Support

A minimal level of psychosocial support is expectable as part and parcel of the functioning of any well-run service organization that deals with clients exposed to stress. In a hospital or clinic, where stress may be aggravated by the care process, it is also desirable to include on the staff someone (usually a psychiatrist or a clinical psychologist) who is given the explicit role of providing appropriate support or ensuring that other staff provide it. My experience in a hospital setting includes personally offering support and stimulating and orchestrating support provided by the medical, nursing, and ancillary ward staff. The latter is accomplished by consultation, collaboration on joint cases, and formal and informal staff education. The techniques I have used include the following:

1. *Nurturant care,* i.e., concerned, warm, and personalized.

2. *Mediation,* by collecting, funneling, and interpreting information to family and interpreting needs of patients and family to staff.

3. *Directive guidance* to offset cognitive erosion.

4. *Anticipatory guidance about expectable intercurrent stressors.*

5. *Support strategic withdrawal* at peaks of stress.

6. *Promote problem-solving activity at their own pace.*

7. *Foster hope.*

8. *Foster mutual support inside family. Reduce family tensions that interfere.*

9. *Foster and validate support by relatives, friends, community professionals, and natural helpers.*

10. *Ensure adequate rest to counteract fatigue.*

To illustrate this method, I cite my support of the parents of a 3½-year-old boy, who underwent an operation for a brain tumor and died three weeks later. I met the parents immediately after the neurosurgeons told them the diagnosis and that brain surgery was mandatory. It proved easy to arouse quickly the trust of the young couple by empathizing with their intense distress, shock, and bewilderment and by offering them my active guidance and help. Over the succeeding weeks, and continuing during follow-up contacts for two years after the death of the child, I maintained with them a warm, solicitous, "tender-loving-care" personalized parental type of relationship, to which they responded positively.

Before and after the operation, I visited the parents and child on the hospital ward 3–5 times a day for periods lasting from a few minutes to over an hour. I also made a condolence call on them at their home during the Shivah week of mourning, and subsequently saw them on several occasions in their apartment or in my hospital office to help with the process of mourning and reconstituting their lives.

A central element of my intervention during the first four weeks was that, before each meeting with the parents, I made the rounds of the doctors and nurses involved in the case and collected up-to-date information about the child's current condition and its implications for prognosis and treatment. I then communicated to the parents a balanced summary of this information, emphasizing any hopeful elements. This collection and funneling of information helped to reduce the confusion of the parents, which stemmed from the large number of staff dealing with the case, i.e., pediatricians, neurologists, neurosurgeons, intensive care specialists, anasthesiologists, nutritionists, chest specialists, physiotherapists, nurses, etc. Until I succeeded in establishing this routine, the deterioration in the cognitive level of the parents caused by the stress was further aggravated by the many dissonant scraps of information they obtained from staff of different levels of competence and involvement, whom they met on the ward or buttonholed in the corridors.

I constantly reiterated a message of hope that the child would recover, even though I did not hide the extreme seriousness of the clinical picture. The latter was in any case quite obvious because the patient never fully recovered consciousness following brain surgery; it was clear that his life processes were being kept going only by the machines to which he was attached in the intensive care unit. And yet, I emphasized that the staff was actively persuing a series of sophisticated treatments designed to help him recover. I told the parents that the brain of a 3½-year-old child is sufficiently flexible that there is always the possibility of recovery despite massive damage that would be fatal to an adult. In my contacts with staff, I helped them mold their own communications with the parents along similar lines.

I urged the parents to stay close to the child 24 hours a day, and I helped them work out a system so that the "off-duty" parent could go home to rest or sleep. I helped them arrange for their other child, a one-year-old daughter, to live with relatives, and for the mother to visit her once a week. This gave the mother an additional respite from the fatiguing vigil at her son's bedside. I arranged for hospital visits by a network of nonprofessional religious volunteers, whom I convened and linked with the parents. I emphasized to visitors whom I encountered (family friends, relatives, and the neighborhood rabbi) the importance of their contribution in offering emotional support and in chatting with the parents in the day room to divert their attention for a while from their ordeal.

I also guided the parents in making an active contribution to the child's welfare. This helped them support the child during the days before surgery. I was with them before the child was taken to the operating room, and I enabled the mother herself to insert the premedication suppository and to comfort the boy until he fell asleep and was carried to the operating room in his father's arms. During the bedside vigil after surgery, my task was more complicated. I guided the parents on how to talk to the child and express their love to him, even though most of the time he showed no response, on the assumption that if he was even dimly conscious he would feel reassured by hearing the familiar voices of his parents. I also helped them, during the first two weeks after surgery, monitor occasional movements of his eyelids or fingers, which indicated minimal levels of intact functioning.

I urged the parents to be sensitive to each other's strain and help each other grapple with the tragic problems. When this mutual support was disturbed by bickering and mutual recriminations, linked probably with long-standing problems in their relationship, I forcefully directed them to put these quarrels aside for the time being. These flare-ups appeared to be an attempt to divert attention from the burdens of current reality, and I urged them to refocus on the issues of dealing with the child and with their own associated distress. By that time, I had enough influence with them to succeed in this effort; I did not try to uncover or understand the source of this squabbling in their relationship. I continued a similar approach after the child died, particularly three months later, when the bereaved parents told me that they were contemplating divorce. I persuaded them to stop talking about divorce, which I interpreted to them as a characteristic attempt to evade the painful problems of their mourning. The unfolding of events over the following two years validated this approach. At the end of that time the parents individually and as a couple apparently were behaving more maturely than before their child's illness.

Convening a Support Group for a Target Individual

The goal is for the intervenor to ensure that a stressed individual or family receive essential support during the crisis or while long-term stressors are operating. The signs of distress emitted by individuals under stress normally evoke a converging movement in their social environment: People almost instinctively move in to support them. In a healthy family someone usually takes on the task of calling in the helpers. A professional who undertakes the role of intervenor needs only to monitor this situation in order to make sure that all is well. But in a hospital, the relatives of a patient may feel inhibited by the setting, and the intervenor may need to facilitate or sanction this spontaneous process.

Where the latter does not take place, the professional intervenor must actively invite members of the family, relatives, and friends, or community caregivers, to come together to support a stressed individual or family unit. In cases where such natural supporters are inadequate in number or effectiveness, the intervenor must fill the gaps with paraprofessionals or professionals.

For instance, I was called to an orthopedic ward to help a ten-year-old boy shortly after he was admitted because of fractures of his ribs, pelvis, and femur, which he had sustained in an accident involving the family car. The father had been driving, had been slightly injured, and was being treated in another ward; the mother had died after admission to the hospital. I was asked by the orthopedic surgeons about how and when to tell the boy that his mother had been killed. I advised them to delay this news for a few days—until the boy had recovered from the physical shock of his injuries. I suggested that the father should then tell the boy in the presence of the rest of the family, including his uncle, aunt, and cousins, who had been traveling with them in a second car when the road accident occurred. This plan was implemented. Meanwhile, I provided direct support to the boy and later satisfied myself that the family did in fact provide him with the help that he needed.

In another case a boy of 14, suffering from sarcoma of the thigh, had to be told that his leg would be amputated. I helped the orthopedic surgeon do this in a group meeting attended by the ward staff, the boy's widowed mother, and her sister and brother-in-law, who happened to be visiting the boy at the time. I learned that an older brother of the patient was doing his army service, and that there were three younger siblings living at their home in Naharia in the north of Israel, who were being taken care of by an aunt. I told the mother that she must stay with her son for the next few weeks until he had recovered from his operation and had received intensive chemotherapy in the oncology department. I also arranged for an urgent message to be sent to the army authorities to obtain compassionate leave for the brother, so that he could join his mother at the bedside. He arrived the following day.

Unfortunately, the mother turned out to be quite ineffectual, and the brother was not very bright. So, in addition to my spending a lot of time with the patient, I augmented his support system by recruiting a student nurse who was assigned the special duty of befriending him, helped by a young male physiotherapist. Even these additions to the boy's support group were not completely adequate, and, after a couple of weeks, I added another element, which I will discuss in the next section.

A third instance led me to an important new insight into the intricacies of convening an effective support system for a target individual. This was a case in which I had to organize support for the five children (aged 4, 8, 13, 17, and 19) of a woman suffering from advanced metastatic carcinoma of the pancreas. The patient was of North African background. She had eleven siblings, most of whom lived with their children and grandchildren close to her home in a congested, low-income neighborhood of Jerusalem.

At first, I felt that I would not have to exert myself unduly in organizing a support system in this case. Whenever I visited the patient, I found her bed surrounded by her siblings and their spouses and children, as though the whole clan had rallied round to support her and her family in their time of need. But when I talked individually to her husband and three older children, they each reported that they were getting little useful help from their relatives. For example, nobody was willing to help out by shopping for supplies, cooking, and cleaning their home or by caring for the two younger children when the older girls were visiting their mother. The usual excuse for refusing to help was that the relatives all had problems in their own homes. My experiences with the extended family confirmed this picture. One day one of the patient's sisters asked me in a tone of ghoulish excitement whether the patient was now moribund. I had the feeling that the sister was eager for the thrill of spreading the news round her community. Once, I sought the help of another of the mother's sisters to calm the older son who had just made a dramatic suicidal gesture after returning on leave from army service and finding his mother in an apparently terminal state. The aunt said to her nephew, "Stop this nonsense. *You are burdening me!*"

After a number of unsuccessful attempts to persuade members of the extended family to provide obviously needed support to the children in their home, I was forced to recruit help in the community. I enlisted the services of local welfare workers, the classroom teachers of each of the children, and a home-help worker from a municipal agency to come into the home to cook and do some housework and lay volunteers to take the smallest children out to play. These outsiders supplied the supportive functions that members of the extended family were unwilling to undertake.

This case and a number of similar examples taught me that convening a sufficiently large supportive group and linking it with a stressed individual may be a necessary step, but is certainly not always sufficient in satisfying the need for effective support. The intervenor must monitor the services actually provided by the so-called supporters and must ensure that all the basic supportive elements are indeed present. It became clear that ostensible helpers may be geared more to satisfying their own self-centered needs than the needs of the stressed individual and that the quality of the interaction with the patient is more significant than the number of actors or the quantity of interactions. Apart from its meaning for support system methodology, this finding has important implications for planning research to test the effectiveness of social support in preventing the harmful effects of stress.

Organizing a Mutual-Help Couple

In this method the intervenor recruits someone who in the past has suffered from and successfully mastered the stresses currently faced by the index person, brings the two together, and provides an opportunity for the former to offer nonprofessional guidance and help to the latter on the basis of personal experience. For example, the boy who had suffered from sarcoma of the thigh was having difficulty believing my predictions that the loss of his hair (caused by chemotherapy) would be only temporary and that he would also eventually learn to use a prosthesis, continue his schooling, and return to a full social life. I asked the physiotherapist to find another adolescent boy who had undergone a leg amputation for sarcoma about a year earlier and had been successfully rehabilitated. The pool of potential candidates was rather small, but an appropriate ex-patient was located; the two boys were brought together with very successful results.

My patient was tremendously impressed by seeing the other boy walk with almost no limp. He was even more impressed by seeing a luxuriant head of hair and being told that this had replaced a completely bald head, which had been produced by the same chemotherapy he was having. The two boys quickly developed a close relationship because of the mutual benefit derived from their interactions. My patient was able to get an authentic account of how the tribulations of the illness and its drastic treatment could be mastered; he could see the other boy as living proof of what I had told him and as a role model to emulate. The other boy was able to reinforce his own feelings of mastery by acting as mentor to someone with whose passive victimization he could identify; he saw before him someone in the same state in which he had been a year previously.

Recruiting a Panel or Network of Natural Helpers

In preparation for their use as part of a support system for future patients, I have found it valuable to develop a cumulative list of the names and addresses of potential informal caregivers and natural helpers in the community. In a well-organized community, particularly one with well-developed religious institutions, such people may be widely known. If not, we should search them out and systematically build relationships with them. They may be generalists who are prepared to help in any predicament or specialists who have themselves suffered from or helped someone in their family deal with a particular stress or privation.

They may be utilized as individual helpers, as in the mutual-help couple method, or we may link them with each other as a supportive network, which we may then articulate with our patient and his family. Opinions differ with regard to the amount or type of training we should give such nonprofessional helpers. I am opposed to systematic training because of the danger of damaging their self-confidence and their power as experiential experts by giving them a smattering of subprofessional or paraprofessional theory and techniques. Instead, I am in favor of continually emphasizing that they possess experiential expertise, which may be qualitatively different from the expertise of professionals but which equips them to be particularly helpful to stressed people in ways that are not easily available to professionals.

Fostering the Development of Mutual-Help Organizations

The first task is to build and maintain an up-to-date list of specialized mutual-help organizations in the community. Usually, there are many more in existence than professionals are aware of (Caplan and Killilea, 1976). Informants who can tell us about them can usually be found in religious, ethnic, and fraternal organizations or among our former patients.

Whenever no mutual-help organization exists to assist patients with particular conditions, we should seek to foster their development. Preferably, we should not ourselves play a central organizing role because, even with the best intentions in the world, such actions may inadvertently lead to the development of a professionally subordinate or dependent type of organization instead of one that is autonomously nonprofessional.

The best approach is to identify and recruit one or more persons of leadership caliber from our former patients and their families—and then to persuade *them* to undertake the task of organization. We can help initially by offering sponsorship and, perhaps, by making suggestions about steps in the organizational process. We can also legitimize the importance of this work by our own willingness to provide behind-the-scenes backing and should make ourselves available as consultants. But, as soon as possible, we should move into the background, ensuring that the organizational leadership remains firmly in the hands of the nonprofessionals.

Supporting the Supporters

Those who support others—particularly during periods of peak stress and when the supporters are nonprofessionals who are personally identified with and involved in the predicament—are usually themselves in need of support to enable them to persevere in their helping efforts. A specialist with an interest in primary prevention may play a valuable role in supporting the supporters. This has both a cognitive dimension and an emotional dimension.

As usual, the primary task of the specialist is to monitor the situation and intervene only if things are not going well. Cognitively, the specialist seeks assurance that the supporters are allowing the target person to withdraw or to maintain distance from the stress and its consequences until personally capable of confronting these painful issues—and, then, that they help foster understanding of what is happening, provide guidance in problem solving, and share necessary tasks. The specialist also must be satisfied that the supporters help the target person remember prestress self-identity and adaptational strengths and help to maintain hope that he or she will succeed in mastering this situation with their assistance, in spite of inevitable confusion and discomforts. And finally, the supporters must be sensitive to the levels of fatigue of the target person and members of the person's family; they must insist on rest periods, during which the supporters will take over essential aspects of the others' roles.

Whenever any of these elements is missing, the intervenor should offer guidance to introduce it. Care must be taken not to obtrude too much and not to reduce the power and self-confidence of the nonprofessionals, such as by trying to inculcate professional-style techniques.

Supporting the supporters emotionally usually focuses on validating the crucial importance of their efforts and sharing with them the intervenors own feelings of involvement and human strain. In regard to the latter, I personally and in common with many professionals, do not seek to hide my own feelings of anxiety, depression, and insecurity that are evoked by the human predicament in which I am participating. This is no place for the aloof, distant, professional posture when closeness, warmth, and communication by bodily contact are called for. I have shed many a tear at the peak of a crisis, particularly in traumatic or wartime situations, or where I am confronted by imminent death and bereavement. I frankly share this information with nonprofessional or professional supporters whom I seek to support, and I offer myself to them as a role model. Only by mutual support among supporters can there be long-term mastery of the cognitive and emotional burdens of this type of work and burn-out be prevented.

Prevention Research During the Next Decade

Focus on Specific Stressors and Populations

I predict that the study of mixed situations, such as the effect of rises in the intensity of stress linked with a heterogeneous set of life-change events in a heterogeneous population, will decline. I further predict that much of the research over the coming years will focus on the effect of single, circumscribed stressors on defined populations, such as the effect of parental or sibling cancer on children or adolescents, the consequences of a period of severe illness from which a child or adult has recovered, the effect of parental divorce on children of different ages, and the like. Each of these stressors is likely to be associated with characteristic expectable adaptive demands that will increase the risk of specific patterns of proximal and distal unhealthy consequences, unless adequate supports operate to prevent them. The content of these needed supports may vary in accordance with the nature of the stressor (Mitchell, Billings, and Moos, 1982), and in line with the competence of the stressed individuals. Despite idiosyncratic personality differences, I expect that a focused study of each stressor will reveal its own generic picture, which should lead to the development of precise prescriptions for preventive intervention in each type of stress and population.

In Jerusalem, my colleagues and I are beginning such studies on the stress in adolescence of cancer of a parent or a sibling and the effects on children and adolescents of divorce involving contested custody. In Haifa, Ciporah Tadmor is just completing a similar focused study on the stress of caesarian section birth, together with an evaluation of specific preventive intervention (Tadmor and Brandes, 1984).

Proximal and Distal Outcome Variables

An obstacle that has burdened researchers ever since systematic studies of stress and of the crisis model began 40 years ago, has been that a stressor experience, however severe and however aggravated by low competence and by the absence of support, rarely results within a short time in manifest psychopathology. In fact, the model does not lead us to expect such an outcome. Rather, it leads us to expect an increase in vulnerability, which eventually will result in illness, usually after other harmful events have cumulatively exerted their influence.

We are beginning to define these short-term outcome conditions of increased vulnerability. And I predict that, over the coming few years, researchers will succeed in clearly specifying them and in developing instruments for their measurement. In Jerusalem, preliminary studies of the sequelae in adolescents of an episode of successfully treated cancer in a parent 2–4 years earlier show a characteristic picture of manifest increased maturity and poise that appears to be a defense against underlying feelings of personal bodily fragility and negative expectations about the future. This defense seems in most cases to be adequate, but the underlying feelings may also constitute a continuing source of weakness in withstanding stress. We are also working on instruments for assessing this situation. These include manifest-anxiety and depression scales and sentence-completion tests of coping capacity, which provide a picture of the manifest competence, and projective tests that reveal the underlying sense of fragility and pessimism.

I imagine that other researchers who, like us, will be focusing on delimited stressors, covering similar ground. I further expect that, within a few years, batteries of appropriate tests of increased vulnerability will be developed and normed.

It will then be necessary to validate that such short-term outcome, in the nature of increased vulnerability, is indeed a precursor of eventual psychopathology. This issue presents problems of research strategy and tactics that I predict will require changes in policy regarding funding and cooperative efforts within the coming decade. First, it will be necessary to modify research-grant policy to stimulate and support follow-up studies lasting at least 5–10 years, so that the long-term pathological outcome of increased vulnerability cases can be determined. Second, in order to control for intervening events over long periods of time, it will be necessary to study fairly large numbers of cases. This is almost certain to overtax the resources of most individual research settings and lead to greater use of consortiums in conducting this type of research.

As we seek to master the problems of multifactoriality by narrowing our focus to homogeneous samples of persons fulfilling precise criteria and exposed to a narrowly defined stressor, the number of available research subjects in most settings will shrink. This is especially true if we take into account the problems of arousing the motivation to participate of stressed individuals and their families. The result is that, although it is possible to gain access to the relatively limited number of cases needed to study proximal outcomes, it is currently not feasible to enlarge our sample sufficiently to implement a follow-up study of distal sequelae.

This leads me to the conclusion that it will be necessary to organize consortiums of research centers, which will use similar research designs and methods of data collation, so that they can pool their cases. Our Jerusalem group is already exploring this possibility with research groups in New York and at Stanford, Minnesota, Toronto, and Dublin universities. I envision that a number of such consortiums will be organized within the coming decade, if adequate simultaneous funding can be obtained.

Development of Standard Research Instruments

I predict that, over the next few years, batteries of multiple tests and structured interviews will be developed and normed for measuring competence, support, intensity of specific stressors, proximal changes in vulnerability, and the other variables involved in our models. When these measures are used in a standard way by different researchers, we will be in a better position than at present to compare their results. This will be particularly true when definitions of stressor and support systems become more precise and, eventually, when methods of preventive intervention geared to the stress experience in a defined population are also explicated in the kind of detail I have suggested.

A Better Balance in Research Strategy

I end this brief forecast not with a prediction but with a hope: I hope that during the coming decade funding agencies and researchers will work out a more productive balance among the successive steps in prevention research. These efforts should be focused on:

- *Exploratory studies,* to identify and define meaningful variables and promising interventions.
- *Pilot studies,* to develop and test techniques for recruitment of subjects and the collection and analysis of data.
- *Retrospective studies,* to determine proximal and distal consequences of stressors.
- *Prospective studies,* to investigate the transactions of the stressor–competence–support equation and, eventually, to *evaluate* the efficacy of *specific interventions* in modifying these transactions and their results, in terms of lowering both the incidence of increased vulnerability and eventual psychopathology.

At present, the most common drawback in our field is that sufficient weight is not given to the early stages of exploratory studies and pilot investigations. Undoubtedly, hypothesis testing is essential for scientific advance, but undue haste in the early stages of research often leads to choosing hypotheses that lack meaningful links with the eventual goal of developing and evaluating feasible preventive interventions and to choosing overly simplified research instruments of questionable validity. This premature closure in research planning is fostered by dominant values in funding agencies, which underestimate the importance, complexity and duration of sophisticated exploratory investigations. Moreover, expertise in the different research stages is rarely uniform among research workers and institutions. This means that reliance must be placed on cross-fertilization of ideas and findings, so that studies in one setting may benefit from those in others. Unfortunately, researchers committed to a particular style of work—because of disciplinary background, an interest in one part of the overall model, or their base in a service institution or a nonservice research setting—are not sufficiently familiar with each other's publications and sometimes have little respect for each other's specialized sophistication and unique contributions. I do hope that over the coming decade, as recognition increases of the problems posed by the complexities of our common mission, we will see an improvement in mutual respect among different groups of workers, a more detailed knowledge of each other's work, and a greater cross-fertilization of ideas.

References

Bordow, S., and Porritt, D. (1979). An experimental evaluation of crisis intervention. *Social Science in Medicine, 13A*, 251–256.

Caplan, G. (1954). The mental hygiene role of the nurse in maternal and child care. *Nursing Outlook, 2*, 14–19.

Caplan, G. (1955). The role of the social worker in preventive psychiatry. *Medical Social Work, 4*, 144–160.

Caplan, G. (1956). *Mental health aspects of social work in public health*. Berkeley: University of California Press.

Caplan, G. (1959). Practical steps for the family physician in the prevention of emotional disorder. *Journal of the American Medical Association, 170*, 1497–1506.

Caplan, G. (1961). *An approach to community mental health*. New York: Grune and Stratton.

Caplan, G. (1964). *Principles of preventive psychiatry*. New York: Basic Books.

Caplan, G. (1970). *Theory and practice of mental health consultation*. New York: Basic Books.

Caplan, G. (1974). *Support systems and community mental health*. New York: Behavioral Publications.

Caplan, G. (1981). Master of stress: Psychosocial aspects. *American Journal of Psychiatry, 138*(4), 413–420.

Caplan, G., and Killilea, M. (Eds.) (1976). *Support systems and mutual help*. New York: Grune and Stratton.

Cassel, J. C. (1974a). Psychiatric epidemiology. In G. Caplan (Ed.), *American handbook of psychiatry, Vol. 2* (pp. 402–410). New York: Basic Books.

Cassel, J. C. (1974b). Psychosocial processes and "stress": Theoretical formulations. *International Journal of Health Services, 4*, 471–482.

Cassel, J. C. (1976). The contribution of the social environment to host resistance. *American Journal of Epidemiology, 104*, 107–123.

Cobb, S. (1976). Social support as a moderator of stress. *Psychosomatic Medicine, 38*, 300–314.

Egbert, I. D., Battit, G. E., and Welch, C. E. (1964). Reduction of postoperative pain by encouragement and instruction of patients. *New England Journal of Medicine, 270*, 825–827.

Eliot, T. D. (1930). The adjustive behavior of bereaved families: A new field for research. *Social Forces, 3*, 543–549.

Henderson, S. (1981). Social relationships, adversity and neurosis: An analysis of prospective observations. *British Journal of Psychiatry, 138*, 391–398.

Langer, E. J., Janis, I. L., and Wolfer, J. A. (1975). Reduction of psychological stress in surgical patients. *Journal of Experimental Social Psychology, 11*, 155–165.

Lindemann, E. (1944). The symptomatology and management of acute grief. *American Journal of Psychiatry, 101,* 141–148.

Mitchell, R. E., Billings, A. G., and Moos, R. H. (1982). Social support and well-being: Implications for prevention programs. *Journal of Primary Prevention, 3,* 77–99.

Skipper, J. K., and Leonard, R. C. (1968). Children, stress, and hospitalization: A field experiment. *Journal of Health and Social Behavior, 9,* 275–287.

Tadmor, C. S., and Brandes, J. M. (1984). The perceived personal control crisis intervention model in the prevention of emotional dysfunction for a high risk population of caesarean birth. *Journal of Primary Prevention, 4,* 240–251.

Zohar, J., Meiraz, D., Maoz, B., and Durst, N. (1976). Factors influencing sexual activity after prostatectomy: A prospective study. *Journal of Urology, 116,* 332–334.

Translating Stress and Coping Research into Public Information and Education

Julius Segal

This chapter covers two seemingly disparate, but nevertheless related topics. The initial material describes some of those factors that seem to be helpful in "inoculating" children who might be expected to crumble in the face of severe stress. Then it addresses the question: How do we translate such research findings about child development into information that the user and the public-at-large can understand and act on?

Studies of Resilient Children

Consider the following case history:

Sandra is 16. She was born in poverty and raised in violence and deprivation. In her short lifetime, she had endured the death of two older sisters, the bitter separation and divorce of her parents, and a series of illnesses that seriously threatened her life. In one of the foster homes that sheltered Sandra, physical abuse and neglect were her daily lot.

By all known criteria, Sandra should be a psychological casualty, engulfed by symptoms or outright disabilities, reflecting her young career of trauma and stress. In fact, the opposite is true. Sandra is an apparently well-adjusted adolescent, living now with a benevolent aunt who is newly arrived in this country, enjoying the rewards of close friends, and zestfully planning a college career.

How did Sandra avoid the penalties that we have learned to expect as sequels to deprivation and trauma? What is it that allowed her—and countless other children like her—not only to escape the ravages of pathology that so often follow prolonged and crushing stresses, but instead to grow to maturity graced with a sense of optimism and an aura of well-being? Answers to this enigma are only now beginning to emerge, primarily because in the past psychologists focused much more heavily on finding the roots of pathology rather than of mental health.

Garmezy (1983) points out that for decades mental health researchers, perhaps especially in the area of human development, have devoted their energies to the study of maladaptation and incompetence. The emphasis has been on symptom patterns characteristic of the various psychopathological states and their etiology, treatment, and outcome. To this end, researchers have sought out those predisposing factors, whether genetic or environmental, that could be related to the origins of disorder states and to the precipitating factors that produced actual breakdown.

In recent years, Garmezy notes, especially with the growth of risk research in psychopathology, attention has moved from the adult patient to the normal child. The previous emphasis on predisposing factors described by Norman Watt in his chapter of this volume has been joined by a growing concern about *protective* factors, i.e., those traits, conditions, situations, and episodes that appear to alter, or even reverse, predictions of psychopathology based on a child's at-risk status.

Rutter (1983) has identified some of the family variables strongly associated with child psychiatric disorder. These include severe marital discord, low social status, overcrowding or large family size, paternal criminality, maternal psychiatric disorder, and admission of the child into the care of the community.

Moreover, there is some evidence to suggest that we can begin to identify those children who are especially at risk. Children encountering only one of the array of risk factors identified above, for example, were found by Rutter to be no more likely to suffer psychiatric disorders than children experiencing no risk factors at all. On the other hand, when any two of the stresses occurred together, the risk increased by a factor of 4; with still more concurrent stresses, the risk climbed further still. In Rutter's words, "The stresses potentiated each other so that the combination of chronic stresses provided very much more than a summation of the effects of the separate stresses considered singly."

Rutter has also portrayed the cumulative effects of specific stressors, such as family breakup or hospitalization for a medical or surgical condition. He has found strong evidence that the longer the family disharmony lasts, the greater is the risk to the children. Similar results emerge in studies of hospitalized children: One hospital admission was found to do no long-term harm, but two admissions were damaging.

Garmezy and Neuchterlein (1972) reviewed all existing studies bearing on disadvantaged children who somehow display a high degree of competence in spite of the stressful environments in which they are mired. Other investigators (Anthony, 1974; Rutter, 1979) have focused on the surprisingly resilient children among the offspring of disturbed parents. Out of their combined findings there begins to emerge a profile of the *invulnerables*.

Social Skills

To begin with, these children are socially skillful, bringing a tone of warmth and ease to their relationships with both peers and adults. They are open, easygoing youngsters, popular and well liked, standing in sharp contrast to more fragile children of comparable background, who are often lethargic, tense, sullen, restless—and considerably less accepted by their peers.

Competency

Competent children are well regarded not only by their peers but also, and perhaps more importantly, by *themselves*. Such children operate out of a sense of power rather than impotence and of self-regard rather than self-derogation; they emphasize their pluses rather than their minuses. They feel capable of exerting control over their environments—of influencing events, rather than becoming the passive victims of fate. The extensive study by Coleman and Associates (1966) of 645,000 students drawn from the third, sixth, and twelfth grades of 4000 American public schools provides strong evidence of the power of this attitude in the achievements of disadvantaged youth. A sense of *personal control* was more closely related to achievement than were a variety of other school or family characteristics measured in the survey. A survey by Epps (1969), describing 2800 black and white children from inner-city schools in Atlanta and Detroit, showed similarly that the best predictor of academic achievement was the child's sense of control over the environment.

Competent children also reveal a reflective rather than an impulsive approach to life. They seem to operate with a sense of caution and self-regulation, keeping a sensible rein on their impulses. Rather than reacting immediately such children will pause to reflect when challenged—not only in their academic work but in their social relationships as well. They manage, in effect, to keep their visceral reactions under control. For example, when confronted by children who want to fight, they are able to ignore the challenge or simply walk away; there is no insistent need to act out every impulse that bubbles to the surface.

Motivation

The child who survives adversity is motivated from within to perform well. Studies have shown that, contrary to the stereotype of disadvantaged children as lacking in drive, many children emerge as quite the opposite. Their reactions to school success and failure appear to be much like those shown by highly motivated, middle-class schoolchildren. Teachers rate such youngsters as goal-directed, eager to learn, doing more than is required of them, and participating fully in class discussion. Moreover, the children themselves express a preference for educational pursuits and aspire to high vocational goals; they take responsibility for learning, accept blame for failure, and display a willingness to defer immediate gratification for the sake of long-range achievement.

Family Environment

The families of disadvantaged but achieving youngsters show more concern for education, which is reflected in the parents' aspirations for their children's educational achievement and their willingness to assist actively with homework and to participate in school-related organizations. Even the physical aspects of the homes of achieving, lower-class children are different—less crowded, for example, and neater and cleaner—and there are more books in the home.

Parents of disadvantaged but competent children appear to permit them considerable self-direction in everyday tasks and to recognize the validity of their personal interests and goals, thus helping them in their struggle for growth and autonomy. In spite of omnipresent parental interest, support, and encouragement, the roles of parent and competent child remain well-differentiated. Mothers of underachieving youngsters, in contrast, appear to behave more as siblings; they are more heavily involved in fulfilling their own needs and expect their children to assume responsibilities far beyond their age and capabilities.

Inspiration by Others

A significant factor emerging from the life histories of competent children from disadvantaged families appears to be the presence in the environment of a charismatic, inspirational person. These children seem to identify with and be responsive to at least one figure among the adults who touch their lives, often a parent. Consider a boy named James, who was born and raised among desperate living conditions. He was one of seven children, two of whom died in infancy. He was surrounded by trouble and illness. His father was an alcoholic. James early began working at odd jobs and had a regular one at age 14. He and his brothers brought every cent home so that the family would have enough to eat; even so, the family sometimes did not have enough. A number of his schoolmates and street companions wound up in the penitentiary; one died in the electric chair. What saved him and his brothers? Here are the words of James himself: "We had a mother to answer to. . . . We loved her profoundly, and our driving force was to do what she wanted because we knew how much it meant to her." The speaker? James Cagney.

The inspirational person is not necessarily a member of the family. He or she may be a playmate's parent, an older friend, a teacher, a member of the clergy, a physician—anyone who can help a child acquire self-assurance and a vision of what can be achieved.

Self-Identity

Resistance to the stress of living with a psychotic parent appears to require in a child a well-developed sense of personal identity. At the Washington University School of Medicine in St. Louis, Lander and associates (1979) found that such children appear to be less submissive and less suggestible than others. They are able to maintain a safe psychological distance from the psychotic parent and thus are not drawn into the preoccupations and delusions of the abnormal adult world about them. Anthony (1974) regards this loss of closeness in relationships as the price such children must pay for their invulnerability. Invulnerables seem to develop an objective, dispassionate, and remote relationship to people, thus allowing them to maintain their own integrity and to fend off disturbing influences.

Insight

Finally, children who appear invulnerable in spite of a psychotic parent are able somehow to find promise in the heavy emotional environment around them. Bleuler (1974) reminds us that some psychotics can be incredibly good parents and that some children can see beyond a schizophrenic mother's pathology to her true parental qualities. They learn to distingish what is strange or sick in a parent from what is good and lovable. Moreover, a nonschizophrenic parent can make up for the devastating impact of the one who is ill. "Sometimes," Bleuler (1974) observed, "gifted, warmhearted marriage partners are able to nullify all the evil influences of the other, schizophrenic partner."

Implications for Further Research

The foregoing portrait of invulnerable children is beginning to serve as a base for significant research explorations. It has sparked a number of investigators in their attempts to find, early in the lives of children, the signposts of competence and psychological strength. If they are successful, their results may enable us to build into the lives of all high-risk children the capacities to conquer the psychological obstacles strewn in their developmental path.

Although the characteristics described remain descriptive correlates of stress resistance rather than proven "causes," a cogent question for mental health education is this: Can such characteristics be facilitated through public information and education efforts? The task of doing so—of translating existing knowledge about both childhood stressors and the characteristics of "copers" into information of utility to broad consumer audiences—is not without its impediments.

Impediments to Public Education

A growing number of education efforts are being devoted to informing the public about the stressors encountered by children and to giving advice in regard to the development of effective coping responses. These efforts provide suggestions for helping children to cope with such crises as divorce, bereavement, placement in foster care, and hospitalization; and to deal successfully with major developmental disorders, such as dyslexia, delinquency, hyperactivity, and depression (Sobell, 1978; Wehrle, 1978; Sargent, 1978, 1979, 1980; Brenton, 1975; Bienvenu, 1967; Hill, 1973).

Unwarranted Assumptions

A number of public education publications do take account of individual variability in children's coping responses. Most frequently, however, they are based on the assumption that, because certain childhood stressors are related to negative outcome, we can conclude that the guidance offered for improved coping is equally relevant to all intended recipients. This assumption may arise, in part, from what Kagan (1979) has described as "an obsession with finding absolute principles which declare that a particular set of external conditions is inevitably associated with a fixed set of consequences for all children."

Rarely acknowledged in the preparation of child-related public education materials is the notion that the ultimate consequences of stressful experiences depend heavily on a variety of personal and situational factors. There is an assumption of homogeneity when, in fact, responses of children to the challenge of a particular stressor may vary considerably.

Three specific childhood stress experiences—divorce, abuse, and maternal absence—may be cited on behalf of variance. In the case of divorce, for example, Wallerstein and Kelly (1980) find that key factors in children's responses include not only age and developmental stage but also individual differences in lifestyle and culture. In the case of abuse, Starr (1979) emphasizes the need to take account of the total ecology of the family and the social forces that impinge on it; and in the case of maternal absence, Hoffman (1979) underscores the variations in effects among boys and girls with different patterns of relationships operating between themselves and their mothers and fathers. The complexity of factors affecting the outcome of such stressful childhood experiences, although well documented, are rarely described or even acknowledged in typical public information materials available today.

The dangers inherent in attending to the nature of stressful situations without regard to the characteristics of the "victims" may be dramatized by turning to studies other than those of children. Such data offer a reminder once again of the fragility of generalizations made only from the knowledge of a stressful episode, without taking account of the characteristics of the individuals subjected to that episode. Like many items of advice provided to parents, the education and orientation programs provided to wives and parents of POWs, prior to their return from Vietnam, were wide of the mark. They were based on a knowledge of the sequelae of captivity (for example, posttraumatic stress syndrome), assumed to be typical, and did not take account of the nature of the individuals themselves.

A second and equally important impediment to effective public education programs lies in the unwarranted assumption that children actually experience the degree and quality of responses to stressors that adults assume they do. Many of the public education interventions introduced on behalf of children are defined not necessarily by the child's perceptions and experiences, but by adult projections of them. Kagan (1979) has offered a note of caution regarding the tenuousness of such projections:

> Every interaction between adult and child is embedded in a matrix of implicit understandings created from past interactions. It is not possible to know the psychological significance or future consequences of a particular set of encounters independent of the larger mural of which it is a part. . . . The child's private constructions are the critical consequences of familial experiences, but the transduction from external event to personal interpretation is not yet understood. (p. 887)

Kagan's observation is relevant not only to the child's encounters with acute stressors, but with everyday life experiences as well. Episodes apparently innocuous to the bystander, for example, may leave a wound in the child—a sudden and inexplicable harsh word, a diffident response of parents, the slight of a teacher or friend. In a letter to his father, Franz Kafka (1954) mourned the fact that the empathy and communication for which he searched was not forthcoming during his childhood:

> I cannot believe that a kindly word, a quiet taking by the hand, a friendly look, could not have got me to do anything that was wanted of me. Now you are,

after all, at bottom a kindly and soft-hearted person . . . but not every child has the endurance and fearlessness to go on searching until it comes to the kindliness that lies beneath the surface. (p. 142)

We do not know from Kafka's words what his father was actually like, but it is at least possible that the child's response arose from an inner reality rather than an objective one. The assessment of a parent as hostile or accepting, Kagan (1979) contends, cannot be made simply by observing the parent's behavior; parental love or rejection arises from a belief held by the child rather than a set of actions by a parent.

Yamamoto (1979) attempted to ascertain whether children assess their experiences of stress in the same terms as adults perceive them. Children in the fourth, fifth, and sixth grades rated 20 life events on a seven-point scale. The children were found to make distinguishing judgments of perceived stressfulness that often differed from those of professionals. The arrival of a new baby sibling, for example, often regarded by adults as a "shocker" for youngsters, was not very highly rated. More traumatic was "a poor report card," "being sent to the principal," "getting lost," "being ridiculed in class," "a scary dream," "not making 100," or "being picked last on a team."

Mental health information specialists have depended primarily on adult judgments to describe the relative importance to children of various stresses. Few investigators have recognized, as Anthony (1974) puts it, that "stress as experienced by the child and stress as estimated by the adult observing the impact of the stress on the child are frequently of a very different order of magnitude." The lack of that recognition defines a major limitation in the quality of public education materials available in the child development field.

Behavioral Medicine

Recent years have brought a crescendo of activity in the field of behavioral medicine and an increasingly widespread acceptance of the notion that major alterations in behavior and lifestyle provide one of the strongest weapons in the armamentarium of prevention. A host of factors underlie this trend, among them the increasing interest among researchers and clinicians in data that relates disease and poor health to living styles and habits and a growing wave of therapeutic nihilism—an attitude that "questions medical intervention and is more friendly to health efforts that begin and end at home" (Wikler, 1978). The practical implications of behavioral medicine have been expressed by many writers, among them, for example, Fuchs (1974), who concludes that "the greatest current potential for improving the health of the American people is to be found in what they do and don't do for themselves."

Not all citizens, however, readily accept the notion that they should be urged to alter their style of life in order to win good health and long life. Many patients recoil at their doctors' preaching to them about the ravages of smoking, eating foods that will reduce their cholesterol level, or—moving more closely to the mental health field—working too long hours, being too achievement-oriented, or using corporal punishment in rearing their children. The following observation by Mencken (1927) epitomizes the revulsion some feel at the contraceptive, preventive, or—as the author calls it—the *hygienic* approach to medicine and mental health:

> Hygiene is the corruption of medicine by morality. It is impossible to find a hygienist who does not debase this theory of the healthful with a theory of the virtuous. The whole hygienic art, indeed, resolves itself into an ethical exhortation. This brings it, at the end, into diametrical conflict with medicine proper. The true aim of medicine is not to make men virtuous; it is to safeguard and rescue them from the consequences of their vices. The physician does not preach repentance; he offers absolution. (p. 269)

The issue sardonically highlighted by Mencken cannot be dismissed, especially by those in the mental health field—and particularly by those working in the twin fields of child development and family life. In the latter areas, a great deal of what experts have to offer does, indeed, comprise "ethical exhortations." Moreover, there are those who argue that preventive interventions, however well intentioned, may have unfortunate consequences. Although they may right one "wrong," they frequently cause yet another to develop; this becomes likely when we do not fully understand all of the mechanisms involved in the behavior at issue (Thomas, 1974).

As Thomas points out, it is even more complicated to intervene in pathological social systems. Certainly this is the case where interventions in the child-and-family system are concerned; these need to be assessed carefully in terms of unforeseen consequences that may flow from the intervention itself.

Governmental Involvement

Especially problematic is the involvement of the government in attempts to alter individual and group behavior. Such governmental efforts to promote patterns of living thought to be healthful is not wholly new; public health and labor laws have existed for a long time. In recent years, however, the government has steadily increased its investment in programs to reform lifestyles as a vehicle for promoting health and preventing the onset of illness. Major health policy documents both in the United States (DHEW, 1979) and Canada (Lalonde, 1974) herald a change of emphasis from "attempts to rescue us from the consequences of our vices" to making us "virtuous."

Given the fact that, in many areas of child development and family life, a need exists for providing guidance on childrearing and family functioning, what is the proper role of a government agency? The issue deserves scrutiny, especially considering the apparent fragility of the guidance that has been provided over time. It would appear that the behavioral medicine offered to the public shifts dramatically, in part, with alterations in the values and mores of the culture. Today's best guidance on childrearing and family life may be tomorrow's anathema.

Evaluating Public Education Programs in Stress and Coping

Mental health education programs in child development—indeed, mental health education programs in general—have rarely been subjected to rigorous evaluation. A number of factors account for the gap, among which are those identified by Hall (1977): Evaluative studies require research expertise that generally is not among the major strengths or interests of those who actually plan and direct information and education programs; the conduct of evaluation studies requires a difficult administrative coordination of research interests and talents with communications skills; evaluation studies are costly, since they typically must be longitudinal in scope, requiring long-term investments of energy and resources; and persons devoted to information and education programs, faced with a choice between funding new programs or funding the evaluation of existing ones, typically perceive greater advantage in initiating new programs.

Methodological Problems

The major impediment in the pursuit of evaluation studies, however, has been methodological. Although precise evaluation methodologies do exist for the assessment of mental health education programs, they are typically applied to small projects in which the outcome measures are narrow, and the results cannot be generalized usefully. The studies, therefore, appear to be trivial in the light of the serious questions being asked about public education initiatives.

Even in the case of direct parent education programs in which the target audience is known and available to the researcher, evaluation studies have been inadequate in both number and quality. The numerous publications on the subject provide, for the most part, only programmatic descriptions, not the outcome of attempts to measure results. When premeasurements and postmeasurements have been made, changes have typically been attributed to the program, without benefit of evidence from a comparison or control group. Moreover, evaluation is most often accomplished by the same individual who communicates the information, and, in many cases, comments by participants are cited as the only evidence of positive results (Croake and Glover, 1977).

Most successful evaluations have been made primarily of experimental parent education programs in which the content is carefully programmed and the information is delivered directly to a target audience that is available for study. Training procedures for families intended to help them deal with extremely aggressive youngsters, for example, provide a model for carefully crafted education programs relatively amenable to evaluation (Patterson 1980).

In contrast, most mental health education programs do not involve a direct relationship between the intervenor (in this case, the mental health educator) and the client. They depend on the input of either printed or electronic media, or what Cowen (1980) describes as the "indirect technologies" of community psychology—specifically, the consultation and education functions of community mental health programs. For such programs to be considered as effective initiatives in primary prevention, the outcomes for the ultimate beneficiaries must be assessed and evidence of benefits for the target audience shown. In Cowen's (1980), view, "Much of what has gone on, and is still going on, in parent education . . . should be seen, at best, as preliminary flirtations with models that may, or may not, prove to be true primary prevention in mental health." (p. 269).

It should be acknowledged that the absence of evaluation data does not necessarily mean that mental health education programs are without impact. Leon Eisenberg's (1981) cautionary note regarding the difficulty encountered in the measurement of distant outcomes is as relevant here as in the case of more traditional interventions in the child mental health field. Childhood interventions, he points out, must be powerful indeed to be able to show a clear effect, despite the vicissitudes of subsequent life experience. Although overwhelming evidence exists on the importance of infant nutrition, even the best fed baby will not grow to healthy adolescence if it is starved in later childhood. That fact, Eisenberg contends, does not demonstrate, however, that feeding infants well is not worthwhile.

The Need for Structure

Public education programs in child development carry a potentially significant impact, but there is a pressing need to structure sound evaluation programs to demonstrate such an impact. Unfortunately, sound evaluation models do not abound in child development education, but those in other health fields reveal potentially useful approaches.

Evaluative studies need to be addressed first to programs of limited scope and with modest goals, i.e., programs with potential for yielding precise but generalizable results. Next, it is important to develop large-scale evaluation systems to make possible the study of broadly based communication programs. The design of such systems continues to be of concern to a number of investigators, some of whose efforts have been described earlier. Other investigators include Mielke and Swinehart (1976), Haskins (1978), Robertson (1976), Green (1975), Kline (1972), Blane and Hewitt (1973), and Sundale and Schanie (1978), who have directed their attention to such areas as health promotion, auto safety, alcohol and drug use reduction, and mental health practices. The repeated implication drawn from such efforts is that the successful solution of methodological problems in evaluation will require the combined attention and skills of clinicians, behavioral scientists, and communication experts. Given the potential for effective prevention initiatives through public education in the arena of child mental health, continued efforts to overcome existing problems in the design of evaluation research are surely warranted.

References

Anthony, E. J. (1974) A risk–vulnerability intervention model for children of psychotic parents. In E. J. Anthony and C. Koupernik (Eds.), *The child in his family: Children at psychiatric risk,* Vol. 3. New York: Wiley.

Bienvenu, M. (1967). *Helping the slow learner.* New York: Public Affairs Committee, pamphlet no. 405.

Blane, H. T., and Hewitt, L. C. (1973). *Mass media, public education and alcohol: A state-of-art review.* Rockville, Md.: National Institute of Alcohol Abuse and Alcoholism; Alcohol, Drug Abuse, and Mental Health Administration (ADAMHA).

Bleuler, M. (1974). The offspring of schizophrenics. *Schizophrenia Bulletin,* No. 8 (pp. 93–107).

Brenton, M. (1975). *Playmates: The importance of childhood friendships.* New York: Public Affairs Committee, pamphlet no. 525.

Coleman, J. S., Campbell, E., Hubson, C., McPartland, J., Mood, A., Weinfeld, F., and York, R. (1966). *Equality of educational opportunity.* Washington, D.C.: U.S. Government Printing Office.

Cowen, E. L. (1980). The wooing of primary prevention. *American Journal of Community Psychology, 8,* 258–284.

Croake, J. W., and Glover, K. W. (1977). A history and evaluation of parent education. *The Family Coordinator,* 26, 153–154.

Department of Health, Education and Welfare (1979). *Healthy people: The Surgeon General's report on health promotion and disease prevention.* DHEW Publication No. PHS 79-55071. Washington, D.C.: U.S. Government Printing Office.

Eisenberg, L. (1981). A research framework for evaluating the promotion of mental health and prevention of mental illness. *Public Health Reports, 96,* 3–19.

Epps, E. G. (1969). *Family and achievement: A study of the relation of family background to achievement orientation and performance among urban negro high school students.* Final report of Contract No. oE-6-85-017, Survey Research Center. Ann Arbor: University of Michigan,

Fuchs, V. R. (1974). *Who shall live?* New York: Basic Books.

Garmezy, N. (1983). Stressors of childhood. In N. Garmezy and M. Rutter, (Eds.), *Stress, coping and development in children.* New York: McGraw-Hill (pp. 43–84).

Garmezy, N., and Nuechterlein, K. H. (1972). Invulnerable children: The fact and fiction of competence and disadvantage. Abstract in *American Journal of Orthopsychiatry, 42,* 328–329.

Green, P. (1975). The mass media and anti-smoking campaign around the world. *Proceedings of Third World Conference on Smoking and Health 2,* 245–253.

Hall, J. J. (1977). *Evaluation of mental health education programs.* Unpublished manuscript. Washington, D.C.: National Institute of Mental Health.

Haskins, J. B. (1978). Evaluative research on the effects of mass communication safety campaigns: A methodological critique. *Journal of Safety Research, 2,* 86–90.

Hill, M. (1973). *Parents and teenagers.* New York: Public Affairs Committee, pamphlet no. 490.

Hoffman, L. W. (1979). Material employment. *American Psychologist, 34,* 859–865.

Kafka, F. (1954). *Letter to his father.* In *Dearest Father: Stories and Other Writings.* Translated by Ernst Kaiser and Eithne Wilkins. New York: Schocken Books.

Kagan, J. (1979). Family experience and the child's development. *American Psychologist, 34,* 886–891.

Kline, F. G. (1972). Evaluation of a multimedia drug education program. *Journal of Drug Education, 2,* 229–239.

Lalonde, M. (1974). *A new perspective on the health of Canadians: A working document.* Ottawa: The Government of Canada.

Lander, H. S., Anthony, E. J., Cass, L., Franklin, L., and Bass, L. (1979). A measure of vulnerability to the risk of parental psychosis. In E. J. Anthony and C. Koupernik (Eds.), *The Child in his family: The vulnerable child.* New York: Wiley.

Mencken, H. L. (1927). *Prejudices, third series.* New York: Octagon Books.

Mielke, K. W., and Swinehart, J. W. (1976). Evaluation of the Feeling Good television series. New York: Children's Television Workshop.

Patterson, G. R. (1980). Mothers: The unacknowledged victims. *Monographs of the Society for Research in Child Development, 45,* monograph no. 186).

Robertson, L. S. (1976). The great seat belt campaign flop. *Journal of Communications, 4,* 41–45.

Rutter, M. (1979). Protective factors in children's responses to stress and disadvantage. In M. W. Kent, and J. E. Rolf (Eds.), *Primary prevention of psychopathology: Social competence in children,* Vol. 3. Hanover, N.H.: University Press of New England.

Rutter, M. (1983). Stress, coping and development: Some issues and some questions. In *Stress, coping and development in children,* New York: McGraw-Hill (pp. 43–84).

Sargent, M. (1978). *Caring about kids: Stimulating baby senses.* Department of Health, Education and Welfare Publication No. ADM 77-481. Washington, D.C.: U.S. Government Printing Office.

Sargent, M. (1979). *Caring about kids: Talking to children about death.* Department of Health, Education and Welfare Publication No. ADM 80-838. Washington, D. C.: U.S. Government Printing Office.

Sargent, M. (1980). *Caring about kids: Pre-term babies.* Department of Health and Human Services Publication No. ADM 80-972. Washington, D.C.: U.S. Government Printing Office.

Sobell, S. (1978). *Caring about kids: Helping the hyperactive child.* Department of Health, Education and Welfare Publication No. ADM 80-561. Washington, D.C.: U.S. Government Printing Office.

Starr, R. H. (1979). Child abuse. *American Psychologist, 34,* 872–878.

Sundel, M., and Schanie, C. F. (1978). Community mental health and mass media preventive education: The alternatives project. *Social Science Review,* 52, 297–306.

Thomas, L. (1974). *The medusa and the snail.* New York: Viking Press.

Wallerstein, J., and Kelly, J. B. (1980). *Surviving the breakup: How children and parents cope with divorce.* New York: Basic Books.

Wehrle, S. (1978). *Caring about kids: Dyslexia.* Department of Health and Human Services Publication No. ADM 80-616). Washington, D.C.: U.S. Government Printing Office.

Wikler, D. I. (1978). Persuasion and coercion for health: Ethical issues in government efforts to change lifestyles. *Health and Society, 56,* 303–338.

Yamamoto, K. (1979), Children's ratings of the stressfulness of experiences. *Developmental Psychology, 15,* 581–582.

Support Groups as Preventive Intervention

Frank Riessman

The Needs–Resources Ratio

While I will address the issue of prevention and its relation to self-help, my own predilection is to view mental health and general human service issues along a different axis and to offer a strategy, which, while encompassing prevention, is not focused directly on it. I am essentially concerned with what might be called the needs–resources ratio. By that I mean the relationship of mental health and human services needs to existing resources for meeting these needs.

The demand for human services today far outstrips what the nation is willing to provide, or as Alice Rivlin, the former Director of the Congressional Budget Office, put it: "We want more services than we want to pay for." This problem is endemic to our society, with its expanded awareness of need; but, of course, it is heightened considerably by the Reagan Administration's service cutbacks. Nevertheless, the problem would continue to exist even if we were to restore the services that have been reduced or eliminated, and a critical question relates to how we would restore them: Would we provide a reorganized, more effective, more efficient service delivery system or simply return to the way services were provided prior to the Reagan onslaught. This issue has enormous significance for both prevention and the selfhelp movement.

The formal human services system, as presently organized, is clearly incapable of serving all those in need. More than 30 million people have hypertension, 10 million are alcoholics, 22 million suffer from arthritis, 25 million have emotional problems— and on and on goes the list.*

*Frequently in the reports on the needs–resources problem, there is the assumption that the formal human services system is the requisite form of help. So, for example, the *President's Commission Report on Mental Health,* Vol. 1, 1978, p. 4, states: "At any given time 10–15 percent of the nation's population is in need of mental health services." It might be more appropriate to state that 10–15 percent of the population have serious emotional problems. What they need in order to deal with these problems may be far broader than formal mental health services or even informal help. (Changes in the social structure such as increased

Moreover, the media constantly dramatizes new needs in vivid fashion, while simultaneously noting the limitations of the services as they are currently delivered. For the coming decade, we need a resource-building strategy that geometrically expands the help-giving potential of the society and also changes it qualitatively. The most ready resource is the enormous amount of nonprofessional helpgiving that is taking place, often unrecognized. This is an existing resource that could be integrated efficiently with the professional system. Much of this help is provided by laypeople or consumers and, as we will see, self-help mutual aid is only one of its forms. Before going further, I want to address some general definitional issues; perhaps the most important of these is the distinction between help and practice.

Help versus Practice

The self-help understanding of the nature of help can be contrasted with the professional theory of practice. Professional practice, which is based on systematic knowledge and scientific methodology, is always contextualized by the fact that the help provided is a commodity to be bought, sold, promoted, and marketed. This dimension affects every phase of professional practice, sometimes in the most overt manner, at other times in a highly subtle manner. But it is something that is always there—and typically ignored.

The help provided by mutual-aid groups, on the other hand, is freely given (with a few exceptions like Weight Watchers), and is generally based on less systematic knowledge and conscious use of methodology. It is based on experience, codified experience (like AA's 12 steps), and wisdom. Furthermore, it is rooted in the experience of people who have the problem and have found methods of giving each other help. Simple and self-evident as this concept may be, the implications are important for understanding the nature of help.

In general, I believe there is a highly useful creative tension (or positive dialectic) between professional practice and mutual help. However, this creative tension should not hide the differences or obscure the useful conflict and mutual questioning and criticism.

Because self-help does not have to encounter the constraints of the market, it can begin to develop helping combinations and patterns in novel, fresh ways, unencumbered by professional assumptions. So, for

employment appear to reduce these emotional problems, independent of any increase in mental health services.)

Moreover, people do a great many things about their problems other than receive professional help. The various forms of lay help described in this paper as well as the help seeking from other nonprofessional sources is witness to this observation.

example, retarded 20-year-olds in England have functioned as caregivers for small children; the jobless build self-help unemployed committees; burned-out professionals provide mutual support to each other; offenders and their victims meet together for support; lay leaders of self-help groups form support groups of their own; "little people" meet together for mutal assistance and to destigmatize their condition.

The help given does not have the constraints of time, place, and format. It can be a 24-hour hotline, a friend or partner on call at any time, immediate concrete assistance as well as emotional help, a 3-hour meeting, or a 5-minute telephone call. It can take place in a basement, an apartment, on a street corner, in a community center, in a church, in an office, on a boat, at a fair, in a rap-room in school, in a hospital, or in a funeral parlor.

People in need are converted into resources: An arthritic, who is seen in a professional system as a dependent helpee, is converted into a helper, a giver whose indigenous inside knowledge of living with the illness becomes a treatment force. Thus, not only is the quality of help changed and viewed differently, but the quantity is enormously expanded as it is freed from the market and professional assumptions.

Two Kinds of Self-Help

Two forms of self-help itself need to be distinguished: (1) self-help mutual aid, which refers to groups of individuals who have the same problem or need and come together to help each other; and (2) being helped through helping. The second form of self-help is individual, self-initiated help. For example, there are 32 million people who have given up smoking by themselves without belonging to either a professional or informal group (Surgeon General's Report, 1979); 65–85 percent of all health and medical care is provided by individuals to themselves (Levin, 1983); studies indicate that a considerable number of people lose weight on their own and cure themselves of various drug addictions (Schachter, 1982); college students who have academic problems and/or sexual problems have overcome them on their own (Perri and Richards, 1977).

In addition, of course, there is what Warren (1981) describes as the invisible network of over 70 million helping transactions a month that are provided informally by friends and intimates to people in need of help. Cowen (1982) describes another variant of this form of informal helping given by four groups of people: hairdressers, bartenders, divorce lawyers, and industrial supervisors.

There are, of course, a host of other forms of help taking place in our society: telephone hotlines, newspaper columns such as "Dear Abby," the help given by psychics, EST, paraprofessionals, the clergy, and many more.

Empowerment

Another issue that needs clarification is the role that the various forms of self-help have in empowering individuals. Empowerment is one of the most noteworthy trends of the 1970s and 1980s. What I am referring to here is the fact that when people help themselves—join together with others who have similar problems to deal with these problems, whether they are human services, mental health, or neighborhood problems—they feel empowered in so doing; they are able to control some aspect of their lives. The help is not given to them from the outside, by an expert, a professional, or a politician; These forms of help have the danger of building dependency and have the directly opposite effect of empowerment. Empowerment expands energy, motivation, and helpgiving power that goes beyond helping oneself or receiving help. This is why the helper-therapy principle is so critical in self-help mutual aid and to some extent in other forms of informal helpgiving. It provides a multiplier effect; that is, help is expanded by giving help and by the unique helpgiving properties attached to an individual who has the same problem and may, therefore, have a special understanding of that problem and ways of dealing with it. All of this is empowering and, I believe, empowerment is extremely important for positive mental health as well as the expansion of the helpgiving system.

In addition, however, such empowerment may have significant political relevance because, as people are enabled to deal with some aspects of their lives in a competent fashion, the skills and positive feelings they acquire may contagiously spread and empower them to deal with other aspects of their lives, including larger political dimensions. Frequently, the competencies they develop at the smaller or more immediate level can be and are applied to larger issues. I believe that most of the significant movements that have arisen in the 1970s and 1980s are really movements *for* empowerment and *of* empowerment. The consumer movement, the environmental movement, the neighborhood movement, the self-help movement, the tenants movement, and the movement for the freeze—all have arisen from an empowerment constellation.

This is particularly important to consider because we professionals in the mental health field (and human services fields in general) frequently have a strong tendency to *medicalize, pacify, and divert* from *social or structural analysis*. Forms of helpgiving that are empowering and have a political potential provide an important counterweight to these tendencies.

In my view, a future helpgiving system must unite the positive dimensions of professional caregiving with that of informal helpgiving. And in this dialectic integration, the limits of both professional practice and informal helpgiving need to be faced and curtailed.

Prevention and Self-Help

Within the broader context of the needs–resources ratio, a preventive strategy is important to consider because its aim, essentially, is to provide resources or services in a more economical or cost-effective manner. The self-help approach to prevention opens the door to a vast new prevention constituency—namely, the large numbers of people in self-help mutual-aid groups and the potential population for these groups. In essence, the self-help approach generally begins from an experienced problem, need, or condition, whether it is widowhood, the birth of a premature child, obesity, single parenthood, the loss of a child, becoming a new parent, and the like. The preventive potential deriving from self-help behavior comes afterward, is frequently implicit, and (when recognized) often secondary. Nevertheless, as I will demonstrate, self-help groups often have a clear preventive function, and, if this were to be made more visible to the self-help community, a significant new constituency might be added to the prevention movement. Reciprocally, this preventive aspect strengthens the case for support of self-help modalities and increases the appeal of the self-help movement.

The importance of social support is seen in the prevention equation, adapted from George Albee (1981):

$$\text{Incidence of dysfunction} = \frac{\text{Stress} + \text{Constitutional vulnerabilities}}{\text{Social supports} + \text{Coping skills} + \text{Competence}}$$

The equation suggests two major strategies for preventing dysfunction: (1) decreasing stress or constitutional vulnerabilities, or both; and (2) increasing social supports, coping skills, and competence (Swift, 1979). Self-help groups provide social support to their members through the creation of a caring community, and they increase members' coping skills through the provision of information and the sharing of experiences and solutions to problems.

Thus far the argument accents what can be done with regard to the denominator of the equation, i.e., through strenghtening social supports, coping skills, and competence. Prevention theorists sometimes overlook what might be done in relation to the numerator, or at least one portion of it: the stressors. In many cases, of course, stressors cannot be eliminated or reduced by the individual. Illness or death of a loved one, accidents, and economic setbacks are not easily controllable and in some cases are impossible to control. But here we must consider the empowering attributes of self-help groups and their recent turn to an advocacy orientation. This allows for the possibility that the groups may strive for institutional and social changes, which may, in fact, affect stressors such as accidents and economic events such as unemployment.

For example, a self-help group, Mothers Against Drunk Drivers (MADD), which now has 200 chapters in 40 states and a mailing list of 150,000 people, is concerned not simply with mutual support of those who have lost children as a result of drunk drivers; it is also concerned with making an impact on legislation and other forms of institutional change. So too, Parents of Murdered Children of New York State is concerned with affecting legislation in that state including a Victims Bill of Rights. In the home of the woman who started the program, Odile Stern, a bumper sticker on the wall says it all: "Stop the American Handgun War." (*New York Times,* June 4, 1984.)

Traditionally, self-help groups have not engaged in advocacy. Alcoholics Anonymous (AA) has always seen the problem it deals with as residing solely in the alcoholic, not in social conditions. It does not call for restricting the sale of alcoholic beverages or relieving the social conditions that affect drinkers. And AA is not alone; many self-help groups today remain apolitical.

Many newer self-help groups, however, like the Sisterhood of Black Single Mothers, the Disabled in Action, Self-Help for the Hard of Hearing, the Center for Independent Living, the Gray Panthers, women's health groups, and so on, advocate social change, and some have been deeply involved in legislative action. A prime example is the Association for Retarded Citizens. Chapters of ARC were started in the early 1950s as parents' self-help groups. Parents of children born with Down's Syndrome, spina bifida, or other handicaps got together because doctors were telling them they should institutionalize these children. "It will be better for you and the child," they were told.

At first, the parents shared mutual concerns: "Why did this happen to me?" "This is tearing my family apart." "I can't face my neighbors." "I feel guilty." Then they started to look at the options for keeping their handicapped children at home. They created and paid for educational programs until the early 1970s, when their lobbying efforts resulted in legislation guaranteeing every child with a handicap a free, appropriate education in the least restrictive environment.

While other legislative efforts continue, local ARC chapters keep up their mutual support functions. Parents still help each other cope with a difficult situation, but the burden they carry has been made less onerous by their social action.

In another area, neighborhood self-help groups originally concerned mainly with traffic issues and local crime have taken on a more political character, becoming involved with such issues as pollution and utility rates. Citizen Action, a national federation of 20 statewide groups totaling more than a million members, has organized broad-based coalitions around such issues as gas prices, Social Security, and toxic waste. It has 1500 full-time staff members and an annual budget of $12 million.

It is also worth noting that in the early 1970s the women's movement consisted mostly of small consciousness-raising and health groups. Today, while such groups still exist, the women's movement has become far more political, as the gender gap well illustrates.

Specific Examples of Prevention Efforts

Let me now turn to some specific illustrations of mutual-aid groups functioning in preventive fashion. Self-help groups exist in a variety of areas that have clear implications for prevention: groups for the unemployed, for the parents of premature children, for the families of the mentally ill, for the divorced, for the single parent, for smokers who want to give up the habit and overeaters who wish to do likewise, for the depressed, for drug users, for peers in high schools and colleges, and for people with hypertension, to mention but a few.

Groups for New Mothers

A study of the effectiveness of mutual aid in helping new mothers improve their coping skills sheds important light on the preventive implications of the self-help model (Gordon et al., 1965). A total of 298 mothers who belonged to mutual-support education groups experienced less emotional distress in the six months after childbirth than did 362 control subjects, and their infants were healthier (Parkes, 1964). Follow-up studies 4–6 years later show that, compared with the control subjects, the new mothers in the experimental self-help group had maintained their emotional gains, had subsequently given birth to greater numbers of healthier children, and had suffered fewer physical illnesses, marital conflicts, sexual problems, and divorces. The data showed that, although preparing for problems of postpartum adjustment is helpful to new mothers, developing a self-help network is more critical.

Groups for the Widowed

Bereavement following the death of a spouse has been recognized as a period of extreme stress—a period in which the surviving spouse is vulnerable to emotional and physical illness, particularly in the months immediately following the loss. Research shows heightened impairment in widowed persons' mental health (Parkes, 1964; Clayton, 1974; Carey, 1977; von Rooijen, 1981) and physical health (Marris, 1958; Maddison and Viola, 1968; Frederick, 1981; Helsing and Szklo, 1981), when compared to married populations of the same age.

In the last 15 years, a growing number of self-help groups have been established to serve the needs of the widowed, e.g., NAIM (a Catholic-sponsored organization), THEOS (They Help Each Other Spiritually), Widowed Persons Service, Widow-to-Widow, and Community Centers for the Widowed.

Lieberman and Borman (1981) report that active participation in THEOS positively affects the mental health status of the members. Both current and former THEOS members who helped each other through their social network consistently showed better outcome on seven variables: depression, anxiety, somatic symptoms, use of psychotropic drugs, self-esteem, coping mastery, and well-being. Similar findings were demonstrated in a two-year study of postbereavement adaptation by 162 widows (Vachon et al., 1980).

The importance of these findings is underscored by the size of the population currently and potentially at risk. The 12 million widowed persons in the United States already number almost 5 percent of the total population. The projected increase in the size of the older population suggests the probability that the proportion of widowed persons will continue to increase.

A recent report shows the need for social support may be particularly great among widowers (Greenberg, 1981). Researchers at the Johns Hopkins University School of Hygiene and Public Health conducted a 12-year survey of more than 4000 widowed persons aged 18 and over. They found that the death of a spouse appears to be much more devastating to men. The survey found that widowed men as a group had a mortality rate 28 percent higher than that of their married counterparts. Moreover, widowed men between the ages of 55 and 65, who made up more than one-fourth of the people in the study, had a mortality rate 60 percent higher than that of married men of the same age.

The National Self-Help Clearinghouse, through grants from the Administration on Aging and the Retirement Research Foundation, is in the process of developing widower self-help groups that are being styled to involve men who may be more resistant to the traditional self-help emphasis on shared expression of their feelings. If successful, the prevention implications may be considerable, even having an impact on mortality rates.

Effective Tertiary Prevention

While the preceeding studies have dealt with acute mental health needs, the following project demonstrates a self-help approach to a chronic condition. With the growth of deinstitutionalization, self-help groups are bridging the gap between hospitalization and community living for ex-patients.

The Community Network Development Project at the Florida Mental Health Institute illustrates how the creation of a mutual-aid network can be an effective method for reducing hospital recidivism among mental health clients (Gordon et al., 1982). The project's development was guided by the belief that a self-help program for aftercare clients should strengthen the members' abilities to take an active part not only in their own rehabilitation, but also in the rehabilitation of their peers.

The project consisted of the establishment of a mutual-aid network of self-help groups for aftercare clients. Members of the support groups were trained in leadership and given responsibilities such as teaching psychoeducational classes, telephoning members to remind them of the next group meeting, driving members to meetings, baking cakes for the group, and arranging outings. Not only did this program help individuals improve their personal functioning, but it also contributed to the survival of the group.

Eighty patients who were being discharged from a nine-week intensive treatment unit were randomly assigned to the project or to a control group for traditional aftercare services. Both groups received equivalent discharge planning, including appropriate referrals to a local mental health center for follow-up treatment, if necessary. The groups did not differ significantly according to age, sex, race, marital status, diagnosis, previous hospitalization, or length of follow-up time. At an average follow-up interval of ten months, only one-half as many project members as control subjects had required rehospitalization (17.5 percent to 35 percent), and their average length of stay was less than one-third as long as that of the controls (7 days versus 24.6 days). Finally, twice as many project members were able to function wihout any contact with a mental health system (52.5 percent versus 26 percent).

Integration of Self-Help and Professional Service Delivery

Recognizing that self-help mutual aid is a potentially useful preventive strategy, let me now return to the overall concern for expanding resources to meet needs. Assuming that preventive approaches represent one useful strategy for dealing with the problem, I have attempted to show that self-help mutual aid can function in a preventive fashion. But that still leaves the larger question of how to expand effectively the potential help-giving resources of the society.

First, it is necessary to become aware of the enormous latent healing power in the various forms of informal help that I have outlined in this chapter.† The next step is to consider and build ways of integrating these forms of help with the formal professional helpgiving system. These include activities such as the development of materials by professionals for lay use, training of lay group leaders, sponsorship of self-help groups, referrals, and so forth. It also means having professionals learn from self-help and other forms of lay help by attending self-help group meetings, including laypeople in training sessions for professionals, and having professional curricula in social work schools and health education programs include information on the various forms of lay help.

The seeds of integration are beginning to take root. Thus there are, at present, 27 regional self-help clearinghouses that bring professional expertise to bear on the building of mutual-aid groups. These local clearinghouses typically provide the following functions: publishing a directory of local self-help groups; developing a hotline for information and referrals; providing technical assistance to existing groups; conducting conferences and fairs; and publishing relevant self-help materials.

Some further examples of lay and professional integration are:

- The American Hospital Association (AHA) has developed a whole self-help resource packet directed at assisting and encouraging health professionals in hospitals to work with and develop self-help groups.

- The American Association of Retired Persons (AARP) has developed a series of programs relating to widow self-help groups.

- In Holland a pattern described as a *Duo* has developed in which patients with chronic illnesses are helped by a team consisting of a professional and a person who has the same problem (Bremer-Schulte et al., 1982).

- Reevaluation counseling, an approach that is widespread in the United States, utilizes a trainer to provide training to lay individuals in how to counsel each other.

- The self-care project directed by Levin at Yale is concerned with em-

†It would be valuable to describe and enumerate the various forms of helpgiving that are in fact taking place. Second, it would be useful to conduct research evaluating the various helpgiving forms and to investigate the processes underlying them. For example, how do people go about giving up smoking by themselves? What preceded the self-initiated act? What factors affected the quitter?

powering self-help groups in the community by providing technical assistance, etc., but always relating this assistance to the mode, style, and skills that already exist in the client or consumer population (Savo, 1983).

• Peer counseling approaches in schools and colleges typically utilize a professional psychologist to train students in peer counseling other students.

• Gendlin, who developed the focusing technique in psychotherapy is concerned with transferring the skills involved in that approach to a consumer population who can then do it themselves. (Most self-help books are written by professional experts to give lay people the skills and approaches they can use in helping themselves.)

• In Westchester County (N.Y.) professionals in the county's self-help clearinghouse have been training natural helpers in the community, adding skills and techniques to their already existing repertoire, but being careful not to violate the natural approaches and strengths they possess.

• Groups that have an advocacy orientation, such as self-help for the hard-of-hearing or single parents. This allows for commitment to institutional change as well as personal help.

• Groups in which there is shared and distributed leadership of various kinds, both formal and informal.

• Groups that provide extra motivation for participating, e.g., recognition, publicity, professional attention.

• Groups that have an ideology or rationale that explains the problem they are addressing and the methodology for coping with the problem.

• Groups that are dealing with a strongly felt need, problem, or illness.

• Groups that have built definite traditions and structure, e.g., meeting at the same time and place, meeting frequently (once a week), providing refreshments.

• Groups that develop a strong experiential knowledge base.

• Groups that maintain some relationship to the professional system from which they may receive assistance, recognition, resources, referral, sponsorship, training, or consultation.

• Groups that have a good balance between the informal, open ethos and the structured dimension related to continuity, group maintenance, and follow-up.

• Groups that provide, in addition to their main agenda of mutual support and help, related activities. For health-oriented groups, this may include various stress-reducing techniques at the meetings or jogging at other times.

• Groups that deal realistically with problems of relapse or regression.

• Groups that believe in themselves; believe that they are effective in dealing with the problems and needs of members.

• Groups that are composed of people with similar background, age level, education, and interests.

• Groups that have access to resources, e.g., meeting place, mailing facilities, phone, publicity.

• Groups that use a variety of behavioral and cognitive principles, either knowingly or unknowingly.

• Groups that are related to a national organization (e.g., AA, Recovery, Inc., Parents Anonymous), although the relationship may be loose and informal.

• Groups that meet in settings that are reinforcing, such as a senior center or at the workplace.

• Groups that have at least one and preferably two "energy" people.

• Groups that add a social aspect at the meeting itself and carry out recreational activities, such as parties and trips.

Two-Way Relationship

However, the new integration of the informal and formal help systems should not be a one-way relationship.‡ As the ethos and style of the more natural self-help system begins to rub off on the professional system, it may become less distant, more humane, and more informal. The result could revitalize and transform the human services delivery system, making it more participatory and appealing to a public that often has been critical of bureaucratic, wasteful, and inefficient service delivery. The delivery system could be dramatically expanded, and the services provided would be more people-based and personalized.

The news media generally depict self-help quite attractively, and the public sees it as an inexpensive, nonbureaucratic, participatory expansion of services that make people less dependent in general. This makes the services more attractive and is likely to win much-needed support against conservative budget cutting.

The new *prosumers* (to use Toffler's term) are no longer dependent consumers or public critics because they are involved directly in the production and delivery of services. Since the self-helpers are not employed workers, they are not subject to the same bureaucratic controls that

‡Apart from what professionals may add to the informal helping mode, there is the potential value of their criticism of abuses and negative aspects of this mode, e.g., the special dependency-producing aspects of many self-help groups.

might apply to the paid employee. Their more direct involvement with services may reduce somewhat a supercritical public stance, to say nothing of the possibility that the newly restructured services may actually be less deserving of criticism or attack.

At the present time, two vastly different human services systems exist side by side with only occasional articulation: the self-help system and the professional system. Each has its weaknesses and strengths. A dialectic integration of the two may provide not only a useful balance that gives them the chance to learn from each other, but also a vastly expanded, restructured, and cost-effective production of human services that is responsive to the growing human services crisis in our society.

In building the human services system of the future, we need to restore what has been cut—but in a new fashion, because the present system cannot possibly fulfill the enormous unmet needs in our society. What we have proposed is a fuller integration of the vast informal helpgiving structure with the professional formal system. This integration should help each system, with the added bonus of consumer involvement in the helpgiving activities. The consumer then is the hidden resource that needs to be mobilized for a new dimension in service productivity.

References

Albee, G. (1981). An ounce of prevention: Reorienting mental health priorities. Remarks made at a conference, New York, January 16, 1981. *Self-Help Reporter, 5,* 1–2.

Bremer-Schulte, M., et al. (1982). Oorspronkelijke Stukken. *Ned. T. Geneesk 126,* nr. 45.

Carey, R. G. (1977). The widowed: A year later. *Journal of Consulting Psychology, 24,* 125–131.

Clayton, P. J. (1974). Mortality and morbidity in the first year of bereavement. *Archives of General Psychiatry, 30,* 747–750.

Cowen, E. L. (1982). Help is where you find it. *American Psychologist, 37,* 385–395.

Frederick, J. (1981). The biochemistry of acute grief with regard to neoplasia. In O. Margolis et al. (Eds.), *Acute grief.* New York: Columbia University Press.

Gordon, R. D., et al. (1965). Factors in postpartum emotional adjustment. *Obstetrical Gynecology 25,* 156–166.

Gordon, R. E., et al. (1982). Reducing rehospitalization of state mental patients: Peer management and support. In A. Yaeger and R. Slotkin (Eds.), *Community mental health.* New York: Plenum.

Greenberg, J. (1981). Researchers find widowers die earlier than widows do. *New York Times,* July 30, 1981 (p. 1).

Helsing, J. J., and Szklo, M. (1981). Mortality after bereavement. *American Journal of Epidemiology, 114,* 41–52.

Levin, L. S. (1983). Self-care in health. *Annual Review of Public Health.*
Lieberman, M. A., and Borman, L. D. (1981). The impact of self-help groups on widows' mental health. The National Research and Information Center's *National Reporter, 4,* 2–6.
Maddison, D. C., and Viola, A. (1968). The health of widows in the year following bereavement. *Journal of Psychosomatic Research, 12,* 297–306.
Marris, P. (1958). *Widows and their families.* London: Routledge and Kegan Paul.
New York Times, Style, Monday, June 4, 1984.
Parkes, C. M. (1964). Recent bereavement as a cause of mental illness. *British Journal of Psychiatry, 110,* 198–204.
Parkes, C. M. (1972). *Bereavement: Studies of grief in adult life.* London: Tavistock Publications.
Perri, G., and Richards, C. S. (1977). An investigation of naturally occurring episodes of self-controlled behaviors. *Journal of Counseling Psychology, 24,* 178–183.
Savo, C. (1983). Self-care and empowerment: A case study. *Social Policy, 14,* 19–22.
Schachter, S. (1982)."Recidivism and self-care of smoking and obesity," *American Psychologist, 37,* 436–444.
Smoking and health (1979). Report of the Surgeon General.
Swift, C. (1979). The prevention equation and self-help groups. *Self-Help Reporter, 3,*(4), 1–2.
Vachon, M. L. S., Lyall, W. A. L., Rogers, J., Freedman-Letofsky, K., and Freeman, S. J. J. (1980). A controlled study of self-help intervention for widows. *American Journal of Psychiatry, 137,* 1380–1384.
Van Rooijen, L. (1981). Widows' bereavement: Stress and depression after 1½ years. In I. Sarason (Ed.), *Stress and anxiety,* Vol. 6. New York: Wiley.
Warren, D. I. (1981). *Helping networks: How people cope with problems in the urban community.* South Bend, Ind.: University of Notre Dame Press.

Education for Prevention

Richard H. Price

Introduction

The choice of words in the title is deliberate. I have chosen to write about *education* rather than training for prevention for several reasons. Training is an idea that implies the acquisition of a narrowly circumscribed set of skills, with little expectation of searching inquiry. Education, on the other hand, is a liberating idea—one that implies questioning and fully exploring choices and possibilities. I believe that it is education rather than training that we and our students will need over the coming decades if the field of primary prevention is to flourish. Furthermore, there are a great many different kinds of people and experiences that can further our education. Not only texts and courses, but also field experiences and direct encounters with those whom we wish to serve will be essential.

The field of prevention is an incredibly broad and diverse enterprise. Because of its vast range we have tended to compartmentalize our knowledge, focusing narrowly on a single aspect of the prevention enterprise and worrying very little about what our co-workers are doing in different parts of the field. If we are to move ahead, we must develop a more articulated view of the broad panorama of the prevention research field.

Education for prevention has had a short and varied history. Thus far, the efforts have been piecemeal. There has been little penetration into academic programs, and, when there has been an academic context for prevention, it has usually been reflected in an apprenticeship model adopted by a few pioneers in the field. Nevertheless, there are important historical milestones to review. In addition, I will review some data that have been collected on educational efforts in prevention because, while the data are relatively modest, they reflect some important trends and needs. I will then turn my attention to the years ahead. Just as the history of education in prevention is brief, so is the future potentially long and

Work on this chapter was supported in part by Grant MH38330 from the Office of Prevention Research, National Institute of Mental Health.

promising. Before we can chart that future, however, we need to systematically map the domain of prevention research and to describe some of the roles for which researchers and practitioners can be educated.

A Short Look Back

As Zolick (1983) has observed:

> The tap root of the current fervor for primary prevention is located in President Kennedy's 1963 historic message to congress which resulted in the passage of the Community Mental Health Centers Act. This legitimation of prevention in 1963 at the highest national level, did not result in immediate major innovations in practice and training. It was, however, the necessary agent and provided the authoritative sanction for beginning the engagement. (pp. 273–274)

A second major milestone and legitimizing event at the national level was the President's Commission on Mental Health (1978). The Commission affirmed the need for prevention by including primary prevention as one of the eight major areas recommended for federal action. While education for prevention did not receive much attention in the president's report, the report was clearly instrumental in identifying primary prevention as a major activity for researchers and practitioners in the field. By the end of the 1970s, the idea of prevention was in the air, and the report of the surgeon general (U.S. Department of Health, Education, and Welfare, 1979) on healthy people identified the need for prevention efforts if significant improvements in the health of the nation were to be achieved.

Each of these historic events was clearly an important milestone for the field of prevention, legitimizing the need for prevention activities and implying the need for educational efforts. But these were largely symbolic efforts. They pointed in important directions, but by themselves only set the scene for action.

On the other hand, the 1963 Community Mental Health Centers Act did provide the conditions for an initial action effort in the field of prevention. One of the five essential services under the act was to be consultation and education. The intention clearly was to develop primary prevention efforts as one aspect of those consultation and education functions. In the arena of action, then, consultation and education came to be identified as a major thrust in the field of prevention. But results have not yet lived up to the promise: Only about 5 percent of the total amount of community mental health center staff time has been devoted to consultation and education activities. Other observers estimate that only half of this small effort could legitimately be identified as primary prevention

(Vayda and Perlmutter, 1977; Bass, 1974; NIMH Survey Reports Branch, 1978). Furthermore, it appears that, when community mental health centers could no longer rely on federal funding to support consultation and education efforts, attention devoted to this activity dropped precipitously.

There have been notable exceptions, however. Training in the John F. Kennedy Hahnemann Community Mental Health Center in Philadelphia has created a rich array of prevention-oriented field experiences under the direction of Marshall Swift. The consultation center at Yale University is a second notable exception, and the Northside Community Mental Health Center in Tampa, Florida, under Tony Broskowski, is a third. Unfortunately, these exceptions are few, and primary prevention efforts in the field of consultation and education remain underrepresented.

Interest in the promise of prevention was not confined to practitioners in the field of community mental health. Pioneers in the field of community psychology also identified prevention as an important thrust for community research and service. Indeed, the Swamscott Conference, which marked the beginning of the field of community psychology, identified preventive efforts as a major goal. Soon afterward, leaders in the field, including Albee and Joffe (1977), Cowen (1977), Bloom (1979), and Iscoe (1981), all exhorted the field of psychology—and community psychology in particular—to move forward on this new intellectual and action front. Albee (1967) established the idea that, while mental health problems will continue to increase, manpower for treatment could not possibly keep pace. Preventive efforts were the logical and compelling alternative. Cowen (1977) cautioned us to move ahead steadily in our research and program delivery efforts, taking "baby steps" toward a fully developed field of primary prevention. By the mid-1970s, Klein and Goldston (1977) could assert that primary prevention was "an idea whose time has come."

Seminal ideas mark the beginning of any new field, and as Kuhn (1970) has observed, no idea is a candidate for adoption without convincing examples. Those examples began to proliferate (e.g., Price and associates, 1980). By the beginning of the 1980s, real examples of prevention programs and research began to appear in increasing numbers. Cowen (1982) edited a special issue of the *American Journal of Community Psychology*, which was devoted to prevention programs that had been rigorously enough evaluated to provide evidence that they could be systematically designed, delivered, and evaluated. Furthermore, it appeared that the programs could indeed have an impact on the incidence of mental health problems. Felner and colleagues (1983) went further, identifying preventive psychology as an important thrust in the field. They examined competence-based perspectives, ecological and environmental viewpoints, and life stress questions, as well as practice and training, as important arenas in the rapidly developing field.

At about the same time, Albee and colleagues had begun convening prevention researchers and practitioners at annual Vermont conferences for the primary prevention of psychopathology. The published proceedings of those conferences have added still further to the knowledge base on which a field of prevention and education for prevention might be built. As the Vermont conferences developed over the years, some—perhaps many—of the participants did not initially identify themselves as prevention researchers. They were experts on specific problems and content areas, some of whom for the first time discovered that the knowledge they were developing could actually be applied to primary prevention efforts. Nevertheless, the stage was set for a rapid series of developments in the field.

Academic Education in Primary Prevention

While legislative and commission declarations, as well as action efforts, continued to move forward, each on its own trajectory, the idea of actually educating people to conduct research and program development in the field of prevention has lagged behind. Academic institutions, as Zolik (1983) observes, are often politically liberal but organizationally conservative when it comes to creative change in their own departmental programs. Consequently, the penetration of the idea of prevention as an action science into the halls of academe remains today relatively limited and unsystematic.

However, thanks to the efforts of Schneider (1982) at the National Institute of Mental Health, the last decade has seen a consistent growth in the number of academic departments where course work and programmatic elements on prevention have, indeed, developed. Barton et al. (1977) conducted a survey of 141 mental health education programs, which indicated that approximately 67 percent of those programs did indeed have prevention represented somewhere in the course content. Course coverage, however, was primarily aimed at applied programming and was considerably less oriented to developing theoretical and empirical foundations for prevention research. Furthermore, course coverage still reflects a failure to address important needs in the field: Only one-half of the programs were concerned with the relationship between the social environment and psychological disorders; only 35 percent of the programs were concerned with the etiology of disorders or with epidemiology. While these programs were training graduate students in the technology of program delivery, considerably less sensitivity to the importance of an epidemiological understanding of mental health problems was evident. It appears that the link between academic study and training in the field was even weaker. Education for the most part extended only as far as the classroom door, and, in many cases, students were on their own if they wanted to obtain a real field experience to enrich their education in prevention.

There have been some notable exceptions, however. Programs under a variety of organizational arrangements and under strong leadership have managed to turn out a second generation of prevention researchers and practitioners. The Laboratory for Community Psychiatry at Harvard University, under the direction of Gerald Caplan, was a clear example. Other examples include the Primary Project at the University of Rochester, under the direction of Emory Cowen, the Community Psychology Program at the University of Texas, under the direction of Ira Iscoe, and the Clinical/Community Psychology Program at the University of Colorado, under the direction of Bernard Bloom.

What can we conclude from this brief history of training and education in the field of prevention? Certainly, while there is a second generation of prevention researchers and practitioners in the field, they have been educated primarily in the apprenticeship mode rather than in a systematically designed program. The coverage of prevention course content has been largely oriented to program delivery and has systematically undervalued epidemiological and etiological research.

Why is this the case? I conclude that *it is because we have no complete and shared map of the domains of prevention research and practice*. We are only beginning to develop a systematic description of the goals and activities of prevention research, and we lack systematic descriptions of the roles to be designed to achieve prevention goals. Without a map of the domain, a description of the salient activities, and a specification of the potential roles for research and practice, education in prevention will continue to be a haphazard affair. In the following section, I will attempt to map the domains and describe some of their conceptual underpinnings. My intent is to improve our understanding of how to educate our students and ourselves, so that we can better pursue *systematic* research and practice in the field of primary prevention.

A Map of the Prevention Field

The field of prevention is too complex to be accommodated by a single role or educational model. Prevention research is actually a chain of linked activities. These activities are very different from each other. They are also interdependent, sequential, goal-directed, and presently isolated from each other. And they require that we create an educational and social structure in which they can flourish.

We badly need a shared map of the field of primary prevention for a number of reasons. First, many preventionists have taken a global view of their work. Global views can be useful because they cover a great deal of territory, but they have severe limitations because they are weak on detail. If you actually try to use a global map to travel in a particular area, you may find yourself lost or dealing with terrain that you are not equipped to handle.

Paradoxically, many prevention researchers have also taken a parochial view of prevention research and practice. They seem unable to look beyond the narrow territory of their own domains. Some of them seem to think prevention research should involve only certain groups; others, that prevention must necessarily involve only certain types of interventions. While this kind of parochialism is comforting in the same sense that ostriches find the sand comforting, it does not necessarily promote research and education with the vision that we need.

We also need a map of the field because the terrain is so varied. Mine suggests that you cannot use the same conceptual and methodological equipment and skills in different parts of the field and that some people are better adapted to travel in some parts of it than in others.

There are several major domains in the field of prevention. Each of these domains has its own native groups who speak their own languages and have different customs and world views. These domains do not necessarily engage in much commerce with each other. Consequently, we need boundary spanners: people who are capable of moving from one domain to another and have some idea of what they are importing, what they are exporting, and why. Obviously, boundary spanners would find a map helpful.

Finally, we need a map because it would help to make our work public. Our efforts are in the interest of society as a whole, and our map should be open to scrutiny by our fellow scientists, policymakers, and citizens' groups with whom we work. A map will enhance communication if it is effectively drawn and shown to potential collaborators. This map is crude in its outlines, and each of its parts could be made into a detailed map in its own right.

Some Features of the Prevention Map

The map shown in Fig. 1 delineates four major domains of activity: (1) problem analysis; (2) intervention design; (3) field trials; and (4) diffusion of preventive interventions. You should read the map by beginning at the upper left-hand corner and moving clockwise. Other maps

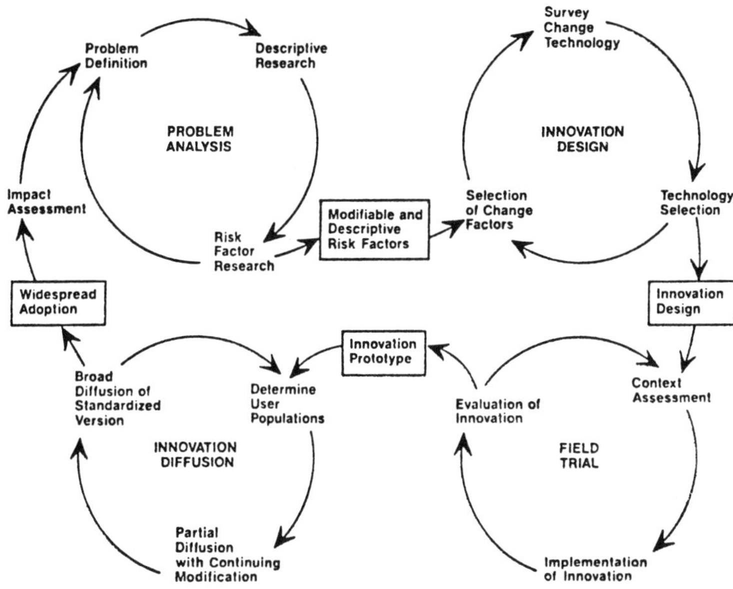

Figure 1 . Four domains of prevention research.

may divide the territory differently, but from where I stand these represent the major areas to be explored. An additional feature of the map is that each domain is portrayed as a cycle. Within the domain of problem analysis, for example, initial considerations of problem definition should lead to descriptive and analytical epidemiological research, which should produce a useful outcome. In addition, this map is goal-oriented. In the context of prevention, the goal in each domain is to generate an output or product (shown in boxes) that can also serve as an input for the next domain.

It is my impression that most of us spend much of our time somewhere in the right-hand side of the map, designing and field testing preventive programs. We now need to spend more time on the left-hand side of the map—in the domains of epidemiologically and theoretically based problem analysis and in the activity of innovation diffusion. More effort in these domains will yield dividends in conceptual sharpness and in the ultimate impact of our efforts.

I have no illusions that this process unfolds in an unerring and mechanical fashion, producing research, educational, and prevention programs from some scientific conveyor belt. We know far too little about each stage of this process and how these stages can be interconnected.

Nevertheless, in its broad outline, I find this map helpful in thinking through the nature of research and education programs in the field of prevention.

If we accept the framework implied by this map, we can begin to sketch some of its implications for the education of prevention researchers and practitioners. Havelock and Havelock (1973) have observed that a useful way to begin thinking about designing new educational programs is to try to envision the role that a graduate of that program might occupy. The roles that I will describe are in some ways quite different from each other, although it is important to note that they interlock at various points. I do not believe that any single role is capable of encompassing the enormous diversity of research and practice activity undertaken in the name of prevention. Let us now look at the various domains of prevention research and the roles implied for prevention practitioners in more detail.

Epidemiologically Oriented Problem Analysis

Although problem analysis can proceed in a number of different directions, there is growing agreement that a promising approach involves the identification of risk-producing situations. These are transitions or events that open the possibility of maladaptation by those who encounter them. Such *risky situations,* as I have called them (Price, 1980), may involve changes in role, status, available interpersonal or material resources, or performance demands. Examples of risky situations include marital separation, job loss, school transitions, the death or loss of a loved one, and life-threatening illness or injuries. At the University of Michigan Prevention Research Center, we have focused on work transition and job loss as a major risky situation to be understood. A hallmark of these events is that their consequences are not simple and are likely to produce a number of complex, interrelated problems involving changes in psychological well-being, health, and legal and financial status. Bloom (1981) calls this a "problem complex" in his book *Primary Prevention: The Possible Science.*

From both a theoretical and practical point of view, the interrelatedness and contingent nature of the outcomes of risky situations are intriguing and important. In our work at Michigan, we think that job loss is, for example, a life event that triggers a variety of other events in financial, marital, parental, and work or career dimensions. These additional events may further increase the period of unemployment and accompanying distress and demoralization, each of which, in turn, may increase the probability of more serious psychological outcomes. The point is not just that outcomes are multiple and diverse but also that they unfold over time and are to some degree contingent on preceding events in the career of the displaced worker. If risky situations have these properties, our problem analysis efforts will need to be capable of appreciating them. A lifespan developmental orientation and longitudinal surveys and case control studies will have to become the norm rather than the rare exception in problem analysis.

Epidemiologists have developed some helpful descriptive and analytical tools for the assessment of risk, and these tools can provide crucial guideposts in working our way through the problem analysis portion of the map. While these concepts and operations are commonplace in epidemiology, they are seldom discussed in the context of primary prevention in mental health. They should be fundamental to any educational program in prevention. Gruenberg (1981) has published an overview on strategies for quantifying risk. In this review, he examines concepts such as *relative risk* (a measure of how much the risk factor affects the incidence rates for the problem in question) and *attributable risk* (the proportion reduction in incidence associated with the removal of a particular risk factor).

Information about risk is, of course, fundamental to making an informed decision about whether it is worthwhile or feasible to develop preventive interventions for a particular problem or population. Our students need to learn how to gather and evaluate such information. In most cases this means doing prospective or retrospective case control studies with representative samples.

Of course, survey research and epidemiological studies are not the only way to measure attributable risk. In some cases, we can measure it directly by engaging in a preventive trial where we can evaluate the degree to which we reduce the probability of a particular problem or disorder and where we can evaluate the causal status of a risk factor. Thus part of the domain of problem analysis should involve the effective teaching and use of risk-factor research methods.

However, the use of analytical concepts from epidemiology in no way implies that we must limit our research to the distribution of risk factors associated with diseases or diagnostic categories. Long ago, Bloom (1968) observed that we did not have to focus on major diagnostic categories just because we want to take an epidemiological approach to understanding problem behavior. We can study the distributional characteristics of any event or behavior.

The outcome of risk-factor research, then, should be sets of risk factors, some of which are modifiable, which are correlated with a complex of interrelated problems, at least some of which should be preventable. A promising path involves the identification of risky life situations that have multiple, contingent, and negative outcomes.

In my view, a problem analyst is someone who has quantitative skills. Problem analysts must have something to say about the distribution of the problem, both demographically and geographically. In this sense, they share some of the characteristics of epidemiologists and are comfortable in doing risk-factor research. On the other hand, problem analysts are not narrowly tied to a single methodological tradition. They are equally comfortable conducting and learning from ethnographic research involving participant observation and interviewing people presumed to be at risk for a particular problem or disorder. For example, the Michigan Prevention Research Center is conducting a series of in-depth group interviews with unemployed people as part of the process of problem analysis. The problem analyst will not be content only with survey results but will want to see the problem from the perspective of the population thought to be at risk.

Innovation Design and Field Trial

Let us now consider the next two portions of the map. The domains of innovation design and field trial have been somewhat better explored by prevention researchers over the last decade or so. I have separated the domains of innovation design and field trial, although in practice they may frequently overlap. Decisions in the domain of innovation design are complex, often not well thought through, and deserve more attention than they receive in our teaching and research efforts (Thomas, 1984). We should educate students to be aware that several critical steps in the design of preventive innovations need careful consideration. First, we need to consider the question of the level at which our efforts should be focused. Frequently drawing on analogies from clinical treatment, we have been inclined to develop labor intensive individual-level interventions without considering possibilities at other levels. An interesting exception is the recent work of Felner, Ginter, and Primavera (1982). They choose to prevent the predictable negative effects of the transition to high school by using an organizational intervention that restructured the role of teachers and reorganized the regularities of the school environment to reduce the flux of the social setting confronting the student. This organizational change strategy is likely to be less labor intensive and less costly than elaborate individually oriented change strategies.

This brings us to a second point, the selection of change strategies. In many cases, the availability of change technologies is much broader than we first imagined. We can choose among organizational innovations, educational approaches, behavior modification methods, and the organization of self-help groups, for example. Unfortunately, our choice of change technologies is often more heavily governed by what is immediately available than by a searching analysis of the nature of the problem and the risk factors that we wish to modify. In selecting a change technology, and in educating preventionists to do so, we need to take into account a wide range of criteria. They include issues of cost, efficiency, the nature of the setting, previous evidence of effectiveness, and even political feasibility. Why have these factors not been considered more carefully? They are critical ingredients in the prevention process; we should be teaching our students about them, and we should be sensitive to them ourselves.

Perhaps the most familiar territory to most of us is in the domain of field trial. Anyone engaging in a field trial for a preventive intervention should first spend considerable time and energy assessing the potential context in which the innovation will be delivered. Not every setting or community is equally hospitable to an innovative program or trial, and yet there is little discussion in educational programs about these considerations. For example, we have deliberately chosen community colleges, YMCAs, and other community settings for our intervention work in Michigan because displaced workers are more comfortable there. The setting is not a clinical one but instead is educational in nature and was designed at the outset to serve the community.

In evaluating programs within the domain of field trial, Heller, Price, and Sher (1980) distinguished between proximal programmatic objectives of the field trial and distal prevention goals. In some cases, field trials will be able to demonstrate an impact only on proximal objectives, even though we would like evidence that more distal goals are also achieved. This distinction between proximal and distal objectives of prevention programs must be central to the education of field researchers. Considerable thought and attention should be given to the natural history of the development of various patterns of adaptation, both for purposes of program design and for the purposes of evaluation (Kessler, Price, and Wortman, 1985).

So what, then, are some of the role characteristics and skills of innovation designers and field researchers? Innovation designers must be able to use the information produced by problem analysts in formulating the design of an intervention. Innovation designers are people with a broad knowledge of change methods. One of their capabilities should be able to make informed choices about the appropriateness, cost, potential effectiveness, and impact of a particular change technology. Field researchers must be able to transform a design for a preventive intervention into a reality and so needs not only research design skills but also must be able to collaborate with administrators and local community groups that will serve as hosts for preventive innovations. The skills of the field researcher may seem familiar to most of us, but they are seldom described in ways that allow us to appreciate the subtle blend of political sensitivity and scientific hard-headedness that is needed to enact this role successfully.

Diffusion of Preventive Innovations

Many prevention researchers find it hard to accept the fact that the fruits of their labors, no matter how effectively evaluated or elegantly packaged, will not be spontaneously embraced by school systems, communities, or other institutions for which they have been designed. Just because you have a better product does not mean that the world will beat a path to your door (Caplan, 1975). Still another activity and role we need to consider in designing educational programs for preventionists is that of diffusion researcher.

Fortunately, there is a substantial body of research on the diffusion of innovations that we can consult in developing principles for effective prevention program dissemination (Rogers and Shoemaker, 1971; Arnt, 1968; Rothman, Erlich, and Teresa, 1976; Rothman et al., 1983; Kotler, 1975; Munson and Pelz, 1982; Zaltman, Duncan, and Holbek, 1973). These researchers have suggested that, in diffusing our innovation to broader systems, we consider a variety of factors, including the nature and quality of the program itself and the principle of partial implementation (Rothman, Erlich, and Teresa, 1976).

The principle of partial implementation is an empirical generalization based on a substantial amount of communication and diffusion research. Briefly, it suggests that innovations which can be tried on a partial basis will have a higher adoption rate than innovations that require total adoption without an initial partial trial. This principle applies to trial of part of an innovation throughout a whole network of users or the trial of an entire innovation in part of a potential user network. The point is that partial trials appear to activate a number of processes that reduce resistance to later total adoption. The last domain in our map reflects this two-step principle of diffusion and the last output in this domain is, of course, broad program acceptance in numerous user groups or networks. Once preventive innovations have reached this stage of development, we can assess the impact of our efforts on the ultimate goal: reduction in the incidence of problems or disorders in the community.

So another critical role in the prevention research process is that of diffusion researcher. We have recognized only recently that to "give psychology away" as Miller (1969) has suggested, is not as easy as it sounds. Even low cost, effective interventions focused on important problems will not necessarily be spontaneously adopted. A diffusion researcher must be able to assess the adoption potential of various groups and involve potential users in examining the innovation and modifying it to suit local concerns, needs, and interests.

The Two-Culture Problem: Linking Key Roles

Because education for prevention will require interlocking activities of groups of researchers who have seldom had commerce with each other, thoughtful planning about future priorities for prevention education must address the issue of *boundary spanning*. Unless we can successfully cross the boundaries between the research domains I have described, the final goal of our efforts is less likely to be achieved. Let me focus on some of the most crucial gaps between these domains.

There are now at least two distinctly different research traditions working in the name of prevention. Each focuses on different points in the research sequence and currently has little communication with the other. One of these research traditions is derived from the field of mental health epidemiology. Gruenberg (1981) observes:

> Epidemiology is the basic science of public health practice and preventive medicine. It is an action science, directed at a set of practical problems. Many useful epidemiologic studies do not lead directly to action. But the goal of epidemiologic inquiries is to find a modifiable risk factor, a risk factor that can be manipulated to social action or individual action so as to lower the frequency of a disease, of a disability, or of a death. (p. 9)

Researchers who have been observing the activities of mental health epidemiologists over the last two decades might be surprised at the description of epidemiology offered by Gruenberg. They are much more likely to think of mental health epidemiologists as being concerned with the definitions and measurement of psychological disorder, the identification of risk factors, and the measurement of the incidence and prevalence of disorders in the community. I've seen little epidemiological research that convinces me that much energy has been directed at actually producing preventive trials to reduce the incidence of disorder. While epidemiology has concerned itself with the precise definition and distribution of disorders, it has seldom been an "action science."

The second research tradition that I see as central to the field of prevention in mental health is that of intervention research. A number of intervention researchers have developed programs at the individual, group, and organizational level that are concerned with the removal of stressful circumstances and other pathogenic conditions or are aimed at strengthening the coping capacity of people so as to make them more resistant to later stresses and their sequelae (Jason, 1980; Cowen, Gesten, and Weissberg, 1980; Felner, Ginter, and Primavera, 1982; Shure and Spivack, 1982; Muñoz and Glish, 1982).

These researchers have their own strengths and blind spots. As a group, they have developed a number of effective change technologies, and they are sensitive to what it takes to actually establish programs in community settings. These are very great strengths and not to be underestimated. On the other hand, as a group, intervention researchers have been much less sensitive to questions of the precise definition of groups at risk and the degree to which interventions are aimed at large or truly vulnerable populations.

I find it interesting that two groups with such complementary sets of skills and knowledge should have had so little interaction in the past. Why this is so is probably a matter for historians of science, but nevertheless this lack of commerce has important implications. Unless we can find ways to link these fields, we are not going to make much progress toward our prevention goal. In fact, a great opportunity is now emerging for linking epidemiological research and training with training and education on program delivery and evaluation. Epidemiological field experiments have the dual possibility of manipulating risk factors to assess their causal status and to build prototypes of prevention programs to be disseminated widely. Here we see something very unusual in science: a genuine convergence of interest.

The possibility of a curriculum and related field experiences oriented to the prevention map I have outlined is an attractive one. Courses and field experiences in community epidemiology, innovation design and operations research, the conduct of field experiments, and the diffusion of innovations could provide both the needed content for the field of prevention as well as broadly educated and trained boundary-spanning prevention researchers, rather than narrowly focused specialists.

Local circumstances and opportunities will certainly guide the actual design of educational experiences for prevention researchers. Still, it is possible to specify some of the exit competencies that one might expect prevention researchers to derive from their education. A provisional list is shown in Table 1, which in effect summarizes some of the suggestions I made earlier. The competencies listed are arranged according to role and imply a fair amount of specialization. This is at least in part inevitable in such a diverse and complex field.

Nevertheless, one of the most critical challenges in the field has to do

TABLE I
Exit competencies for prevention roles

Prevention Role	Exit Competencies
Problem analyst	• Substantive knowledge of problem area • Epidemiological methods, risk assessment, survey methods • Quantitative skills • Qualitative ethnographic skills • Knowledge of ethical principles
Innovation designer	• Benefit/cost analysis skills • Operations research knowledge • Planning and organizational design • Knowledge of intervention technology • Collaborative skills • Knowledge of ethical principles
Field researcher/evaluator	• Experimental design knowledge • Evaluation skills, formative and summative • Knowledge of measurement and psychometric principles • Quantitative/analytic skills • Knowledge of ethical principles
Diffusion expert	• Knowledge of diffusion of innovation principles • Marketing, consumer analysis, forecasting skills • Knowledge of mass communication theory • Knowledge of social influence principles • Knowledge of ethical principles

with how we move from one domain on the map to another. Researchers in different domains speak different languages, have different customs, and carry on precious little commerce outside their own domain. We need people trained for and capable of conceptual boundary spanning; people who are able to cross effectively from one of these areas to another. My map has implications for the way in which we organize prevention education efforts in the future. Certainly, to paraphrase Gruenberg (1981), if we do not wish to have our students keep acquiring new doctorates, we will have to learn to collaborate with those outside our own domain and teach our students to do so as well.

References

Albee, G. W. (1967). The relation of conceptual models to manpower needs. In E. L. Cowen, E. A. Gardener, and M. Zax (Eds.), *Emergent approaches to mental health problems*. New York: Appleton-Century-Crofts.

Albee, G. W., and Joffe, J. M. (Eds.). (1977). *Primary prevention of psychopathology. Volume I: The issues*. Hanover, N.H.: University Press of New England.

Arnt, J. (1968). A test of the two-step flow in diffusion of a new product. *Journalism Quarterly, 45*, 457–465.

Barton, A. K., Andrulis, D. P., Grove, W. P., and Aponte, J. F. (1977). Training programs in the mid '70s. In I. Iscoe, B. L. Bloom, and C. D. Spielberger (Eds.), *Community psychology in transition*. Washington, D.C.: Hemisphere.

Bass, R. D. (1974). *Consultation and education services: Federally funded community mental health centers*. Department of Health, Education, and Welfare Publication. Washington, D.C.: U.S. Government Printing Office.

Bloom, B. L. (1968). The evaluation of primary prevention programs. In L. M. Roberts, N. S. Greenfield and M. H. Miller (Eds.), *Comprehensive mental health: The challenge of evaluation*. Madison: University of Wisconsin Press.

Bloom, B. L. (1979). Prevention of mental disorders: Recent advances in theory and practice. *Community Mental Health Journal, 15*, 179–191.

Bloom, M. (1981). *Primary prevention: The possible science*. Englewood Cliffs, N.J.: Prentice-Hall.

Caplan, N., et al. (1975). *The use of social science knowledge in policy decisions at the national level*. Ann Arbor: Institute for Social Research, University of Michigan.

Cowen, E. L. (1977). Baby-steps toward primary prevention. *American Journal of Community Psychology, 5*, 1–22.

Cowen, E. L. (1982). The special number: A compleat roadmap. *American Journal of Community Psychology* (Special issue on primary prevention).

Cowen, E. L., Gesten, E. L., and Weissberg, R. P. (1980). An integrated network of preventively oriented school-based mental health approaches. In R. H. Price and P. E. Politser (Eds.), *Evaluation and action in the social environment*. New York: Academic Press.

Felner, R. D., Jason, L. A., Moritsugu, J. N., and Farber, S. S. (1983). *Preventive psychology: Theory research and practice*. New York: Pergamon.

Felner, R. D., Ginter, M., and Primavera, J. (1982). Primary prevention during school transitions: Social support and environmental structure. *American Journal of Community Psychology* (Special issue on primary prevention).

Gruenberg, E. M. (1981). Risk factor research methods. In D. A. Regier and G. Allen (Eds.), *Risk factor research in the major mental disorders*. National Institute of Mental Health, DHHS No. (ADM) 81-1068). Washington, D.C.: U.S. Government Printing Office.

Havelock, R. G., and Havelock, M. C. (1973). *Training for change agents: A guide to the design of training programs in education and other fields*. Ann Arbor: Center for Research on the Utilization of Scientific Knowledge, Institute for Social Research, University of Michigan.

Heller, K., Price, R. H., and Sher, K. J. (1980). Research and evaluation in primary prevention: Issues and guidelines. In R. H. Price, R. F. Ketterer, B. C. Bader, and J. Monahan (Eds.), *Prevention in mental health: Research, policy and practice*. Beverly Hills, Calif.: Sage.

Iscoe, I. (1981). Conceptual barriers to training for the primary prevention of psychopathology. In J. M. Joffe and G. W. Albee (Eds.), *Prevention through political action and social change*. Hanover, N.H.: The University Press of New England.

Jason, L. A. (1980). Prevention in the schools: Behavioral approaches. In R. H. Price, R. F. Ketterer, B. C. Bader, and J. Monahan (Eds.), *Prevention in mental health: Research, policy and practice*. Beverly Hills, Calif.: Sage.

Kessler, R., Price, R. H., and Wortman, C. (1985). Social factors in psychopath-

ology: Stress, social support and coping processes. *Annual Review of Psychology, 36*, 531–572.
Klein, D. C., and Goldston, S. E. (Eds.). (1977). *Primary prevention: An idea whose time has come*. Washington, D.C.: National Institute of Mental Health.
Kotler, P. (1975). *Marketing for nonprofit organizations*, 2nd ed. Englewood Cliffs, N.J.: Prentice-Hall.
Kuhn, T. S. (1970). *The structure of scientific revolutions*, 2nd ed. Chicago: University of Chicago Press.
Masterpasqua, F. (1981). Toward a synergism of developmental and community psychology. *American Psychologist, 36*, 782–786.
Miller, G. A. (1969). Psychology as a means of promoting human welfare. *American Psychologist, 24*, 1063–1075.
Muñoz, R. F., and Glish, M. (1982). The San Francisco mood survey project: Preliminary work toward the prevention of depression. *American Journal of Community Psychology, 10*(3).
Munson, F. C., and Pelz, D. C. (1982). *Innovating in organizations: A conceptual framework*. Ann Arbor: Center for Research on Utilization of Scientific Knowledge, Institute for Social Research, University of Michigan.
National Institute of Mental Health, Survey Reports Branch. (1978). *Provisional data on federally funded community mental health centers, 1976–77*. Washington, D.C.: Division of Biometry and Epidemiology, National Institute of Mental Health.
President's Commission on Mental Health. (1978). *Report to the President*, Vols. 1–4. Washington, D.C.: U.S. Government Printing Office.
Price, R. H. (1980). Risky situations. In D. Magnusson (Ed.), *Toward a psychology of situations: An interactional perspective*. Hillsdale, N.J.: Lawrence Erlbaum Associates.
Price, R. H., Ketterer, R. F., Bader, B. C., and Monahan, J. (Eds.). (1980). *Prevention in mental health: Research, policy, and practice*. Beverly Hills, Calif.: Sage.
Rogers, E., and Shoemaker, F. F. (1971). *The communication of innovations*. New York: Free Press.
Rothman, J., Erlich, J. L., and Teresa, J. G. (1976). *Promoting innovation and change in organizations and communities: A planning manual*. New York: Wiley.
Rothman, J., Teresa, J. G., Kay, T. L., and Morningstar, G. C. (1983). *Marketing human service innovations*. Beverly Hills, Calif.: Sage.
Schneider, S. F. (1982) *Ambiguity, power, and credibility: A public servant's dialogue with psychology*. Paper presented as the Harold M. Hildreth Memorial Award for Distinguished Public Service address at the meeting of the American Psychological Association, Washington, D.C., August 24, 1982.
Shure, M. B. (1979). Training children to solve interpersonal problems: A preventive mental health program. In R. E. Muñoz, L. R. Snowden, and J. G. Kelly (Eds.), *Social and psychological research in community settings*. San Francisco: Jossey-Bass.
Shure, M. B., and Spivack, G. (1982). Interpersonal problem-solving in young children: A cognitive approach to prevention. *American Journal of Community Psychology, 10*(3), 341–356.
Thomas, E. J. (1984). *Designing interventions for the helping professions*. Beverly Hills, Calif.: Sage.
U.S. Department of Health, Education, and Welfare. (1979). *Healthy people: The*

Surgeon General's report on health promotion and disease prevention. Washington, D.C.: U.S. Government Printing Office.

Vayda, A., and Perlmutter, F. (1977). Primary prevention in community mental health centers: A survey of current activities. *Community Mental Health Journal, 4*, 343–351.

Zaltman, G., Duncan, R., and Holbek, J. (1973). *Innovations and organizations*. New York: Wiley-Interscience.

Zolik, E. S. (1983). Training for preventive psychology in community and academic settings. In R. D. Felner, L. A. Jason, J. N. Moritsugu, and S. S. Farber (Eds.), *Preventive psychology: Theory, research and practice*. New York: Pergamon.

PART IV

The Politics of Prevention

Advocates and Adversaries of Prevention

George W. Albee

My children sometimes have accused me of writing the same paper over and over, and my students often complain that I say the same things in half a dozen different ways. One can find an aphorism to apply to nearly every situation. I have often envied Klein's and Goldston's (1977) title: *Primary Prevention: An Idea Whose Time Has Come*. I shudder at the enemies of prevention who add "and gone" to this catchy title, but then I also think of applying to them Jonathan Swift's appropriate aphorism: "*There's none so blind as they that won't see.*"

This chapter reviews some of the highly predictable arguments in opposition to efforts at primary prevention and suggests why many of these arguments are not valid. But weak arguments, coming from powerful people, have a way of taking on weight and credibility far beyond their validity. As a child, youth, and young man, I lived with the illusions that people occupying the seats of power usually knew whereof they spoke. It was only slowly and gradually that I have come to realize that economic and political ideology often influences the script, and that there is no "divine providence" guaranteeing the validity of the statements of the powerful.

Many of us were permanently disillusioned when we read transcripts of the "Nixon tapes." Perhaps even more destructive of our idealism is the recent biography of *The Kennedys* (Collier and Horowitz, 1984), which reveals how power-driven, petty, and immoral (like his father) was JFK. It is sobering to have to abandon the illusion that U.S. presidents were men of principle and wisdom or that they had wise and principled counselors. Who among us can take seriously any recent American president? Are the people who hold power within the mental health field any better? For the most part, I fear not.

Sir Cyril Burt's biographer, Hearnshaw (1982) frequently asked, in puzzlement and wonderment, how Burt could distort reality by repeatedly changing his version of events when the objective record proved him to be lying. How could he claim that he had invented factor analysis, and other techniques in the field of mental measurement, when the objective record was available for anyone who cared to go back and read it? Did Burt actually believe what he was saying, or did he need to believe it so desperately that he tried to fool even himself with his distortions?

I wonder, for example, how responsible textbook writers could have stated all these years, with bland assurance, that schizophrenia is largely genetically determined, and support their argument with quotations from Kallmann whose work has been shown (by Pastore, 1949, for example), to be distorted and incredible; and how can so many experts refer blandly to the Kety et al. (1976) Danish studies as conclusive proof of the genetic basis of schizophrenia when there are telling critiques undermining Kety's position that have been published by Lidz and Blatt (1983) and by Sarbin and Mancuso (1980).

Understand, I do not argue that other evidence may not provide convincing evidence of a genetic factor in a redefined and more reliable condition now covered today by the global term schizophrenia. It is simply that the "clear" evidence cited in texts is inconclusive. Nearly every textbook in psychiatry and in abnormal psychology perpetuates the illusion that we already know the truth in this matter.

Am I exaggerating? Those two intrepid and articulate antipreventionists, Lamb and Zusman (1981), say:

> Recent research has increasingly suggested the operation of genetic and biochemical factors in the causation of mental illness. The adoption studies of Kety and associates indicate that schizophrenia is in large part genetically determined. The same is true for major affective disorders. (p. 845)

These leading antipreventionists argue that this "organic position" has gained further support from other recent adoption studies that indicate essential genetic factors in alcoholism, antisocial personalities, and depression (p. 845).

Lamb and Zusman (1981) go through all the conventional arguments against primary prevention, all over again. While I hesitate to increase their *Citation Index* count, their papers are condensations of the antipreventionist argument:

1. They argue that we should not be spending money on applied prevention programs when there is so much treatment that needs to be done. (They do not mention the vast unmet needs for treatment, needs that will never be met, or the inappropriate focus of most mental health professionals on the milder emotional problems of the middle class rather than on the serious problems of the lower classes, the elderly, the unserved minorities, etc.)

2. They argue that "there is no evidence that the incidence of mental illness has decreased as a result of earlier prevention efforts." (They neither mention the many successful prevention programs nor take notice of the difficulty of demonstrating effectiveness in the absence of research funds.)

3. They stress the importance of distinguishing between *real* mental illness and feelings of unhappiness, distress, and social incompetence. They do not mention the contradictory fact that the official Diagnostic and Statistical Manual III (DSM III) identifies all of these latter conditions as genuine psychiatric illnesses.

4. They argue that the correlation between rates of mental illness and poverty and other damaging social conditions does not establish a *cause and effect relationship*, and they even question whether any such causal relationship exists.

5. They argue against getting involved in attempts at the resolution of social problems without a societal mandate that they say has not been given mental health professionals—this in spite of the long history of such involvement.

6. They dredge up the tired and invalid old argument that it is necessary to know the *cause* before primary prevention efforts can be more than shots in the dark. This is demonstrably invalid, and anyone who knows the history of public health recognizes this fallacy.

7. They stress genetic and biochemical factors as primary causation of a wide range of mental disorders and imply that a fatal flaw in people makes their conditions beyond the realm of effective prevention efforts. We know many conditions that can be prevented in spite of genetic factors that contribute.

8. They argue that the development of competence has nothing much to do with preventing true mental disorder. Seven volumes from the Vermont conferences demonstrate otherwise.

9. They assert that even where research (such as they quote by Leighton and associates) shows a clear relationship between social disintegration and symptoms of mental illness this does not prove a *causal* relationship, and they drag out the old argument that the higher rate of disturbance among poverty-stricken neighborhood dwellers may be due to downward drift.

10. Finally, they wind up with the argument that in a world of shrinking resources, where there is not enough money to support urgent direct-service programs, it is dangerous and foolish to fund expensive prevention efforts.

In one sense we should be grateful to Lamb and Zusman because they are able to pack into such a short space all of the standard and predictable arguments, common to most of the antipreventionists. Bloom's (1981) companion piece in the same journal answers and even anticipates most of their arguments in a masterful way. I will not repeat his arguments here, but I commend them to your reading.

While opposition to prevention does not come exclusively from people in the field of psychiatry, I think it is fair to say that many leaders in American psychiatry have spoken out strongly against prevention efforts and that support for prevention programs has been lukewarm at best with the leadership at the National Institute of Mental Health.

John A. Talbott last year was President of the American Psychiatric Association. When science columnist, Darrell Sifford (1983) of the *Philadelphia Inquirer,* asked him if it were possible to lay out a program for the prevention of mental illness, Talbott responded that "There is no preventive medicine for mental illness." The problem, Talbott said, is that prevention cannot be a reality until researchers uncover "the root causes of mental illness—and nobody so far has been able to do that." The Catch 22 nature of this argument (to say nothing of its lack of validity) should be obvious, but often is passed over unnoticed: How can evidence of cause—or anything else—be accumulated without research funds? And, further, what other area of psychiatric activity has been delayed because of a lack of convincing data?

There is an *Alice in Wonderland* quality to many of the objections to primary prevention efforts made by contemporary clinicians. A favorite argument holds that little evidence exists for the effectiveness of primary prevention efforts.

Melvin Sabshin, Medical Director of the American Psychiatric Association, argued recently that the new emphasis on primary prevention is premature and "not yet truly supported by sufficient or adequate empirical evidence." And: "What would be ideal is if we had data about prevention that were top-notch and convincing for large preventive programs. That'd be marvelous. I'd put the priority there right away, if the data were convincing. Now, it's not convincing." Sabshin goes on to say that:

> Even with all the discussions in the President's Report and elsewhere, with the theoretical work about prevention, we know very little about prevention. So, it'll be more like 20 or 30 years before it makes sense to put a lot of money into prevention, whereas now, we should put money in to clarify what really can be done, and defining high risk groups. Talking about preventive action for the population as a whole, or for large populations, is premature. (See Klein, 1980, pp. 1–2, 4.)

It is instructive to see how effectively the mental health bureaucracy could divert and delay a major presidential commission's efforts at refocusing national priorities and goals in the area of prevention. In 1978, following a year-long intensive study of the nation's needs and resources in the mental health field, the President's (Carter) Commission on Mental Health (1978) identified the mental health needs of the following groups as unserved or underserved: children, adolescents, the elderly, minorities, the urban poor, the rural poor, migrant farm workers, the mentally retarded, and abusers of drugs and alcohol. Also described in the commission's report as "inappropriately served" were women, people whose first language was not English, and the physically handicapped. In short, a majority of the population.

The report pointed out, clearly, that the model of one-to-one treatment is a hopeless approach to bringing any significant amount of help to all those in need of help—that there would never be enough professionals to meet the need. The obvious solution recommended was an intensified effort in *primary prevention*. Despite the opposition of a number of defenders of the status quo (see Albee, 1979; Hebert, 1979) from the ranks of psychiatry, the President's Commission made as one of its major recommendations the establishment of a Center on Prevention within the National Institute of Mental Health.

One might think that the strong recommendation of a president's commission, followed by the enactment of a law containing provisions for the establishment of such a center—and focusing national goals and priorities in mental health on prevention—would have an immediate energizing effect on NIMH. But resistance from the bureaucratic structure supporting the mental health establishment can give the appearance of cooperation without any real cooperation. When the bureaucracy wants to resist a president, or even the Congress, it has many resources. For example, there is the device of the appointment of a task force to study and develop planning and coordinating efforts. This slows the process of compliance considerably. And when the task force wants to erect its own roadblocks, it develops a language that sounds cooperative but involves stalling and passive resistance:

> A PCMH "strategy for prevention" provides an important start, *but* many conceptual issues still need to be considered. Developing a focused and coordinated prevention effort requires that first the conceptual issues must be addressed, then a careful planning and evaluation process must be initiated *before* a comprehensive program can be undertaken. (See Albee, 1979.)

After President Carter had left office, and in nominal response to the congressional mandate, a modest prevention effort was mounted at

NIMH but with definitions and administrative rules and regulations, such that no really effective prevention program is likely to be funded. And the political in-fighting has been intense, with the result that enormous energy has been dissipated with little result.

The Group for the Advancement of Psychiatry (GAP) was formed shortly after World War II by a group of "young turks" who undertook the task of shaking up the traditional conservatism of organized psychiatry and injecting social concern and responsibility into the field. They are now "old turks" and have grown conservative. Recently GAP (1983) published *Community Psychiatry: A Reappraisal,* which reflects a dramatic switch to conservatism by this once-liberal group of psychiatrists. One of the most depressing aspects of this "reappraisal" is the degree to which it spins, distorts, and twists facts, ignores data, distorts or invents history, and ignores inconsistencies in its own arguments in reaching its conclusions. These, briefly, hold that the field of psychiatry was unduly influenced in the 1960s by political activists within its ranks and was naive in proposing social and community change as appropriate efforts at mental health maintenance and in supporting primary prevention. The group has now come to its senses and is redirecting its attention to individual treatment and rehabilitation. In considering this GAP Report, I believe that it is important to set forth some factual statements as benchmarks with which to compare some of the incredible statements made.

First, most U.S.-trained psychiatrists work with middle-class patients in private offices and in general hospitals; often, but not necessarily, those general hospitals have psychiatric wards. (For documentation of this statement, see Albee, 1959, 1979; Marmor, 1975).

Second, American medicine in general, and American psychiatry in particular, strongly *opposed* (in the mid 1960s) the use of federal funds to staff the community mental health centers (CMHCs). When the bill that proposed the construction and staffing of centers was being considered by the Congress, following President Kennedy's 1963 message, every member of Congress received a telephone call from his or her personal physician urging the defeat of the proposal to allocate money to staff the centers. Indeed, this effort was initially successful. Funds for the construction of CMHC centers were appropriated with conditions that forced the construction of centers by general hospitals in affluent communities rather than in the deteriorated centers of cities, as had been originally envisioned by the Joint Commission on Mental Illness and Health (1960). It was not until Lyndon Johnson became president and exercised his large influence with the Congress that modest federal staffing funds became available. The NIMH regulation that insisted that each community mental health center be directed by a psychiatrist was changed only after it was discovered that relatively few psychiatrists were available—and an even smaller number was willing to work full-time for the salaries paid by CMHCs. (For a detailed discussion of this whole political scenario, see Williams, 1965.) Williams was the science writer in residence for the Joint Commission on Mental Illness and Health and was largely responsible for writing the staff summaries and the final report *Action for Mental Health* (1960).

Third, the major change in the pattern of care of mental patients in the United States, recommended in the final report of the Joint Commission on Mental Illness and Health, was that *no new state hospitals be built,* that existing state hospitals be reduced in size, and that community alternatives to hospitalization be developed. It is crystal clear in the final report of the joint commission itself that the cost of expanding the existing state hospital systems, terribly overcrowded and understaffed, was more than most states could possibly accomplish with their limited tax resources. It was also clear that the state hospitals long had served as a dumping ground for the mentally ill poor, that they were largely staffed by incompetent and often brutal attendants, and that most of the medical staff were poorly trained foreign physicians from Third World countries, unqualified to be licensed and unable to communicate effectively with the persons in their charge. Because U.S.-trained psychiatrists were unwilling to take positions in these overcrowded pestholes, the only solution was to reduce the hospital census by getting people out of the back wards and into the community by whatever means. (A detailed examination of the economic factors leading to the mass decarceration movement of the 1950s, 1960s, and 1970s is presented in detail by Scull, 1977).

Fourth, the community mental health centers from their inception down to the present have devoted the lion's share of their time to one-to-one treatment, usually in the form of individual psychotherapy, although increasingly they have concentrated on less frequent visits devoted to providing and checking medications. (For a detailed examination of the early community mental health centers, identified as "among the best," see Glasscote et al., 1964; Kiesler, 1980, 1982).

Fifth, because of the chronic shortage of operating funds in community mental health centers, the one-to-one treatment orientation, and the frequent unavailability of professional staff trained in consultation and education (C&E: one of the required activities under federal regulations), the amount of community consultation and mental health education has always been a very minor part of the centers' activities. In recent years, with even more drastic reductions in funding, many centers have eliminated their consultation and education activities or have demanded that C&E staff spend a majority of their time in one-to-one patient contact in order to generate income for the center to help deal with chronic budgetary problems.

And finally, the expenditure of funds for community mental health centers has always been a small fraction of money spent for state hospitals and, more recently, for nursing home care for chronic mental patients. At the present time, something like 4 percent of all federal dollars spent for intervention with persons with mental conditions goes to the community mental health centers. Seventy percent of all monies spent are soaked up by inpatient hospital costs and nursing home fees for the elderly mentally disabled (see Kiesler, 1980, 1982).

The recent GAP (1983) report is highly critical of community psychiatry, community mental health, and efforts at primary prevention, while maintaining a pretense of objectivity. In the report, Goffman is alleged to have seen mental institutions as "sinister" (p. 42); it was Goffman's view, according to the report, that state hospitals tended to "foster rather than cure 'psychopathological behavior'" (p. 42). And it was "a core of politically-minded psychiatrists" who believed it would be possible to attack successfully the "causes of mental illness in the social environment." The GAP report disagrees with President Kennedy's recommendations that the general strengthening of our fundamental community, social welfare, and educational programs can do much to eliminate or correct the harsh environmental conditions that are also associated with mental retardation and mental illness. The report criticizes psychiatrists like Leonard Duhl, who are said to have jumped on the CMHC bandwagon. Psychiatrists like Robert Felix and Gerald Caplan joined in recommending political activism and social change and are responsible for leading the field astray, according to GAP.

All of the arguments and enthusiasms for social change, they conclude, were premature because "It has not been demonstrated that community organization can improve mental health within the community" (p. 45). GAP finds little validity for prevention efforts, which have "led to a disregard for disease models which were seen as irrelevant to mental illness" (p. 51).

Eisenberg was once a staunch advocate for prevention programs based on social change (see Eisenberg, 1962). But recently he has moved back, taking a more conservative, cautious position affirming the first importance of individual treatment of real mental illness. In an editorial in the *New England Journal of Medicine* he says, "Even if we could deliver on the uncertain promises of prevention, we have not the right to abandon those who are already ill and in need of care that they cannot obtain" (1977, p. 1231). He writes about the possible prevention of genuine mental diseases and points out that many of these are multifactorial in origin: that they depend in part on life-style and that preventive efforts require educational, legal, and economic changes. He concludes his editorial by saying, "Prevention? Of course! As we know what can be delivered and how to deliver it. But not at the expense of treating the sick, whom we are sworn to 'keep from harm and injustice' by the Hippocratic Oath that we have taken" (p. 1232). His present views are a pale shadow of the same Leon Eisenberg who, as President of the American Orthopsychiatric Association in 1962 (in an address entitled, "If Not Now, When?") spoke these ringing words:

> As citizens we [professionals] bear a moral responsibility, because of our specialized knowledge, for political action to prevent socially induced psychiatric illness. This implies fighting for decent subsistence levels in public housing, health care, education, and the right to work for all. (p. 790)

Back then he stressed the "social roots" of orthopsychiatry, criticized the preoccupation with individual psychotherapy which he felt held "no promise" for public health. He added:

> When systems in the social organism go awry, it is as absurd to attempt their correction by medicating the individuals whose aberrations are second- and third-order consequences of the basic lesion as it would be to treat the white count in meningitis rather than to eradicate the offending meningococci. (p. 789)

Oh Leon! Leon of 1962! Where are *you now* that we need *you?* If not now, when, Leon?

Much of the confusion that characterized certain common arguments of the antipreventionists is a result of double-think about the *illness model* of mental disorder. It may be useful to consider this logical problem briefly. On the one hand the *number* of conditions officially classified as mental illnesses by *The Diagnostic and Statistical Manual III* (DSM III) of the American Psychiatric Association keeps expanding from edition to edition. There is good reason for this expansion. So-called health insurance programs cover the treatment of real illness. The insurers do not want to pay also for interventions aimed at distress over life's critical problems in living. Nor do insurers want to pay for nonmedical interventionists, such as nutrition counselors, acupuncturists, herbal experts, meditation teachers, yoga gurus, divorce counselors, or encounter group leaders. The chronic and growing shortage of psychiatrists is an advantage for the insurance companies, and it is to the advantage of both groups to keep the definitions and diagnoses *medical,* the therapists medical, and the treatments medical. Common sense assures us that people in distress over broken marriages, in despair over the death of loved ones, or seeking escape from boredom or loneliness at work or in the home are not really sick with a genuine medical illness. But it suits the insurance companies to define these conditions as illnesses. So to get psychotherapy in a private office, or at a community mental health center, each client must have an official diagnosis from DSM III to enable the therapist to collect from the insuring group. The more conditions that are listed as mental illnesses the better for therapist, client, and insurer.

So, are these conditions mental illnesses or not? At this point in the discussion we usually hear about the inseparability of the mind and body, about how psychological conflict disrupts the physical substratum; we even hear about the latest ultimate approach—*medical psychotherapy,* counseling with a drug-assist, for which there ought to be a state law! The danger, of course, is that this argument inevitably leads to identifying every human problem as illness, even including school learning problems, poverty, crime, and delinquency. When we add up all the people suffering from all these problems, we find that a majority of the population has a diagnosable psychiatric illness! Obviously, this is a difficult position to defend, especially with the small number of troops in the illness-model command. Also, and more relevant to our present concern, there is the embarrassing problem that many of these "illnesses" *can* be prevented. This brings up the other position often heard: Prevention efforts have not been shown to be effective in reducing the rate of "real" mental illnesses like schizophrenia and bipolar depression. Problems in living, those hard-nosed realists say, may respond to efforts involving competence training, coping-skills acquisition, and support groups, but let us not mistake these adjustment problems for *real* mental illnesses. The contradiction is obvious. A large majority of the people in treatment do *not* have one of the *real* mental illnesses; but most of the people in treatment *are* given a DSM III psychiatric diagnosis so that their therapy can be paid for through insurance. Either DSM III is a hoax—a giant conspiracy either to protect or defraud the health insurance industry—or spokespersons should stop making statements about *real* mental illness because DSM III defines officially the existence of these disorders as real illness! And many of them can be prevented.

Now let me explore a highly sensitive and delicate area that may be involved in opposition to preventive efforts. For nearly a century, clinical experience in psychotherapy has pointed to the important role played by the early social familial environment in the complex developmental model of psychopathology. Overstated, this model suggests that *bad parenting leads to disturbed social development.* Certainly this model is at the heart of clinical and psychoanalytic thinking, and it is at the center of the emerging set of theoretical developments known as *ego psychology.* The ego psychologists talk about the importance of the early symbiotic relationship between infant and caregiver, about the importance of individuation and separation, and about the critical importance of successfully negotiating each stage of development throughout infancy and childhood. Most of us, as clinicians, stress the importance of not oversimplifying this issue, of stressing the interaction model that makes causation a complex mosaic. But no matter how much we emphasize the complexity, we meet strong resistance from groups interested in protecting parents from the unjust accusation that they are somehow to blame. The American Schizophrenia Foundation (1965) says in a widely distributed booklet that:

> Some psychoanalytic theorists have, unfortunately, encouraged the schizophrenic to blame his ailment on his mother, his father, his spouse, the society he lives in, or all of these together. . . . [*N*]*o one is to blame* [because] . . . laboratory evidence has been steadily growing that a defect in his body chemistry causes the schizophrenic to brew—perhaps in his liver, perhaps in his adrenal glands—some substance that distorts the working of his brain. (pp. 8–9; italics in original.)

The American Schizophrenia Foundation (1965) hastened to announce (prematurely, it turns out), that:

> Scientists have succeeded in extracting from the blood and urine of schizophrenics various poisonous substances which, when injected into the blood of normal persons, create many of the classic symptoms of schizophrenia. The origin of these toxins is still something of a mystery, and much inspired research remains to be done to track down the source of the defect or defects. (pp. 2–3)

It should not surprise us to learn that a recent major contributor to the establishment of a new foundation to study the physical origins of mental illness has come from John Hinckley, Sr., the father of the young man who shot the president and was later found to be not guilty by reason of insanity. Hinckley, Sr., expressed surprise and distress that so little is known about the chemical origins of mental illness. Clearly and understandably, some of the most spirited and strong support of the biochemical explanation has come from the families of disturbed people.

Resistance to models other than the illness model often characterize people with a disturbed family member. John Hinckley, Sr., was quoted recently in the *APA Monitor* (December, 1983) as saying:

> We hope to do for mental illness what the American Cancer Society has done for that disease. I was astounded to find out that mental illness was so prevalent and yet the public was so unaware of it. (See Tarkington, 1983.)

Hinkley, Sr., has provided seed money for a new organization, The American Mental Health Fund, and hopes that this group will be able to raise funds to support research into the "cause and treatment of serious mental illness." Now this is a highly laudable goal. Anyone with a shred of human empathy will feel some of the anguish that the Hinckleys must have felt because of the erratic and violent behavior of their son. At the same time, it is understandable that people like the Hinckleys will much prefer an organic explanation for deviant thinking and deviant behavior to a social learning environmental model.

Sarbin is quoted in the same issue of the *APA Monitor* (p. 2) as saying that establishing a research institute to try to prevent the kind of behavior that young Hinckley exhibited is laudable, "but to go about it in a way that equates mental conditions to cancer will have two unfortunate effects." First, the public will be encouraged to think that unethical conduct can be blamed on a disease; and second, Sarbin adds, financial resources will be wasted in search of a biochemical or neurological defect, rather than addressing family circumstances and social conditions that are linked with behavior considered antisocial.

Zek (see same *APA Monitor* issue, p. 2), Director of Neuropsychology at the Adult Psychiatry Branch of NIMH, reacted strongly against such sentiments. Zec argues that schizophrenics often perform like brain-damaged clients, that the effects of biological treatments suggest that there is a biological basis to the disease, and that CAT scans show some schizophrenics to have enlarged ventricles, suggesting brain atrophy. In addition, Zec claims that there is some evidence of decreased cerebral blood flow to the frontal lobes in some chronic schizophrenics, as well as brain abnormalities in certain autopsies of schizophrenics. These findings support an organic model, he argues. I must simply take note of the fact that reported findings of organic factors in schizophrenia have a way of appearing over and over—and disappearing when replication fails to confirm the original results.

Opponents of prevention frequently challenge us to produce evidence that prevention has been successful. Show us, they sneer, one example where the rate of psychopathology has been reduced by the efforts of preventionists, and we will stop trying to block the funding of prevention programs. On the off-chance that they are sincere, I would like them to read the special issue of the *American Journal of Community Psychology*, edited by Cowen (1982), which contains descriptions of carefully evaluated prevention programs. Other programs also have produced changes as a result of social action.

The total number of persons considered to be mentally ill, with a historically acceptable psychiatric diagnosis, was reduced by approximately 13–14 million following the social challenge in the 1960s to the validity of the diagnosis of homosexuality and the resulting decision to remove homosexuality from the official American Psychiatric Association nomenclature. Some might try to argue that this is not *really* prevention because nothing has changed (no *rate* of the actual behavior has been reduced), but the fact is that the rate of a mental disorder affecting something like 6 percent of the population was reduced suddenly to zero!

Similarly, the decision to change the definition of mental retardation as including those whose IQs are below 70, rather than the earlier cutoff of 80 IQ, immediately reduced by several million persons the size of the pool of the retarded.

Let me give a more real research-based illustration. Mariner (1980) has recently joined the ranks of those psychiatrists critical of efforts at primary prevention. Interestingly, half of the references he cites are to publications appearing before 1965, and two-thirds predate 1970. He seems unaware of, or has neglected to consider work in the field of prevention since 1975. Mariner says:

> It might be expected that the sort of "deprivation" involved in the inculcation of a poor self-image would be likely to play a significant role in the development of still less severe disturbances. At this level, unfortunately, there are no controlled studies to supply supportive evidence—only rhetoric . . . and a mass of anecdotal material from the case files of psychotherapists, who are daily confronted with patients whose deficient sense of self-worth and lack of confidence often appears traceable to the denigrating "messages" transmitted by their parents (and, less often, their teachers). . . . If just one major research effort in the field of prevention could be mounted, a long-term prospective study of children indirectly influenced by such programs should have high priority. (p. 103)

Fortunately, Mariner's yearning has been fulfilled! A carefully controlled and well-designed scientific study has been reported, demonstrating the relationship between negative attitudes in the mother and subsequent emotional disturbance in the children. And then a further study by the same investigator qualifies as an experimental demonstration of the effectiveness of an intervention program with measured consequences in reducing subsequent emotional disturbances.

I refer to the work of Broussard, who is professor of public health psychiatry, among numerous other appointments, at the University of Pittsburgh. Mariner failed to read Broussard's papers and chapters (Broussard, 1976, 1976b, 1977, 1979; Broussard and Cornes, 1981; Broussard and Hartner, 1970; Broussard and Hartner, 1971). Back in 1963 she developed the Neonatal Perception Inventories (NPI), which she administered to mothers of first-born children who were healthy, full-term infants without any observable defects—a group that would not be considered at special risk for later psychosocial problems. The inventories were given to 318 mothers within a 2½-month period. The mothers interviewed came from all socioeconomic and racial groups in Pittsburgh. The NPI asked the mother to rate her own infant in comparison with her concept of the "average baby." If she considered her baby to be better than average, her perception was rated positive, and the infant was considered to be at low risk for later emotional problems. If she did not rate her baby as better than average, the rating was seen as negative, and her infant was judged to be at high risk. The same inventory was administered to the mother when the infant was one month old. Four-and-one-half years later, 120 of the original group were evaluated by one of two child psychiatrists with no knowledge of the original ratings; then 10½ years later 104 of these children were evaluated by one of three psychiatrists with no knowledge of the earlier ratings. At each age the children who had been perceived negatively (and therefore judged to be at high risk at one month of age) were found to have emotional disorders much more frequently than those earlier judged to be at low risk. Then at age 15, 99 of the children were seen by one of four psychiatrists without knowledge of the earlier risk ratings. Broussard (1982) concludes: "The odds ratio indicated that one-month-old infants who were considered to be high risk were 5½ times more likely to have psychosocial disorders at age 15 than those one-month-old infants who had been considered low risk" (1982, p. 181). She reports that *not one* of the high-risk infants appeared free of psychosocial disorder in at least one of the follow-up evaluations. She says: "The *absence* of a positive maternal perception of the neonate is associated with a very high rate of subsequent psychosocial disorder" (p. 182).

Broussard's preventive intervention study needs to be read in detail (see Broussard, 1977; Broussard, 1982) but a brief summary is in order. She offered a new group of mothers with negative images of their babies an opportunity to join an experimental intervention program for biweekly meetings and home visits. Some mothers accepted and some refused. Two-and-one-half-years later she did a careful and objective evaluation of 25 low-risk and 43 high-risk (13 intervention, 12 intervention-refused, and 18 comparison) children. All of her univariate statistical tests were significant. The low-risk and the high-risk intervention groups had scores reflecting more optimal functioning, whereas the high-risk comparison group and the high-risk intervention-refused groups had scores showing considerably higher psychosocial distress. In short, the intervention was successful in reducing risk in children for the high-risk group of mothers who chose to participate. This brief account fails to do justice to the meticulous care with which Broussard designed her studies and analyzed her data, which includes case examples (see

Broussard, 1982). The important point is that critics of primary prevention like Mariner (if they read the literature) will never again be able to say, "Measures of behavioral changes are conspicuous by their rarity; and there are, predictably, no reports whatever of long-term effects on the target population of children influenced by these parents or teachers." (Mariner, 1980, p. 100.)

Cassel (1973), a physician and major contributor to public health knowledge, demonstrated repeatedly that the risk of disease and of emotional distress is significantly greater in individuals with low levels of meaningful social contacts and an absence of social support systems. He argued that:

> Preventive action in the future should focus more directly on attempts at modifying these psychosocial factors, on improving and strengthening social supports, and reducing the circumstances which produce ambiguities between actions and their consequences. (p. 110)

Bloom (1981) reviews other major research efforts that support Cassel's position. People with good social supports have lower mortality from heart disease, and women with good support systems have fewer difficulties in pregnancy and childbirth. Sameroff and Chandler (1975) review the evidence that a variety of developmental defects occur largely in high risk social environments. In spite of all this evidence of the importance of social factors, in 1981 ADAMHA ordered its research and training programs to focus exclusively on biomedical factors, a process that Bloom (1981) calls an effort "to biologize the mental health field" (p. 841). Bloom adds:

> The hope that the key to controlling the major, currently unpreventable, disorders lies exclusively in our biology seems not only illusory but defies an overwhelming amount of evidence. Culture invades physiology, and symptoms are an exquisite final common pathway of a complex, but ultimately comprehensible, interaction of biological, psychological, and sociocultural forces. (p. 841)

One would expect psychotherapists, particularly those with a dynamic orientation, to be more sympathetic to explanatory models of mental disorder that emphasize early damaging personal interaction; in short, to support a model of social origins of stress and distress. But this is not universally the case. Henderson (1975), a psychoanalyst, is vehement in his criticisms of preventive psychiatry, community psychiatry, and efforts at social change aimed at prevention. He says:

> Since human suffering is prevalent if not universal, the role of the mental health professional is not so much to venture into the community with ill reasoned . . . and sometimes naive claims of preventing that which is innate to human exis-

tence, but rather to get on with the job of helping his fellow man. That help, of course, is therapy, not prevention. Early therapy by all means, thorough therapy if at all possible, but above all, therapy. To do otherwise is a neurotic and ineffectual compromise. (p. 243)

Henderson does accept evidence that childhood trauma, bad parenting, and even social disorganization may all play their role in causing, or at least exacerbating, mental conditions. But he sees no way that community efforts can change these things. This position is curious because anyone who accepts the value of individual therapy accepts an environmental effort to reduce suffering through a change involving social learning. Why is an effective approach to the individual not possibly an effective approach to groups? Many psychotherapists attempt to change the destructive behavior or the confused thinking or the inappropriate emotionality of their clients through their personal influence in the psychotherapeutic exchange which, when one thinks about it, is a strictly environmental approach. These same people often criticize prevention efforts, asking how we can really know that poverty or bad social environments produce later pathology; but then they attempt to remediate emotionally disturbed behavior in adults by providing a more nurturant, more understanding, and more supportive environment.

At the risk of possibly offending some good-hearted people who are truly committed to the prevention effort, I am impelled to focus attention for the moment on those who constantly talk about the urgent need for more systematic and controlled preventive interventions, with control groups and rigorous statistical tests of effectiveness, and who deny that we know very much about prevention. How can anyone disagree with the need for careful research? But I disagree with the implicit or explicit implication that underlies this assertion that we know very little about prevention because there have not been enough carefully controlled and rigorous studies. I have the distinct impression that this issue reflects more about personality styles than anything else, but I worry about the issue because it often gives aid and comfort to our adversaries. There are vast areas of meaningful prevention efforts where it is difficult to control all but one or a few variables and where it is impossible to follow experimental and control groups over years to measure changes in rate. Do we need more research to prove the devastating damage that racism and sexism and ageism do to people?

Let me try to illustrate what I am driving at. Most attempts at enumerating groups who are at high risk for mental and emotional distress identify premature pregnancy, especially in young teenaged girls and their infants and young children. Assessment of the many problems associated with these girls may lead to the identification of their poor sex information, their loneliness, their need to have someone to love, their poor prenatal care and poor nutrition during pregnancy, their lack of knowledge of child care and child rearing, and so on. Each one of many identifiable associated causes may be seized on as the focus for a preventive intervention effort. Courses in sex education may seem promising as a way of reducing the risk of pregnancy. Group interventions with teenaged boys to help counteract the macho cultural image could also be assessed using experimental and control groups. High school courses in value clarification, preparation for marriage, and the like seem indicated. All such intervention, while suited to fairly rigorous experimental designs, seems frighteningly like "blaming the victim." As Joffe (1981) has pointed out, we would do much better to seek the *cause of the causes*.

What is the common cause? Is it low socioeconomic status? Is it simply poverty? Indeed, is it not likely that the high rates of nearly every form of psychopathology among the poorest of the poor reflect the stresses, the feelings of powerlessness, the low self-esteem that are part of occupying an inescapable island of poverty in a sea of affluence? These statements do not lend themselves to easy manipulation as independent variables. But must we be hung up on our obsession with tidy experimental design? We can strengthen our hypothesis about the pathological role of social and economic powerlessness by looking at major sociological variables that have changed over time with a resulting change in the incidence of mental and emotional disturbance, and we can also look at cross-cultural similarities and differences for further elucidation of the problem.

My favorite example of data that are clear, and that we cannot replicate (and my friends and students are weary of hearing this), is the clear observation that each immigrant group into the inner cities of the United States has had high rates of emotional disorder, alcoholism, and mental retardation during the time that the group occupied the lowest rung on the socioeconomic ladder, but then this rate decreased as each of these groups moved into economic security and eventually into middle-class status. I have written frequently about the high rate of every kind of psychopathology among the Irish in 1850–1860; and then the Scandanavians; and then the Eastern Europeans, including the Poles, the Slovaks, and the Eastern European Jews—all followed by the southern Italians and, most recently, by southern blacks, Puerto Ricans, and Chicanos. Let me be sure that my point is clear. It seems to me that we do not need experimental data to confirm the observation that any group occupying the lowest social class position has high rates of the conditions we seek to prevent and that, when they move out of abject poverty and into relative economic security, their rates of disturbance drop. Clearly these impoverished groups might have been shown to exhibit ignorance about the complex details of human reproduction and lack of knowledge of proper nutrition and to have poor school achievement and high rates of family pathology. But the changing social conditions that led to their escape from poverty resulted in a reduced rate of distress. Is it poverty alone that was and is responsible? Here cross-cultural comparisons can help us answer the question. In those societies where a large majority of the population is poor, we do not find poverty alone to be the cause of emotional distress. In Haiti, for example, where nearly everyone is grindingly poor, the rate of mental disorder is reportedly quite low. In crowded countries like India and China, where the poor are the majority, the rate of mental disturbance is not obviously higher. I recognize the extreme difficulty of doing reliable epidemiological studies under such conditions. But I still would argue that there is good reason to believe that in our society, where the prevailing ethos emphasizes conspicuous consumption and one's worth as a person is significantly defined by one's ability to consume, the stress of being a member of a minority poverty group—being a nonparticipant—is a major source of distress.

Another converging set of observations is the devastating consequences of involuntary unemployment. The work of Brenner (1973, 1977) on the damaging physical and psychological consequences of unemployment in this country and in England is convincing. To get back to my original point—it does not seem to me inappropriate or unscientific to suggest that a major cause of emotional problems, including premature pregnancy, alcoholism, and all of the other conditions found to be most common in Class 5 (the poorest of the poor), could be cleared up by a successful major social effort at reducing the incidence of poverty. Here, I do not imply that we should make the same mistake as was made in Lyndon Johnson's War on Poverty, which sought to deal with many of the consequences of poverty without doing anything to eliminate the causes of poverty itself.

I do not expect that every person interested in primary prevention will find advocating massive social change entirely congruent with their own orientation as preventionists with more modest aspirations. But at the same time I do not want the hard-nosed researchers to undermine those of us who believe that many effective prevention programs *will* involve social change and political action. (New York State and other states now require the use of seat belts at all times for people in the front seats of cars being driven in that State. Legislation proposed in Congress would raise the drinking age to 21. Frankly, I see both of these steps as making potentially large contributions to primary prevention. Reducing the speed limit to 55, requiring seat belts, getting young, especially male, drunken drivers off the highways, will reduce significantly the number of deaths, brain damage, and mutilations; this reduction, in turn, will reduce significantly the trauma of premature death or disfigurement or paralysis of loved ones. Do we need statistical tests of this statement?)

Another example. I regard sexism as another major cause of emotional distress in women and men. Can we as preventionists fail to support vigorously programs for equal opportunity and affirmative action and proposals like the Equal Rights Amendment without waiting for critical statistical analyses? I am sure I do not need to add an elaborate qualification reassuring you that I am all in favor of the best possible research. I simply do not want to be done in by our friends who insist on focusing prevention efforts only on strict research designs dealing only with a specific DSM III condition. I see the obsessives sometimes as counterrevolutionaries. I believe the social revolution is made by acting.

Some community psychologists who are ideologically opposed to primary prevention efforts are adept at suggesting plausible-sounding reasons why prevention efforts are premature or less than hopeful. One of the most distressing examples comes from a well-published community psychologist (whom I will not name) who raises questions about the potential dangers of primary prevention programs based on his careful description of failures of *secondary* prevention programs! I have read and re-read his papers and they only distressed me the more because I believe that he, too, really knows better. He describes in some detail two major efforts at *secondary* prevention involving early identification of people with problems and early efforts at remediation, both of which failed to show positive results. In one of these, the intervention group later showed "negative effects" in seven of 57 variables examined. Somehow these examples are supposed to make us cautious about primary prevention efforts! He cautions us about possible negative side effects in primary prevention and even in health promotion programs. Straining for an example, he describes one major program that resulted in significant improvement in inner-city children's mental test performance and on other measures of their ability. This group of inner-city children received several years of intensive intervention to foster better mental and emotional functioning. The group showed dramatic growth when compared with a contrast group. But our critic asks whether inner-city children are *really* happier in their interaction with family and peers following successful change, i.e., improvement in their general ability level. Are there also not likely to be unfortunate consequences, he asks, for these now well-functioning inner-city children because, with their greater abilities, they don't fit in with their old environment? Is it too inappropriate to suggest that he might also find good health in older persons something other than an unmixed blessing because these healthy individuals would not fit in with sick people in their environment? And what of the individual who escapes syphilis, or ringworm of the scalp, when a high proportion of other teenagers in the school are afflicted? May they not feel out of place? Perhaps my reaction is excessive, but I don't think so.

Another group of friends of prevention, who make enemies for us unnecessary, are those who deliberately stretch the definition of primary prevention to include early treatment. Early treatment, of course, is a desirable approach in itself, and it may forestall much greater difficulty later. It simply is *not* primary prevention (and I think some of the proponents for its inclusion in grant programs know this), but it opens a door for the support of a wide range of one-to-one interventions that soak up funds earmarked for the support of primary prevention efforts. I find this group particularly troublesome because they really know better but often seem to be seeking to ally themselves with the treatment establishment, which is so heavily committed to one-to-one intervention and which would like to have access to prevention funds.

Let us all understand that anyone has the right to oppose prevention programs. What distresses me is the knowing use of invalid arguments to oppose prevention. Simply saying, "I'd rather put the money into treatment of children," is perfectly okay. It is the assumption that preventionists are not bright enough to detect illogical arguments that I find unacceptable.

One of the other foci of resistance to primary prevention comes from those psychotherapists in the mental health professions who have been self-selected early to be interested in one-to-one relationships and, particularly, in seeing the results of their efforts: helping the real, living, suffering persons in their offices. Here is another clue to a source of opposition. Wertheimer (1981) has pointed out the difference between our perception of real lives and statistical lives. When we do individual treatment we see the results in the real-life, flesh-and-blood person we help. That individual may even thank us for our help, but, gratitude aside, we get direct feedback from our efforts. This is not true with most efforts at primary prevention. Because primary prevention interventions are always proactive rather than reactive, and because they are directed at groups of persons not yet affected, we must acknowledge the fact that we rarely, if ever, know the identities of the people we have helped to save from disorder. Even with the best follow-up evaluation, the most we can hope for is a decrease in rate. A declining rate curve may mean that dozens, or hundreds, or thousands of persons have *not* developed a disturbance or disorder, but it is impossible to point to those who would have been stricken but were not. We must be content with changing statistical lives. As a friend of mine in public health told me recently: "No one ever calls to thank me that they have not had cholera!" Nor, we could add, typhoid, measles, polio, and plague—or Down's syndrome, brain damage, or depression.

How can we be sure that, as proponents of primary prevention, we are not guilty of the same faults, inclined to invalid assertions and irrational objections, as our opponents? Certainly we know from experience that it is easy to see flaws in others, and in their arguments, while being blind to similar defects in our own perceptions. Perhaps only neutral, unbiased persons can judge us. But I submit that, in spite of the ambiguous and uncertain evidence concerning the effectiveness of psychotherapy I do not oppose its use, nor do I know any preventionist who does. I have never heard the argument that "while we are in favor of research on psychotherapy we do not think it should be applied until the evidence for its effectiveness is clear." Nor have I heard this argument about the careful and selective use of drugs in emergencies involving severe psychoses. I do not ever argue that the higher incidence of depression in the conscience-laden middle class is due to "upward drift," even though one could assemble compelling evidence that upwardly mobile people (such as white-collar school teachers with blue collar origins), are at high risk for all the stresses associated with social class change. I do not oppose support for biochemical research, and I hope that Kety gets all the money he needs for even more careful statistical analysis of his Danish adoption studies. So why do these people say all of those mean things about us preventionists?

One of the most interesting findings of Kelly's (1984) dissertation research was that few mental health professionals overtly are likely to oppose publicly the concepts and content of primary prevention. But she found that there are significant and striking differences between those who strongly endorse prevention efforts and those who moderately support them—the latter group who says, "Yes, but. . . ." The "Yes, but . . ." group spends significantly more time doing psychotherapy and are more often engaged in administrative tasks than the strong supporters who spend more time in consultation. The strong supporters, understandably, are more likely to explain mental disorders as having a social etiology, while the "Yes, but . . ." group are more inclined to a biochemical explanation. The "Yes, but . . ." group also seeks ways to include early secondary prevention as a variant that can be included as primary prevention. And we often encounter the argument that because early treatment is sometimes clearly unsuccessful this somehow tells against primary prevention.

With all of these people opposing prevention, with all the forms of resistance I have suggested, is there any hope for one approach? Of course there is. The overwhelming majority of members of the general public understand exactly what is meant by primary prevention and most of them are in favor of it. They also understand that mental disturbances and emotional distress are *not* diseases but are a result of the interaction of intense stress and inability to cope with it (lack of competence and coping skills). I have yet to sit down with anyone who is genuinely interested in hearing about primary prevention where the reaction was not positive and supportive. The only *real* enemies we have are our friends in the field! As more and more courses in primary prevention are taught in graduate programs (in schools of social work and elsewhere) and as the literature and ideas about prevention pervade the professional culture, we can anticipate a major shift in professional emphasis in the allocation of resources and in the explanatory models used in the field. Let me suggest that we be generous in our reaction to those who oppose us, that we work to convert those we can to our cause, and that we keep political pressure at maximum strength on our adversaries. I say all these things rather lightheartedly because I am optimistic that our approach ultimately will prevail and that we will help to build a more just society: a society that will follow Rawls' (1972) principles that emphasize equal opportunity for all and first priority for the support of the least advantaged.

References

Action for Mental Health (1960). Final Report of the Joint Commission on Mental Illness and Health. New York: Basic Books.

Albee, G. W. (1959). *Mental health manpower trends.* New York: Basic Books.

Albee, G. W. (1979). Psychiatry's human resources: 20 years later. *Hospital and Community Psychiatry, 30,* 783–786.

Albee, G. W. (1979). The prevention of prevention. *Physician East, 1,* 24–26.

Albee, G. W. (1981). Politics, power, prevention, and social change. In J. M. Joffe and G. W. Albee (Eds.), *Prevention through political action and social change: Primary prevention of psychopathology,* Vol. 5. Hanover, N.H.: University Press of New England.

Albee, G. W. (1982). Preventing psychopathology and promoting human potential. *American Psychologist, 37,* 1043–1050.

American Schizophrenia Foundation (1965). *What you should know about schizophrenia.* Pamphlet. Ann Arbor, Mich.: American Schizophrenia Foundation.

Bloom, B. (1981). The logic and urgency of primary prevention. *Hospital and Community Psychiatry, 32,* 839–843.

Brenner, M. H. (1973). *Mental illness and the economy.* Cambridge, Mass.: Harvard University Press.

Brenner, M. H. (1977). Personal stability and economic security. *Social Policy, 8,* 2–4.

Broussard, E. R., and Hartner, M. S. S. (1970). Maternal perception of the neonate as related to development. *Child Psychiatry and Human Development, 1,* 16–25.

Broussard, E. R., and Hartner, M. S. S. (1971). Further considerations regarding maternal perception of the first-born. In J. Hellmuth (Ed.), *Exceptional infant: Studies in abnormalities,* Vol. 2. New York: Brunner-Mazel.

Broussard, E. R. (1976a). Evaluation of televised anticipatory guidance to primiparae. *Community Mental Health Journal, 12,* 203–210.

Broussard, E. R. (1976b). Neonatal prediction and outcome at 10/11 years. *Child Psychiatry and Human Development, 7,* 85–93.

Broussard, E. R. (1977). Primary prevention program for newborn infants at high risk for emotional disorder. In D. Klein and S. Goldston (Eds.), *Primary prevention: An idea whose time has come.* Washington, D.C.: U.S. Government Printing Office.

Broussard, E. R. (1979). Assessment of the adaptive potential of the mother–infant system: The Neonatal Perception Inventories. *Seminars in Perinatology,* Vol. 3, No. 1.

Broussard, E. R., and Cornes, C. C. (1981). Identification of mother–infant systems in distress: What can we do? *Journal of Preventive Psychiatry, 1,* 119–132.

Cassel, J. (1976). The contribution of the social environment to host resistance. *American Journal of Epidemiology, 104,* 107–123.

Collier, P. and Horowitz, D. (1984). *The Kennedys.* NY: Summit Books.

Cowen, E. (1982). Special Issue on Primary Prevention. *American Journal of Community Psychology.*

Eisenberg, L. (1962). If not now, when? *American Journal of Orthopsychiatry, 32,* 781–793.

Eisenberg, L. (1977). The perils of prevention: A cautionary note. *The New England Journal of Medicine, 297,* 1230–1232.

Glasscote, R. M., Sanders, D., Forstenzer, H. M., and Foley, A. R. (Eds.) (1964). *The community mental health center: An analysis of existing models.* Washington, D.C.: Joint Information Service, American Psychiatric Association and National Mental Health Association.

Group for the Advancement of Psychiatry, Committee on Psychiatry and Community (1983). *Community psychiatry: A reappraisal.* New York: Mental Health Materials Center, Vol. XI, No. 113.

Hearnshaw, L. (1979). *Cyril Burt Psychologist.* Ithaca, N.Y.: Cornell University Press. Vintage Books Edition, 1981.

Hebert, W. (1979). The politics of prevention. *APA Monitor, 10*(7), 8–9.

Henderson, J. (1975). Object relations and a new social psychiatry: The illusion of primary prevention. *Bulletin of the Menninger Clinic, 39,* 233–245.

Joffe, J. M. (1982). Approaches to prevention of adverse developmental consequences of genetic and prenatal factors. In L. Bond, and J. Joffe, (Eds.), *Facilitating infant and early childhood development.* Hanover, N.H.: University Press of New England.

Joint Commission on Mental Illness and Health (1960). *Action for mental health.* New York: Basic Books.

Kelly, L. D. (1984). Primary prevention ideology: An examination of the attitudes and activities of mental health professionals. Ph.D. dissertation. University of Vermont.

Kety, S., Rosenthal, P., Wender, P., et al. (1976). Studies based on a total sample of adopted individuals and their relatives: Why they were necessary, what they demonstrated, and failed to demonstrate. *Schizophrenia Bulletin, 2,* 413–428.

Kiesler, C. A. (1980). Mental health policy as a field of inquiry for psychology. *American Psychologist, 35,* 1066–1080.

Kiesler, C. A. (1982). Public and professional myths about mental hospitalization: An empirical reassessment of policy-related beliefs. *American Psychologist, 37,*(12), 1323–1339.

Klein, K. J. (1980). An interview with Dr. Melvin Sabshin, Medical Director, American Psychiatric Association, *SPAA Newsletter, 2,* 1–3, Division 31, American Psychological Association.

Klein, D. C., and Goldston, S. E. (1977). *Primary prevention: An idea whose time has come.* Washington, D.C.: U.S. Government Printing Office.

Lamb, H. R., and Zusman, J. (1981). A new look at primary prevention. *Hospital and Community Psychiatry, 32,* 843–848.

Leighton, A. H. (1959). *My name is legion.* New York: Basic Books.

Lidz, T., and Blatt, S. (1983). Critique of the Danish–American studies of the biological and adoptive relatives of adoptees who became schizophrenic. *American Journal of Psychiatry, 140,* 426–435.

Mariner, A. S. (1980). Benevolent gambling: A critique of primary prevention programs in mental health. *Psychiatry, 43,* 95–102.

Pastore, N. (1949). *The nature–nurture controversy.* New York: Columbia University Press.

President's Commission on Mental Health (1978) *Report to the President.* Washington, D.C.: U.S. Government Printing Office.

Marmor, J. (1975). *Psychiatrists and their practice: A national study of private office practice.* Washington, D.C.: Joint Information Service, American Psychiatric Association and National Mental Health Association.

Rawls, J. (1971). *A theory of justice.* Cambridge, Mass.: Harvard University Press.

Sameroff, A. J. and Chandler, M. J. (1975). Reproductive risk and the continuum of caretaking casualty. In F. D. Horowitz, E. M. Hetherington, S. Scarr-Salapatek, and G. M. Siegel (Eds.), *Review of child development research. Vol. 4.* Chicago: University of Chicago Press.

Sarbin, T., and Mancuso, J. (1980). *Schizophrenia: Medical diagnosis or moral verdict.* New York: Pergamon.

Scull, A. (1977). *Decarceration.* Englewood Cliffs, N.J.: Prentice Hall.

Sifford, D. (1983). Are there ways to keep mental illness from getting a grip? *The Philadelphia Inquirer,* July 24 (pp 1F, 6F).

Wertheimer, A. (1980). Statistical lives. Op-ed page. *The New York Times,* April 25.

Williams, G. (1964). The help we need. *The Atlantic, 214,* 112–114.

Statewide Prevention Programs
The Politics of the Possible

Betty Tableman

To use Richard Price's terms, some people in state government are linkers or boundary spanners, responsible for searching out program possibilities and moving ideas and resources into the community service system. This chapter explores how this can happen for prevention programming through the politics of the possible: how the context that enables prevention programming to take hold and prosper can be established in a state department of mental health.

My review of the current status of prevention programming in the state departments of mental health is based on 39 responses to a brief survey. Some axioms, propositions regarded as self-evident truths, for the politics of the possible are proposed. These self-evident truths have been extracted from my experience in Michigan and from conversations with prevention staff in other states. Finally, some directions for the future are presented.

State Survey

In 1975, I was given the assignment to develop recommendations for prevention programming for the Michigan Department of Mental Health. At that time there was a small literature on prevention, and Klein and Goldston (1977) were just about to issue their manifesto: *Primary Prevention: An Idea Whose Time Has Come*. At that time, also, there were rumored to be prevention staff in the state departments of mental health in Ohio, Massachusetts, Kentucky, and Florida.

By 1984, there was a proliferating literature; four journals on prevention, specialized program journals, a bookshelf from the annual Vermont Conferences on the Primary Prevention of Psychopathology, monographs and proceedings from NIMH workshops, and a small but respectable—and growing—number of replication manuals and service models. In 1984, there were ostensibly 17 state departments of mental health (and one department of children and youth services responsible for mental health services for children) that had some identifiable prevention programming. These departments had assigned staff resources or allocated state funds for service development. In a few instances, both staff resources and program funding were provided.

The states that have some identifiable prevention programming are:

- State funds for local programming:
  - Florida
  - Maine
  - Mississippi
  - New Jersey
- Assigned staff and state funds for local programming:
  - New York
  - New Hampshire
- Designated prevention unit:
  - Alabama
  - California
  - Connecticut
  - Georgia
  - Hawaii
  - Michigan
  - North Carolina
  - Ohio
  - Oklahoma
  - South Carolina
  - Virginia
  - Wisconsin

In addition to these states, Missouri and Arkansas are currently requesting prevention program funds; Vermont has a legislative mandate to develop a prevention plan. Not included are states which, in response to the survey, reported that 5–10 percent of a staff person's time was assigned to consultation and education or to prevention but did not provide explicit information about activities.

In the states listed, staff resources range from as little as one-third of a person (New Hampshire) to a staff of five (California). Program resources, reported in 8 states, ranged from $16,000 in New Hampshire to $815,000 in California to $1.3 million in Michigan. No state at that time was putting as much as 1 percent of its budget into prevention programming.

State prevention units carry out a variety of activities. They may fund community services or encourage their development through the provision of models, conferences, and training workshops. They may issue newsletters and provide informational materials. They may place emphasis on participating with other state and nonpublic agencies in planning and developing services. Finally, prevention units may develop guidelines and policy statements for providing services.

Although it is difficult to impose order on this diversity, there are several identifiable patterns:

1. Prevention services for children are being developed as part of the continuum of services for children (Maine, Mississippi, and Connecticut).

2. Prevention services directed at mental disorder are part of the unit that administers the federal bloc grant for substance abuse prevention (Alabama, Ohio, Oklahoma, and Hawaii).

3. Prevention programming is located in a unit responsible for training, education, or public information (Virginia, New Hampshire, Ohio, Alabama, and Oklahoma).

4. Prevention staff, located within the agency's executive office, concentrate on promoting internal, interagency, and public–private prevention initiatives (Virginia, North Carolina, and Wisconsin).

5. Prevention programming has been placed in a research and development or policy bureau. Of these states, California and Georgia develop resource materials and service models but do not provide funds to local agencies for service development; Michigan and New York are developing service models by funding local projects.

Program areas vary as widely as organization. Some states have selected a single focus. California (Friends Can Be Good Medicine) and New Jersey have targeted their programming solely at promoting self-help and social support. New York is funding projects for children in disordered and stressed families. Maine is developing infancy programs.

Other states have multiple interests. Georgia has developed resource materials for community mental health agencies on social–emotional learning in the schools and life crisis management by adults. Virginia has two initial projects: (1) facilitating employee health promotion in state agencies; and (2) better beginnings for children of adolescent parents as an interagency effort with public health funds. Michigan is funding community mental health agencies to implement new or existing service models in such program areas as infant mental health, stress-management training for low-income women, parent training, interpersonal cognitive problem-solving training, children of disordered adults, children of divorce, and unemployment transition. New Hampshire is supporting a needs assessment for latchkey children, a geriatric health promotion program, and public information on child mental health. North Carolina proposes to develop seven target areas: family violence, family crises, children of substance abusers, childhood accidents and illnesses, teenage pregnancy, health risks to workers, and genetic screening.

Axioms

Based on this limited review, the first axiom has to be: *There is no one way; there is no one right way.* Prevention programming develops within the context and idiom of a particular state, and each state is different.

States have edged into prevention programming in two divergent ways. Some states assign resources to local services and then proceed to develop an identifiable state-level staff and program (Florida is at this stage, requesting a temporary position to write a state plan.) On the other hand, most states assign staff to develop prevention programming and then move to obtain state or other funds for local services. (Georgia and North Carolina have had state staff since the late 1970s but have been unable to secure a state appropriation for local services.)

The initial impetus for prevention programming at the state level may be an interested state mental health director (as in California) who initiates prevention activity because he or she believes in prevention. Or the initial impetus may be a department-sponsored conference (North Carolina), a new mental health code (Michigan), or a resolution by the legislature (Virginia). But the initial impetus and its translation into ongoing programming requires a constituency. Absolutely nothing happened in any of the states without a constituency. So, axiom two is: *There must be field support for prevention.* In most of these states, it has required both internal and external support to get prevention activity started, and it has certainly required external support to be sustained.

In Michigan and Georgia, the Mental Health Association was the constituency encouraging the director of mental health to set up a prevention unit. In Michigan, the Mental Health Association has consistently bypassed the executive budget and lobbied in the legislature for increases in the prevention appropriation. In New York, a small group of community mental health directors lobbied the state department for prevention funding. In California, a department director with an eye for innovations started the Mental Health Promotion Branch, but the program's continuance through four administrations is a reflection of community support and the sponsorship of a prominent legislator. In Florida, a special appropriation for prevention projects emerged from a legislative initiative.

Whatever the initial constituency, active programming should build further support. In Michigan, for example, an early decision was made to develop service models by funding small community projects. This was in part a prudent decision to spread the risk, but it was also a political decision to widen the base of involvement and interest.

Some states have developed statewide organizations around prevention programming. Thus the Georgia prevention unit has nurtured an active organization of consultation and education professionals. In Michigan, an association for infant mental health evolved out of department-sponsored training, which predated the prevention unit. Such organizations, developed for educational purposes, suggest the existence of a constituency; as they mature, they take on advocacy roles.

An advisory committee to the prevention unit is an important way to generate support. Prevention programming inevitably is a very small operation in a very large and crisis-burdened department. Even if the prevention unit starts out at the top in the organization (in terms of placement and support), it will tend to slide downward over time as other exigencies and other issues take precedence.

In Michigan, an advisory committee was organized as part of the initial exploratory process and was formalized when the unit was established. Michigan's Advisory Committee for Prevention and Community/Caregiver Services is composed of community mental health directors from various regions of the state, representatives of interested organizations, and knowledgeable individuals with a particular interest in prevention. The advisory committee is appointed by the director of the department to provide advice and recommendations on policy direction and the conduct of the program. It is a visible reminder of constituency interest in prevention and a channel for field input, and it can at any time open a dialogue with the director of the department. It has played a significant role in the survival and accomplishments of the Michigan program; for example:

• When the evaluators wanted to wipe out infant mental health projects, the advisory committee defused this internal attack.

• It has monitored departmental fiscal and program policies as they affect prevention programming.

• It has been closely involved in the development of guidelines and has brought a field perspective to this task.

• The periodic meetings provide an ongoing mechanism for reporting prevention developments and assessing progress.

• It has continually broadened the scope and direction of the prevention enterprise.

In the politics of the possible, a politically skilled and credible advisory committee is an essential constituency and an invaluable support system for a small staff, who can easily feel beleaguered and isolated. It is equally important for a state office and for the survival and well-being of a local program. There are local prevention programs in Michigan today that were kept alive by the actions of their advisory committees.

Axiom three: *There should be a plan of action, and it must specify what is meant by prevention.* When developing prevention programs, most states start out by formulating a plan. This plan should be both a selling document and a road map. It should have two main components: (1) a clear articulation of the program proposed; and (2) an outline of the administrative steps required to integrate prevention within the department.

Even with the best definition in the world, the way in which prevention becomes operational is not immediately self-evident. The term *primary prevention* can encompass quite diverse programming initiatives. Further, the term *prevention* has been severely handicapped by the primary, secondary, and tertiary formulation that expands that diversity and blurs boundaries. However, the more precise the specification of parameters of prevention programming, the less likely it is that prevention programming will be co-opted by traditionalists within the department, who will want to redefine prevention to mean alternatives to hospitalization.

The more precise the specification of parameters, the more likely it is that support will be obtained from departmental decisionmakers and legislators. Legislators tend to think in concrete terms. They can deal with specific populations and specific problems, but they have difficulty understanding what exactly is subsumed under preventing mental illness or such broad concepts as empowering people. But they know what they are buying if the plan proposes specific examples.

Whenever possible, plans, position papers, or legislative proposals should specify what you are proposing to prevent, the population you propose to serve, what you propose to do, and the documentation from the risk factors and intervention literature that says this is a reasonable thing to do. This point cannot be emphasized enough.

Axiom four: *Prevention programming should not be perceived as a threat.* This axiom argues for small, even tentative, beginnings. A prevention proposal that says 25 percent, or even 10 percent, of existing resources should be reallocated to prevention may be reasonable. It is also unrealistic: Even small reallocations of funds are threatening.

It is threatening to say, as the mental health director of one state did, that the private sector can handle outpatient services and that public funding and activity should be redirected to prevention services. In the context of that state's service capabilities, that may well be a realistic proposal. It was, however, not accomplishable by a frontal attack, and the service providers coalesced against him.

Michigan's program started with a $400,000 line-item appropriation for pilot demonstration projects. Pilot demonstrations are not threatening because they do not imply a commitment. They imply several decision points down the road, which a department can tolerate. It is, in fact, an extraordinarily effective way to feed innovation into a state system.

Axiom five: *Prevention should be perceived as relevant to the department.* Prevention programming inevitably is isolated from the mainstream of departmental activity. The issue of relevance, however, is part of the politics of the possible. One aspect of relevance is language: Most departments of mental health (California excluded) generally do not relate to the term *health promotion.*

For most states, relevance will be a demonstrable connection between the prevention caseload and the department's clients. This connection can be shown most clearly for children of mentally ill adults, but it can also be identified for other areas (e.g., stress-management training for low-income populations and infant mental health). For New York, it is understandable that prevention programming concentrates on children living with mentally ill adults or siblings or in similar chaotic situations.

For other states, relevance may be the goodwill engendered and the connections made with citizens and organizations not ordinarily interested in or supportive of the department's mission. California's Friends Can Be Good Medicine program has generated credibility and support for mental health activities in local communities and among ethnic groups. Virginia's involvement with the state board of realtors has had similar payoffs. In Michigan, where the governor is encouraging public and private sector collaboration, the department is participating with a bank to fund interpersonal cognitive problem-solving training in the Detroit schools.

For some states, relevance will be the opportunity provided by a prevention office to participate meaningfully in gubernatorial or interagency task forces or committees to develop recommendations for state initiatives. These planning efforts, directed at such issues as school health education, adolescent parent programming, and delinquency prevention are a recurring and time-consuming activity in state government. Relevance also will be prevention programming as a way of reaching otherwise unserved groups.

Over the long run, relevance resides in the concept of a continuum of services starting with prevention, on the evidence that the prevention caseload is the treatment caseload at an earlier point in time, and on the evidence of impact.

Some prevention modalities can be shown to be appropriate and effective in treatment settings, and this unintended benefit from prevention programming is peculiarly relevant to a department of mental health. For example, Michigan's stress-management training for low-income women has been evaluated as an alternative to traditional outpatient therapy and has been found to be both more effective in promoting independence and less expensive.

Axiom six: *There must be a good product.* It is important to have prevention programming that is perceived as good. What is defined as good work will vary from state to state. In California, good media is good work. In Georgia, community satisfaction with resource packages is good work.

In Michigan, good work is a well-operating pilot demonstration and evaluation results that show a difference between served and unserved groups. All of our pilot demonstration projects have an evaluation component. We look at those indices that might be expected to change in the short run because of the intervention. We have not tried to measure long-term impacts because the politics of the possible, in terms of the level of funding available and the pressure for closure and results, dictates a short time frame. We review process, and we collect anecdotal material.

The state-of-the-art in evaluation is less than perfect, field research is vulnerable, and it is easy to get caught in a no-win situation. In the politics of the possible, it is important not to make unrealistic promises. Oregon lost a prevention appropriation in the 1970s because, after one year, the projects did not show the outcomes that had been promised.

In the politics of the possible, evaluation may be less significant for actual results than as a surrogate for careful work and scrutiny—and a means for ongoing refinement of process. Few states have been willing to undertake full-fledged evaluations. As evaluated models become available, this activity should become less necessary, but some feedback process is essential.

In the politics of the possible, it is important to have an identifiable product. Idiosyncratic, undocumented efforts rapidly become invisible. Michigan's product is a service model, which is outlined in a replication manual. The process of putting a replication manual together forces us and the provider to understand all the dimensions of the service model. Once the replication manual is available, community agencies can implement the service in another setting.

Not only should the work be good, but it also should be reported.

Again, there are various ways by which this can be done: memos, project reports, and annual reports are useful in informing departmental decisionmakers, the legislature, and the prevention constituency. Journal articles and conference presentations may be valued in some departments and not in others. Such efforts document what is going on and are useful as a means of organizing material and providing information. Further, these opportunities are, in effect, an outside validation through recognition of the state or local program, as well as a means for information dissemination.

Axiom seven: *Prevention must be institutionalized within the state system.* State departments operate through an intricate management system. Laws, rules, policies, standards, and guidelines establish various service parameters; budget documents and performance contracts allocate funds; data systems monitor and report. Implementation of prevention at the local level through the state funding process requires attention to all of these internal processes.

It is through these internal processes that prevention programming becomes sanctioned and supported as part of ongoing operations. If prevention programming is not incorporated over time into state directives and decision processes, then it exists only as a peripheral and ephemeral activity.

Incorporating prevention programming into state structures takes time, and it must occur in a meaningful way. Mention in an official document contributes to awareness and official sanction. But inroads into rules, state plans, and budget instructions will be regarded as pious platitudes by the field agencies, unless they perceive that prevention has indeed been incorporated into the decision-making and funding structure. Such processes and structures are state specific, so that what is required in North Carolina may differ in timing and context from what is required in Michigan.

The Michigan Experience

In 1975, a new mental health code for Michigan specified prevention as a possible community mental health activity; this statutory authority was the initial sanction. (Other states have had legislative resolutions or gubernatorial directives but such expressions of intent provide no more than the opportunity.)

The new code, with an assist from the Mental Health Association, resulted in the generation of a position paper, which led to assignment of staff and a line item for prevention projects in the department's 1976 appropriation.

Rules and regulations were developed pursuant to the code. The community mental health section included prevention as a mandated community service. Another section permitted community boards to request a waiver for those services that they currently were unable to provide. Because so few boards had prevention services and because we were just embarking on pilot demonstrations, the department issued an automatic waiver for prevention services. The mandate was there, but it was on hold.

The pilot demonstration projects proceeded. This program included evaluation of pilot projects, replication in another setting to test generalizability, and then widespread dissemination as a service model.

Over the years, paragraphs on prevention programming were included in the state's health service plan and in the department's management plan, program policy guidelines, and budget instructions. All to the good—but resources, as always, were limited. Predictably any requests by boards for expansion money for prevention or for community–caregiver services were sidelined in favor of the department's real priorities.

As we began to get involved in programming, the decision was made to develop departmental guidelines as a part of the public mental health manual, which is the explicit statement of policy and procedures for the department and its contractual agencies. Over a period of two years, four guidelines were developed, guided through a public hearing and legislative review process, and formally adopted by the department. The adoption of guidelines on community–caregiver services and on infant mental health services represented a formal sanction by the department of these categories of services. For the first time, the department and community staff had an explicit reference for what was meant by the community–caregiver services and infant mental health services that were funded by the department.

A third significant guideline spelled out the procedures for continuation and transfer of projects. It tackled the issue of funding after the pilot demonstration or replication was completed. Under the all-too-usual state and federal pattern of funding projects, local sponsors are expected to find resources when project funding terminates. This practice means that in the majority of cases the project is dropped, and the investment in service development is lost. Under today's fiscal conditions, asking for funds to be reallocated at any level is unreasonable.

The third guideline grew out of the cutbacks and an active appeal by the sponsors of two projects that had been terminated. It was apparent that the same disruption of all projects would occur under normal circumstances, if there were no orderly process for the transfer of projects to continuation funding. Adoption of the third guideline meant that evaluated prevention services which had been initiated as projects could be transferred as a matter of course to continuation funding. The department director promptly added $300,000 to his request for continuation funds to accommodate the transfers. And it began to look like prevention was not just projects any longer, but could move with funding into base programming.

It was also encouraging that, during this period, prevention services were spelled out in the report establishing the framework for a children's continuum. (One of the most positive developments for prevention programming is the widespread conceptualization in state departments of a continuum of children's services.)

An overall prevention services guideline was the last to be developed. This guideline is a clear signal of departmental sanction for the provision by local boards of four categories of prevention services: (1) infancy programming; (2) services to enhance the competent development and life-coping skills of children; (3) services to enhance the coping skills of adults; and (4) services to facilitate coping with life crises.

A later administrative action was an even more significant step. On the recommendation of the advisory committee, the director of community services rescinded the automatic waiver for prevention services. Thus community mental health boards that do not provide prevention services now have to request a waiver each year and to plan what they propose to do in this area of services.* However, one piece of the puzzle is still missing: We have not yet been able to get prevention services into the data system; that is the next major effort required.

This recital of the Michigan experience is but a brief outline of our efforts in prevention programming and services since 1975. It does not communicate very well the dynamics of the process, so I feel constrained to add an eighth axiom, which brings in the operational dimension: *The politics of the possible is in large measure composed of patience, persistence, realism, creativity, and a sense of timing.*

Making Things Happen

The politics of the possible for prevention programming is no different than the politics of the possible for any other category of service development. We have to know when to lie low and when to move ahead. We need to recognize the windows of opportunity within the bureaucratic system. And we need to recognize and take advantage of the serendipi-

*In 1985, the four prevention guidelines were specified in the performance contract documents with community mental health boards. That step makes prevention an integral part of the community services system.

tous occurrences that are totally unplanned but that create an opportunity for forward movement. At the state level, making things happen requires knowing what it is you want to accomplish and focusing and targeting activities. It requires nurturing, encouraging, and protecting local efforts. The politics of the possible requires being willing to make progress one step at a time in good times and, in bad times, being willing to perservere until the situation changes.

Making things happen is a function of credibility. It is important to know about those advances in the rest of the world that give credibility to your efforts. The Vermont conferences build credibility, as do the activities of the Office of Prevention and the Center for Prevention Research at NIMH, the prevention resolutions passed by the National Association of State Mental Health Program Directors and their workshops on prevention research for state directors.

Making things happen is a function of constituency, as has been previously discussed and a function of resources. Protected resources are required, including staff who can concentrate on prevention and funds that are not in competition with other departmental initiatives.

Making things happen is also a function of the people who happen to occupy particular positions at particular times. A great advantage comes from presently having in Michigan, for example, both a supportive state director and colleagues in key positions in research, budget, and community services. Further, the Michigan service models are developed at the local level, and the caliber of the state program rests on the solid work of local project staff who can take an idea and successfully resolve recruitment and intervention issues.

Future Directions

With respect to the next decade of prevention programming in the states, I predict that states will develop some prevention services whether or not there is a designated prevention unit. I expect to see prevention services implemented in states as part of the continuum of children services and to see the number of infant mental health services and self-help clearinghouses increase steadily. The implementation of prevention services will be energized as validated service models become more widely available. The greatest energizer of all would be if Congress were to follow the pattern for substance abuse and require that 20 percent of the mental health bloc grant be devoted to prevention services. But that outcome is probably well beyond the politics of the possible for the foreseeable future.

References

Klein, D. C., and Goldston, S. E. (Eds.) (1977). *Primary prevention: An idea whose time has come.* Proceedings of the Pilot Conference on Primary Prevention, April 2–4, 1976. Department of Health, Education, and Welfare Publication No. ADM 77-447. Washington, D.C.: U.S. Government Printing Office.

The View from the Top: National Prevention Policy

Beverly Benson Long

Since being asked to address this topic, I have been trying to decide where the top might be. If I could find it, perhaps I could play Moses, ascend the mountain, and receive *THE* word. I spent days seeking the place from which to see the totality of national prevention policy. I kept coming back to Burlington, Vermont and the Vermont conferences, the one place that thus far has offered an opportunity to coalesce thoughts, ideas, and concepts. At present, there is no other focal point that encompasses the consumer, private, governmental, and volunteer efforts except these annual conferences.

Now, a comment about the higher authorities whom I sought to give me the true word. Those higher authorities, it turns out, also attend the Vermont conferences. Somehow, they don't seem to reside on high with streets paved with gold and harps playing, nor are they garbed in white robes with magic wands ready to cause the seas to recede, or the skies to part. These authorities appear to be more like the old man of the mountain: tough, rugged, self-reliant. Or like the pioneers of our country: reaching out, pushing, enduring, determined to reach a new beginning. Some of them have been around for more than the decade we celebrate, but the Caplans, the Albees, the Goldstons, and the Cowens, together with perhaps a half dozen more, *are* the founders of the prevention movement. History may or may not vest the prevention promotion revolution in these true pioneers, but when the dust settles, my guess is that most of the view from the top originally will have been articulated and based on the evidence summarized in these conferences.

Since my assignment is to view national prevention policy from whatever height I can manage, this chapter is written from the view of my own window of experience. My view is essentially one of a *citizen advocate*. As a volunteer citizen advocate, I have had the opportunity to serve on many local, state, and national councils, advisory groups, and commissions. Those affiliations that have most affected my thinking include the Georgia Governor's Advisory Council on Mental Health, Mental Retardation and Substance Abuse, which I chaired for three years; the local and state chapters and the National Mental Health Association, with which I have worked and served in leadership roles for many years; the NIMH National Advisory Mental Health Council, on which I have been a liaison representative for six years; and the President's Commission on Mental Health in 1977–1978. These mental health organizational experiences, together with a variety of health planning activities stemming from now-repealed health planning legislation, I believe, have afforded me a fairly wide-angle view of how citizen and consumer advocates relate to national and local policy matters.

In this chapter, I first want to take note of several very tall mountains that must be conquered as we move toward realization of the goal of prevention of mental and emotional disability. Then I will review some activities relating to the prevention field, especially political and turf matters. To conclude, I will share my ideas of where and how we might proceed.

Tall Mountains to Be Conquered

There are tall mountains (obstacles) standing in our way that must be overcome. The first and tallest mountain is often forgotten. The basic obstacle in achieving our mental health goals is *not* when we start looking at mental health problems but at the time when resources are targeted for overall health needs. The most fundamental barrier to our prevention goals is the unremitting discrimination of mental health in the allocation of health resource dollars. Everyone knows that mental and physical health are two sides of the same coin: that to be healthy a person needs a healthy mind in a healthy body. (Although if we look at the cliché closely, we would probably decide that it is more possible to have a healthy mind in an unhealthy body than the other way around!) Slogans aside, we can agree that optimum health encompasses a balance of good mental and physical health.

We can agree, that is, until that point is reached at which our tax dollars are divided and allocated, ostensibly to improve the health of the people of these United States. Despite reason and common sense, tax monies are allocated not on the basis of the magnitude of the health problems—and the resulting nonproductivity and tax drain—but on illogical, tradition-bound ideas that are supported by the special interests they engender. Federal tax dollars, as well as most state and local taxes, are spent without a process to determine the health priorities in relation to the scope of the disabilities, the source of the problems, or the relative cost to the taxpayers.

Let us look at two facts. The care and treatment of the diagnosed mentally ill accounts for 12 percent of the total health dollars spent in the United States; in 1983 that cost amounted to $43 billion. That amount does not include the costs hidden in general physical health care; those stress-related, behavior-related physical manifestations of ill health that have basic or associated psychological causes. If a method were used by which all the costs of emotional and mental disorders were totaled, there is little doubt that at least one-half of what is spent on health results from mental and emotional problems.

How much of our tax money is allocated to the mental side of the health coin? In research, as an example, about 4½ percent. In other allocations of money and resources, such as Medicare, Medicaid, housing assistance, most private insurance, etc., the discrimination is blatant and irrational.

Until some semblance of reason is brought into the use of public dollars for health, our efforts to prevent mental and emotional disorders will continue to be severely penalized. Each of us has a responsibility to recognize this overarching problem and to educate the officials responsible for making program and funding decisions.

The next most urgent need is *within* the mental health field. It is the allocation that shapes the balance between the attention and resources afforded efforts to prevent disability and to treat disability. We need to have a better understanding of how allocation decisions are made and how fact and reason can be brought to bear on those who make them.

A third challenge is to find ways to fully recognize, integrate, and celebrate the advances and efforts being made in related fields and activities, such as behavioral medicine, biomedical, epidemiological, and other research, and in the technologies that serve as tools for the advancement of knowledge. We must welcome the many new advocates who are related to or are entering the field. All of these aspects of cross-fertilization are part and parcel of future advances in prevention.

The fourth and last of the major hurdles is the need to remind ourselves—and the need to remind the broader field—that mental health and mental ill-health are *at least* as complex as physical health and physical ill-health, and that the interaction is pervasive and real. The prevention of mental and emotional disability is not a simple goal; it is multifaceted, intertwined, and infinitely complex.

Background to A Decade of Progress

The decade of progress recorded in this volume prompts our sense of history:

• The first hospital in the United States for "persons of insane and disordered minds" was built in 1773.

• The first organized effort to identify and eliminate the causes of mental illness in the United States was promoted in 1909 by Clifford Beers and his National Society for Mental Hygiene, the precursor of the Mental Health Association.

• The first unified governmental effort in mental health resulted in the Report of the Joint Commission on Mental Illness and Health. This document entitled *Action for Mental Health* was completed in December 1960 (Joint Commission, 1961).

• In 1961 the American Medical Association (AMA) stated: "The major health problem facing the nation today is mental illness" (AMA, 1961).

President Kennedy in his special message to Congress on February 5, 1963 said:

> Mental illness and mental retardation are among our most critical health problems, they occur more frequently, affect more people, require more prolonged treatment, cause more suffering by the families of the afflicted, waste more of our human resources, and constitute more financial drain upon both the public treasury and the personal finances of the individual families than any other single condition. (Kennedy, 1963)

One-fourth of all the hospital beds in the United States are occupied by persons diagnosed as schizophrenic (Hamburg, Elliot, and Parron, 1982), and conservative estimates place one-third of the hospital beds (including those diagnosed as schizophrenic) as being occupied by mentally disordered individuals; in the early 1960s and until recently, the statistics were one-half of all beds. But whatever the precise figures, more people are hospitalized for mental problems than for any other category of disorder, and this has been an accepted fact for years.

So, for the last 50–100 years there has been growing recognition of mental and emotional disability as a serious problem. Strangely, our celebration of progress in *prevention* efforts speaks only to the last 10 years, not the last 100.

The Welsh, in ancient times, had a simple test of sanity. When they questioned someone's sanity, they placed the person in a room with a faucet running into a large container and handed the "candidate" a bucket. The task presented was to empty the large container of the water. If the person attempted to empty the container by filling the small bucket over and over, he was deemed insane. If the person first turned off the faucet, he or she was found to be sane. If we consider the analogy to our efforts in the mental health field, there is little doubt about how the Welsh would have described us.

Prevention History

At the time of the Joint Commission's report in 1960, prevention was not a priority in the mental health world. The Commission mentioned prevention as important but did not emphasize the potential, instead directing its recommendations to early and community-based treatment.

It is interesting, however, to note what the Joint Commission reported, what President Kennedy said, and what then actually occurred. When Kennedy sent his message to the Congress he said:

> Our attack must be focused on three major objectives: First we must seek out the causes of mental illness and of mental retardation and eradicate them. Here, more than in any other area, "an ounce of prevention is worth more than a pound of cure." For prevention is far more desirable for all concerned. It is far more economical and it is far more likely to be successful. (Kennedy, 1963)

As recommendations from commissions and other official groups are translated into legislation, there are many opportunities for change. In this case, the president chose to *add* an emphasis on prevention.

The laws that resulted from the Joint Commission's report, the community mental health centers legislation, include *consultation and education* as one of the five required essential services. To this category of service the Congress assigned the role of prevention of mental illness and the promotion of mental health.

As we are aware, the prevention responsibility of the community mental health centers (CMHCs) was never adequately defined, either by the Congress or by the federal agencies. The National Institute of Mental Health placed practically no emphasis on prevention programs. However, despite the lack of administrative support from the federal side, there were enough people in the field who had a grasp of the concepts so that some of the centers made creative and effective prevention efforts (Swift, 1980). A slow ferment began. That consultation and education was one of the five original essential services of the CMHCs was, I believe, the seed of the coming new emphasis.

Other happenings in the 1960s and early 1970s influenced the prevention movement. In the early 1960s, there was some activity in mental health education in the schools. In 1962, when I worked as a psychologist at the Georgia Division of Mental Health, a coworker and I discovered and developed great enthusiasm for Ojemann's (1969) program of mental health educational units. Currently, there are several well-researched and promising programs for increasing coping and other positive mental health skills using classroom settings.

In 1971, prevention was the theme of the National Mental Health Association's (NHMA) annual meeting, and in 1973 a task force was formed to plan and conduct a pilot conference on prevention, which was held in 1976 in Philadelphia. That conference, financed by the National Institute of Mental Health (NIMH), stimulated both the National Mental Health Association's *Action Guidelines for Prevention* (NMHA, 1976) and the NIMH publication *Primary Prevention: An Idea Whose Time Has Come* (Klein and Goldston, 1976).

Another significant event that increased the evolving interest in prevention as a viable avenue in reducing mental and emotional disability was the work of the President's Commission on Mental Retardation in 1971. That group declared that by using present knowledge and techniques from the biomedical and behavioral sciences, the occurrence of mental retardation could be reduced by 50 percent by the end of this century. President Nixon adopted that figure as a national goal, and President Ford reaffirmed it in 1974. The importance and benefits of a prevention effort in mental retardation gave impetus to securing a focus on prevention of mental and emotional disability. (Report to the Congress by the Comptroller General of the United States, 1977.) In 1976, the Alcohol, Drug Abuse, and Mental Health Administration (ADAMHA) conducted a prevention conference attended by officials from the governments of Canada, Great Britain, and the United States (ADAMHA, 1976).

In my view, one of the most influential events basic to prevention activity was the work of the Canadian government in its assessment of the health needs of their people. The official document, entitled *A New Perspective on the Health of Canadians* (Lalonde, 1974), set forth the health field concept that categorized human biology, environment, and lifestyle as at least equal in importance to the health care system. The health field concept has significantly shifted emphasis to factors outside medical treatment, providing a broad base for engendering personal responsibility for wellness, promotion of health, and prevention of illness.

Also in 1975, the first Vermont prevention conference was held in Burlington. The effect of that conference and subsequent meetings is the sine qua non.

Currently, there is growing interest in prevention at the state level, and we hope to see continued enthusiastic state involvement. I was involved in the efforts that resulted in the inclusion of language mandating a separate prevention unit in Georgia's Mental Health System Act of 1976. The process by which that was accomplished was almost parallel to the processes associated with the subsequent federal legislation, thereby exemplifying the importance of constituency and political know-how. These breakthroughs rarely, if ever, come without being fought for at every level, and increasingly I have come to recognize the need for legislation. Laws are not sufficient but are necessary. Personnel changes occur so rapidly in agencies and interests vary so greatly that, without a specific law, new program dimensions often are lost.

In retrospect, I think it fair to say that by the time of the President's Commission on Mental Health in 1978 there were significant areas of interest in prevention and growing activity, but no structure equal to giving any real order to the field.

The President's Commission on Mental Health

What was behind the President's Commission on Mental Health? How do such interests come about, and what does the power of high office contribute to specific endeavors? We think of Franklin D. Roosevelt and his interest in poliomyelitis. We think of John F. Kennedy and Community Mental Health Centers. Similarly, we think of Jimmy Carter and the President's Commission on Mental Health (1978).

In the fall of 1983, I attended a conference held at the John F. Kennedy Library in Boston, which focused on an oral history of the role that presidents have had in mental health and mental retardation policy. The interchange between the 20 some participants was fascinating and embraced many viewpoints. I came away impressed by the divergent views, by the differences in emphasis and memory, and with a little skepticism about how well history reflects truth. In this chapter, I relate observations to you from *my* viewpoint, hoping to add to the accuracy and balance of the mental health movement during the Carter years and since.

How was it that Jimmy Carter, President of the United States, in his first month in office set in motion the President's Commission on Mental Health? In Georgia, Carter, as Governor, had a keen interest in making human services more effective. He provided strong leadership in the development of the department of human resources, which consolidated many separate services. He soon became involved in mental health activities not only because of the humane issues, but also because the mental hospital system consumed a large part of the state's health costs. He understood the politics and moved quickly to break the tradition-bound and disgraceful pork-barrel, central mental hospital situation. The changes caused much turmoil. The resulting turf guarding by some professionals, and the unbridled and often unprincipled maneuvering of a few politicians, eventually caused the departure of the young and progressive mental health director that the governor had brought in. The tensions created when priorities and structures are reordered in bureaucracies are basic to the difficulty of carrying out effective management practices.

Governor Carter was receptive to and worked very closely with the Georgia Mental Health Association. In fact, several of his key staff people, both while in Georgia and later at the national level, came from the ranks of the association's volunteers. My own involvement with Governor Carter and later with Mrs. Carter was related to my role as president, first of the Georgia Mental Health Association and, later, of the National Mental Health Association.

James A. MacKay, former congressman and then president of the Georgia Mental Health Association, conceived of and initiated, with the encouragement and cooperation of Governor Carter, the Governor's Commission to Improve Services for Mentally and Emotionally Handicapped Georgians. The commission was chaired by John L. Moore (1971), an active volunteer of the mental health association. Mrs. Carter was a member of the commission.

The President's Commission on Mental Health was a direct outgrowth of that Georgia commission, and I and other mental health association members were directly and closely involved from its inception.

I believe we can learn from these antecedent conditions about special interests of persons in power. In my view, individuals in key positions must come into power with their special interests already in place. The Carters could not have become mental health advocates after his election to the presidency; the pressures were too demanding. The lesson here is that it is necessary to educate and involve *potential* leaders as they ascend to power.

So, how did the PCMH come about? It emerged from realistic need and from political opportunity. The commission was made up of a diverse group of people. Each of the 20 members fought for what she or he believed in, and the final report came reasonably close to reflecting a balanced digest of all views. The report did not have the benefit of even a final consensus meeting; it was completed by Dr. Bryant and his staff through innumerable telephone conversations with the individual members, thereby obviating an exchange of views and the resulting weighting of various sections and recommendations. But, on balance, I think it is a good example of what can happen when a group is brought together who genuinely represent most of the diverse interests that are a part of broad-based policy decisions. One recommendation called for an ongoing commission or advisory group. This recommendation has not been implemented. In my view, such a body, not aligned with governmental agencies, but with an oversight and advisory role, would have potential in keeping mental health in a visible position and in cutting through bureaucratic inertia.

The President's Commission and Prevention

Because the prevention mandate, now the law of the land, came out of the repealed Mental Health Systems Act, which resulted from the President's Commission on Mental Health—and because the process is symbolic of the political process and policymaking, I want to trace some of the steps involved.

When the commission was formed, prevention was one of the original categories, and the task panel, chaired by George Albee, was created. The fact that both President and Mrs. Carter had expressed a special interest in prevention protected the emphasis to some extent. And referring back to the prior interests of persons who are in positions of power, I might point out that the president's interest in the prevention aspects of mental illness went back to a focus brought to the attention of and discussed often with Carter while he was governor of Georgia. It is of utmost importance that such interests be expressed publicly. Unless reference can be made to leaders' interests, these interests can quickly be buried in other peoples' agendas, and persons in positions of great power cannot constantly be affirming where they stand.

During the deliberations of the commission, careful and constant monitoring to ensure that prevention meant prevention and not treatment was necessary. There were many times when attempts were made to blur the definition and to broaden the boundaries. The report of the Albee panel was clear, however, and because the commission members had respect for each other, and understood that there were positions that could not be diluted, a reasonably strong prevention recommendation emerged. There were times, however, when I did not dare leave the room and absolutely would not unless another advocate, Dr. George Tarjan, was there. As I noted, individual commissioners had strongly held special concerns and interests and fought for their particular beliefs.

During the deliberations of the commission, the relevant governmental agencies were involved and the staff people were aware of the evolving directions. It was clear that prevention was not going to be abandoned.

Shortly after Dr. Gerald Klerman became Director of ADAMHA, a small group of us from the Mental Health Association had dinner with him. As we talked, he spoke of the increasing interest in prevention, and he told us that he was going to make prevention one of the four agency priorities.

From a personal standpoint, I could only marvel at the way things change. It had not been many months since I was saying in talks and speeches around the country that if you were to call the NIMH and ask for the Prevention Department, you found that there was one prevention person who had neither budget nor staff nor could be found on an organizational chart!

Since the result of the commission report was obviously going to require new attention to prevention, and since the parent agency (ADAMHA) had announced its new awareness, it was appropriate that an Office of Prevention should be established in the Director's Office at NIMH. This was done in 1979.

As most of you are aware, the commission found that the NIMH had been essentially ignoring prevention. The report stated:

> At present our efforts to prevent mental illness or to promote mental health are unstructured, unfocused, and uncoordinated. They command few dollars, limited personnel, and little interest at levels where resources are sufficient to achieve results. If we are to change this state of affairs, as we believe we must, the prevention of mental illness and the promotion of mental health must become a visible part of national policy. (p. 53)

The report contained recommendations for a center for prevention and for funding that would support a viable effort (PCMH, 1978).

The process through the system after the PCMH Report was delivered to the President and the commissioners had gone home is interesting in terms of policymaking. The route from such administration-backed reports, or for that matter for most proposals, to actual legislation and hence policy change is complex and vulnerable to distortion at many points. The road from the President's endorsement at the White House ceremony, to the NIMH, to the Senate and House subcommittees, committees, and through the Congress was long and filled with detours, potholes, and delays. Because of my position then as President of the National Mental Health Association, I was involved in the proceedings. It quickly became clear that the various constituencies had to get their act together, if the recommendations were to be held together through the processes. The people actually writing the bills were being besieged at every point by the same special interests that had tried to influence the PCMH, and in addition the agency personnel had their own turfs and interests. Also, before the bill was out of the Senate committee, chaired by Senator Kennedy, he and President Carter were competing for their party's 1980 nomination. In my view, the principals steered clear of the pending legislation; in fact, I am convinced that they cooperated on the basis of their mutual desire to produce the best content. Inevitably, however, there was political maneuvering on the part of some of the staff and other interested and involved parties.

In order to influence the pending legislation, the NMHA formed a coalition with the National Association of State Mental Health Program Directors and the National Council of Community Mental Health Centers, and forged liaisons with some of the other powerful constituencies. With the coalition speaking as one, it was evident that any legislation that was unacceptable could be stopped. Thus we had a position of power from which to negotiate.

You can imagine that the coalition itself, composed of state mental health officials, community mental health representatives, and voluntary association persons, had some problems to resolve. There were innumerable meetings, telephone calls, drafting and redrafting of positions, and lots of good will. I won't go into the internal swapping other than to indicate that we became quite sophisticated. Once we reached consensus, we stood absolutely together, and prevention was one of the absolutes.

Let's trace what happened to the prevention package. The first language that was sent forward in the NIMH-written and backed version was completely and totally unacceptable to prevention advocates. It did not reflect the commission's recommendations for the NIMH to have a national leadership and coordinating role. It did provide that the states could request grants to do a variety of things that might be called prevention. The proposed bill would have allowed the NIMH to go back to the neglectful state of affairs that the commission had reported. Why the agency and the White House people allowed that to happen will be left to the readers' speculation.

The NMHA proposed new language, which was agreed to by the coalition and, in addition, such organizations as the American Psychological Association and the National Consortium for Child Mental Health Services. However, when Senate staff rewrote the bill, the resulting subcommittee markup was even worse than the original NIMH version.

Representatives of our group met with Dr. Stuart Shapiro, a physician, who was then the proposed Systems Act lead staff member for Senator Kennedy's committee. Dr. Shapiro indicated that he was personally opposed to the prevention title in the proposed legislation because of the same kind of opposition that we had all heard before—you can't prevent if you don't know how or know what it is you want to prevent; knowledgeable sophisticated people do not favor allocating resources to fuzzy ideas, etc.

It was fascinating to note how intense the opposition became. The sources of opposition were not altogether clear. I knew some of them and some of the sources of the sources. The more outspoken were psychiatrists and other medically-oriented individuals, and there was considerable overlap with those who protested that the comprehensive community mental health centers were a failure and that the idea should be abandoned in favor of something less than that systems-type approach. That the small number of protestors were able to mount such an extraordinary effort to dislodge the prevention focus was in keeping with much that happens in the world of politics and turf guarding.

To convince Dr. Shapiro and his cohorts that there were savvy medical people who endorsed the prevention effort, we called in extra troops, spearheaded by such distinguished and respected psychiatrists as George Tarjan and Roy Menninger. We enlisted an outstanding group from North Carolina, some from Georgia, and a variety of other medical heavyweights. They had an effect, and we never felt it necessary to alert the mental health association network.

When it was recognized that not only was prevention backed by solid forces but was likely to be an important part of the give-and-take to get a Systems Act through the Congress, another level of negotiation came into the picture. Prevention became a good target for which to barter, and the prevention title became a political football.

The language relating to prevention of mental disability was put in, dropped out, put in again, altered, strengthened, and weakened in an unprecedented political engagement relating to the overall proposed legislation. On at least one occasion the entire bill was held up because of the prevention provision.

The language relating to the separate administrative unit for prevention stayed in only because late one afternoon my intuition told me that "they" were bluffing about other key issues that "they" would strike unless we gave in on the point. I said no and "they" backed down. We lost the line-item funding in the same engagement—I backed down. It was not softball that the actors were playing, and had not the coalition been able to hold together and know what was going on, the prevention part could have been either entirely lost or watered down to virtually nothing.

I want carefully to emphasize that without key medical figures, we would not have been able to prevail. I think that most of the opposition to prevention comes from general medical and psychiatric bias, but I also am sure that the medical people who understand the concepts and know the potential are at least equal in number and certainly equal in prestige and status. We must be certain that we do not generalize from the shortsightedness of a few.

So in 1980 a battle was won: Prevention efforts to reduce mental and emotional disablement were mandated by the Mental Health Systems Act (PL 96-398). In 1981 the law was repealed. However, the part of the Act that directed the NIMH to give specific attention and action to efforts to prevent mental disability was retained. The Congress amended the Public Health Service Act, which is the foundation for all health related federal activity, to add a paragraph to the section of the Act that defines the role of the NIMH. I am pleased that the prevention language that is now law is almost identical to the language originally proposed by the NMHA.

Section 455d of the Public Health Service Act states:

(d) The Director shall designate an administrative unit in the Institute to—

(1) Design national goals and establish national priorities for—
(A) The prevention of mental illness, and
(B) the promotion of mental health,

(2) Encourage and assist local entities and State agencies to achieve the goals and priorities described in paragraph (1), and

(3) Develop and coordinate Federal prevention policies and programs and to assure increased focus on the prevention of mental illness and the promotion of mental health.

After the President's Commission

I have used my experience and observations of the PCMH as an example of how public laws and policies sometimes come into being. The work and recommendations of that commission were the result of genuine knowledge and experience, balanced against and with power plays of turf guarders and special interest groups. The Mental Health Systems Act was the result of the combined effects of the enthusiasm of a new administration and of power and its benefits. It was sometimes based on idealism untempered by market place reality. There was activism fettered by narrow vision; there were mature, seasoned political leaders who contributed their know-how; there were skillful manipulators who had their own agendas; there were determined constituencies; and there was unremitting determination on the part of a sufficient number of individuals to carry it through. I might add that some of those individuals already have been lost to history, and some who were little involved have been elevated to leadership status.

The fact that so massive and complex a legislative package was put together and enacted is a marvel. That it was so quickly wiped out, or at least most of it, is somehow less a marvel.

If there is a prevention bandwagon, it is because the important prevention language of the Systems Act was retained as part of the Public Health Service Act and because the present administration has strongly endorsed the preventive thrust with money as well as rhetoric. Money directs the focus and, until it was made clear by the Congress and the Administration that money was to be utilized specifically for prevention, little but talk issued from the bureaucracy. Once there was a designated administrative unit in the NIMH, the Office of Prevention, as is now required by law, *and* once money became available for basic functions, some of the needed activities could take place. The visibility needed and called for in the PCMH report and now in the Public Health Service Law had a focal point. Likewise, until money was made available specifically for research in prevention, there was little attention given to such investigations.

The imbalance between prevention and treatment efforts continues to exist at NIMH and the other components of the National Institutes of Health (NIH). One of the most blatant, and amusing in a way, reported results of the emerging emphasis on prevention was printed in the February 3, 1982 issue of the *Blue Sheet*. The National Institute of Allergy and Infectious Diseases (NIAID), it said, had expanded its definition of prevention research so that more work is classified as prevention-oriented. NIAID's original definition focused on intervention before the biologic onset of disease. However, the revised definition included interventions to prevent further progression and complications of already established disease, in other words, treatment.

Use of the public health rubric has confused the picture significantly. The terms primary, secondary, and tertiary prevention encompass everything that NIMH and all the other agencies do to improve physical and mental health. But the essence of the PCMH report with regard to prevention was that treatment and rehabilitation efforts needed to be balanced with efforts to prevent. Treatment called "secondary prevention" and treatment and rehabilitation called "tertiary prevention" simply are attempts to do what NIAID was reported to have done, i.e., expand the boundaries to include what they wanted to include. Those who advocate that a reasonable proportion of resources be directed to prevention, and who have succeeded in getting a congressional mandate as well as having the leadership of ADAMHA and NIMH proclaim a new emphasis on prevention, find it illogical and unacceptable that "prevention" should be used as an overarching rhetoric to define what has been going on all along. The PCMH said do something *different* from what you have been doing all along, rather than keep on doing the same things but now calling it prevention. The law mandates a genuine commitment and allocation of attention and resources to prevention, not early or late treatment.

The Future

In my view, the necessary forces have already converged to provide the zeitgeist for achieving substantial success in preventing mental and emotional disorder. In order for a zeitgeist to exist, the problems must have been long-lasting, far-reaching, ill-defined, mysterious, and devastating. When definition becomes possible and research techniques and tools have been developed, a knowledge base begins to emerge, and there is an expanding potential for solving problems. The accelerating public awareness of the mind-boggling economic costs, both direct and indirect, of the various mental and emotional disabilities is also a factor in the present situation. So, with a substantial scientific base, increasing public awareness of mental and emotional problems, and the awesome economic facts, we probably have conditions that provide the zeitgeist for achieving cost-effective prevention programs.

Can we lose it? Yes, for a decade or so. Yes, unless mental health facts are projected so the depth and scope of the disablements, together with the interdependency with physical health, are effectively presented and unless such facts are reflected in the allocation of resources. And yes, unless the prevention constituencies, which, in my opinion, have reached a critical mass, work in a coordinated and carefully orchestrated manner. Political realities must be recognized and effective strategies developed.

Despite the "bandwagon" it is predictable that actual dollar resources for prevention will be scarce at the federal, state, and local levels. Only if such resources as become available are managed in goal-directed and politically astute ways, utilizing the available business techniques of management, will a genuine turn-around result.

It is essential that the available knowledge about prevention of mental disability be put together in a way that the layperson and professional can understand. Existing models and programs must be cited, and new results must be made available much more rapidly than has been true in the past. In the vernacular, we have to continue to get our act together, and we must be able to project it so that it sells itself.

With the mental health resources now available (as relatively miniscule and out of balance as they are), prevention must be brought into reasonable balance with the treatment aspects of NIMH. The urgency of designing national prevention goals and priorities (as required by law); in fostering coordination, and in disseminating knowledge demands an administrative unit that is supported as a valuable and productive entity. The days of neglect and internal strife must be replaced with effective management practices. The fact that certain organizational structures have existed in the past is not relevant. Basic management principles demand that form follows function, not the reverse. The Office of Prevention at NIMH, which is the administrative unit required by law, must have appropriate autonomy, adequate funds, and staff to function.

We are enthusiastic, encouraged, and greatly pleased with the increase in prevention research spearheaded by the NIMH Center for Prevention Research. But research is not all of the mandate, nor will research without application of the knowledge get us to our goal.

In addition to the need for equitable distribution of health funds at the first level of allocation and for a better balance of mental health funds for efforts to treat as compared with efforts to prevent, we must improve the communication among our networks. These networks must grow and must be effective. In my view, in the long run there must be a permanent, carefully balanced commission that reports to a governmental level high enough to afford objectivity and autonomy and to generate attention and resources to make a genuine difference.

If the view from the top is to be one of a vibrant and happy people, we must succeed in bringing into balance the attention and resources needed for mental health as well as physical health. We must get the decisionmakers to understand the interrelationship and to allocate the resources, which we as a people make available, according to a rational process to determine need rather than according to traditional and political expediency.

Prevention is not only an idea whose time has come; it is indispensible if we as a people, are to improve our well-being, that overall mental–physical health which is true health.

References

Alcohol, Drug Abuse, and Mental Health Administration (1976). *Summary proceedings, tripartite conference on prevention*. Department of Health, Education, and Welfare Publication No. (ADM) 77-484. Washington, D.C.: U.S. Government Printing Office.

American Medical Association, Council on Mental Health (1961). *Program of the council on mental health*. Pamphlet extracted from the AMA's Preliminary Program Conference on Mental Illness and Health, September, 29–October 1, 1961. Chicago: American Medical Association.

Blue Sheet. February 3, 1982. Allergy institute expands definition of prevention research so that more work is classified as prevention-oriented; other institutes may follow.

Hamburg, D. A., Elliott, G. R., and Parron, D. L. (Eds.) (1982). *Health and behavior.* Washington, D.C.: Institute of Medicine.

Joint Commission on Mental Illness and Health (1961). *Action for mental health.* New York: Basic Books.

Kennedy, J. F. (1963). Special Message to the Congress. *Mental illness and mental retardation*. Washington, D.C.: U.S. Congress.

Klein, D. C., and Goldston, S. E. (1976). *Primary prevention: An idea whose time has come*. National Institute of Mental Health. Department of Health and Human Services Publication No. (ADM) 80-447. Washington, D.C.: U.S. Government Printing Office.

Lalonde, M. (1974). *A new perspective on the health of Canadians*. Ottawa: Ministry of National Health and Welfare, Government of Canada.

Moore, J. L. (1971). *Governor's Commission to improve services for mentally and emotionally handicapped Georgians*. Report to Governor Carter.

National Mental Health Association (1976). (Formerly National Association for Mental Health.) *Primary prevention of mental disorders action guidelines*. Alexandria, Va: The Association.

Ojemann, R. H. (1969). Incorporating psychological concepts in the school curriculum. In H. P. Clarizio (Ed.), *Mental health and the educative process*. Chicago: Rand McNally.

President's Commission on Mental Health (1978). *Report to the President*. Washington, D.C.: U.S. Government Printing Office.

Public Health Service Act, Part G, 455(d), National Institute of Mental Health.

Report to the Congress by the Comptroller General of the United States (1977). *Preventing mental retardation—more can be done*. HRD-77-37 October 3, 1977. Washington, D.C.: U.S. Congress.

Swift, F. (1980). Primary prevention: Policy and practice. In R. H. Price, R. F. Ketterer, B. C. Bader, and J. Monahan (Eds.), *Prevention in mental health* (pp. 207–236). Beverly Hills, Calif.: Sage.

The Federal Scene
Ten Years Later

Stephen E. Goldston

Prologue

This chapter addresses the history of primary prevention as viewed from the Federal scene, with an emphasis on the activities proposed and conducted by the National Institute of Mental Health. Chronicling the past decade and some of the affect aroused in preparing this chapter has best been described (and aptly so) 70 years ago by Robert Frost (1955), the famed Vermont poet, when he wrote in *The Road Not Taken:*

I shall be telling this with a sigh
Somewhere ages and ages hence:
Two roads diverged in a wood, and I—
I took the one less traveled by,
And that has made all the difference.

I hasten to note that this poetry is cited not merely to indicate a road that I personally chose, but that many of the advocates of primary prevention chose as well. And it is our common journey on that road that has brought us to Burlington each June (but one) since 1975.

Some find history boring; others find bureaucracies boring, as well. So my task is compounded by the fact that the content and context of this chapter deals with historical bureaucracy or, if you will, bureaucratic history.

As I examined files and located memos, reports, notes prepared for the record, and other documents, three notions emerged:

1. Prevention has a rich history that provides guidelines for future endeavors. As tempting and seemingly efficient as it may be to favor a nonhistorical approach, Santayana's (1906) famed words of caution apply: "Those who cannot remember the past are condemned to repeat it." Nonetheless, there will always be those among us who prefer Henry Ford's (Wheeler, 1916) dictum: "History is more or less bunk." Yet, how

we got where we are today is as important to understand as the reality of what presently exists.

2. The history of primary prevention cannot be told in a chapter. Accordingly, consistent with available space, this chapter reflects my view of the most important events and ideas. Of necessity, much is abbreviated, much omitted.

3. Preparation of this chapter convinces me that there is a book to be written on the history and emergence of primary prevention. This view evokes a commitment to write a social and personal history of an idea and ideal that merits special consideration in the ongoing story of the mental health movement and the effort to advance human welfare.

Early Responses of Government to Prevention, 1968–1975

All stories have a beginning, and this one is no exception. For convenience, this story starts a decade ago—in 1974—thus coinciding with the decade of progress recorded in this volume.

In the spring of 1974, two documents of major significance were released, one issued by the Government of Canada and the second by the United States Government. The Canadian document, a working paper entitled *A New Perspective on the Health of Canadians,* which appeared under the imprimatur of the then Minister of National Health and Welfare, Marc Lalonde, and subsequently to be known as the Lalonde Report, presented a new framework for addressing the issues of health and sickness. In short, the Lalonde Report introduced the health field concept, which identified four major elements of the health field: human biology, environment, lifestyle, and health care organization. The fundamental position expounded in the Report stated:

> Marvelous though health care services are in Canada in comparison with many other countries, there is little doubt that future improvements in the level of health of Canadians lie mainly in improving the environment, moderating self-imposed risks and adding to our knowledge of human biology. (Lalonde, 1975, p. 18)

The report went on to note:

> There is the paradox of everyone agreeing to the importance of research and prevention yet continuing to increase disproportionally the amount of money spent on treating existing illness. (Lalonde, 1975, p. 30)

Further, this document stated: "It is apparent therefore, that vast sums are being spent treating diseases that could have been prevented in the first place" (Lalonde, 1975, p. 32).

The logic was compelling, but prevention was neither a new idea nor an approach that originated in the Lalonde Report. The next important question was not scientific but political: What effect might the Lalonde Report have on modifying priorities and perspectives?

Interestingly, 2 months after publication of the Lalonde Report, in June 1974, the U.S. Department of Health, Education, and Welfare (DHEW) (DHEW) issued its first *Forward Plan for Health* covering the five-year period FY 1976–80. Listed first among the five themes in the plan was prevention, an area that previously had rarely been referred to in any federal publication on health. This plan, covering both physical health and mental health indicated that:

> Preventing illness, injury and premature death must be a major component of this Nation's health strategy. . . . A fundamental component of our emphasis on prevention is a full commitment to research, evaluation, and the generation of new knowledge. . . . [P]revention not only alleviates human suffering, it also holds the key to the lock on our present and foreseeable health care problems, including their costs. (DHEW, 1974, p. 7)

The similarity of ideas expressed in both the U.S. and Canadian documents would lead to a speculation that either (a) Lalonde had a "mole" on his staff, who sneaked a copy of the report over the border, or (b) a truly international, cooperative planning effort was operating, which involved health planners on both sides of the border.

Beyond the general comments about prevention, the U.S. plan contained the following statements about mental health prevention:

1. One goal in our mental health strategy for FY 1976–80 is to extend services beyond the traditional direct methods of treating persons in need and to mobilize the concern of the community in providing effective programs of prevention of mental illness.

2. Our preventive thrusts will include not only the diagnosed illnesses such as schizophrenia and depression or the more recently, more clearly defined areas of alcoholism and drug abuse, but will extend as far as possible to addressing such social stresses as the influence of violence on television, racism, crime and delinquency, poverty and suicide.

3. Special initiatives will place specific emphasis on family problems. These efforts will be directed at such problems as child abuse and neglect, and youth who run away from home. Minority group mental health

problems and metropolitan mental health problems are two more areas which will be dealt with in a preventive perspective.

4. In coping with the preventive aspect of mental health in all of these high-risk groups, continuing research for identifying needs, providing a sound basis of information, and *formulating agency policy* will be stressed. (DHEW, 1974, pp. 32–33; italics added.)

Finally, the 1974 document specified the following NIMH prevention plans:

NIMH will continue its prevention activities through direct community mental health services, such as emergency and crisis management, outpatient outreach services, and medical and psychotherapeutic aftercare. Research and evaluation of consultation and education and community care programs will be supported to distinguish which interactions have most impact on the populations.

In addition, NIMH will give priority to programs concerned with prevention of impairment in children and youth through early detection, management of developmental and situational crises, through training in coping skills, and through the study of effective developmental environments. Attention will also be given to increasing personal effectiveness and development of coping skills among teachers. The NIMH preventive thrusts will also include the diagnosed illnesses, such as schizophrenia and depression, and areas such as racism, crime and delinquency, poverty, and suicide. (DHEW, 1974, p. 89)

Two points merit comment. First, the emphasis on prevention came from planners in the *physical* health sphere who managed to include mental health. Second, this new emphasis on prevention certainly wasn't *primary* prevention but, rather, secondary prevention (early diagnosis and treatment) and tertiary prevention (rehabilitation). The semantic and conceptual issues remain a source of contention and debate to this very day, as will be pointed out later.

But for now, let us not bicker about terms and meanings. Rather, let us suspend reflection on such matters so that we can keep our eye on the donut and not the hole. For the overarching fact was that in June 1974 prevention appeared officially on the departmental agenda as a priority theme for health planning and implementation. In short, the plan accorded a sanction to prevention. Historians should note that prevention's coming-of-age in the modern era can be traced directly to the *Forward Plan for Health, FY 1976–1980* (DHEW, 1974).

As important as the remarks about prevention contained in the Departmental plan were, by June 1974 NIMH already had a history of *planning efforts* aimed at advancing prevention and mental health promotion. In June 1968, a group of prestigious mental health workers (e.g., George

Albee, Eli Bower, Leonard Duhl, M. Brewster Smith, Reginald Lourie, John Clausen, and Julius Richmond) constituted a consultant panel to advise NIMH on program development in the area of primary prevention, including program strategies and specific proposals. This group met three times and in March 1970 sent to the Director of NIMH a report entitled *Promoting Mental Health* (NIMH, 1970).

After reviewing existing efforts the Panel concluded: "NIMH's current involvement in primary prevention activities is *underdeveloped* and *unfocused*" (italics added). The panel advocated a primary prevention program for NIMH including specific priority areas (viz., activities related to early child development and to increased parental competence and programs focused on the mental health aspects of public school education and adolescence), numerous programmatic functions, linkages with other key agencies and organizations, and an NIMH self-study of ongoing primary prevention efforts. The panel's report went on to state:

> Major gaps in program efforts in this area can be filled only by creating a specific program focus with sufficient budgetary allocations. . . . [I]t would not seem unreasonable to consider building up to a level of support equal to approximately one-half of the NIMH budget. . . . The Panel proposes that an organizational structure and focal point be established within NIMH which would have visible responsibility and authority for programming in the areas of primary prevention. (NIMH, 1970)

The report further indicated that: ". . . assigned staff, adequate budget, clear lines of authority and responsibility, a defined relationship to other parts of NIMH, and a clear program mandate are required if NIMH determines to develop this area." And the panel concluded:

> It is now timely and appropriate for NIMH to devote the same maximum effort of talent, energy, and resources which went into the community mental health centers program, schizophrenia research, manpower development, and hospital improvement toward a national program in primary prevention. (NIMH, 1970)

In spite of the compelling arguments put forth by the panel, in March 1970 primary prevention apparently was not yet an idea whose time had come. Nor had an earlier staff working paper calling for a National Center for the Prevention of Mental Illness and the Promotion of Mental Health (Goldston 1968), prepared prior to the panel's work, proved sufficiently persuasive in terms of the political realities of that time to bring prevention to center stage. Nor were recommendations put forth in 1975, 1976, and 1977 to establish an administrative unit for prevention acted on favorably. Almost a decade after the panel's report, the first administrative structure for prevention at NIMH, the Office of Prevention, was established in the fall of 1979. Three years later, in April 1982, a second administrative unit for prevention was created, the Prevention Research Branch, now the Center for Prevention Research. But, I get ahead of the story. . . .

If the *Forward Plan for Health, FY 1976–80* (DHEW, 1974) is viewed as the first official U.S. Government sanction for prevention, the following year's report can be perceived as a confirmation of prevention. The *Forward Plan for Health, FY 1977–81* (DHEW, 1975) once again included prevention as one of its major emphases or themes. The report contained the following specific ideas:

> A basic premise of the prevention strategy [is] that much greater attention and resources must be directed at preventing the underlying causes of disease rather than at the disease itself. . . . Enough is known about the underlying causes to justify major preventive action now. . . . An overwhelming proportion of them [diseases] are caused by man and his institutions and can be controlled by man. (p. 16)

> Over the next several years, all programs of the Public Health Service will seek ways to concentrate their energies and talent on attacking the underlying causes of disease and on helping people and communities to take direct responsibility for protecting their own health. (p. 19)

> For planning purposes, we believe it is more productive to focus our attention on the underlying conditions or antecedent causes of preventable diseases than to concentrate on the diseases themselves. (p. 98)

With this comment, the U.S. report indicated similarities with the Lalonde Report.

> While we propose that a higher priority be given to the development of primary prevention programs directed at the underlying causes of disease, we recognize that in some instances our capacity to affect these problems is limited or unknown. Many of them involve fundamental changes in the behavior of people and in the traditional practices of social and economic institutions. It would be unrealistic to expect significant improvements within a short time. Efforts will therefore continue to be directed toward improving the scope and utility of prevention programs for the early detection and treatment of disease and for the reduction of disability and dependence. This must be accompanied by an assessment of the efficacy and costs of all preventive approaches. (p. 98)

Well, just when it appeared that the planners had finally gotten around to mentioning primary prevention, they apparently proceeded quickly to pull the rug out from under it. But, the report continued:

> A basic assumption underlying our approach is that despite major gaps in our knowledge, enough is known about the links between these diseases and their

antecedent conditions to justify a special emphasis on *primary prevention action*. (p. 99; italics added.)

While that comment certainly was a pat on the back for primary prevention, the following statement was an unqualified endorsement:

Perhaps more important at this time than agreement on specific proposals is the explicit *commitment* of the Public Health Service and the Secretary of HEW to the goals of primary prevention and the determination to apply the energies and resources of this Department to help find practical ways of achieving those goals. (p. 99; italics added.)

How enthusiastic and "redeemed" I felt on first reading those words, almost a decade ago. I believed them. I wanted to believe them. I needed to believe them. But as events demonstrated, in a bureaucracy even word from the top often takes time both to reach the operating units below and to be acted on after the message has been received.

The 1975 DHEW report went on to state some specific options for mental health action:

Develop mental health programs that give special emphasis and support to programs helping individuals to cope with life crises. Such programs would include anticipatory guidance, parent and family life education, health education, and counseling. (p. 118)

Increase communications between mental health programs and family planning services, neighborhood health centers, schools, and similar institutions to increase the potential for mental health promotion in these facilities. (p. 118)

Support extensive research and demonstrations on techniques to prevent developmental failures in children, e.g., stimulating forms of preschool care, education of parents as enhancers of development, and intensive enrichment programs in early childhood. (p. 119)

The report proceeded to specify the Public Health Service responsibility with respect to prevention:

• Identify and call public attention to the major causes of disease and death in the country and recommend alternative ways to prevent or control them.

• Assist States and localities and the private sector to improve their capacities to deal with these problems.

• Provide short-term technical and specialized assistance and training in prevention techniques and procedures.

• Promulgate uniform national prevention objectives, standards, and norms for planning programs and assessing progress.

• Provide funds to states and localities to carry out their prevention programs.

• Assure that all people have equal access to preventive programs and that the programs preserve each person's rights and freedom of choice.

• Compile and publish data on the nature, extent, and consequences of the principal causes of death and disease.

• Conduct and support research on the etiology of preventable diseases and on techniques for the prevention or control of the principal causes of such diseases. (pp. 119–120)

Finally, the following material about NIMH prevention activities appeared in the DHEW report:

Since its inception, NIMH has emphasized the importance of understanding the basis of, and promoting, positive mental health as well as the importance of being concerned with the etiology, incidence, and treatment of mental illness. However, activities related to prevention have for the most part been developed and carried out within a variety of programs ranging from basic studies on the relation of culture to identity formation, or early infant stimulation and cognitive development, to demonstration projects to improve the climate of early child care centers and schools.

Thus, while the Institute's involvement in prevention has been extensive, it has also been *undirected and unfocused.* A major Institute objective for the planning period is to bring organized thinking and program planning to bear on its prevention-related efforts. (pp. 250–251; italics added.)

So far, this chapter has presented the background needed to show where NIMH was programmatically when prevention became an official, mandated activity within the Public Health Service and the then Department of Health, Education, and Welfare. From this vantage point, we can proceed to review the decade beginning in 1975, to note the road traveled.

A Decade of Progress

We turn now to another "coincidence" in time. For just as the second *Forward Plan for Health* was appearing in June 1975, the first Vermont Conference on the Primary Prevention of Psychopathology was being convened. For that occasion, I was asked specifically to address the status of primary prevention as viewed from the federal scene.

In the text prepared for that occasion, I indicated in restrained and understated terms that: "A more favorable climate for primary prevention is still evolving. Only the sanction has been forthcoming [as a result of the Department's *Forward Plan for Health, FY 1976–80*]—not the mandate for action" (Goldston, 1977a). With that comment as preface, I informed the conferees about existing unmet needs in preventive mental health programming at the federal level, which were identical, with minor variations, to those typically found in mental health agencies at the state and local levels (Goldston, 1977b).

These unmet needs, enumerated almost a decade ago, stand as baseline points of comparison to assess where we were then and where we are now, thus offering some guideposts to understanding where our emphases and resources must be placed in the decade ahead.

The 12 unmet needs cited in 1975 have been grouped into 9 areas and are discussed in terms of then and now.

Unmet Need No. 1—Policy, Resources, and Administrative Structure:

- A commitment at the policy and operating levels to provide support, encouragement, resources, and sanction for prevention activities.
- A specific program focus with sufficient budgetary allocations and an organizational structure with visible responsibility and authority for programming in primary prevention.

In the fall of 1979, NIMH made a programmatic and policy commitment to prevention. That commitment was translated into action by the establishment of the Office of Prevention within the Office of the Institute Director and the allocation of $4 million as a specific budget item for prevention. Thus, by creating an administrative structure, spelling out its functions and responsibilities, assigning staff, and allocating funds, policy through practice (in effect) was devised and implemented. As indicated earlier, a second administrative unit for prevention, the Center for Prevention Research, was established in 1982. Whereas the Office of Prevention is charged with coordination and policy and program development, the Center for Prevention Research operates the various NIMH prevention grant programs. By fiscal year 1983, $8.7 million had been expended for prevention research grants (Alcohol, Drug Abuse, and Mental Health Administration [ADAMHA], 1984, p. 19). In terms of staffing, the Center for Prevention Research has the approximate equivalent of six full-time professionals, and the Office of Prevention one full-time professional.

In addition, prevention has received the sanction of law. The Mental Health Systems Act, signed into law by President Carter in October 1980, contained the following provision under Section 325:

> The Director of the National Institute of Mental Health shall designate an administrative unit in the Institute to—

(1) design national goals and priorities for—
  (A) the prevention of mental illness, and
  (B) the promotion of mental health,

(2) encourage and assist local entities and State agencies to achieve the goals and priorities described in paragraph (1), and

(3) develop and coordinate Federal prevention policies and programs and to assure increased focus on the prevention of mental illness and the promotion of mental health.

Although enactment of the Omnibus Budget Reconciliation Act of August 1981 repealed the Mental Health Systems Act, four sections remained in force, including the above provisions, which now are known officially as Section 455(d) of the Public Health Service Act.

Unmet Need No. 2—Active Program Planning:

• Reorientation of priorities so that planned active programming will replace reactive responsiveness to the field.

This issue concerned the extent to which prevention research activities should be agency initiated versus investigator initiated; this writer's bias continues to favor the former approach. Viewing programmatic developments over the past five years, it is apparent that considerable progress has been made. Active efforts by the agency, in many instances in cooperation with recognized experts in particular areas, have increased.

The following requests for proposals (RFPs) have been issued, inviting prevention grant applications in specific areas:

1. Special Initiative on the Impact of Marital Disruption of Children (fall 1979).

2. Special Initiative on the Effects on Children of Having a Severely Disturbed Parent (fall 1979).

3. Special Initative on High-Risk Factors in Depression (fall 1980).

4. Special Initiative to Study Preventive Interventions Targeted to Infants and Families within High Risk Populations (1981).

5. Preventive Intervention Research Centers Notice (April 1982).

6. Prevention Research General Notice (December 1982).

7. New Investigator Research Awards in Prevention (January 1983).

8. Research Notice on the Prevention of ADM (Alcohol, Drug Abuse, and Mental Health) Disorders in Children and Adolescents (June 1983).

9. Research Notice on the Prevention of ADM Disorders at the Worksite (July 1983).

In addition to these special initiatives and notices, which eventuated as grant programs, various program mechanisms have been utilized to identify the cutting edge of prevention research and to facilitate pregrant program activities in promising areas. The three major program mechanisms include: (1) research planning and state-of-the-art workshops; (2) commissioned monographs, literature reviews, and bibliographies; and (3) contract studies to explore approaches to potentially promising areas.

The research planning and state-of-the-art workshops have proved to be key initial steps in the process of program planning and program development. Operationally, the workshop mechanism calls for convening a group of 12–14 research scientists and related professionals for a 2–2½-day period to discuss in depth a specific problem area or set of research issues. The agenda of each workshop includes consideration of the following elements:

(a) a review of state-of-the-art research knowledge with respect to the problem area on which the workshop is focusing;

(b) identification of the gaps in research knowledge and promising areas for further research;

(c) an indication of the readiness of the field to pursue preventive intervention research on that specific subject;

(d) delineation of a prioritized research agenda for the support of both basic and preventive intervention research; and

(e) preparation of a set of recommendations to NIMH and to other groups or organizations about research concerns related to the specific theme of the workshop.

The workshop mechanism may be viewed as a pipeline for program development in the sense that, where the experts indicate the readiness of the field for preventive interventions, budget planning may proceed to set aside funds and to invite applications in that specific area relevant to preventive intervention research. Finally, the intent was to produce a proceedings document or, at minimum, a descriptive final report from each workshop in order to make the information generated readily available to the field and thereby promote knowledge transfer and information dissemination.

The workshop series was initiated in September 1981; over the subsequent 33 months, 27 workshops on the following topics were convened by the Office of Prevention:

- Use of the media to prevent and reduce stress and anxiety.
- Prevention of mental disorder in American Indian and Alaska Native communities.
- Prevention of stress-related psychiatric disorders.

• Preventive interventions to reduce the harmful consequences of severe and persistent loneliness.

• Psychiatric epidemiology and primary prevention: The possibilities.

• Preventive intervention programs for family units with a mentally ill relative.

• Key issues in the planning and implementation of prevention research.

• Research issues in preventive psychiatry.

• The design and conduct of cost-effectiveness and cost-offset research in primary prevention.

• Prevention and mental health promotion: The interpersonal cognitive problem-solving (ICPS) model.

• Conquest of two agents that endanger the brain: Measles and rubella.

• Preventive aspects of suicide and affective disorders among adolescents and young adults.

• Preventive child psychiatry and childhood chronic illness.

• Prevention research on the assessment, correlates, and treatment of disabling anger.

• Primary prevention research relevant to state mental health programs.

• Depression prevention research: The potential and the limits of psychological interventions.

• Ethics and primary prevention.

• Assessing and promoting healthy family functioning.

• Primary prevention of aggressive and violent behavior.

• Preventing health risk behaviors and promoting coping with illness.

• Preventing stigma: How the media show mentally ill people.

• Coping with mental stress: The potential and the limits of exercise intervention.

• Prevention research and state mental health programs.

• Medical anthropology: Implications for stress prevention.

• The utilization of mutual support groups as a prevention approach for victims of personal violence.

• Roles of the core mental health professions in preventing and reducing the incidence of black homicide.

• A decade of progress in primary prevention: Retrospective and prospective analyses.

The office specifically commissioned manuscripts,* which aimed to contribute to the development of future research proposals by facilitating research planning among investigators, including:

• Mobilizing Support Networks for the Prevention of Psychopathology (Monograph by B. H. Gottlieb).

• Stressful Life Event Theory and Research: Implications for Primary Prevention (Monograph by B. L. Bloom, 1985).

• Social Support, Loneliness, and Social Isolation (An Integrative Literature Review by K. S. Rook).

• The Toll of Loneliness: Clinical Practice and Prevention (Monograph by L. M. Horowitz).

• Primary Prevention: An Annotated Bibliography (by J. C. Buckner, E. J. Trickett, and S. J. Corse, 1985).

• The Process of Prevention Research (Monograph by J. G. Kelly).

• Social Networks and Mental Health: An Annotated Bibliography (by D. E. Biegel, E. McCardle, and S. Mendelson, 1985).

Two examples of contract studies are (1) the study performed by the Institute of Medicine (IOM) on the health consequences of the stress of bereavement (Osterweis, Solomon, and Green, 1984); and (2) the data analysis and report by R. Novaco on anger in a community population and implications for the prevention of violent behavior (in preparation). The first cited study will increase knowledge about bereavement and particularly the harmful mental health consequences for specific subpopulations. Since the IOM report points out numerous areas for prevention research, NIMH staff have proposed a research-grant program on preventive intervention research related to the stress of bereavement (NIMH, 1984). The Novaco study will address key issues about opportunities for research on preventing violence as a function of the epidemiological evidence being analyzed.

Unmet Need No. 3—Focus on Major Problem Areas:

• Devoting resources to studying and devising means of helping people deal with real-life problems—those ever-occurring crises that require specific coping capacities and ego strengths in order to maintain health. We need to identify

*Those that have seen the light of day are cited. (Eds.)

coping methods, develop educational programs, and find means and resources for helping people deal with crises through the life cycle.

The requests for proposals (RFPs), program notices, and the IOM bereavement study cited earlier attest to significant progress in addressing this observed unmet need. Moreover, the research program notice issued by the Center for Prevention Research, NIMH (1982) states:

> Increasingly, research is making evident the contribution of episodic (e.g., a brief traumatic event) or enduring (e.g., an emotionally ill parent or family instability) stressful life events to the onset and maintenance of disorders and dysfunction. The Center for Prevention Research is interested in research specifically linking stressful life events to individual vulnerability and resistance to specific disorders or dysfunctions with the intent of applying these research findings directly to the development of preventive interventions. Also encouraged is research assessing the impact of preventive interventions on at-risk individuals which enables them to cope effectively with the emotional consequences of stressful life events or ameliorate their pathogenic influence.

The task that remains is to produce relevant research findings and package them in appropriate form and format, making such information accessible to and understandable for a wide variety of specific populations that may be at risk.

Unmet Need No. 4—New Research Techniques and Approaches:

- Supporting research into new techniques and approaches in primary prevention.

The research program notice of the Center for Prevention Research (NIMH, 1982) highlights the priority for methodological advances:

> The Center for Prevention Research (CPR) seeks research projects which develop innovative means for conducting evaluations of the salient processes and short- and long-term mental health effects of preventive interventions. CPR encourages projects which demonstrate and validate new methods for dealing with the design, subject selection, analysis, and measurement problems common to the assessment of short- and long-term preventive outcomes. Also encouraged are projects which use cost-effectiveness, cost-offset, and/or cost-benefit measures to assess the differential costs of preventive interventions relative to each other and relative to treatment. Projects which use or combine pre-existing or longitudinal studies are supported as well as the use of forecasting and decision-making strategies in the assessment of preventive outcomes. Finally, research on methods for exploring cost-effective dissemination of validated preventive interventions is supported.

Clearly, the opportunity to address this unmet need is contained in the Center for Prevention Research's stated program priorities.

Unmet Need No. 5—Mental Health Aspects of Health Problems:

• No longer regarding mental health as separate and distinct from somatic health. As a consequence of present policies and practices, mental health workers have abdicated responsibility for involvement in public health programs that have clear mental health components and implications—for example, maternal and child health services, nutrition and diet counseling, and family planning.

The past decade has witnessed tremendous interest among both mental health and health professionals with respect to behavioral health concerns. The subspecialties of behavioral medicine and health psychology have risen to prominence. In addition, the amount of mental health-related research in the following areas has increased substantially: nutrition, drug compliance, exercise, Type A behavior and coronary heart disease, and the effects of the physical environment on mental and emotional status.

Although the linkages between physical and mental health *research* have expanded, need continues to forge cooperative working relationships at the service delivery level.

Unmet Need No. 6—Relationships with the States:

• Providing resources to help States develop primary prevention programs within their departments of mental health. Currently, formal primary prevention programs at the State level exist only in Kentucky, Massachusetts, Michigan, and Ohio.

A decade later the following States have established a formal office of prevention within their departments of mental health: Georgia, North Carolina, South Carolina, Michigan, Texas, California, Ohio, Virginia, and Hawaii. The former offices of prevention in Kentucky and Massachusetts were abolished years ago. Describing—and, in some cases, even identifying—the prevention function in the mental health agencies of the various states is complex because: (a) in some States there may be a designated person but no formal office; (b) in other States there may be an administrative entity for prevention, but the mission includes, in addition to mental health, the areas of mental retardation, alcoholism, and drug abuse; and (c) in some States there are no identifiable prevention activities within the department of mental health.

Over the past decade, NIMH staff have provided technical assistance to various states, both to encourage the establishment of offices of prevention as well as to facilitate ongoing programs. In recent years, the NIMH Office of Prevention has served a clearinghouse function by sharing research and program information with the various state office directors, as well as convening annual meetings to discuss mutual concerns.

In addition, at NIMH's request each state has identified a person to serve as a prevention contact with the Federal government. Plans have been developed to initiate regional meetings, bringing together the prevention contacts, various prevention research and program specialists, and NIMH staff members. The purpose of the meetings is to share information, create an interstate prevention network to encourage program development, and reduce the professional isolation that exists in instances when a single staff member carries the prevention portfolio.

As the listing of workshops indicated, two meetings were held with state mental health program directors to provide information about prevention research relevant to state concerns, e.g., interventions with children of severely disturbed parents, psychoeducational interventions with family units having a mentally ill family member, support groups for families of Alzheimer's patients, and ongoing research on risk-factor identification. In addition to the knowledge-transfer function, these workshops aimed to create a more favorable attitude toward an understanding of prevention, to encourage those states without a formal prevention office to explore the merits of establishing such a unit, and to prompt those states having research programs to consider investing funds in prevention research. The feedback from the two workshops convened to date has been sufficiently positive to suggest that NIMH should also support an advanced workshop on prevention program and policy issues for state program directors who attended the initial sessions.

Progress has been achieved in the area of federal–state relations regarding prevention. However, as the recent resolution of the National Association of State Mental Health Program Directors (1984) indicates, much remains to be done with respect to continuing communications; technical assistance; state input in the development of national goals and priorities for the prevention of mental illness and the promotion of mental health; and the development of research priorities and budget planning.

Unmet Need No. 7—Consultation and Education Services:

- Strengthening consultation and education services within community mental health centers.

With enactment of the Omnibus Budget Reconciliation Act of 1981, which provided for block grants to the states for funding of community mental health centers, NIMH no longer has responsibilities for services. Accordingly, rather than direct monitoring of consultation and education services, NIMH's role became limited to technical assistance and knowledge transfer or information sharing.

NIMH funded a study to review the status of consultation and education services in community mental health centers as a result of the block grants, funding limitations, and resulting impacts on programming (Backer, Levine, and Erchul, 1983). This study remains under review to determine appropriate federal roles with respect to community mental health center operations.

Unmet Need No. 8—Training in Prevention:

• Developing training programs in primary prevention among professional and paraprofessional groups at both the basic and the continuing education levels.

• Inservice training to familiarize mental health workers with public health principles and epidemiology to give them a better balance in their approaches and values between public health and community considerations and their accustomed clinical considerations.

Among all the unmet needs cited in 1975, perhaps the most neglected continues to be training. No formal degree programs with a specialization in primary prevention exist. While single courses in primary prevention are appearing with greater frequency in the curriculums of various departments of psychology and schools of social work, a prevention *sequence* is not offered anywhere. The situation is no more promising with respect to the prevention training of paraprofessionals or for continuing education of a variety of mental health and other human-services workers.

Indeed, we know little about the content presented in existing prevention courses. An exception involves schools of social work and the information about prevention curricula gathered by the Council on Social Work Education (Nobel, 1981).

Further, I know of no evidence that indicates any attempt to familiarize mental health workers on a formal basis with public health content by means of *inservice* training opportunities. However, the early efforts of two universities to develop joint psychology–public health training programs (Miller, Fowler, and Bridges, 1982; Tanabe, 1982) represent optimistic developments in mental health and public health.

In 1984, the Federal administration proposed once again to phase out support for clinical training. If this plan is implemented, NIMH will support only research training. Under these circumstances, it is unlikely that prevention training opportunities will be available with NIMH funding. Therefore viable ways of meeting this need have not yet been found.

Unmet Need No. 9—Knowledge Transfer:

• An information and retrieval system that identifies activities dealing with prevention.

• Developing publications about prevention activities for distribution to mental health programs across the nation.

There is a continuing need for some form of clearinghouse that would collect, store, retrieve, and disseminate prevention program information. Both preventive intervention researchers and frontline prevention service deliverers require information for the planning and implementation of their activities. Presently, such information is available on more or less of a hit-and-miss basis, since no central or even large-scale regional repository of prevention information exists.

Progress has been made toward addressing the need to develop a variety of publications on prevention subjects. NIMH initiated the Prevention Publication Series with the proceedings document, entitled *Primary Prevention: An Idea Whose Time Has Come* (Klein and Goldston, 1977). To date the following additional titles have been released:

Mutual Help Groups: A Guide for Mental Health Workers (Silverman, 1978).

Preventive Intervention in Schizophrenia: Are We Ready? (Goldstein, 1982).

New Directions in Prevention among American Indian and Alaska Native Communities (Manson, 1982).

In FY 1981, the Office of Prevention initiated a formal publications program by commissioning monographs, literature reviews, bibliographies, and program manuals. In addition to the manuscripts cited in connection with unmet need number 2, the following works have been commissioned:*

• A Guide to Evaluating Preventive Programs in Mental Health (Monograph by R. H. Price and S. Smith, 1985)

• An Introduction to Conflict Resolution: A Community Mental Health Worker's Guide to the Basic Principles of Negotiations and Mediation (Monograph by W. F. Lincoln).

• Prevention of Psychological Casualties Related to Community Disruption (Handbook by J. Zusman).

• Approaches to Creating Competent Communities (Monograph by D. C. Klein).

*As of January 1986, only Price and Smith's monograph had been issued. (Eds.)

• Preventing Mental Health Problems: The Community Challenge (Booklet by M. Sandmaier).

• Integrating Research on High-Risk Infants into Health/Mental Health Settings: A Primer (Monograph by F. Masterpasqua).

• Primary Prevention Primer (Monograph: various contributors).

• A Sourcebook of Stress Management Programs for Consultation/Education/Prevention Staffs in State and Local Prevention Units (Program Manual by M. Swift).

• A Sourcebook for Mental Health Professionals on Family Education for Relatives of Schizophrenic Patients (Program Manual by M. J. Goldstein)

In addition, the Office of Prevention is preparing proceedings documents from many of the workshops identified earlier. Publications anticipated by the close of calendar year 1984 included:

• Preventing Stress-Related Psychiatric Disorders (edited by H. H. Goldman and S. E. Goldston, 1985).

• Preventing the Harmful Consequences of Severe and Persistent Loneliness (edited by L. A. Peplau and S. E. Goldston, 1985).

Over the period 1985–1986,† the following titles were scheduled for release:

• Psychiatric Epidemiology and Primary Prevention: The Possibilities.

• Preventive Intervention Programs for Family Units with a Mentally Ill Relative.

• Use of the Media to Prevent and Reduce Stress and Anxiety.

• The Design and Conduct of Cost-Effectiveness and Cost-Offset Research in Primary Prevention.

• Prevention and Mental Health Promotion: The Interpersonal Cognitive Problem-Solving (ICPS) Model.

• Ethics and Primary Prevention.

• Assessing and Promoting Healthy Family Functioning.

• Medical Anthropology: Implications for Stress Prevention.

Because of both time and money limitations, some workshop documents are being processed by private publishers; the majority of these publications were scheduled to appear in calendar year 1985.

Thus a publications program has been put in place, with the expecta-

†As of February 1986, these were still in preparation. (Eds.)

tion that between 6–10 documents will be produced each year. The continued support, production, and distribution of prevention publications should remain a high priority in view of the continuing need for such information in the field.

Summary

In summary, I believe that even the most hardened critic can look back over the past decade and admit that considerable progress has been made, although most of that progress came during the last five years. Much basic work remains to be accomplished: training programs, a clearinghouse, a publications program that produces documents in a timely fashion, formulation of national goals and priorities for the prevention of mental illness and the promotion of mental health, a more responsive federal–state relationship, and a variety of forms of assistance to prevention practitioners at the local level. The scorecard reveals that the highest marks have been earned at NIMH in the following areas: establishment of administrative structures for prevention, assignment of personnel to staff these prevention units, creation of a separate and distinct prevention budget, formulation of a research agenda and special announcements inviting applications, and, consequently, the initiation of a research grants program of varied components. These are no small achievements!

One further issue addressed in 1975 merits consideration, namely, the matter of how prevention is defined. At the first Vermont conference, I stated:

> Some standard meaning of the term *prevention* is needed to avoid semantic difficulties. Accordingly, this writer advocates that *prevention* be used solely to refer to actions which either aim to (1) anticipate a disorder or (2) foster optimal health. In short, only activities that deal with health promotion or health maintenance, or what in the mental health field has been called positive mental health, should bear the label of prevention; the term prevention, then, would be synonymous with primary prevention. (Goldston, 1977a, p. 20)

Little progress appears to have been made in dispelling the prevailing confusion about the meaning of the term *prevention*. As a result, primary prevention seems to be diminished. Over recent years the prevention vocabulary has been increased with the addition of such terms as "early preventive intervention" and "preventing the *progress* of a disorder." As these terms indicate, rather than narrowing the definition of prevention to the point where its meaning becomes uniform, the term has taken on additional meanings, thereby blurring, not clarifying, what had been identified a decade ago as a confusing matter. One obvious consequence of an expanded definition of prevention is that this fosters the continuance of a Tower of Babel, prevention meaning no more or no less than what its user may have in mind.

Within the federal bureaucracy, discussions and debates have gone on during the past two years about arriving at a uniform definition of prevention research for the entire U.S. Public Health Service. The final, established definition of prevention research cites three categories of activity: (1) preintervention research; (2) intervention research; and (3) prevention-related research. This categorization hardly provides for primary prevention, deliberately omits health promotion, and thereby redefines prevention research. One outcome may be that the majority of the research portfolio for almost every component of the U.S. Public Health Service will be identified as prevention. In short, by the stroke of consensus on definition within the bureaucracy, budgets that in previous years may have shown barely 5 percent for prevention (that is, *primary* prevention as I recommended in 1975) will now reveal high proportions of resources directed toward prevention research. Confusion is bound to accompany interpretations of program statistics on prevention research.

Factors Promoting Progress

What factors account for the achievements of the past decade? In answering this question, I would say that the significant determinants in advancing primary prevention have been:

1. The convening of the annual Vermont Conferences on the Primary Prevention of Psychopathology, thereby creating a forum for prevention advocates to meet each year. In addition, the volumes produced have been major contributions, demonstrating that prevention is substantive and scientific, not a cloud, an illusion, or patent medicine.

2. The growing body of research evidence showing that prevention works.

3. The National Mental Health Association–NIMH Pilot Conference on Primary Prevention held in Philadelphia in April 1976. The proceedings document, entitled *Primary Prevention: An Idea Whose Time Has Come* (Klein and Goldston, 1977), provided hope, inspiration, content, sanction, and a glimpse of the possible to many lonely professionals who were struggling in communities across the country, believing in prevention, and needing to be told that they were on the right track and that prevention was worth doing.

4. The extraordinary report of the Task Panel on Prevention of the President's Commission on Mental Health (1978), which stimulated serious review by the commission in their deliberations about prevention.

5. The recommendations about prevention in the Report of the President's Commission on Mental Health (1978), especially those recommendations dealing with needed administrative structure(s) and budget at NIMH.

6. The enactment of the Mental Health Systems Act with its inclusion of specific sections on prevention, thereby providing sanction and legal status for prevention, including the mission to establish national goals and priorities for the prevention of mental illness and the promotion of mental health.

7. The FY 1980 budget, which for the first time allocated funds for prevention, and the administrative actions taken to ensure that those funds were used for prevention programming.

8. The declaration from the then Administrator of the Alcohol, Drug Abuse, and Mental Health Administration, Dr. Gerald Klerman, that prevention was the fourth mission of the agency, thus joining research, services, and training.

9. The constituency-building efforts of the Office of Prevention, particularly: (a) the inclusion of all major mental health organizations in the planning and implementation of NIMH prevention efforts; and (b) the series of 27 research planning and state-of-the-art workshops during a 33-month period, which served to enlist the support and collaboration of more than 350 senior researchers who increasingly identify their work as preventive in scope and endorse NIMH's prevention efforts.

10. The support, cooperation, and active collaboration of the leading prevention advocates in the nation, viz., George Albee, Beverly Long, Emory Cowen, Bernard Bloom, Marshall Swift, and virtually all the contributors to this volume.

11. The political reality, which the NIMH leadership translated into administrative structures, staffing patterns, and prevention budgets.

In addition to these factors, each conference, each workshop, each publication, and each grant award has added to advancing prevention. Prevention constitutes a professional and political force of growing proportion. Prevention is part of the present and will continue to be a major part of the future of the mental health movement.

Some Continuing Issues

As we move into a new decade, several issues remain on the agenda for consideration. First, the need exists to clarify the boundary line between primary prevention and early preventive intervention. Official definitions should recognize and include primary prevention as well as mental health promotion. If this is not done, then what is labeled "prevention" may well neglect or omit primary prevention. In short, the trend of overlooking primary prevention must be halted; primary prevention must be reclaimed as *the* banner for prevention advocates.

Second, the tensions between research and practice must be resolved. Currently, from a bureaucratic perspective, the NIMH role is almost exclusively focused on research, and the state and local roles are concerned with service delivery via the block-grant funding mechanism. Yet, in reality, research and service cannot be separated either bureaucratically or programmatically. Practitioners must inform researchers of their needs, the types of outcome studies that should take high priority, and the program and replication manuals needed to advance practice. Researchers, on the other hand, should focus on the major aspects of major problems, i.e., significant areas for preventive intervention, being mindful always of the ultimate objective of their research—its translation into practice.

With respect to these tensions, let us conjecture about the effect of a hypothetical congressional mandate: The use of funds for any further prevention research is banned for the next three years; in its place, two times the amount of funding currently available is provided to identify everything that is already known and applicable and to put this information into suitable "packages," e.g., replication manuals, so that service deliverers can develop a wide range of community-located, data-based preventive service programs.

Another key issue concerns priority setting. Major concerns include decisionmaking about agency-initiated research versus investigator-initiated research; the roles of constituency groups; goal setting over a five-year period; establishment of national goals and priorities for the prevention of mental illness and the promotion of mental health; an appropriate mix within the prevention research portfolio on DSM-III, symptom relief, and mental health promotion outcomes; and a continuing need for the support of high-risk, potentially high-payoff projects.

And finally, much would be lost if prevention—the best hope for transforming the mental health field—were to become just like every other grant program, subject without exemption to rules and regulations that may thwart creativity and innovation. Prevention must lead the way, not risk losing its special identity.

Future Outlook

The future for prevention, broadly defined, appears bright indeed. Whether that future will be as promising for primary prevention remains uncertain at this time.

Further, there is no lack of subject areas for investigation and program development. The research planning and state-of-the-art workshops have identified a cutting edge of prevention research, thereby establishing a research agenda for the decade ahead. On that cutting edge, I believe, will be the priorities of controlling disabling anger, preventing violence, and preventing the harmful consequences of severe and persistent loneliness.

Conclusion

Nothing in the prevention field has come easily. What has been achieved has been gained by persistence and constant struggle. That level of effort must continue if we are to maintain our gains and further advance the cause of prevention. Realizing the promise and potential of prevention is necessarily a partnership enterprise involving federal, state, local, and voluntary efforts. So long as concerned professionals and citizen groups remain active advocates of prevention, there is good reason to believe the decade ahead will result in prevention being a significant NIMH program area having sufficient resources.

Let me offer two final thoughts in closing. First, when assessing the present status of primary prevention, we might well inquire whether the cup is half empty or half full. And, with the continued support of prevention advocates, we can hope that the story will have no end, but rather a continuing, rich future.

(Editors' postscript: In October 1985, a reorganization plan was implemented at NIMH. The Office of Prevention was abolished.)

References

Alcohol, Drug Abuse, and Mental Health Administration (1984). *Prevention activities of the Alcohol, Drug Abuse, and Mental Health Administration—fiscal year 1983 report to Congress*. Rockville, Md.: ADAMHA.

Backer, T. E., Levine, I. S., and Erchul, W. P. (1983). *Consultation and education activities in mental health programs*. Los Angeles: Human Interaction Research Institute.

Biegel, D. E., McCardle, E., and Mendelson, S. (1985). *Social networks and mental health: An annotated bibliography*. Beverly Hills, Calif.: Sage.

Bloom, B. L. (1985). *Stressful life event theory and research: Implications for primary prevention.* Department of Health and Human Services Publication No. (ADM) 85-1385. Washington, D.C.: U.S. Government Printing Office.

Buckner, J. C., Trickett, E. J., and Corse, S. J. (1985). *Primary prevention in mental health: An annotated bibliography.* Department of Health and Human Services Publication No. (ADM) 85-1405. Washington, D.C.: U.S. Government Printing Office.

Frost, R. (1955). *Complete poems of Robert Frost.* New York: H. Holt.

Goldman, H. H., and Goldston, S. E. (Eds.). (1985). *Preventing stress-related psychiatric disorders.* Department of Health and Human Services Publication No. (ADM) 85-1366. Washington, D.C.: U.S. Government Printing Office.

Goldstein, M. J. (Ed.). (1982). *Preventive intervention in schizophrenia: Are we ready?* Department of Health and Human Services Publication No. (ADM) 82-1111. Washington, D.C.: U.S. Government Printing Office.

Goldston, S. E. (1968). Proposal for a national center for the prevention of mental illness and the promotion of mental health. Unpublished manuscript.

Goldston, S. E. (1977a). Defining primary prevention. In G. W. Albee and J. M. Joffe (Eds.), *Primary prevention of psychopathology—Volume I: The issues* (pp. 18–23). Hanover, N.H.: University Press of New England.

Goldston, S. E. (1977b). Primary prevention: A view from the federal level. In G. W. Albee and J. M. Joffe (Eds.), *Primary prevention of psychopathology—Volume I: The issues* (pp. 297–315). Hanover, N.H.: University Press of New England.

Klein, D. C., and Goldston, S. E. (1977). *Primary prevention: An idea whose time has come.* Department of Health, Education, and Welfare Publication No. (ADM) 77-447. Washington, D.C.: U.S. Government Printing Office.

Lalonde, M. (1975). *A new perspective on the health of Canadians: A working document, April 1974.* Ottawa, Canada: Information Canada.

Manson, S. M. (Ed.). (1982). *New directions in prevention among American Indian and Alaska Native communities.* Portland, Oregon: Oregon Health Sciences University.

Miller, H. L., Fowler, R. D., and Bridges, W. F. (1982). The public health psychologist: An ounce of prevention is not enough. *American Psychologist, 37,* 945–948.

National Association of State Mental Health Program Directors (1984). *Primary prevention resolution requesting a report from NIMH.* Washington, D.C.: The Association.

National Institute of Mental Health (1970). *Promoting mental health.* Unpublished manuscript.

National Institute of Mental Health (1982). *Research program notice: Center for prevention research.* Rockville, Md.: NIMH.

National Institute of Mental Health (1984). *Forward plan for research 1986.* Rockville, Md.: NIMH.

Nobel, M. (Ed.). (1981). *Primary prevention in mental health and social work: A sourcebook of curriculum and teaching materials.* New York: Council on Social Work Education.

Novaco, R. (in preparation). *Anger in a community population: Implications for the prevention of violent behavior.* Rockville, Md.: National Institute of Mental Health.

Osterweis, M., Solomon, F., and Green, M. (Eds.). (1984). *Bereavement: Reactions, consequences, and care.* Washington, D.C.: National Academy Press.

Peplau, L. A., and Goldston, S. E. (Eds.). (1984). *Preventing the harmful consequences of severe and persistent loneliness.* Department of Health and Human Services Publication No. (ADM) 84-1312. Washington, D.C.: U.S. Government Printing Office.

President's Commission on Mental Health (1978). *Report to the President.* Washington, D.C.: U.S. Government Printing Office.

Price, R. H., and Smith, S. (1985). *A guide to evaluating prevention programs in mental health.* Department of Health and Human Services Publication No. (ADM) 85-1365. Washington, D.C.: U.S. Government Printing Office.

Santayana, G. (1906). *The life of reason, Vol. I.* New York: Scribner's Sons.

Silverman, P. R. (1978). *Mutual help groups: A guide for mental Health workers* Department of Health, Education, and Welfare Publication No. (ADM) 78-646. Washington, D.C.: U.S. Government Printing Office.

Tanabe, G. (1982). The potential for public health psychology. *American Psychologist, 37,* 942–944.

Task Panel on Prevention (1978). *Report of the task panel on prevention to the President's Commission on Mental Health—Volume IV.* Washington, D.C.: U.S. Government Printing Office.

U.S. Department of Health, Education, and Welfare (1974). *Forward plan for health FY 1976–80.* Washington, D.C.: U.S. Government Printing Office.

U.S. Department of Health, Education, and Welfare (1975). *Forward plan for health FY 1977–81* Washington, D.C.: U.S. Government Printing Office.

Wheeler, C. N. (1916). Interview with Henry Ford. Reported in the *Chicago Tribune,* May, 25, 1916.

PART V

Summary

Current Issues in Prevention

Summary of the 1984 Vermont Conference on the Primary Prevention of Psychopathology

Ricardo F. Muñoz

In 1975, when the first Vermont Conference on the Primary Prevention of Psychopathology was held, I was midway through my graduate work at the University of Oregon. I remember the excitement I felt that such a conference was being planned. I did not dream that one day George Albee would be introducing me to summarize this celebration of ten years of progress. As I reviewed the earlier volumes from the conference, I found it personally meaningful that the first chapter in the first volume of the series is by Jim Kelly (1977), who nurtured my interest in prevention while he was at the University of Oregon. The point I'm making is that one of the things that has occurred in the last ten years is that the leaders in the field of prevention have brought new people, like myself, into the field. We who are newer in the field need to do the same in the next ten years.

In this summary, I would like to underscore those themes and concepts from the presentations that we should keep in mind as we chart the next decade of progress.

The first very important theme is the monitoring of *the definition of prevention*. Emory Cowen clearly espoused maintaining a strict definition of prevention. Beverly Long's presentation highlights why this is so important to ensure that funding for prevention is not siphoned into other areas during the political process. We need to strike from our vocabulary the adjectives *primary, secondary,* and *tertiary* when referring to preventive interventions. *Prevention* and *treatment* must be clearly differentiated.

Empowerment (as distinguished from prevention)—a concept that Emory Cowen brought to us from Julian Rappaport's writings—has much potential. However, there is a substantial political risk involved in defining prevention efforts by focusing on empowerment. Betty Tableman refers to this in her chapter, stating that if she were to propose empowerment programs they would have little chance of being funded. But the concept of empowerment does stretch the concept of prevention into what may be a fruitful direction. We will need to walk a tightrope between what is politically feasible and what is truly needed to advance effective prevention efforts. The concept of prevention ultimately will not be constrained by political expediency or boxed in by bureaucratic guidelines.

Gerald Caplan discusses two points that I would like to emphasize. One deals with the need to *reduce the intensity of incapacitating stress*. Caplan's suggestion that chronic stress produces a reduction in cognitive functioning and in the clarity of self-concept is supported by experimental work in memory and mood described by Bower (1981). When a list of words is learned in a certain mood, it is easier to remember it when that mood is again present. If you learn the list in a happy mood, it is easier to remember that list when you are in a happy mood. When you learn something in a sad mood, it is easier to remember it in a sad mood. These findings have implications for depression and demoralization. When we are depressed, we tend to remember things that we have learned in periods of depression earlier in our lives. This may have something to do with the "cognitive distortions" that we observe in depression, which may not necessarily be distortions. Our memories may be picking up accurate data from the same type of (depressed) period in the past. This process is a version of "state dependent learning". (This phenomenon has implications for epidemiological work: If you depend on self-reports, as most of our psychiatric instruments do, you may get a higher memory for negative events and negative feelings from people who are experiencing such feelings at interview time. Thus current states may bias estimates of lifetime diagnoses). From a preventive standpoint, it may be beneficial to counteract this natural cognitive mechanism and purposefully elicit memories and behavioral patterns that help individuals to recall healthy self-concepts. Caplan's second point deals with the concept of *reverberative self-identification*. This concept, as well as Osofsky's description of *reciprocal dynamic interactions* between child and mother, reminds us that we should not limit our thinking to unidirectional phenomena but consider phenomena that affect each other: If at one point something is an effect, at another point it can be a cause. This latter concept, called *reciprocal determinism* by Bandura (1977), will be very helpful in prevention.

Another clear and recurrent theme is that prevention professionals must pay more attention to *learning from the people they serve*. Riessman's suggestion that self-help systems can integrate with formal systems and be mutually helpful is very important. Marshall Swift reminds us that sometimes systems do not adopt "successful" programs because we are just going in the wrong direction for a particular setting; that sometimes our pet ideas will not work in the real environment. Swift highlights the importance of *constituent validation,* in addition to scientific validation, by which he means learning what will work from the people we serve, i.e., learning from the real world. Price gives us an example of people altering his design by forming their own social support group after the experimental intervention was supposedly finished.

Another theme sounded in many forms throughout this conference—and which validates what George Albee has been saying for many years—is that, given the great need for resources, treatment alone is not sufficient. Bruce Dohrenwend makes the statement that serious psychopathology, for example, is not rare in the aggregate. Riessman reminds us of the millions of people who are in stressful life situations, as attested to by the great number of self-help organizations that have been formed.

Still another theme heard repeatedly in the last ten years was echoed in a number of presentations: the need to study the precursors of health instead of the precursors of pathology. Cowen spoke of it in terms of engineering health versus pathology. Segal called on us to seek the roots of mental health instead of the roots of pathology. McGuffin offered interesting examples of how even genetic approaches, which sometimes are considered to be totally deterministic, can be combined with the study of the effect of life events and chronic adversity to tease out the contributions made by each. He also reminded us that *familial* does not mean *genetic.* Both of these ideas can serve to light a path toward many advances in genetics in a truly preventive manner, in which the roots of health can be studied in persons with a family history of psychological problems.

Now, I'd like to turn to concerns that have to do with research methods. Cowen stated that hard-nosed research evaluation is our short suit. I believe that he is right. There have been many advances of note in the last ten years. There have been measurement advances, for example, in identifying specific diagnoses by means of structured interviews and in ways to measure microenvironments. The advances in genetics that McGuffin recounts are amazing. None of these advances has been used sufficiently in prevention. Price mentions the two research traditions that need to be brought together by the prevention field: mental health epidemiology and intervention research. Osofsky brings to our attention the information to be obtained from clinical work. The divisions between clinical and prevention *research* need not be emphasized as much as they sometimes are. For example, the issues of attrition in both research arenas are very similar.

We should be learning from each other. The focus of prevention on populations (instead of on individuals identified by the presence of disorders) implies that epidemiological tools are essential in evaluating the effects of interventions. Treatment-outcome research has contributed methodologies for determining the presence or absence of effects, their size, and to which ingredients such effects can be attributed. Prevention research, in turn, will contribute by helping to determine whether theories about disorders are applicable outside the highly selected samples available to clinicians.

The research versus practice controversy is closely connected to the amount of progress made (or not made) by prevention researchers. Many critics of prevention have stated that they are in favor of prevention research but that it is too early yet to fund prevention practice. However, many of the presentations show us that prevention practice can guide prevention research.

Research has practical limitations. Consider treatment-outcome studies of depression. Only about 20 percent of all those who are depressed seek mental health treatment. Because of the screening criteria imposed by the research design and the need to obtain signed consent from prospective participants, those recruited for such studies comprise an even smaller proportion of those who suffer from the disorder in the general population. Thus we should question how generalizable the data from such studies can be. By focusing on entire populations, prevention projects can sample a larger proportion of those who are depressed, thus obtaining information about persons who are often inaccessible to clinicians. To keep prevention research focused on prevention, only currently nondepressed persons should be included in our studies, which would create a side-benefit: the referral function of our work.

Practice can assist in determining research questions. If you want to understand the theories and methods involved in prevention, you must take part in prevention practice. For example, treatment professionals have sometimes accused prevention workers of trying to get away from dealing with the pain of severe problems. This is not necessarily the case, as Caplan pointed out very clearly in his poignant examples. This is not to say that there is virtue in exposing oneself to pain for its own sake. That is not the point. The point is that prevention is not necessarily doing work with the healthiest people or the people who do not have any life problems. Are there special issues involved in doing work of this sort? How can an interviewer maintain a hope-engendering perspective in the midst of the human suffering that Caplan describes? Caplan's comments about who supports the supporter are very important in this context. (Parenthetically, the celebration in which we are participating is a way of supporting the supporters of prevention. VCPPP, and all the people involved with it, have to be credited with much of the progress in prevention. Acknowledging that is supporting the supporters of prevention). The ideas that Caplan shares with us stem from his experience doing prevention, which can light the way for prevention research.

Prevention research itself needs to be described more candidly. I found Sheppard Kellam's list of what is needed in a prevention intervention research center to resonate well with my own experiences. In journals, things are clear; there is a methods section, a results section and so on, but that is an idealization; it does not explain what it took to get those data and to make sense of them. Kellam's list does, and it will be very useful in helping us to do prevention work in the next ten years.

The providers of research funds also need to be recognized. The research money that we are using now became available because of the efforts of a number of people, many of whom are here. Often when we are busy writing a grant, we do not realize where the money comes from, money without which we will not be able to do the work that we will be doing in the next ten years. It is good to remind ourselves that there are different roles for people in prevention: the roles of the politician, the conceptualizer, the researcher, the practitioner, and so on. All these roles must be respected. There are still few enough of us that if we start to create distinctions and then to feel that the researcher is better than the practitioner or the politician is really the only person who can make a difference, we will not be able to move forward as a group.

Many goals for the next ten years are embodied in the chapters of this volume. Cowen lists three: (1) showing that our interventions are demonstrably related to mental health; (2) that changes produced are real and robust in human terms (and not just as psychiatric labels or scores in psychometric scales); and (3) that these changes are enduring and not ephemeral. Caplan suggests four: (1) that we focus more carefully on specific stressors in specific populations; (2) that we look at both proximal and distal outcomes (which will require longer funding, larger numbers of cases, and collaborative arrangements); (3) that we develop a set of standard instruments with which to measure common concepts, such as stress, support, competence, demoralization, and specific diagnoses; and (4) that we fund a better balance of research strategies, including exploratory, pilot, retrospective, and prospective studies. McGuffin believes that a key question we must attempt to answer is: "What is the pathway from abnormal genes to abnormal mental states?"

Dohrenwend asks us to move from the existing indirect evidence for the link between social stress and pathology to studies looking for direct evidence. He suggests building on large-scale epidemiological studies to set up retrospective case control studies, which would encompass representative samples of cases and well controls, and finally adding prospective features to such studies. He also expresses interest in finding out whether demoralization is a risk factor for specific disorders. Finally, he brings up the issue of including a third group (in addition to well controls and persons with a specific disorder) in our studies. I believe that he is referring to the deviation hypothesis: If you examine any group that deviates from another group, you are likely to find differences between those groups merely because they are different. With a third group, which deviates from the other two, you can start to tease out which of the risk factors or prevention intervention effects are functionally related to, say, depression as opposed to schizophrenia or another disorder.

A number of caveats are advanced, generally addressing issues that have been commonly misunderstood or misinterpreted in the last ten years. McGuffin's presentation clearly points out that, even if every person diagnosed with schizophrenia swore off procreation, there would still be schizophrenics for generations to come. Most schizophrenics do not have schizophrenic parents, nor do most schizophrenics have schizophrenic children. Although there is a large body of evidence that there is a genetic component to this disorder, much of it based on studies of twins, and the practical implications of these findings are far from clear. Watt's comments that there are differences in the rates of giving children up for adoption based on the severity of the schizophrenic process in the mother should also give us pause. If more mothers who have severe symptoms of schizophrenia give up children than those with less severe symptoms, any differences that emerge could be a spurious biasing of the data, which would artificially inflate the size of the effects for the genetic contribution to schizophrenia.

Cowen warns us that, although prevention has made tremendous structural progress (in terms of associations, journals, books, etc.) in the last ten years, substantive progress leaves much to be desired. He also warns us that our efforts to promote programs based on competencies and skill learning should be tempered by Rappaport's suggestion that such programs could be a cruel joke if they are offered to people who are being exploited by a society that will not allow them equal access. In his usual even-handed manner, he asks whether Rappaport's concept of empowerment assumes that empowered people would not develop psychological problems. The issue is one of a possible tautological definition: If you assume that anyone who develops psychological disorders is not empowered, obviously you will always be right. There is a need to define empowerment in a way that allows it to be measured.

Segal shares with us his view of three problems with the way prevention has been practiced in the last ten years. The first is an implicit assumption that the populations served are homogeneous and that there are absolute principles that can be used for all recipients of preventive programs. The second is the ethical dilemma in not distinguishing between giving information and giving advice. Will prevention programs take the form of ethical or moral exhortations? The third is the lack of evaluation of results, including negative ones. I should point out that, even in areas in which there are clear-cut interventions and outcome measures, efforts to produce measurable changes are sometimes discouraging. In the first VCPPP volume, McNeil and others (1977), cite a study in Sweden that found that only 2–3 percent of all pregnancies had been actively planned. This means that most people (even in places where contraception is easily available) are coming into the world by chance. What would happen if the proportion of actively planned pregnancies were to increase to 30, 60, or 90 percent? This would be a relatively easy outcome to measure (though a hard one to bring about).

I would like to end my summary with some personal reactions to the conference. The underlying basis for the Vermont Conference on the Primary Prevention of Psychopathology is an enduring belief in human self-direction. I believe that is why the issue of genetics produces such tension. Like psychodynamic and behavioral theories, genetic theories appear to take away the possibility of self-direction. In fact they are felt to be the ultimate insult because they imply that our destiny is built into the very fiber of our beings. It is important not to give in to that kind of immediate reaction to a discipline that may in fact be very helpful to prevention in the future. The genetic determination of behavior, like prevention, is still a revolutionary concept, and, as such, it has great potential for producing benefits as well as harm to humanity.

The revolutionary nature of prevention is one of the reasons that it provoked so much fervor in the past—and, I believe, still does. But, as prevention becomes more established, will the prevention movement be co-opted? Price suggests that we are nearing the end of prevention as a cottage industry. Albee shares his belief that the Group for the Advancement of Psychiatry has become conservative in the last few years. Could that happen to the proponents of prevention? My guess is that this will not happen within the next ten years, but it is not too early to begin to watch for warning signs.

One such sign is a failure to ask the crucial questions: the philosophical ones. Someone has said, "The big questions are those that a child asks and, not getting an answer, stops asking. That is known as growing up." We need to keep on asking these questions, especially in the area of prevention. And these questions *were* raised at this conference.

The questions of uncertainty as a basic element of human existence is touched on by Osofsky in her description of the concept of discontinuities as an expectable part of growth. This raises the issue of the limits of predictability. Bandura (1982) has addressed the same idea in another context, in terms of "the psychology of chance encounters." As George Albee spoke about his "conversion" to prevention in 1958, I was thinking that, in 1958, I was an eight-year-old child in the small South American town of Chosica, Peru. I defy any psychologist, or anyone else, to come up with a way to have predicted that today I would be addressing this conference. There are many things we cannot predict. That is part of the fun of psychology and part of the fun of living.

Another question has to do with the relevance of truth. There is some evidence that depressed people may be more accurate than nondepressed people in perceiving certain aspects of reality. When human beings are not depressed, they tend to distort reality in a positive direction. There may be an evolutionary advantage in doing so. Should we propose purposeful adjustment of people's perception of reality in the name of prevention? In the studies in which the perceptions of mothers changed from thinking that their children were below average to thinking that they were above average, there is the possibility that their initial perceptions were accurate. But even if they were accurate, perhaps it was good to change those perceptions because, by changing it, they helped the children become more than "below average." Distortion of the "truth" caused the original truth to change.

The word *hope* is mentioned repeatedly throughout. Caplan mentions the need to maintain active hope, perseverance, and problem-solving processes, even if it means temporary *strategic withdrawal* from a stressful situation. Segal talked of hope as remaining open to the idea that throughout development there is room for surprising change and that change is possible throughout human life. Interpersonal cognitive problem solving (ICPS) utilizes the generation of alternatives as a way of increasing options, which means increasing hope.

As people dedicated to prevention, we need to maintain this hope. We should end the celebration of this decade of progress remembering the clear advances made, the number of people who are in the field doing preventive work, writing about prevention, the funding from the NIMH Center for Prevention Research, and participation in meetings that Steve Goldston's Office of Prevention has put together. A number of people have said that now it is respectable to say that you are doing research in prevention. Much of the credit goes to a number of people at this conference. At the same time, there is still uncertainty regarding how far we can take the prevention concept, especially in conducting carefully controlled experimental studies (which, as I said before, have their own intrinsic limits in terms of reflecting generalizable effects). But uncertainty and probabilities are what prevention and human lives are all about. Both prevention and human life are processes, not end products. Therefore there will always be uncertainty and probabilities to confront.

By ending on an optimistic note, we increase the probability of producing effective preventive work. That is, believing that we can do it will motivate us to try and, as we try, the likelihood increases that we will in fact achieve our goals. We need to remind ourselves that the goal of prevention is to push back the boundaries of the unavoidable and inescapable. By doing so we will not just be discovering reality in a scientific sense: We will be changing reality so that human suffering that is inevitable now will not be inevitable in the future.

References

Bandura, A. (1977). *Social learning theory.* Englewood Cliffs, N.J.: Prentice-Hall.

Bandura, A. (1982). The psychology of chance encounters and life paths. *American Psychologist, 37,* 747–755.

Bower, G. (1981). Mood and memory. *American Psychologist, 36,* 129–148.

Kelly, J. G. (1977). The search for ideas and deeds that work. In G. W. Albee and J. M. Joffe (Eds.), *Primary prevention of psychopathology—Vol. 1: The issues* (pp. 7–17). Hanover, N.H.: University Press of New England.

McNeil, T. F. and Kaij, L. (1977). Prenatal, perinatal, and post-partum factors in primary prevention of psychopathology in offspring. In G. W. Albee and J. M. Joffe (Eds.), *Primary prevention of psychopathology—Vol. 1: The issues* (pp. 92–116). Hanover, N.H.: University Press of New England.

Contributors

George W. Albee, Ph.D., is one of those luminaries who needs no introduction. Currently Professor of Psychology at the University of Vermont, Dr. Albee has been involved with two presidential commissions on mental health; that of Kennedy and that of Carter. As co-author of the classic, *Manpower for Mental Health,* which was prepared for Kennedy's Commission, and as Coordinator of the Task Panel on Prevention for Carter's Commission, Albee has been an advocate of prevention for much longer than the decade covered in this book.

Gerald Caplan, M.D., is another person who truly needs no introduction to an audience of community psychologists and psychiatrists. Currently Professor of Child Psychiatry and Chair of the Department of Child and Adolescent Psychiatry at Hadassah University Hospital in Jerusalem, Dr. Caplan is one of the pioneers of community psychiatry, crisis intervention, and primary prevention.

Emory L. Cowen, Ph.D., is Professor of Psychology, Psychiatry and Education at the University of Rochester and the Director of the Center for Community Study. His Primary Mental Health Project was an early and very succesful program in the field and the model for many others across the country. He was a major contributor to the report of the Task Panel on Prevention of President Carter's Commission on Mental Health.

Bruce P. Dohrenwend, Ph.D. is Head of the Social Psychiatry Research Unit of the College of Physicians and Surgeons and Professor of Public Health at Columbia University. He is one of the most distinguished specialists in psychiatric epidemiology and social psychiatry. His writings with his wife, the late Barbara Snell Dohrenwend, are major contributions to the field of community psychiatry and psychology. Dr. Dohrenwend headed the Task Group on Behavioral Effects of the President's Commission on the Accident at Three Mile Island and was a member of the Task Panel on Problems, Scope, and Boundaries of the President's Commission on Mental Health.

Stephen E. Goldston, Ed.D., M.P.H. was Director of the Office of Prevention at NIMH. He is co-author (with Donald Klein) of the widely-quoted, *Primary Prevention: An Idea Whose Time Has Come,* and numerous chapters, articles, and monographs on prevention. From his office at NIMH, Dr. Goldston was able to bolster prevention efforts by stimulating and providing financial support for more than two dozen workshops on primary prevention around the country.

Kathryn N. Healey, Ph.D., is Associate Director of Consultation and Education of the John F. Kennedy Community Mental Health Center and is the Associate Director of the Hahnemann University Preventive Intervention Research Center.

Randy Katz, Ph.D., is an Honorary Lecturer at the University of London Institute of Psychiatry, where he received his Ph.D. in Psychology and an Honorary Clinical Psychologist at Maudsley Hospital. He has published papers on stress, anxiety, and depression.

Sheppard G. Kellam, M.D., is Professor and Chair of the Department of Mental Hygiene, School of Hygiene and Public Health, Johns Hopkins University. Dr. Kellam is well known for his contributions to child mental health and to elementary education and social change affecting the development of inner-city children. Currently Dr. Kellam directs one of the NIMH-funded Prevention Research Centers.

Beverly Benson Long, M.S., is an individual who should need no introduction but does. While she may lack the visibility of other authors in this volume she does not lack impact. She is Chair of the NMHA's Commission on the Prevention of Mental and Emotional Disorders. She is a past president of the National Mental Health Association and was a member of President Carter's Commission on Mental Health.

Peter McGuffin, M.D., is a Senior Lecturer in the Department of Psychiatry at the Institute for Psychiatry at the University of London. He has written numerous articles and texts on the genetics of normal and abnormal behavior and is recognized as one of the current leaders in discovering the genetic bases of psychopathology.

Ricardo Muñoz, Ph.D., is Associate Professor of Psychology in the Department of Psychiatry at the University of California, San Francisco. Dr. Munoz's major work on the prevention of depression has become a model for similar programs nationwide.

Joy Ossofsky, Ph.D., is a research and staff psychologist at the Menninger Foundation and an adjunct professor in the Department of Human Development at the University of Kansas. She is a member of the Executive Committee of the World association for Infant Psychiatry. She has written extensively on infant development and parenting and her developmental text is rapidly becoming a standard in the field.

Richard H. Price, Ph.D., is Professor of Psychology at the University of Michigan, and Faculty Associate at the Institute for Social Research. He is noted for his contributions to the evaluation of social programs and in training for community psychology.

Frank Reissman, Ph.D., is the Director of the National Self-Help Clearing House and Professor of Sociology in the Graduate School of the City University of New York. He is the editor of *Social Policy,* one of the major periodicals in the field, and the author of more than a dozen books dealing with poverty and the mental health problems of the poor. Dr. Reissman is an active participant in the "self-help" revolution.

Julius Segal, Ph.D., is Director of the Division of Communication and Education of the National Institute of Mental Health. Recipient of the Science Writer's Award of the American Psychological Association, he has devoted his life's work to communicating the results of science to the public.

Marshall Swift, Ph.D., is Director of Consultation, Education and Prevention Programs at the John F. Kennedy Community Mental Health/Mental Retardation Center and Professor in the Department of Mental Health Sciences at Hahnemann University. He is also Associate Director of the Prevention Research Center at Hahnemann. Dr. Swift's work involving community members in the development and evaluation of intervention programs has become a model for the country.

Betty Tableman, M.P.A., is Director of Prevention and Demonstration programs for the Michigan Department of Mental Health. She is a member of the National Mental Health Association's Commission on the Prevention of Mental and emotional Disorders.

Norman F. Watt, Ph.D., is Professor of Clinical Psychology at the University of Denver. As Chair of the Steering Committee of the Risk Research Consortium, he is in a prime position for reviewing risk research and for knowing the future direction of this important line of work. Dr. Watt was the chair of the NIMH Ad-Hoc Review Committee on Prevention Research and has written extensively on risk research and child psychopathology.

Lisa Werthamer-Larrson, M.S.W., is a predoctoral fellow in psychiatric epidemiology in the Department of Mental Hygiene of the Johns Hopkins University School of Hygiene and Public Health.

Name Index

Subject Index